D1187686

COLONIAL LIVES ACROSS THE
BRITISH EMPIRE

This volume uses a series of portraits of 'imperial lives' in order to rethink the history of the British empire from the late eighteenth to the early twentieth century. It tells the stories of men and women who dwelt for extended periods in one colonial space before moving on to dwell in others, developing 'imperial careers'. These men and women consist of four colonial governors, two governors' wives, two missionaries, a nurse/entrepreneur, a poet/civil servant and a mercenary. Leading scholars of colonialism guide the reader through the ways that these individuals made the British empire, and the ways that the empire made them. Their life histories constituted meaningful connections across the empire that facilitated the continual reformation of imperial discourses, practices and cultures. Together, their stories help us to reimagine the geographies of the British empire and to destabilise the categories of metropole and colony.

DAVID LAMBERT is Lecturer in Human Geography at Royal Holloway, University of London. He is the author of *White creole culture, politics and identity during the Age of Abolition* (2005).

ALAN LESTER is Professor of Historical Geography at the University of Sussex. His previous books include *Imperial networks: creating identities in nineteenth century South Africa and Britain* (2001).

COLONIAL LIVES ACROSS THE BRITISH EMPIRE: IMPERIAL CAREERING IN THE LONG NINETEENTH CENTURY

EDITED BY

DAVID LAMBERT AND ALAN LESTER

CAMBRIDGE UNIVERSITY PRESS
Cambridge, New York, Melbourne, Madrid, Cape Town, Singapore, São Paulo

Cambridge University Press
The Edinburgh Building, Cambridge CB2 2RU, UK

Published in the United States of America by Cambridge University Press, New York

www.cambridge.org
Information on this title: www.cambridge.org/9780521847704

© Cambridge University Press 2006

First published 2006

Printed in the United Kingdom at the University Press, Cambridge

A catalogue record for this publication is available from the British Library

ISBN-13 978-0-521-84770-4 hardback
ISBN-10 0-521-84770-2 hardback

To Carolyn, and to Jo, Daisy and Evan

Contents

Figures

x *List of figures*

Maps

Notes on contributors

LAURENCE BROWN is Lecturer in Migration History at the University of Manchester, UK. His publications have focused on the inter-colonial migrations which shaped the construction of indentured immigration in the Caribbean and the Pacific. He is currently completing a manuscript on Caribbean migrants in the modern Atlantic World.

MATTHEW BROWN is Lecturer in Latin American Studies at the University of Bristol, UK. His current research focuses on travel and adventure in Latin America in the nineteenth and twentieth centuries. His *Adventure in Colombia: the birth of new nations in the Atlantic world* will be published in 2006.

LEIGH DALE teaches Australian and post-colonial literatures at the University of Queensland, Australia. She is the editor of the journal *Australian Literary Studies* and the author of *The English men: professing literature in Australian universities* (1999). Her current research is in representations of self-harm and self-mutilation in literary texts.

CATHERINE HALL is Professor of Modern British Social and Cultural History at University College London, UK. Her work focuses on the relation between Britain and empire in the nineteenth century. Her most recent book is *Civilising subjects. Metropole and colony in the English imagination 1830–1867* (2002).

PHILIP HOWELL is University Senior Lecturer in the Department of Geography at the University of Cambridge, UK. His principal recent research is on the regulation of prostitution in Britain and the British empire, on which topic he is working on a book for Cambridge University Press.

JONATHAN HYSLOP is Deputy Director of the Wits Institute for Social and Economic Research (WISER), University of the

Witwatersrand, Johannesburg, South Africa. He has published numerous articles on nineteenth- and twentieth-century South African social history. His most recent book is *The notorious syndicalist: JT Bain – a Scottish rebel in colonial South Africa* (2004).

ANNA JOHNSTON is Senior Lecturer in English at the University of Tasmania, Australia. She has published on colonial and postcolonial missionary writing, settler postcolonialism, travel writing, and autobiography. She is the co-editor of *In transit: travel, text, empire* (2002) and the author of *Missionary writing and empire, 1800–1860* (Cambridge University Press, 2003).

ZOË LAIDLAW is Lecturer in History at Royal Holloway, University of London, UK. Her book, *Colonial connections 1815–45: patronage, the information revolution and colonial government*, was published in 2005. Her current research examines changing conceptions of empire in the long nineteenth century.

DAVID LAMBERT is Lecturer in Human Geography at Royal Holloway, University of London, UK. He is the author of *White creole culture, politics and identity during the Age of Abolition* (Cambridge University Press, 2005). He is currently researching the connections between circum-Atlantic systems of slavery, forms of scientific knowledge and debates about abolition in the early nineteenth century.

ALAN LESTER is Professor of Historical Geography at the University of Sussex, UK. Much of his work has been on historical geographies of South Africa. His current research focuses on contests and connections among British colonial interests in settler colonies during the nineteenth century. His latest book is *Imperial networks: creating identities in nineteenth century South Africa and Britain* (London: Routledge, 2001).

VAL MCLEISH completed a Ph.D. at University College London, UK, in 2002, and since then has been involved in research for family historians. Her personal research interests include aristocratic women in the empire, and she is now considering writing a biography of Lady Aberdeen.

ANITA RUPPRECHT is a lecturer in Cultural and Historical Studies at the University of Brighton, UK. Her current research focuses on the relations between moral sentiment and political economy in relation to the British representation of slavery and antislavery in the late eighteenth and early nineteenth centuries.

NICOLA THOMAS is Lecturer in Human Geography at the University of Exeter, specialising in Historical Cultural Geography. Her current research explores the construction and negotiation of identity in British colonial and imperial contexts.

Acknowledgments

During its gestation period since 2002, this book has benefited from intellectual guidance and helpful suggestions from a variety of individuals. In particular, we would like to thank the contributors, as well as Alison Blunt, Nemata Blyden, Elleke Boehmer, Trevor Burnard, Daniel Clayton, Felix Driver, Saul Dubow, Fae Dussart, Cecily Jones, Gerry Kearns, David Killingray, Miles Ogborn, Christer Petley and Andrew Porter.

The ideas for the book have also been presented and worked through in a number of fora, including the 'Rethinking the colonisers' conference held in 2002 at the University of Warwick; the 'World History Workshop' conference held at the University of Cambridge in 2005; the 'Geographies of Transnational Networks' conference at the University of Liverpool in 2005, and the 'Reconfiguring the British' seminar at the Institute of Historical Research in London in 2005. The 'Reconfiguring the British' seminar series has provided a regular source of intellectual inspiration. Opportunities to present chapters were taken gratefully by the editors at the University of Bristol's 'Geography Research' seminar, the University of Tasmania's 'Colonialism and its Aftermath' research centre, the Institute of Historical Research's 'Imperial History' seminar and the University of Sussex's 'Geography Research' seminar. The staff at the School of Oriental and African Studies (SOAS) Reading Room were especially helpful in assisting the research on William Shrewsbury. We are very grateful to Hazel Lintott of the University of Sussex Cartographic Unit for her diligent preparation of the maps and illustrations.

INTRODUCTION

Imperial spaces, imperial subjects

David Lambert and Alan Lester

This book is about some of the ways that individual people made the British empire, and some of the ways that the empire made them. During the 'long nineteenth century', from the War of American Independence to the First World War, the expanding British empire presented Britons with vastly increased opportunities to settle in or visit other lands. Much has been written about those who carved new lives for themselves by settling permanently within particular colonies. Initially these emigrants reinvented themselves as various kinds of colonial Britons, but subsequently, especially from the late nineteenth century, most of their descendants constructed new national identities – for example as Australians, South Africans, Canadians or New Zealanders – that were distanced both metaphorically and literally from Britain itself. Much has also been written about Britons who travelled through colonial places, reporting their observations and impressions in popular travelogues or creating exciting and exotic narratives of exploration. A number of authors have demonstrated that such narratives were influential in constructing the geographical imaginations of those who had stayed 'at home' in Britain itself.[1]

Many Britons can be considered in a different category, however, from either those who settled in or those who travelled through the empire. These were men and women who dwelt for extended periods in one colony before moving on to dwell in others, developing what we might

Acknowledgments: Our thanks to Elleke Boehmer, Matthew Brown, Daniel Clayton, Leigh Dale, Felix Driver, Klaus Dodds, Saul Dubow, Fae Dussart, Jon Hyslop, David Killingray, Zoë Laidlaw, Steve Legg and Adele Perry for their helpful comments on various drafts of this introduction.

[1] C. Hall, '"Going-a-trolloping": imperial man travels the empire', in C. Midgley (ed.), *Gender and imperialism* (Manchester: Manchester University Press, 1998), pp. 180–99; F. Driver, *Geography militant: cultures of exploration and empire* (Oxford: Blackwell, 2000); D. Clayton, *Islands of truth: the imperial fashioning of Vancouver Island* (Vancouver: University of British Columbia Press, 2000).

call 'imperial careers'. Within each of the colonies they inhabited, these people had opportunities to transcend their initial impressions, to insinuate themselves into personal, business, official, religious and friendship networks. They came, as they saw it, to 'know' the local 'native' peoples, and to articulate more considered and comparative reflections on the colonial societies in which they had dwelt. As Doreen Massey points out, '[a]rriving in a new place means joining up with, somehow linking into, the collection of interwoven stories of which that place is made'.[2] The majority of individuals who feature in this book did so more frequently than most settlers, and they did so in more profound, more interactive, more sustained, and often more personally transformative ways than did the travellers and explorers about whom so much has been written. Their imperial careers are worthy of further study not necessarily because imperial careerists' own comparative insights give us a more objective view of colonial relations, but because their life histories – indeed, their life geographies[3] – constituted meaningful connections across the empire in their own right. And these connections were one kind among many which facilitated the continual reformulation of imperial discourses, practices and culture.

Although the individuals examined in this book are not intended to be in any sense representative of those who careered across the British empire, they do span a good breadth of gender, class, religious and generational subject positions. All but one was 'white', reflecting in part the differential, racialised mobilities of colonial citizens and subjects, and in part the availability of sources. They were English, Scottish, Irish, American and West Indian. They consist of four colonial governors, two governors' wives, two missionaries, a nurse/entrepreneur, a poet/civil servant and a mercenary. Some were motivated to move between colonial sites by profit, some by religion and some by a sense of duty. In different ways, each colonial life provides insight not only into the heterogeneity of the empire and the multiple subject positions that arose from this 'variegated terrain',[4] but also how ideas, practices and identities developed *trans-imperially* as they moved from one imperial site to another.

Telling stories about people who moved across, and dwelt in, different parts of the empire during the course of their lives challenges the structure

---

[2] D. Massey, *For space* (London: Sage, 2005), p. 119.
[3] S. Daniels and C. Nash, 'Life paths: geography and biography', *Journal of Historical Geography* **30** (2004), p. 450.
[4] G. Whitlock, *The intimate empire: reading women's autobiography* (London: Cassell, 2000), p. 2.

of the national archives upon which its very pursuit is necessarily based. As Ann Laura Stoler recognises,

research that begins with people's movements rather than with fixed polities opens up more organic histories that are not compelled by originary narratives designed to show the 'natural' teleology of future nations, later republics, and future states.

The individual trajectories traced in this book 'ran across and athwart state-archived paper trails'.[5] The narratives of the subjects' lives knit together markedly different places, weaving between distanced cultural configurations. This volume therefore seeks to introduce a more explicit discussion of the complex spatiality of empire, as well as of imperial subjectivities.

IMPERIAL SPACES

From the beginnings of British imperial history-writing at the end of the nineteenth century, the differences between spaces and places, particularly 'metropolitan' or 'core' ones, and 'colonial' or 'peripheral' ones, have been absolutely fundamental to scholars' imagination of the British empire. And yet these spatial concepts have rarely been examined explicitly.[6] Between the 1950s and 1980s, the most influential model for understanding Britain's nineteenth-century imperial expansion was that of Ronald Robinson and John Gallagher. Robinson and Gallagher argued that the mid-Victorian British government favoured a low-cost 'imperialism of free trade' over the intricacies of formal empire, but that this preference was often subverted by events on the 'periphery' of empire. The crucial figures deciding when formal intervention was necessary to protect British interests were government officials in the colonial service. These men (and they were all men) shared a common educational background and worldview that Robinson and Gallagher described as the 'official mind', and many of their decisions were taken with the potential for indigenous collaboration with British administrations in mind.[7]

---

[5] A. L. Stoler, 'Tense and tender ties: the politics of comparison in North American history and (post) colonial studies', *The Journal of American History* **88**, 3 (2004), p. 852.

[6] For an extended discussion of the spatiality of imperial history, see A. Lester, 'Imperial circuits and networks: geographies of the British empire', *History Compass* **3**, 189 (2005), pp. 1–18.

[7] J. Gallagher and R. Robinson, 'The imperialism of free trade', *Economic History Review*, 2nd series, **6**, 1 (1953), pp. 1–15; R. Robinson and J. Gallagher with A. Denny, *Africa and the Victorians: The official mind of imperialism*, 2nd edition (Basingstoke: Macmillan, 1981), p. xvii; R. Robinson, 'Non-European foundations of European imperialism', in E. R. Owen and B. Sutcliffe (eds.), *Studies in the theory of imperialism* (London: Longman, 1972), pp. 117–42.

In linking economic and political motivations, and explaining their intersection within the culture of the 'official mind', Robinson and Gallagher's theory inscribed an implicit geographical imagination on their discipline. Imperial historians' role was to study a world of 'core' British metropolitan interests interacting with 'local/peripheral' crises that were generated through the actions of indigenous peoples and rival imperial powers, and to reconstruct the ways in which the 'official mind' would have understood this world. In spatial terms, theirs was a centripetal, or, as they called it, 'ex-centric', analysis, since expansionary initiative moved from the colonial 'edge' of the empire to the British 'centre'.[8]

In the early 1990s, though, a new integrative model of imperial expansion and decline was formulated. In place of Robinson and Gallagher's centripetal framework, the work of P. J. Cain and A. G. Hopkins was based upon a more explicitly centrifugal sense of imperial space. For them, 'gentlemanly capitalism', with its logic structured above all in the City of London, was the driving force of interaction between Britain and its colonies. Cain and Hopkins asserted that '[p]utting the metropolitan economy back at the centre of the analysis ... makes it possible to establish a new framework for interpreting Britain's historic role as a world power'.[9] Britain's imperial expansion was not so much the product of an 'official mind', as it was the result of the work performed by 'gentlemen' operating in the financial and service sectors of the City of London, but maintaining close connections with government. Cain and Hopkins were confident that 'geographical considerations, like the "peripheral thesis" have their place in the story, but only within the context of impulses emanating from the centre'.[10]

'Geographical considerations', however, continued to trouble imperial historians after Cain and Hopkins had sought to lay them to rest. With their metropolitan focus, and the consequent marginalisation of both British and indigenous peoples in the colonies themselves, Cain and Hopkins still did not address the longstanding problem of how to write about such vastly different places, processes and people as those contained within the ever-changing nineteenth-century British empire at the same time – how to link the local and particular (metropolitan *and* colonial)

---

[8] Robinson and Gallagher with Denny, *Africa and the Victorians*, p. xxii.
[9] P. J. Cain and A. G. Hopkins, *British imperialism: innovation and expansion 1688–1914* (Harlow: Longman, 1993), p. 5.
[10] P. J. Cain and A. G. Hopkins, *British imperialism: crisis and deconstruction, 1914–1990* (Harlow: Longman, 1993), p. 297.

with the general and universal (imperialism). In other words, how to connect people, places and events analytically in the ways that colonial relations had connected them historically.

In his influential survey of the state of imperial history in the aftermath of decolonisation, David Fieldhouse seemed to think that only a super-human scholar could properly attain the necessary vantage point to achieve such an overview. His ideal imperial historian would have to be located

in the interstices of his [*sic*] subject, poised above the 'area of interaction' [between the imperial 'core' and its 'peripheries'] like some satellite placed in space, looking, Janus-like in two or more ways at the same time ... [and giving] equal weight to what happens in a colony and in its metropolis ... intellectually at home in both.[11]

The tendency of 'traditional' imperial historians, since Fieldhouse's article, to think in terms of 'interactions', 'linkages' or, as John Darwin suggested, 'bridgeheads',[12] between Britain and its colonies, preserved at least some common ground between the discipline of imperial history and in other respects very different postcolonial accounts of empire. Scholars who approached colonial relations from other disciplinary or sub-disciplinary backgrounds, and with a more postcolonial emphasis on culture, were also recognising the need to analyse metropole and colony in the same analytical frame during the 1990s, even if their theoretical orientation led them to resist Fieldhouse's notional ideal of a panoptic (and exclusively gendered) vision.[13] We do not propose here to enter into the significant theoretical differences between 'traditional' imperial history and post-colonial theory. Nor can we do full justice to the ways that the 'new' imperial history that has emerged since the mid-1990s seeks to blend the attention to empirical detail and historical context of the former, with the post-structuralist understanding of race, class, nationality, sexuality and gender of the latter. But we will attempt at least to draw attention to the different spatial imaginations associated with each tendency.[14]

---

[11] D. Fieldhouse, 'Can Humpty-Dumpty be put together again? Imperial history in the 1980s', *Journal of Imperial and Commonwealth History* **12**, 2 (1984), pp. 18–19.

[12] J. Darwin, 'Imperialism and the Victorians: The dynamics of territorial expansion', *English Historical Review* (June 1997), p. 629.

[13] A. L. Stoler and F. Cooper, 'Between metropole and colony: rethinking a research agenda', in F. Cooper and A. L. Stoler (eds.), *Tensions of empire: colonial cultures in a bourgeois world* (Berkeley and London: University of California Press, 1997), pp. 1–58.

[14] On general differences and points of connection between 'traditional' and 'new' imperial history, see D. Kennedy, 'Imperial history and post-colonial theory', *Journal of Imperial and Commonwealth History* **24**, 3 (1996), pp. 345–63, and C. Hall (ed.), 'Introduction: Thinking the postcolonial,

New ways of understanding the British empire as an interconnected space emerged especially out of prominent literary scholars' reflections on their own diasporic identities, as well as the postcolonial criticism of novels and travel writing that had been produced within, and marked by, colonial discourses. Edward Said's work loomed large in both genres.[15] The growing body of criticism of colonial literatures tended by its very nature to traverse national borders as it linked colonial modes of representation from different sites.[16] While imperial historians tended to dismiss much of the work emanating largely from departments of English for being ahistorical, some of their own work was nevertheless gradually coming into dialogue, often in unacknowledged ways, with its spatial openness.

Darwin's article, for instance, touched on themes that were being explored much more explicitly by anthropologists, historians and geographers who found inspiration in postcolonial writing.[17] In recognising the coexistence of different British interests, each with their own ways of connecting metropole and colony (or their own 'bridgeheads'), Darwin approached Nicholas Thomas' insistence that we identify multiple, and often contestatory, 'projects' of colonialism, rather than try to isolate *the* single driving force behind imperial expansion (such as the 'official mind' or 'gentlemanly capitalism').[18] In emphasising the interaction between each British 'bridgehead' and specific local societies, it gestured towards Mary Louise Pratt's notion of 'contact zones'.[19] In noting that different 'bridgeheads' might not be oriented towards compatible aims, it chimed with Ann Laura Stoler and Fred Cooper's call for greater analysis of the significant 'tensions of empire' among colonists, as well as between them and colonised peoples.[20] And in conceiving of several 'bridgeheads' connecting any one colony with Britain, Darwin was moving closer to the networked or webbed conception of imperial space characteristic of the

thinking the empire', *Cultures of empire, a reader: colonizers in Britain and the empire in the nineteenth and twentieth centuries* (Manchester: Manchester University Press, 2000), pp. 1–36.

[15] E. W. Said, *Orientalism: western conceptions of the Orient* (London: Penguin, 1978) and *Culture and imperialism* (London: Chatto and Windus, 1993).

[16] See E. Boehmer, *Colonial and postcolonial literature: migrant metaphors* (Oxford: Oxford University Press, 1995).

[17] Darwin, 'Imperialism and the Victorians'.

[18] N. J. Thomas, *Colonialism's culture: anthropology, travel and government* (Cambridge: Polity, 1994).

[19] M. L. Pratt, *Imperial eyes: travel writing and transculturation* (London: Routledge, 1992), pp. 6–7.

[20] Stoler and Cooper, 'Between metropole and colony'.

'new' imperial history, and of recent approaches to the historical geographies of colonialism, as we will see below.[21]

Before we explore the utility of networked notions of empire more thoroughly, it is worth pausing at this point to review what it is about the implicit geographies of 'traditional' imperial history that is most problematic. The empiricist approach of this tradition tends, with some recent exceptions, to translate into a notion of the empire as a space for the movement of material things – of capital and commodities especially. These things are propelled (usually by white, male Britons) between discrete, pre-constituted, bounded places. The internal identity of each of these places is self-evident and unassailable. Sometimes that identity is designated by a specific national or regional entity ('Canada' or 'southern Africa'), but often it is captured by the more reductionist designation of 'core' or 'periphery'. These designations have a specific analytical function. From Seeley,[22] through Robinson and Gallagher, and Fieldhouse, to Cain and Hopkins, their function is to explain and locate the (usually singular) motivation for, or cause of, British imperial expansion.

This is a pursuit that seems to be conducted for an audience interested in Britain's 'progress' to 'Great Power' status, rather than one interested in the nature and effects of colonial relations in any one or more places. The main geographical point of difference between authors within the imperial history 'tradition' is whether the 'causes' of Britain's imperial expansion were located in the 'core' itself or in its 'periphery'. What they share is an attempt to retrieve a sense of the imperial whole from the viewpoint of this metropolitan 'core', even if that 'core' is connected to its 'periphery' by 'interactions' or, perhaps, 'bridgeheads'.[23] The places mentioned in this tradition of imperial history, then, are significant as locales only in the Cartesian sense of points on a grid or map, set out in relation to an imperial core which may be Britain as a whole or London

---

[21] A spatial imagination premised on the idea of multiple, coexistent connections between Britain and each of its colonies also features in two recent departures in imperial history that should be mentioned. First, there is A. G. Hopkins' drive to make the discipline more politically relevant as a foundation for understanding contemporary globalisation: A. G. Hopkins (ed.), *Globalization in world history* (London: Pimlico, 2002). Second, there is the series of conferences and resulting publications around the theme of the 'British World': C. Bridge and K. Fedorowich (eds.), *The British world: diaspora, culture and identity* (London: Frank Cass, 2003). Both of these departures are addressed at greater length in Lester, 'Imperial circuits and networks'.

[22] J. R. Seeley, *The expansion of England: two courses of lectures*, 2nd edition (London: Macmillan, 1895).

[23] For a similar critique of imperial history's spatial imagery, see F. Driver, 'Distance and disturbance: travel, exploration and knowledge in the nineteenth century', *Transactions of the Royal Historical Society* **14** (2004), pp. 80–1.

in particular. The purpose of this map is to allow the driving forces of Britain's expansion to be plotted. In such an imperial history, neither colonial nor British places are of interest as configurations of peoples, experiences, things and practices in their own right.

Scholars who have recently proposed a networked conception of empire generally consider it more useful to try to examine multiple meanings, projects, material practices, performances and experiences of colonial relations rather than locate their putative root causes, whether they are 'economic', 'political' or, indeed, 'cultural'. These relations were always stretched in contingent and non-deterministic ways, across space, and they did not *necessarily* privilege either metropolitan or colonial spaces. They remade both metropolitan and colonial places in the act of connecting them. A colonial history which, as Kirsten McKenzie puts it, 'recasts the relationship between metropolitan centre and colonial periphery into a more contested, unstable and mutually constitutive frame' may have more limited ambition in one sense than a history that seeks definitively to name, locate or model the causes of imperial expansion.[24] However, such a history can perhaps fulfil its own aims more effectively.

Importantly, such a history also does a little more to challenge the contemporary acceptance of a European colonial conception of the world. The unquestioning use of categories such as 'centre' and 'periphery' in particular serves not so much to describe, as to reify and perpetuate some of the many spatial distinctions enacted through colonial (and other) unequal relations. At its most damaging, when played out in broader public debates, this reproduction of a language of spatial primacy helps to bolster attitudes and practices of social/racial superiority. Of course, any alternative spatial conceptualisation of colonial relations has to recognise that power relations were never evenly dispersed and that many of the most powerful institutions and individuals were indeed agglomerated in places like Whitehall and the City in London. But we need to see this uneven spatiality as, in large part, a constructed product of colonial relations rather than simply a static and uncontested precondition for them. As Nicholas Dirks puts it, we need to see colonialism less as

---

[24] K. McKenzie, *Scandal in the colonies* (Melbourne: University of Melbourne Press, 2004), p. 3.

'a process that began in the European metropole and expanded outwards' and more as 'a moment when new encounters within the world facilitated the formation of categories of metropole and colony in the first place.'[25]

In the discussion of Darwin's work above, we touched upon two aspects of what has been called the 'new' imperial history that inform its geographical imagination. The first concerns the notion of multiple colonial projects, and the second, the networks through which these projects were pursued. In partial critique of 'traditional' imperial history, 'new' imperial history recognises that there was never a single European colonial project, whether it be the pursuit of industrial or 'gentlemanly' capitalism, or governmental geo-strategising. Neither, accordingly, was there a single colonial discourse, or set of representations and practices of colonialism. Rather, the agendas of colonial interests, their representations of colonised places and peoples, and their practices in relation to them, were not only differentiated, but also often constructed in opposition to one another. Moreover, these projects and discourses always took shape through connections between colonial and metropolitan places. Catherine Hall, for instance, has written extensively about the contested notions of race, class and gender difference that connected Jamaica and Britain, especially Birmingham, within the reformist evangelical project of the nineteenth century; Ann Laura Stoler has studied relations of sexual intimacy and their role in the construction of social boundaries in different imperial contexts; Antoinette Burton has focused on circuits of discussion over the definition of feminism that connected India and Britain; and Kathleen Wilson has explored the varied performances of difference and domination across the eighteenth-century empire.[26]

While the focus of much of the 'new' imperial history has been on links between a specific colony and its metropole, this is founded on an awareness that these interactions were components of much more extensive networks connecting multiple colonial and metropolitan, as

---

[25] N. B. Dirks, 'Introduction: colonialism and culture', in N. B. Dirks (ed.), *Colonialism and culture* (Ann Arbor: University of Michigan Press, 1992), p. 6. See also A. Burton, 'Introduction: on the inadequacy and indispensability of the nation', in A. Burton (ed.), *After the imperial turn: thinking with and through the nation* (Durham, NC: Duke University Press, 2003), pp. 1–26.

[26] C. Hall, *White, male and middle class: explorations in feminism and history* (Cambridge: Polity, 1992), and *Civilising subjects: metropole and colony in the English imagination, 1830–1867* (Cambridge: Polity, 2002); A. L. Stoler, *Carnal knowledge and imperial power: race and the intimate in colonial rule* (Berkeley: University of California Press, 2002); A. Burton, *Burdens of history: British feminists, Indian women and imperial culture* (Durham, NC: University of North Carolina Press, 1994); K. Wilson, *The island race: Englishness, empire and gender in the eighteenth century* (London: Routledge, 2003).

well as extra-imperial, sites.[27] Although the emphasis of each of the studies mentioned above has been on reciprocal cultural and political construction, all recognise that the networks connecting colony to metropole were also of a more material kind. The travel of ideas that allowed for the mutual constitution of colonial and metropolitan culture was intimately bound up with the movement of capital, people and texts between these sites, all dependent in the last resort on the passage of ships, and later, the construction of telegraphic cables across imperial space.[28] The 'new' imperial history may place more emphasis than 'older' imperial history on culture, but it does not artificially separate culture from its material conditions.[29]

Tony Ballantyne has focused recently on circuits of discussion, people and material that connected different colonies, rather than just an individual colony with Britain. He has tracked ideas about Aryanism and racial difference that circulated between India and New Zealand, as well as much further afield. Ballantyne's project has been dependent upon an unusually explicit and extended discussion of the British empire's web-like spatiality. He argues that the image of the web 'captures the integrative nature of ... cultural traffic, the ways imperial institutions and structures connected disparate points in space into a complex mesh of networks'.[30] As Ballantyne notes, the utility of a networked or 'webbed' conceptualisation goes further: it enables us to think about the inherent relationality of nodal points or 'centres' within an empire. Undercutting simple metropole–binary divides, places and people can be 'nodal' in some of their relations with immediate hinterlands or subordinates (Calcutta in relation to Bengal, for instance), and yet simultaneously 'peripheral' in some of their relations with other centres (Calcutta in relation to London).

Of the multiple and continually fragmenting and reconstituting imperial networks of communication that held the empire together, those of colonial governmentality, humanitarian campaigning and settler

---

[27] See A. Lester, *Imperial networks: creating identities in nineteenth century South Africa and Britain* (London and New York: Routledge, 2001), and 'British settler discourse and the circuits of empire', *History Workshop Journal* **54** (2002), pp. 27–50.

[28] See S. Potter, *News and the British world: the emergence of an imperial press system* (Oxford: Oxford University Press, 2003).

[29] See Lester, *Imperial networks*, pp. 1–9; E. Boehmer, 'Global and textual webs in an age of transnational capitalism; or, what isn't new about empire', *Postcolonial Studies* **7**, 1 (2004), pp. 11–26.

[30] T. Ballantyne, *Orientalism and race: Aryanism in the British empire* (Basingstoke: Palgrave, 2002), p. 39.

counter-campaigning, and of natural scientific enquiry, have received the most attention to date.[31] Zoë Laidlaw, for instance, has shown how the governance of Britain's colonies relied for its existence and functioning to a great extent on informal contacts, patronage, nepotism and politicking, especially through contacts in London.[32] But, as the chapters by Laidlaw herself, Laurence Brown, and David Lambert and Philip Howell in this book show, the discourse of colonial governmentality was also profoundly a product of the mobility of governors themselves. Since most governors dwelt in multiple colonies during their careers, so they inevitably made comparisons and connections between those colonies. Colonial governance was thus often a relative and comparative endeavour – one that was dependent on fruitfully imagining the lessons that could be learned and transferred between differently constituted colonial places.[33] Moreover, as Laurence Brown's study of Arthur Gordon shows, the mobility of individual governors could have profound effects for the mobility of other people whose individual experiences are harder to access. In Gordon's case, an individual career was shaped in part by the imperative of ordering the mass migrations of Asian indentured workers. The model of indentureship that Gordon developed can be thought of as a kind of 'travelling theory', which had profound implications for the hundreds of thousands of migrants whose stories the archive does not allow us to tell with any precision.[34]

As these examples demonstrate, a networked conception of imperial interconnectedness is very helpful if one wants to consider metropole and colony, or colony and colony, within the same analytical frame, and without necessarily privileging either one of these places. However, there are still traps into which one might fall. There is a tendency in some discussions of contemporary, much faster, networked flows across the globe, to emphasise their progressive nature and their cosmopolitan

---

[31] On humanitarian networks, see for example, A. Porter, *Religion versus empire: British Protestant missionaries and overseas expansion, 1700–1914* (Manchester: Manchester University Press, 2004) and A. Lester, 'Missionaries and white settlers in the nineteenth century', in N. Etherington (ed.), *Missions and empire* (Oxford: Oxford University Press, 2005), pp. 64–85. On counter-networks, established by settlers, see Lester, 'British settler discourse' and D. Lambert, *White creole culture, politics and identity during the Age of Abolition* (Cambridge: Cambridge University Press, 2005). On the networks of natural science, see, for example, R. Drayton, *Nature's government: science, imperial Britain, and the 'improvement' of the world* (London: Yale University Press, 2000).

[32] Z. Laidlaw, *Colonial connections, 1815–1845: Patronage, the information revolution and colonial government* (Manchester: Manchester University Press, 2005).

[33] See also S. B. Cook, *Imperial affinities: nineteenth century analogies and exchanges between India and Ireland* (New Delhi: Sage, 1993).

[34] E. Said, 'Traveling theory', in *The world, the text and the critic* (London: Faber and Faber, 1983), pp. 226–47.

effects – the ways that they bring together previously discrete populations and allow for the mutually enlightening mobility of knowledge. But, as scholars of any empire should be aware, newly instituted networks have destructive as well as creative effects. If imperial networks allowed previously unconnected activities, lives and practices to be brought together, they also allowed previously connected ones to be wrenched apart.

It is all too easy to imagine the networks instantiated by Britons of various kinds as originary; as the first means by which distanced places were ever connected. Such a move would unrealistically inflate the innovativeness and ingenuity of Britons and elide the significantly interconnected nature of the pre-colonised societies that were assimilated into the British empire. Spatially extensive trading, tribute, diplomatic, intellectual, migration and travelling networks were by no means a British invention. In most cases, the webs structured by British colonial interests were either layered on top of pre-colonial networks and networks constructed by pre-existing empires (such as the Mughal in India), adding new levels of complexity, or those pre-colonial and other imperial networks were fundamentally disrupted and restructured as a result of British interventions.[35]

If we think only about imperial networks that were constructed and maintained by colonial interests, it is also easy to overlook the fact that colonised subjects themselves could and did forge new networks which similarly spanned imperial space, some of which were assimilationist and others more directly anti-colonial in their effects. Fewer colonised and anti-colonial subjects were themselves as voluntarily mobile in this period as the largely colonial figures included in this book. Olaudah Equiano, Mahatma Gandhi and Sol Plaatje are well-researched exceptions, but there are others who deserve more study, such as the pan-Africanists F. Z. S. Peregrino and Henry Sylvester Williams.[36] Aside from pan-Africanism, inclusionary claims-based or counter-imperial networks of communication and agitation could be created by Khoisan, Maori and aboriginal groups, as well as Irish and Indian nationalists and anti-British Boers.[37]

---

[35] See E. Wolf, *Europe and the people without history* (London: University of California Press, 1982); A. Gupta and J. Ferguson, 'Beyond "culture": space, identity, and the politics of difference', *Cultural Anthropology* **7** (1992), pp. 6–23; Hopkins, *Globalization in world history*.

[36] See C. Saunders, 'From Trinidad to Cape Town: the first black lawyer in the Cape', *Quarterly Bulletin of the South African Library* **55**, 4 (2001), pp. 146–61; O. C. Mathurin, *Henry Sylvester Williams and the origins of the Pan-African movement, 1869–1911* (Westport, CT: Greenwood, 1976).

[37] E. Elbourne, 'The Eastern Cape and international networks in the early nineteenth century', Fort Hare Institute of Social and Economic Research, Working Paper series, WP 43 (August 2003),

Finally, there is the danger of imagining imperial networks as reified and ossified infrastructures, rather like a road or rail network at any given point in time. It may be more productive not to use 'systems' language at all to conceptualise such networks, since across any kind of space 'there are always connections *yet to be* made, juxtapositions yet to flower into interaction, or not, potential links which may never be established. Loose ends and ongoing stories'.[38] Colonial networks must be seen not only as provisional and contingent, but sometimes as ephemeral and even fleeting. Rather like the patterns in a kaleidoscope, the precise constitution of the interconnections may be momentary, although the networked nature of interconnectedness itself is constant.

Bearing these qualifications in mind, the notion of an imperial spatiality consisting of networks is one that informs the narrative of each individual life recounted in this book. These lives can themselves be thought of as strands connecting one place contingently with another – strands liable to take new forms and embodying 'loose ends and ongoing stories'. In pursuing their imperial careers, the figures peopling this book helped to produce and alter the spatiality of the empire in ways ranging from the trivial to the historically enduring. As Stoler notes,

one thing is increasingly clear as colonial studies reconsiders the breadth of its locations and its analytic frames. It was not only empires that reshaped the 'interior frontiers' of the nation; people who moved within, between, and outside of imperial boundaries were also reshaping them.[39]

IMPERIAL SPACE, PLACE AND SUBJECTIVITY

The point about networks, of course, is that they connect different places. And what emerges implicitly from a networked conception of imperial *space* is an understanding of *place* that shares many features with recent theoretical approaches within the discipline of geography. In this conception, places are not so much bounded entities, but rather specific juxtapositions or constellations of multiple trajectories. These trajectories may be those of people, objects, texts and ideas. They may also consist of the movements of rock, sediment, water, ice and air – trajectories of a

University of Fort Hare, South Africa; E. Boehmer, *Empire, the national and the postcolonial, 1890–1920: resistance in interaction* (Oxford: Oxford University Press, 2002); E. Boehmer and B. Moore-Gilbert, 'Postcolonial studies and transnational resistance', *Interventions* 4, 1 (2002), pp. 7–21; Ballantyne, *Orientalism and race*, p. 11.
[38] Massey, *For space*, p. 107. [39] Stoler, 'Tense and tender ties', pp. 23–4.

different pace and scale that constitute the physical geography of a given place at a given time. Such material trajectories both impose constraints on the material practices that humans adopt in place, and condition the imagination of place. The differences between places are the result of these trajectories intersecting in varied ways across the surface of the Earth. In their ever-changing coming together, they produce combinations that are unique and thus give 'character' to each place.

Doreen Massey is the most eloquent exponent of this view of place. She notes how, in most humanities and social science literature, more bounded notions of place limit our ability to analyse both historical and contemporary interconnectedness. In this literature – and here we would include 'traditional' imperial history writing – '[f]irst the differences between places exist, and then those different places come into contact. The differences are the consequence of internal characteristics. It is an essentialist, billiard-ball view of place. It is also a tabular conceptualisation of space'.[40] Following their recognition of the networked nature of imperial space, scholars of colonialism are now beginning to conceive of this 'first' (and subsequent) meeting of metropolitan and colonial places, rather, as the throwing together of a set of diverse and complex trajectories that were already spatially extensive, even if in other directions.

In such a conceptualisation, imperial space is 'the sphere of a multiplicity of trajectories',[41] many of which were given impetus and direction by individuals collaborating in pursuit of specific colonial or anti-colonial projects, such as proselytisation, humanitarianism, settler capitalism, commercial enterprise, scientific enquiry, governmentality, or pan-Africanism and resistance to white supremacy. Some of these trajectories may be 'stronger' than others for a while and some of them may become formalised as organisational networks such as those constructed by missionary societies, the Colonial Office, the East India Company or the Pan-Africanist Congress. Both metropolitan and colonial places are specific meeting points of such trajectories, a coming together of them in specific ways at a specific time. Adopting such a conceptualisation allows us to continue insisting on the unique 'character' of different places within the empire, and thus also to emphasise the obvious differences between metropolitan and colonial places. As Massey notes, the 'open, relational construction of place in no way works against specificity and

---

[40] Massey, *For space*, p. 68, quoting P. Kamuf (ed.), *A Derrida reader: between the blinds* (New York: Columbia University Press, 1991), p. xv.
[41] Massey, *For space*, p. 119.

uniqueness, it just understands its derivation in a different way'.[42] This conceptualisation of place and its relation to space also allows us to understand better the relationship between dwelling in new colonial places and the reformulation of individual subjectivity. Place does 'change us', but

> not through some visceral belonging (some barely changing rootedness, as so many would have it) but through the *practising* of place, the negotiation of intersecting trajectories; place as an arena where negotiation [of these different trajectories] is forced upon us.[43]

While we are especially interested in this volume in the changes of subjectivity wrought by dwelling in, and actively experiencing multiple colonial places, it is important to recognise that substantial connections can also exist between subjectivity and the more virtual *imagination* of place. There are different kinds of trajectory that come together to constitute place and thus the revision of the self, and not all are embodied or material. This is a point made in the epilogue by Catherine Hall. Hall's main subject, Harriet Martineau, developed an understanding both of her own, and of Britain's, place in the world through her shifting impressions of colonised places that she had never seen.[44] For her, as for many other Britons who did not travel the empire, the lived reality of daily life was 'utterly dispersed, unlocalised, in its sources and in its repercussions'. Martineau's personal geography was never 'simply ... territorial'.[45] Even if one experiences places only through travelling discourses, such as texts, tales, conversations and the viewing of images, each such encounter with place involves engagement – each produces the 'need for judgement, learning, improvisation'.[46]

Adopting the conceptualisation of imperial space outlined here makes the constitution and significance of certain Britons' trans-imperial career trajectories, and of other, less-travelled Britons' imperialist subjectivities, easier to appreciate. The individuals studied here were 'part of the constant process of the making and breaking of links' which made places,

---

[42] *Ibid.*, p. 169. For a comprehensive contextualisation and discussion of understandings of the 'region' as a similarly, always-already interconnected bundle of trajectories, see A. Baker, *Geography and history: bridging the divide* (Cambridge: Cambridge University Press, 2003), pp. 156–205.

[43] Massey, *For space*, p. 154.

[44] Imaginative geographies are operational in all contexts, whether or not one has seen or been in the place imagined. The point here is that one does not *necessarily* have to have lived in or visited a place for it to meaningfully affect one's subjectivity.

[45] Massey, *For space*, p. 184. [46] *Ibid.*, p. 162.

and those links and places were in turn 'an element in the constitution' of these figures' own subjectivities.[47] These people did not just travel through and inhabit space; they altered it to some degree as they created their own trajectories and as they cross-cut or insinuated themselves into trajectories other than their own, either materially or imaginatively. In doing so, they contributed to the 'active material practices', which allowed colonial and metropolitan places, and the differences between them, to emerge.[48]

WRITING COLONIAL LIVES

In *Civilising subjects*, Catherine Hall provides perhaps the most comprehensive and successful attempt so far to bring colony and metropole into a single analytic frame.[49] To do so, Hall presents two interlaced case studies of Jamaica and Birmingham, delimited chronologically by two overlapping time frames: the first, from just prior to the formal ending of slavery in the British empire to the Morant Bay rebellion of 1865 and the second defined by the Reform Acts of 1832 and 1867. In this way, *Civilising subjects* explores the co-constitution of colony and metropole, and the identities of coloniser and colonised.

Significantly, Hall brackets her pair of case studies in prologue and epilogue with the making of an imperial life – that of Edward John Eyre.[50] The emphasis placed on this man's life is characteristic of the approach of *Civilising subjects* as a whole. Hall quotes from James Baldwin's essay, 'Stranger in the village' (1953) that 'People are trapped in history and history is trapped in them'.[51] In so doing, she is signalling the thoroughly embedded nature of racial thought and discourse that Baldwin addresses, and the practices of colonialism and slavery with which they are associated. This is also, we would suggest, a methodological allusion, a way of suggesting that 'history' can be released from the 'people' it is trapped within. Indeed, *Civilising subjects* is a thoroughly peopled history, complete with a 'cast of characters', potted life histories and the reflexive foregrounding of the author's own personal and intellectual trajectory. Eyre serves a particular purpose, of course. His life

---

[47] *Ibid.*, p. 118.   [48] *Ibid.*   [49] Hall, *Civilising subjects*.

[50] *Ibid.*, pp. 23–65, 434–41. Unfortunately, Julie Evans' *Edward Eyre: race and colonial governance* (Dunedin: University of Otago Press, 2005) was published too late for us to give it the attention it deserves here.

[51] J. Baldwin, 'Stranger in the village' in *Notes of a native son* (Harmondsworth: Penguin, 1953), pp. 151–65. To this we might venture to add that people are also trapped in geography and geography is trapped in them. See the section on 'Imperial space, place and subjectivity' above.

in the empire spans the chronological frame of the study and serves 'as a way into the shifts in racial thinking between 1830 and 1867'.[52] He was the governor of Jamaica in 1865 when, in the aftermath of a riot outside the courthouse of Morant Bay, martial law was declared and over 400 Afro-Jamaicans were executed. The subsequent controversy over Eyre's actions culminated in Eyre's acquittal, a result that for Hall represents the collapse of the humanitarian hegemony of the 1830s and 1840s. But beyond this substantive point, Eyre's life – from migrant to, and explorer in, Australia in 1833, sheep farmer, explorer, colonial official in New Zealand, lieutenant governor in St Lucia, on to Antigua, and finally governor in Jamaica in 1864 – knits together the trans-imperial formation that is Hall's object of study:

His identity, his sense of self and his notions of the world were formed as much by his experiences abroad as by his time in England. His 'imperial identity', his individual history, can be mapped across these different sites of empire. The theatres of empire constructed different possibilities. Metropolitan society, white settler societies, sugar colonies, each provided a site for the articulation of different relations of power, different subject positions, different cultural identities.[53]

An imperial career like that of Eyre affords a substantive, empirical and archival focus amidst the complex 'circuitry of empire',[54] and Hall's account of it provides a broad template for the substantive chapters in this book.[55] Like the notions of racial difference held by Eyre that were informed by his experiences of different sites of empire and transformed as he moved across these sites, the life histories in this book provide insight into trans-imperial ideas and practices. But these imperial subjects are more than just the avatars of ideas and ideologies, they are also people whose colonial lives were cross-cut by 'familial time, private time, the time of birth, emigration, marriage, new home and death'.[56] Charting lives in terms of 'movement and settlement' across the empire[57] provides a powerful way to put into practice the sort of networked approaches we have discussed above.

A focus on the lives of nineteenth-century figures like Eyre raises important questions about the relationship between the historical and the

---

[52] Hall, *Civilising subjects*, p. 20.   [53] *Ibid.*, p. 65.
[54] Wilson, *The island race*, p. 17.
[55] A somewhat similar approach is adopted, albeit for a particular range of figures, in A. Mackillop and S. Murdoch (eds.), *Military governors and imperial frontiers, c. 1600–1800: a study of Scotland and empire* (Leiden: Brill, 2003).
[56] Hall, *Civilising subjects*, p. 65.   [57] Daniels and Nash, 'Life paths'.

biographical.[58] For Eyre's contemporary and supporter, Thomas Carlyle, history was 'the essence of innumerable biographies' and the history of the world 'but the biography of great men'.[59] The Victorian period was characterised by considerable interest in life-writing – perhaps only matched by its popularity today. The era witnessed an outpouring of memoirs, self-portraits and other first-person singular writing, as well as the *Dictionary of national biography* itself.[60] Writing in 1918, Lytton Strachey caustically characterised Victorian life-writing as:

Those two fat volumes, with which it is our custom to commemorate the dead ... with their ill-digested masses of material, their slipshod style, their tone of tedious panegyric, their lamentable lack of selection, of detachment, of design.[61]

Strachey's *Eminent Victorians* was a savage attack on the verbose hagiography that had characterised Victorian biographical writing. It provided a manifesto and blueprint for a more critical, focused and succinct approach to life-writing.[62] As such, Strachey is often credited with seeding the development of the modern biographical form, which eschews didacticism and often explores the psychological dimensions of the subject. Yet despite the development of more revisionist and critical forms of *popular* biography – alongside hagiographic accounts of 'great figures' – life-writing has not always attracted the attention or approval of historical scholars. So, whilst Leon Edel claims that '[t]he writing of lives is a department of history and is closely related to the discoveries of history',[63] there remains a considerable gap between historians and biographers.

The suspicion with which life-writing has been viewed by some academic historians reflects, in part, the lack of engagement by practitioners

---

[58] See L. E. Ambrosius, *Writing biography: historians and their craft* (London: University of Nebraska Press, 2004) and D. Beales, 'History and biography', in T. Blanning and D. Cannadine (eds.), *History and biography* (Cambridge: Cambridge University Press, 1996), pp. 266–83.

[59] T. Carlyle, *On heroes, hero worship and the heroic in history*, 4th edition (London: Chapman and Hall, 1852).

[60] M. Shortland and R. Yeo (eds.), *Telling lives in science: essays on scientific biography* (Cambridge: Cambridge University Press, 1996); E. Baigent, 'The geography of biography, the biography of geography: rewriting the *Dictionary of national biography*', *Journal of Historical Geography* **30** (2004), pp. 531–51.

[61] L. Strachey, *Eminent Victorians* (London: Chatto and Windus, 1993; originally published 1918), p. ix.

[62] L. Edel, *Writing lives: principia biographica* (New York: W. W. Norton, 1984), pp. 76–82; W. H. Epstein, *Recognizing biography* (Philadelphia: University of Pennsylvania Press, 1987), pp. 138–71; L. Marcus, *Auto/biographical discourses: theory, criticism, practice* (Manchester: Manchester University Press, 1994), pp. 90–134.

[63] Edel, *Writing lives*, p. 14.

of biography with social historiography and critical theory.[64] After the Second World War, philosophical and sociological perspectives came to prominence that resulted in the decentring of the individual, an emphasis on the social or structural, and, famously, proclamations about the 'death of the subject'. For example, the 'new criticism' rejected the 'biographical fallacy' by giving primacy to the work or text, rather than the life its author had led.[65] Similarly, critical theory's questioning of 'the real' posed considerable problems for mimetic approaches to auto/biography. Yet, whilst academic *auto*biography has been transformed through its engagement with critical theory and become a key way of exploring issues of reflexivity and positionality,[66] biographical writing has remained 'stuck in a time-warp'.[67]

There have been efforts to develop more critical approaches to biographical writing in academic circles,[68] not least through a shift in focus towards 'minority' subjects, including women, non-whites and non-heterosexuals.[69] It has been suggested, however, that reworked forms of biography must also address taken-for-granted assumptions about the centred and unified individual that lie at the heart of much life-writing. As Mary Rhiel and David Suchoff ask, '[h]ow does the urge to destabilize traditional culture, by telling stories of different lives, mesh with the stabilizing generic conventions of the traditional, unified self on the road to self-consciousness?'[70] We might thus suggest that biographical forms of writing can remain problematic if they evoke an essential character and personality, and thereby sustain what James Clifford has called the 'myth

---

[64] Biographical sketches – particularly of 'great men' – do still remain an attractive narrative mode for some historians. See, for example, Blanning and Cannadine (eds.), *History and biography: essays in honour of Derek Beales* (Cambridge: Cambridge University Press, 1996).

[65] Edel, *Writing lives*; Marcus, *Auto/biographical discourses*.

[66] C. Steedman, *Landscape for a good woman: a story of two lives* (London: Virago, 1986); E. V. Bunkše, *Geography and the art of life* (Baltimore: Johns Hopkin University Press, 2004).

[67] L. Stanley, *The auto/biographical I* (Manchester: Manchester University Press, 1992), p. 126.

[68] For example, see L. Cotterill and G. Letherby, 'Weaving stories: personal auto/biographies in feminist research', *Sociology* 27, 1 (1993), pp. 67–80; L. Stanley, 'On auto/biography in sociology', *Sociology* 27, 1 (1993), pp. 41–52. In anthropology, life history remains among the tools of fieldwork. See D. Bertaux (ed.), *Biography and society: the life history approach in the social sciences* (London: Sage, 1981).

[69] C. N. Parke, *Biography: writing lives* (New York: Twayne Publishers, 1996); P. R. Backscheider, *Reflections on biography* (Oxford: Oxford University Press, 1999); H. Lee, *Body parts: essays in life writing* (London: Chatto and Windus, 2005); Marcus, *Auto/biographical discourses*, pp. 273–96. For reviews of recent work on gender and (auto)biography, see C. Steedman, 'Difficult stories: feminist auto/biography', *Gender and History* 7 (1995), pp. 321–6 and N. I. Painter, 'Writing biographies of women', *Journal of Women's History* 9 (1997), pp. 154–63.

[70] M. Rhiel and D. Suchoff (eds.), *The seductions of biography* (London: Routledge, 1996), pp. 3–4.

of personal coherence'.[71] It is to avoid this that some have sought to distinguish new forms of life-writing – sometimes dubbed the 'new biography'[72] – from the older ones through their representational experiments with narrative discontinuity and polyvocality.[73] Clifford himself called for a less centred biography that seeks to bring the 'background' of a life as close to the surface as possible. In terms similar to Massey's notion of places as arenas where different trajectories are thrown together, he described this as a 'narrative of transindividual occasions'[74] in which '[i]ndividuals become meeting points for influences, no longer static but mobile, effusive, decentred, a process not a thing'.[75]

Despite concerns about biographical writing, we would argue that it remains a powerful way of narrating the past.[76] Barbara Tuchman suggests that it can serve as a 'prism of history' and, whilst we prefer to follow Kali Israel in seeing it as more of a shifting 'kaleidoscope',[77] Tuchman is surely right when she notes that life-writing can attract and hold the reader's interest in the larger subject.[78] More specifically, John MacKenzie argues that biographical lives can serve as convenient case studies for 'addressing some of the historiographical fractures and neglect of imperial diversity' – precisely the issues we have raised above.[79]

Although a broadly defined biographical approach runs through the substantive chapters that follow, each addresses this in particular ways. Nevertheless, all the chapters have at least three things in common. First, each focuses on an individual who settled, was posted or otherwise dwelt

---

[71] J. Clifford, '"Hanging up looking glasses at odd corners": ethnobiographical prospects', in D. Aaron (ed.), *Studies in biography* (Cambridge, MA: Harvard University Press, 1978), p. 44.

[72] Rhiel and Suchoff (eds.), *The seductions of biography*, p. 2.

[73] T. Söderqvist, 'Existential projects and existential choice in science: science biography as an edifying genre', in Shortland and Yeo (eds.), *Telling lives in science*, p. 78.

[74] Clifford, '"Hanging up looking glasses"', p. 52.

[75] Shortland and Yeo (eds.), *Telling lives in science*, p. 14. See also S. Smith and J. Watson (eds.), *Getting a life: everyday uses of biography* (Minneapolis: University of Minnesota Press, 1996), p. 18.

[76] See, for example, N. Z. Davis, *Women on the margins: three seventeenth-century lives* (Cambridge, MA: Harvard University Press, 1995).

[77] K. A. K. Israel, 'Writing inside the kaleidoscope: re-representing Victorian women public figures', *Gender and History* 2 (1990), pp. 40–8.

[78] B. W. Tuchman, 'Biography as a prism of history', in M. Pachter (ed.), *Telling lives: the biographer's art* (Philadelphia: University of Pennsylvania Press, 1981), p. 134. In the course of putting this book together, we have been struck by the number of suggestions for other figures to include. This seems to confirm the appeal of biographical sketches as a means of narrating the interconnected histories of the British empire. Other examples of the use of this narrative mode include Elleke Boehmer's 'Introduction' to R. Baden-Powell, *Scouting for boys* (Oxford: Oxford University Press, 2004; originally published 1908), pp. xiv-xviii and L. Colley, *Captives: Britain, empire and the world, 1600–1850* (London: Jonathan Cape, 2002).

[79] J. MacKenzie, 'Foreword' to Mackillop and Murdoch (eds.), *Military governors and imperial frontiers*, p. xxvii.

across the multiple spaces of the British empire and beyond, roughly between American independence and the First World War.[80] Second, each chapter offers a biographical 'portrait' or 'sketch' of its subject. As a distinct form, the biographical sketch has its own long history and conventions, including the common practice for them to be grouped together in collections of up to a dozen. Tuchman suggests that the advantage of this sub-genre is that

one can extract the essence – the charm or drama, the historical or philosophical meaning – of the subject's life without having to follow him [*sic*] through all the callow years, the wrong turnings, and the periods in everyday life of no particular significance.[81]

Certainly one advantage of the biographical sketch for this collection is that they can be placed side-by-side with others to afford comparative insight into wider trans-imperial phenomena.

The third point deserves more attention: each chapter seeks to draw out the connections between different imperial and extra-imperial sites that are apparent from focusing on a single, though not isolated, life. Developing Hall's treatment of Eyre, this resonates with a networked spatial imagination of the British empire, as well as representing an attempt to produce the sort of 'narrative of transindividual occasions' that Clifford sees as vital for a critical approach to life-writing.[82] To elucidate this, we want to turn to a key theme that frames our mobile and decentred biographical approach to exploring the spatial heterogeneity of the British empire.

IMPERIAL CAREERING

One of the key motifs in this book is the idea of 'career' and, stemming from this, that of 'careering'. The term 'career' is a suggestive one that captures a sense of volition, agency and self-advancement, but also accident, chance encounter and the impact of factors beyond the control of the individual. William Epstein has noted that

---

[80] Charles Murray (chapter eleven) lived longer into the twentieth century, until 1942.
[81] Tuchman, 'Biography as a prism of history', p. 133. In this volume, most of the chapters do not follow their subjects into 'retirement', which often involved a return 'home' to Britain. On this, see E. Buettner, '"We don't grow coffee and bananas in Clapham Junction you know!": imperial Britons back home', in R. Bickers (ed.), *Settlers and expatriates: Britons over the seas* (Oxford: Oxford University Press, forthcoming).
[82] Clifford, '"Hanging up looking glasses"', p. 52.

the word 'career,' meaning 'a person's course through life (or a distinct portion of life), especially when publicly conspicuous, or abounding in remarkable incidents,' enters the English language around 1800, as does the cognate sense, 'a course of professional life or employment, which affords opportunity for progress or advancement in the world'.[83]

The interrelated meanings of life path and a course of employment signified by career gained currency during the nineteenth century with the professional modernisation of British society linked to the development of industrial capitalism, the embedding of middle-class Victorian values and, not least, the opportunities afforded by an expanding empire.[84] This etymology matches the chronological focus of the book.

The term career has other promising connotations. Biography and career are related and reciprocal ideas. As Magali Larson puts it: '[w]hile biography is looking backward on one's life, an after-the-fact search for order and meaning, career is looking forward, with a sense of order to come'.[85] This is a significant association given the importance of life-writing to this collection: biographical sketches provide the means of mapping careers across the multiple sites of empire. Nevertheless, we would want to challenge the emphasis that Larson places on 'order', which is too redolent of Victorian biographical conventions. Although the outpouring of life-writing in the Victorian era provides a useful resource for many of the chapters that follow – such as Mary Seacole's *Wonderful adventures* or the *Memorials* of William Shrewsbury published by his son – the aim of this collection is not to reproduce such forms of hagiography or the centred self-making they imply.

In seeking to avoid and even contest the ordered conventions of career-focused, personally coherent Victorian biographical forms, the etymology of career is of further use. Along with its nineteenth-century meanings, 'career' continued to carry with it an older sense of a head-long gallop along a road or race course.[86] This older meaning – *to* career, career*ing* – is suggestive of a more disordered and uncontrolled path through life than Larson allows. In this way, it serves as a conceptual counterweight to the tendency of biographical approaches to sustain the 'myth of personal coherence'.[87] This is because the notion of 'careering' places an emphasis

[83] Epstein, *Recognizing biography*, p. 139. Epstein is quoting from the *OED*, 2nd edition (1989), p. 895.
[84] Colley, *Captives*, pp. 308–13.
[85] M. S. Larson, *The rise of professionalism: a sociological analysis* (Berkeley: University of California Press, 1977), p. 229.
[86] Daniels and Nash, 'Life paths', p. 454.
[87] Clifford, ' "Hanging up looking glasses" ', p. 44.

on the mobile and spatially distributed qualities of life, which resonates strongly with the decentring impetus of the new biography. As Stephen Daniels and Catherine Nash put it:

The conceptual dispersal, or 'decentring', of the autonomous individual and unified life has, if anything, emphasised the intersection of the geographical and biographical, in overlapping domains of self and place, personality and identity, spatiality and subjectivity.[88]

As this suggests, the connections between biography and notions of the spatial in general, and of movement and travel in particular, are strong. For example, William S. McFeely suggests that 'When we write a biography or read one ... we are embarked on what can be an exciting journey'.[89] It is this association that Nash and Daniels underline when they insist that 'life histories are also, to coin a phrase, life geographies'.[90] The idea of 'life geographies' evokes a sense of the spatial not simply as the location of, or backdrop to, a life, nor as a metaphor (as in the 'journey' of life),[91] but rather as co-constitutive with selfhood and identity, as we have argued above.

In the notion of 'imperial careering' we have a useful and evocative idea. It captures a sense of the professional life of the collection's subjects who made their way in the world as servants of empire, as governors, colonial officials or their wives, or whose professional lives took place in an imperial context, such as missionaries, nurses or mercenaries. But, the older sense of career also has considerable purchase by evoking a less autonomous, more decentred sense of subjectivity and movement. If history – and indeed geography – is 'trapped' in people, as Baldwin put it, then by tracing the careers of those who travelled and dwelt across

---

[88] Daniels and Nash, 'Life paths', p. 450.

[89] W. S. McFeely, 'Preface', in Rhiel and Suchoff (eds.), *The seduction of biography*, p. ix.

[90] Daniels and Nash, 'Life paths', p. 450. See also N. J. Thomas, 'Exploring the boundaries of biography: the family and friendship networks of Lady Curzon, Vicereine of India, 1898–1905', *Journal of Historical Geography* **30** (2004), pp. 496–519. For work by geographers on the British empire that involves biographical elements, whilst often eschewing the label 'biography', see A. Blunt, *Travel, gender, and imperialism: Mary Kingsley and West Africa* (New York: Guilford Press, 1994); F. Driver, 'Henry Morton Stanley and his critics: geography, exploration and empire', *Past and Present* **133** (1991), pp. 134–66; C. McEwan, '"The Mother of all the Peoples": geographical knowledge and the empowering of Mary Slessor', in M. Bell, R. Butlin and M. Heffernan (eds.), *Geography and imperialism, 1820–1940* (Manchester: Manchester University Press, 1995), pp. 125–50; M. Bell, '"Citizenship not charity": Violet Markham on nature, society and the state in Britain and South Africa', in Bell, Butlin and Heffernan (eds.), *Geography and imperialism*, pp. 189–220.

[91] M. Fuchs, 'Autobiography and geography: introduction', *Biography* **25** (2002), pp. iv–xi, and the articles that follow in that special issue reduce geography to physical terrain, site specificity and a metaphor for identity.

trans-imperial spaces through biographical sketches, we can gain insight
into the dynamic trajectories and networks of knowledge, power, commodities, emotion and culture that connected the multiple sites of the
empire to each other, to the imperial metropole and to extra-imperial
spaces beyond. As Bonham Richardson puts it, the relationships between
ideas, popular thought and policy 'are perhaps clearest in specific places,
at particular times, and when set in motion by real people'.[92] Tracing
these colonial lives over time and space provides one way of thinking
about empire that moves beyond dualisms of centre and periphery, global
and local, and contributes to an understanding of trans-imperial (and
extra-imperial) networks.

COLONIAL LIVES ACROSS THE BRITISH EMPIRE

In his foreword to Andrew Mackillop and Steve Murdoch's collection of
studies of Scottish military governors who served in the English/British
empire and beyond, John MacKenzie draws parallels between the careers
explored there and the trajectory of imperial historiography as a whole:

Just as migrations, as well as military gubernatorial careers, proceeded by geographical steps, so is modern imperial scholarship marking out key and dynamic
stages, replacing the old imperial historiographical certainties and simplicities
with a new complexity and multi-faceted approaches.[93]

In bringing together a collection of imperial careers, this book aims to
develop further MacKenzie's observations. As we have already noted,
these careers are not intended to be representative. There are clearly many
other individuals and types of figures who could have been included.[94]
Nevertheless, at least six key themes emerge from the chapters that follow.

---

[92] B. C. Richardson, 'Detrimental determinists: applied environmentalism as bureaucratic self-
interest in the *fin-de-siècle* British Caribbean', *Annals of the Association of American Geographers* **86**
(1996), p. 214.

[93] MacKenzie, 'Foreword' to Mackillop and Murdoch (eds.), *Military governors and imperial
frontiers*, p. xxi.

[94] Military figures are one category that would benefit from future critical research. It was military
networks that, as Anita Rupprecht shows in her chapter, prompted Mary Seacole's journey from
Central America to the Crimea. Military gubernatorial careers are addressed in Mackillop and
Murdoch (eds.), *Military governors and imperial frontiers*, whilst the lives of rank-and-file soldiers
receive attention in C. Steedman, *The radical soldier's tale: John Pearman, 1819–1908* (London:
Routledge, 1988); Colley, *Captives* and E. Spiers, *The Victorian soldier in Africa* (Manchester:
Manchester University Press, 2004). For the role of British and Irish mercenaries in extra-imperial
conflicts, see M. Brown and M. A. Roa (eds.), *Militares extranjeros en la independencia de
Colombia: nuevas perspectivas* (Bogotá: Museo Nacional de Colombia, 2005). The role of
friendships and connections established in the Peninsular campaign in subsequent gubernatorial
appointments is considered in Laidlaw, *Colonial connections*, especially pp. 21–7.

First, as they 'careered' across the empire and beyond, each colonial subject was involved in the introduction of certain modes of gendered, raced and classed thought to new contexts, where these ideas were modified and sometimes rejected in new spaces and circumstances. This suggests that ideas about, for example, race and national identity, and the governance, conversion and 'civilisation' of colonised peoples, were not simply exported from the imperial centre, nor indeed imported from the periphery. Instead, many developed across multiple spaces, especially as attempts were made to transpose and translate them through comparison and generalisation. For example, Laurence Brown's chapter explores Arthur Gordon's efforts to reform and extend state-controlled systems of indentured labour in the Indian and Pacific Oceans based on his paternalistic vision of colonialism and informed, in part, by his experience of the West Indian colonies. Yet, the effects and legacies of Gordon's efforts differed from place to place. Clearly, not all imperial ideas, practices, ideologies and discourses travelled well, and those that did not can reveal the differential mappings of race, class, gender and religion across the empire. Hence, the chapter by Philip Howell and David Lambert demonstrates that 'slavery' was a profoundly mobile and contested signifier. The consequences of John Pope Hennessy's attempt to wrestle with its different meanings in West Africa, the Caribbean and Hong Kong reveal not simply how an abstract idea 'played out' locally, but also how that idea was shaped by its complex travels. If the examples of Gordon and Pope Hennessy are suggestive of how trans-imperial forms of governance were produced, then Jon Hyslop's chapter serves as a reminder that 'national' culture was also produced over transnational space. Charles Murray was a remarkably significant figure in the literary production of Scottishness during the early twentieth century, and yet he made his contribution from a colonial site some 6,000 miles from Scotland. What Hyslop shows is that Murray's trajectory of voluntary colonial 'exile', far from serving as impediment to his brand of Scottish nationalism, was actually productive of it.

There are a host of other trans-imperial lives that could be considered in ways similar to those in this collection. To give just a few examples, there were imperial officials who advised on matters of forestry, botany and agriculture, such as Daniel Morris, who applied the experience he gained in Ceylon in 1879 to later postings to the Caribbean. See B. C. Richardson, *Igniting the Caribbean's past: fire in British West Indian history* (Chapel Hill: University of North Carolina Press, 2004), pp. 76–82, and the picaresque figures in Kirsten McKenzie's *Scandal in the colonies*. For an earlier period, studies of slaving captains, such as John Newton, could provide insight into the networks of the Atlantic world. See J. Rawley, *London, metropolis of the slave trade* (Columbia: University of Missouri Press, 2003).

Second, the colonial lives studied here appear as more than just the embodiments of travelling thought and discourse. Concomitant with the movement of ideas, knowledge and practices across and beyond the networks of empire was the formulation and reformulation of identities. Each biographical sketch reveals the changes in personhood that came from dwelling in different spaces – including, as we have indicated above, the transition from initial impressions to more considered articulations of new imperial sites (such as Lady Aberdeen, who went from disliking anything Irish to 'falling in love' with the people), engagements in local society (as in Charles Murray's involvement in South African Caledonian societies), the construction of friendship and familial networks (as in the case of William Shrewsbury, who married a white West Indian) and feelings of loss and nostalgia for home (as in Mary Curzon's profound sense of alienation in India). According to Matthew Brown, Gregor MacGregor reinvented himself throughout his career as a Scottish rebel, a patriot general, the 'Inca of New Granada' and the 'Prince of Poyais', partly for reasons of expediency and self-advancement. Nevertheless, his sense of identity changed in more profound ways as he established ties and roots – not least through fatherhood – eventually culminating in his recognition as a Venezuelan citizen. Changing personal circumstances would often propel, or curtail, imperial careers. For example, Zoë Laidlaw shows that Richard Bourke's imperial career was initiated through his wife's illness, as the couple sought a better climate to live in, whilst Shrewsbury requested a move back from southern Africa because of his wife's poor health. Professional career, family obligations and love were intertwined, and a historiography that insists on separating them – especially on separating profession from emotion – is likely to be incomplete.

Third, it was not just the physical movement of individuals and their embodied presence in particular places that served to shape their identities or ideas, but also how other places could be present with them. This could be when contrasts were drawn between different colonial sites, as Shrewsbury did when comparing colonialism in the West Indies and the Cape, or when the essential sameness of colonial situations was stressed, as Leigh Dale suggests George Grey did when he attempted to apply the same lessons of governance in Ireland, New Zealand and the Cape. Such comparisons played an important part in the development of transimperial ideas. Other places could also be present as imaginative geographies – in perceptions, memories and idealisations of elsewhere. For example, Nicola Thomas shows that Mary Curzon felt a strong sense of double exile in India from both England and America, and Arthur Gordon drew on a suite of indentureship policies based on his reading, as well as experience, of other colonial situations. Previous sites in an imperial career were also present in reputations that had been established elsewhere. Renown or notoriety could precede and haunt individuals. So when Bourke arrived in New South Wales or Pope Hennessy reached Hong Kong, many members of the colonial community were already predisposed against them because of what was known about their previous postings. Lancelot Threlkeld, as Anna Johnston shows, was marked as a troublemaker by his own mission society as a result of his activities in Polynesia, and was thus already eyed with suspicion by the colonial élite on his arrival in New South Wales. Similarly, as Val McLeish shows, when Lady Aberdeen returned to Ireland she faced mistrust and opposition. McLeish's chapter also shows that time, as well as place, could make a difference in shaping colonial lives. While other subjects moved between differently configured colonial places, Lady Aberdeen was in Ireland in 1886 and again in 1906–15. As we discussed earlier, Massey suggests that 'place' be understood as a meeting point of trajectories that come together in specific ways at a particular time.[95] For Lady Aberdeen, a familiar place was rendered as unfamiliar as a new colony by the development and conjunction of new circumstances there.

Massey's emphasis on intersecting trajectories brings us to a fourth theme running through this collection, by suggesting the other paths that cross-cut these individual colonial lives. Although the trans-imperial life path traced by the travelling and dwelling of these colonial subjects is the most obvious network that the chapters address – a network that can be partially represented in the figurative maps in each chapter[96] – we also see other networks with which these lives intersected. Most obviously, there were the trajectories of other individual lives, some that traced their own imperial careers, such as Mary Curzon's companion, Lord Kitchener; Charles Mitchell, who benefited from Arthur Gordon's patronage; or Edward John Eyre, who was a resident magistrate under George Grey in

---

[95] Massey, *For space*.
[96] The maps in each chapter are intended to convey a general sense of the spatial trajectory of the imperial career in question, or at least a portion of it. As with the variety of approaches to lifewriting adopted across the book, the maps do not – nor could they – conform to a singular format. They are *not* intended to show the 'travels' of each individual, and thus may not show intermediary points between major sites of dwelling. Nor are these maps supposed to be representations of 'time-geography' in the tradition of Torsten Hägerstrand and the Lund School. Rather they provide a particular representation of how each colonial life knitted together different imperial and extra-imperial places.

South Australia, and then Grey's lieutenant governor in New Zealand. Others had distinctly anti-imperial careers, like the Venezuelan leader Simón Bolívar, whose cousin married Gregor MacGregor. But these singular lives also intersected with wider patterns of movement and migration, such as the indentured labours that Gordon was concerned with or the settlers that Lady Aberdeen sought to attract to Canada. Although many of the figures addressed in this collection were members of élites and there are countless trans-imperial life stories that cannot be told as easily, these élite lives can give insight into these other colonial lives, including those of the subaltern colonised.

The life stories here also bear witness to flows of profit and commodity, and the circulation of newspapers, publications and correspondence. Formal and informal communicative networks provided channels that connected the subjects to other individuals and institutions, and through which instructions, requests, petitions and intelligence moved, transmitting past successes and failures, and shaping political ideologies and personal sensibilities. This also underlines the textuality of these lives. The chapters by Anna Johnston, Leigh Dale and Anita Rupprecht remind us that colonial lives are accessible not only to historical scholars, but were also construed by many of their contemporaries, through texts. For instance, Dale shows that Grey's own writings have persuaded many historians that it was his shock at the brutalities of colonialism in Ireland, as a young soldier, that converted him to liberalism. But these writings also persuaded many of his *own* correspondents, most notably those in the Colonial Office, of his essential liberalism. Similarly, as Anna Johnston suggests, Threlkeld's voluminous writings established a reputation for himself as troublemaker among metropolitan reformers and mission directors who had never met him and the resulting marginalisation from humanitarian networks proved costly for his own efforts in New South Wales. Finally, it is mainly the fact that Mary Seacole partook of the Victorian popularity for autobiography that has enabled her to attain a higher profile than many of the other 'black' subjects in British public consciousness.[97] Not only is our historical understanding shaped and confined by these texts, but those lives themselves were lived out in large part through the textual representations that moved within and between different colonies and Britain: appeals, memoranda, letters, despatches and, of course, biographical writing were the forms through which

---

[97] In 2004, Seacole was voted the 'Greatest Black Briton'.

individual agency was expressed, communicated across distance, and effected.[98]

Fifth, although we would want to stress the multiple nature of imperial networks, the chapters clearly show that not all networks were equally powerful and empowering for those associated with them. Many of the broader networks addressed in the chapters were related to the articulation over space and time of different and more or less powerful colonial projects – such as those associated with governmental, settler, commercial and humanitarian interests, or indeed with anti-colonial resistance, as mentioned above – some of which were in conflict. Individuals could find themselves at the centre of the resulting tensions. In standing out against the abuses of aboriginal people, Threlkeld aligned himself with a humanitarian colonial project founded on the 'reclamation of souls' and against the local settler project of land appropriation: his difficulty, as we have hinted, was that he was by no means fully integrated within effective humanitarian political networks. Shrewsbury, on the other hand, seems to have moved during his career, from being hero to pariah within humanitarian networks and, accordingly, from pariah to hero within settler networks. Focusing on the controversies and difficulties these colonial subjects faced, and contextualising them in relation to these broader networks and projects, provides a powerful means of discussing the 'tensions of empire' between competing imperial projects and ideas, and helps to mediate between overly generalised, 'global' models of empire and narrowly particularist, 'local' studies. Understanding colonial projects as being fostered through networked connections also enables us to see why some projects could be implemented more effectively than others and, indeed, why some imperial careers were more successful. Much depended on just how well 'networked' one was. Grey, for example, was particularly well connected in governmental and broader élite circles, while Bourke's use of his son as a kind of personal agent in London was an attempt to achieve the same kind of connectivity. Moreover, Thomas' chapter shows not only how Curzon acted as a go-between and source of intelligence for her husband, the viceroy of India, when she visited Britain, but also how her knowledge of India helped her to establish a position of some importance in metropolitan political life. In contrast, Johnston's chapter shows that the politically active and vocal

---

[98] See M. Ogborn, 'Writing travels: power, knowledge and ritual on the English East India Company's early voyages', *Transactions of the Institute of British Geographers* **27** (2002), pp. 155–71; D. Lambert, 'The counter-revolutionary Atlantic: white West Indian petitions and proslavery networks', *Social and Cultural Geography* **6** (2005), pp. 407–22.

Threlkeld was so isolated from his own London Missionary Society (LMS) and broader humanitarian networks that he remained a lonely voice in Australia. This was why Threlkeld's narratives 'ricocheted' through empire, while those of other LMS figures penetrated straight to the heart of British government in the 1830s. As we discussed above, the chapters confirm the importance of approaching these networks not as reified and ossified infrastructures, but rather recognising that they had to be made and maintained. The formal colonisation of Fiji, as discussed in Laurence Brown's chapter, is but one example of the extension of a governmental network into a new space, albeit one that was already characterised by networks of commercial and missionary activity.

The final theme arising from the chapters is how trans-imperial careers can shed new light on existing historical debates, not least by unsettling taken-for-granted categories and revealing hitherto unsuspected lines of enquiry. A few brief examples will suffice. Laurence Brown insists that in order to understand indentureship, we must recognise it as a product of various trans-imperial migrations, involving officials like Gordon, planters, missionaries, servants and labourers, as well as the migration of ideas and policies. A number of the chapters also provide further insights into the relationship between empire and identity. The studies of Murray, MacGregor, Pope Hennessy and Bourke, for example, show that Scottish and Irish identities were not simply 'taken' overseas to have a potentially different impact on the practice of empire from English identities, but rather how these other identities were articulated through the experience and heterogeneity of empire. In a similar vein, Rupprecht's chapter on Mary Seacole suggests how the trans-imperial mobility of non-white subjects could be a way for them to negotiate the hegemonic racial and gendered binaries associated with geographically specific colonial cultures (such as those of the post-emancipation Caribbean).

In addition to such particular insights into the history of the British empire, tracing trans-imperial networks can also inform a research agenda that goes beyond comparison and looks for actual historical connections and disconnections between different sites of empire. Thus, the chapter on Shrewsbury responds to calls to bring together the histories of the Caribbean and southern Africa.[99] Bourke's imperial career, along with the more famous one of Grey, connects the histories of South Africa and Australia (as well as New Zealand in Grey's case) in very tangible ways,

---

[99] A. G. Cobley, 'Forgotten connections, unconsidered parallels: a new agenda for comparative research in Southern Africa and the Caribbean', *African Studies* **58** (1999), pp. 133–55.

for despite the emergence of the 'British world' paradigm, the historiographies of these places remain largely separate.[100] And it is not only the histories of the colonies within Britain's empire that could be usefully connected more thoroughly. Matthew Brown's chapter, for instance, links British imperial activities in the Caribbean to the fate of other European empires, especially the Spanish. Along with Rupprecht's account of Seacole's trajectory between the British Caribbean, 'independent' Panama, Britain and the Crimea, and Thomas' emphasis on the significance of the USA to Curzon, it shows that imperial networks and the trajectories that constituted them were never contained neatly within empires, but spilled over and across them.

Of course, research on the sort of peripatetic figures addressed in the following chapters may be hindered by the organisation of archives along national lines, which makes the investigation of cross-imperial connections more difficult. To pick just one example, Matthew Brown explains that sources about MacGregor are dispersed across a variety of geographically disparate sites. Antoinette Burton notes the effects of such concentrations of material: 'Historians of Empire have tended to understand archives as a delineated physical space from which to reconstruct an equally delimited imperial past'.[101] Even connecting discrete histories and historiographies within a single empire may require a considerable amount of time and resources, as well as multifaceted expertise. Collaborative research may help in this regard – as in the chapters that follow on Shrewsbury and Pope Hennessy. Furthermore, bringing a number of such trans-imperial lives together almost certainly requires collaboration. In this regard, we hope that this collection, itself a product of multiple and intersecting personal and professional trajectories – or, indeed, careers – can go some way to pointing toward future work on the British empire, though not necessarily based on individual life history, that takes its multiple and networked spaces seriously.

---

[100] Although for some recent examples which do emphasise the co-constitution of such sites, see Lester, 'Settler discourse'; McKenzie, *Scandal in the colonies*, and P. Mein Smith and P. Hempenstall, 'Australia and New Zealand: Turning shared pasts into a shared history', *History Compass* (2003), http://www.history-compass.com/popups/print.asp?items=148, accessed 11/07/05.

[101] A. Burton, 'Archive stories: gender in the making of imperial and colonial histories', in P. Levine (ed.), *Gender and empire* (Oxford: Oxford University Press, 2005), p. 283.

CHAPTER I

Gregor MacGregor: clansman, conquistador and coloniser on the fringes of the British empire

Matthew Brown

Gregor MacGregor (Fig. 1.1) was born in Edinburgh in 1786 and died in Caracas, Venezuela, in 1845. Throughout his life he repeatedly crossed the boundaries nominally separating the British, French and Spanish empires in the Caribbean, adapting his loyalty and identity according to circumstance (see Map 1.1). His diverse and mobile imperial career ended in acrimony in Europe and anonymity in South America. This chapter illustrates the way that a military career allowed British subjects to travel throughout the interdependent and interrelated European imperial outposts in the Caribbean in this period, rethinking their own loyalties and affiliations as they served under old empires and new republics.

MacGregor, a Catholic, liked to claim his ancestry back to the Jacobite rebellion of 1745 and beyond. He served briefly in the British Army in the Peninsular Wars against Napoleon, and in Portugal he was granted a title that, he claimed, made him 'Sir' Gregor. In 1811 he moved to Caracas, and shortly after receiving news of the death of his English wife back in London, he married a cousin of the prominent Venezuelan leader Simón Bolívar, Josefa Antonia Andrea Xeres Aristeguieta y Lovera Bolívar. This represented a more permanent decision to seek his fortune in the troubled American colonies of the Spanish empire. This decision was confirmed by the huge earthquake that hit Caracas in 1812, in which MacGregor lost his substantial travelling library and other possessions. When the Spanish army subsequently reoccupied Venezuela (which had proclaimed its independence from Spain in 1810), MacGregor joined other exiles in fleeing to Cartagena de Indias (the principal port of the viceroyalty of New Granada, present-day Colombia), where his career as a patriot general began. Exploiting his reputation as a battle-hardened British officer, he won command of republican troops under Bolívar and soon gained esteem in the eyes of his subalterns after a series of military victories. Exiled again from Venezuela, he joined an élite band of patriots

Fig 1.1 Portrait of Gregor MacGregor by Constancio Franco Vargas, c. 1886, Museo Nacional de Colombia, MN273. Reproduced with the permission of El Museo Nacional de Colombia.

in Bolívar's celebrated 'Aux Cayes expedition', which sailed for Venezuela from Haiti in 1816. Its success led to the independence of the republic of Colombia (consisting of the present-day republics of Venezuela, Colombia, Ecuador and Panama), which was eventually declared in 1819 after protracted military conflict. Despite his almost complete ignorance of the topography of the region upon arrival, MacGregor established himself as one of the principal patriot leaders in the struggle against Spanish rule and was one of the most prestigious of the almost seven thousand British and Irish soldiers who enlisted in the Venezuelan army in this period.[1] This chapter shows how a quest for identity and

---

[1] For the involvement of these mercenaries in the Colombian Wars of Independence, see E. T. D. Lambert, *Voluntarios británicos e irlandeses en la gesta bolivariana*, Vol. I (Caracas: Corporación Venezolana de Guayana, 1983), Vols. II–III (Caracas: Ministerio de Defensa, Venezuela, 1990)

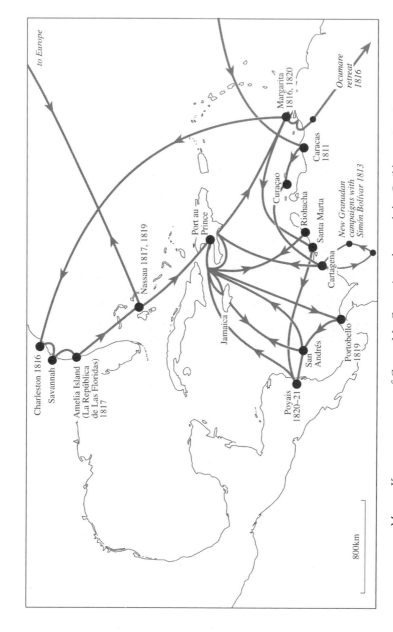

Map 1.1 Known movements of Gregor MacGregor in and around the Caribbean, 1811–1821.

reputation underpinned his subsequent career and attributed to his several successes and failures. By 1817, MacGregor had already left the Venezuelan service and, after spending time in the USA and Nassau, he led an expedition that ended Spanish rule in Amelia Island where he established the republic of Florida. Leaving Amelia he travelled to Britain, where he set about raising a Legion to fight for Venezuelan independence. He returned to the Caribbean in 1818 at the head of this expedition, but disease and desertion severely depleted his forces and he was forced to recruit replacements (and further supplies of food and ammunition) during a tour of Haiti, Jamaica and Barbados. In 1819, MacGregor led attacks on Riohacha and Portobello on the New Granadan coast, and proclaimed himself as the 'Inca' of New Granada. The next year MacGregor negotiated a land grant on the Mosquito Coast of present-day Nicaragua (which at the time was still claimed by the Spanish monarchy), and styled himself as 'the Prince of Poyais'. Returning to Britain – which remained ostensibly neutral in the struggle between Spain and its rebellious colonies – to recruit colonists, write constitutions and attract investment, he spent much of the 1820s in Edinburgh, Paris and London, including periods in jail for fraud and debt. He apparently never returned to Poyais where many of his colonists – a number recruited as indentured servants – had either died of disease or escaped to found another settlement in Belize. After the death of his second wife, who had accompanied MacGregor throughout all his travels, in Edinburgh in 1838, he returned to Venezuela, where he petitioned the government for unpaid wages and pensions, openly admitting that this was a financial decision rather than one motivated by any love of the country. He died in 1845. MacGregor and his compatriots who operated as mercenaries had their British identities fractured by virtue of operating outside the conventional limits of British imperial activity. In this context, MacGregor developed a highly sensitive sense of his own honour and masculinity.

Gregor MacGregor was a successful military leader in the Wars of Independence in Hispanic America, and crossed the Atlantic at least a dozen times seeking finance, resources and supporters for his enterprises. In this period, Spanish imperial identity was in crisis as a result of

and M. Brown, *Adventuring through the Spanish colonies: Simón Bolívar, foreign mercenaries and the birth of new nations* (Liverpool: Liverpool University Press, 2006). This chapter and the book upon which it expands were written with the support of a Carnegie Scholarship from the Carnegie Trust for the Universities of Scotland, several research grants from the University College London Graduate School, and a Marie Curie Fellowship from the European Union.

Napoleon's 1808 invasion of Spain, and this had profound consequences for the way Spain's American subjects viewed their relationships with the metropole and with each other.[2] The formation of republics was by no means inevitable but had its roots in contemporary understandings of liberty and patriotism, the example of the American, French and Haitian Revolutions, and perhaps most importantly, changes in local and regional identities based on colonial boundaries, existing political institutions and patterns of internal and external trade.[3] Within this environment, Mac-Gregor was able to form networks of support and finance amongst colonial élites and republican authorities, as well as with contrabanders, bandits and guerrillas. He often benefited from his reputation, which tended to precede him as a result of extensive newspaper coverage of his adventures. On occasions his inconsistent and often contradictory attitude towards slavery caused worry and distrust on the part of colonial planters in Jamaica who had previously supported him. Operating on the periphery of the British empire, MacGregor was able to thrive in a world where empires and identities were constantly adapted and negotiated.[4]

This chapter consists of four main sections. After a brief introduction to MacGregor's place in the historiographies of Scottish and British imperial activity and the Colombian Wars of Independence, each section examines a different stage or 'site' of his career. Firstly, his 'insurgent' phase, between 1811 and 1820, during which he travelled repeatedly across the Caribbean and four times across the Atlantic and lived for periods in Bermuda, Jamaica, Haiti, New Granada (Colombia) and Venezuela. Secondly, his 'Poyais' phase in the 1820s, in which MacGregor's thoughts and actions were concentrated on the small settlements on the Mosquito Coast but when he was mainly resident in London and Paris. The third section explores the early 1830s when MacGregor was resident in Edinburgh and engaged in reflection and meditation upon his career. The final site is MacGregor's Venezuelan retirement, a period which lasted from 1838 to his death in 1845. Because the archival resources left by MacGregor are fragmentary and scattered, this chapter relies as much upon the testimony of others as it does upon

---

[2] The principal work on this subject is F.-X. Guerra, *Modernidad y independencias* (Madrid: MAPFRE, 1992). In this chapter, references to Spanish language secondary sources have been kept to a minimum. All translations are my own unless stated. For a full bibliography see Brown, *Adventuring through the Spanish colonies*.

[3] On these processes see J. Lynch, *Latin American Revolutions 1808–1826* (Norman, OK: University of Oklahoma Press, 1994).

[4] See for example the many excellent contributions to M. V. Kennedy and C. Daniels, eds., *Negotiated empires: centers and peripheries in the Americas, 1500–1820* (New York: Routledge, 2002).

his own correspondence. The degree of insight offered by these different sites varies considerably according to the type of document preserved, which range from private and public correspondence, to government petitions and autobiography.

HISTORIOGRAPHY

The Wars of Independence in Hispanic America were an integral part of the Atlantic 'Age of Revolution' and as such they witnessed the incursions of revolutionaries, adventurers and curious travellers from across the globe.[5] Gregor MacGregor took part in 'circuits of movement that crisscrossed metropoles and peripheries that disregarded official histories and national borders' and he and others like him 'followed career itineraries and personal trajectories that led them in and out of explicitly racialised contexts, from imperial to domestic missionising projects, through locations where modernity was differently conceived and across imperial maps'.[6] As such he has been filtered out of nation-oriented histories of the period. The very first biographies of MacGregor were generally critical and often lapsed into lampooning him for acting outside the conventional British imperial world.[7] Histories of Scottish overseas activities tend to neglect South America entirely.[8] English-language biographies emphasise what they see as the absurdity of MacGregor's situation.[9] David Sinclair played up this angle to the extent that he marvelled that MacGregor continued to get away with his 'fraud' for as long as he did.[10] Whilst a little more prosaic, the few Hispanic American historical studies of MacGregor have also portrayed him as a foreign fool whose failures

---

[5] On the 'Age of Revolution' in Hispanic America see E. Van Young, 'Was there an Age of Revolution in Spanish America?', in V. M. Uribe Urán, ed., *State and society in Spanish America during the Age of Revolution* (Wilmington, DE: Scholarly Resources, 2001), pp. 224–39.

[6] These phrases are taken from A. L. Stoler, 'Empires and intimacies: lessons from (post) colonial studies: a round table: tense and tender ties: the politics of comparison in North American history and (post) colonial studies', *Journal of American History* **88**, 3 (December 2001), pp. 847–8.

[7] See for example M. Rafter, *Memoirs of Gregor M'Gregor; comprising a sketch of the revolution in New Granada and Venezuela, with biographical notices of Generals Miranda, Bolivar, and Horé and a narrative of the expeditions to Amelia Island, Porto Bello, and Rio de la Hacha, interspersed with revolutionary anecdotes* (London: Stockdale, 1820).

[8] M. Harper, *Adventurers and exiles: the great Scottish exodus*, (London: Profile, 2003), p. 257.

[9] A. Hasbrouck, 'Gregor MacGregor and the colonization of Poyais, between 1820 and 1824', *Hispanic American Historical Review*, **7** (1927), pp. 438–59; V. Allan, 'The Prince of Poyais', *History Today* (January 1952), pp. 53–8; R. T. Gregg, *Gregor MacGregor, Cazique of Poyais 1786–1845; on the trail of the gullible* (London: International Bond and Share Society, 1999).

[10] D. Sinclair, *Sir Gregor MacGregor and the land that never was: the extraordinary story of the most audacious fraud in history* (London: Headline, 2003). See also the entry in the *Oxford dictionary of national biography* (2004) written by Frank Griffith Dawson.

were due to his inappropriate ambitions and desires in a land that he never understood. Although more sympathetic than Sinclair, Tulio Arends traced the progression from the young MacGregor's enthusiasm and desire for glory, to his eccentric imaginative wanderings in middle age, to his sad and lonesome death, forgotten and ignored by friends and family alike.[11]

Whereas MacGregor does not emerge well from his various biographical 'lives', excellent documentary collections have presented individual episodes in good detail. Nevertheless, they have done little to dent the overall perception of MacGregor as an incongruous and peripheral figure in the early nineteenth-century Caribbean.[12] Subsequent narratives have provided some new sources, but retained the assumption that MacGregor was largely irrelevant and unconnected to wider contemporary issues.[13] Even in Clément Thibaud's excellent treatment of the period, MacGregor is little more than a diverting footnote.[14]

In the Spanish historiography there is a growing movement towards the study of such apparently incongruous figures. In particular, historians are increasingly exploring the ambiguous space occupied by men and women of Scottish and Irish descent in the multiple identities that made up the Hispanic colonial world.[15] MacGregor, like his distant relation William Semple two centuries before, used his military career to move between Scotland and the Hispanic world, using professions of Catholicism to convince allies of his loyalty but at times fighting against the Spanish crown.[16] Importantly, this was often a conscious decision.

---

[11] T. Arends, *Sir Gregor MacGregor: Un escocés tras la aventura en América* (Caracas: Monte Avila, 1988).

[12] J. Friede, 'La expedición de Mac-Gregor a Riohacha – Año 1819', *Boletín cultural y bibliográfico* 10, 9 (1967), pp. 69–85; D. Bushnell, ed., *La República de las Floridas: Text and Documents* (Mexico DF: Pan American Institute of Geography and History, 1986).

[13] J. R. Fortique, *Sir Gregor MacGregor: general de división del ejército venezolano* (Maracaibo: Published by author, 2001) was a brief narrative relying heavily on the secondary literature, but in addition provided a transcript of an 1824 letter from MacGregor, taken from the author's private collection. Sinclair, *Sir Gregor MacGregor*, also cited from unpublished letters.

[14] C. Thibaud, *Repúblicas en armas. Los ejércitos bolivarianos en la Guerra de Independencia (Colombia-Venezuela, 1810–1821)* (Bogotá: Planeta, 2003), p. 454.

[15] See for example J. M. Serrano, 'La familia O'Farrill en Cuba', and other papers presented in L. Navarro, ed., *Élites urbanas en hispanoamérica* (Sevilla: Universidad de Sevilla, 2005). For the nineteenth century see M. Brown, 'Scots in South America, 1810–1830', in I. H. McPhail and K. Kehoe, eds., *A panorama of Scottish history: contemporary considerations* (Glasgow: Glasgow University Press, 2004), pp. 124–44.

[16] G. Redworth, 'Between four kingdoms: international Catholicism and Colonel William Semple', in E. García Hernán, M. A. de Buenes, O. Recío Morales, B. J. García García, eds., *Irlanda y la monarquía hispánica: Kinsale 1601–2001, Guerra, política, exilio y religión* (Madrid: Universidad de Alcala, 2002), pp. 257–64.

Like Semple, MacGregor was 'more than capable of looking back on his life and reshaping his memory'.[17] MacGregor's career took him back and forth across the Atlantic and Caribbean, where local and regional conceptions of patriotism, masculinity and competence were contrasted with MacGregor's often singular approach to matters.[18] This chapter takes a more personalised perspective, examining documentation produced by MacGregor, and his friends and allies, held in Spanish and Scottish archives, to show how MacGregor's identity – as a freedom fighter, as a paternal colonist or Catholic, as a Scot, as a Venezuelan, and as a father – evolved and changed according to the circumstances of place and context during the four broad sites of his career.

MACGREGOR'S INSURGENT CAREER, 1811–1820

There is little evidence to testify for MacGregor's service in the British army during the Napoleonic Wars. As was relatively common in the period, documents were lost and witnesses died. MacGregor exploited this lack of information to talk up his early interventions in the political turmoil that followed Napoleon's invasion of the Iberian Peninsula in 1807. In Scotland, he developed a sympathetic reputation as a friend of freedom. *Scots Magazine* described him in 1818 as a Scottish defender of liberty across the world:

In Spain he fought to free a patriotic people from a tyrannical usurpation; but when he saw the beloved monarch, whom his courage had assisted to restore to the Spanish throne, reward the friends of liberty with dungeons and death, he indignantly resolved to join the party in America, who are endeavouring to emancipate themselves from the oppressions of the mother country. From Scotland he set out on his chivalrous expedition with retinue in every respect suited to a chieftain's state. Sir Gregor, to considerable talent, and perhaps more enthusiasm, adds rather superior literary attainments; and among his camp equipment has not forgotten to include a library of the most choice and valuable books.[19]

Some commentators viewed him rather more cynically. The Spanish ambassador in Washington, Luis de Onis, assessed MacGregor's intentions

---

[17] Redworth, 'Between four kingdoms', p. 264.
[18] M. Brown, 'Inca, sailor, soldier, king: Gregor MacGregor and the early nineteenth-century Caribbean', *Bulletin of Latin American Research* **24**, 1 (January 2005), pp. 44–71. I am grateful to the editors of *BLAR* for their permission to draw on some sections of this article.
[19] *Scots Magazine* **79**, pp. 64–5, cutting in NAS GD50/184/104/34.

in 1818 on the basis of rumours and the correspondence sent to him from London. MacGregor was engaged in the 'business' of recruiting and arming mercenaries, with the support of 'various capitalists in Scotland and London'.[20] The plan of the expedition was 'neither conquest nor to join the insurgent leaders, but rather limited to individual strikes on vulnerable ports, sacking and robbing with impunity'.[21] Differing views of MacGregor's intentions produced an array of terminological diversity: other Spanish colonial officials described MacGregor as a 'pirate',[22] an 'adventurer',[23] a 'revolutionary',[24] and a 'bandit'.[25]

Those who served with him saw MacGregor as a man who worked for his own ends regardless of national affiliations, collecting 'a thousand men of every class, colour and nation'.[26] The New Granadan representative Lino de Clemente recorded that MacGregor's aim in liberating Florida was to 'gain control of a point where all the Emigrants of all the world – of whom today there are very many – can go to and where they can join similar people in expeditions to strike mortal blows against our enemies'.[27] MacGregor was rumoured to be expecting reinforcements from Ireland, the Low Countries, North America and Haiti.[28]

While this was so, MacGregor was careful to make sure that he was not wholly associated with this diversity of human experience, particularly the lower orders. In the negotiations with South American representatives in Philadelphia in 1817, which led to his expedition to Amelia Island, he put strict conditions on his participation.[29] At this stage in his career, MacGregor sought to differentiate himself from the uncivilised 'others' often under his command by stipulating the insertion into his contract that he would undertake his expedition 'without

[20] L. de Onis to Captain-General of Cuba, 16 December 1818, Washington, AGI Cuba Legajo 1898.
[21] *Ibid.*
[22] J. Cienfuegos to Marqués de Casa Trufo, 24 May 1819, Habana, AGI Estado Legajo 12 No. 13, fo. 1.
[23] Testimonies made in Trinidad, 2 April 1819, attached to J. Cienfuegos to F. de Eguia, 29 April 1819, Habana, AGI Estado Legajo 12 N.15 (2), fos. 1–3.
[24] L. de Onis to J. Pizarro, 16 April 1817, Washington, AGI Estado Legajo 88 N.16.
[25] Solis to Samano, 13 October 1819, Riohacha, AGI Cuba Legajo 745.
[26] Testimony of P. Camiruaga, Bilbao-born Captain of a Danish-registered vessel, Trinidad, 2 April 1819, attached to J. Cienfuegos to F. de Eguia, 29 April 1819, Habana, AGI Estado Legajo 12 N.15 (2), fo. 2.r.
[27] L. de Clemente to Bolívar, 4 September 1817, Philadelphia, AGI Estado Legajo 69 No. 48, fos. 12–13.v.
[28] T. Berridge, Interrogation, 20 October 1819, Riohacha, AGI Cuba Legajo 745.
[29] L. de Clemente to Bolívar, 28 July 1817, Philadelphia, AGI Estado Legajo 69 No. 48, fo. 7.v.

deviating from the traditions and models of Civilised Nations'.[30] MacGregor sought to avoid 'the Civilised Nations judging his actions as without authorisation'.[31]

In October 1819, MacGregor's forces occupied the New Granadan port of Riohacha, which had hitherto remained loyal to Spain. Their six-day occupation of the town, before MacGregor retreated after realising that he did not have the full support of the local population, had profound consequences for the way people in Riohacha thought about their identities as colonial subjects.[32] Fundamental to the fears held by the Governor of Riohacha, José Solis, in the wake of the occupation, was the apparent ease with which Riohachero men had developed relations of familiarity with MacGregor that went against what should have been their natural loyalty to the king of Spain. It seemed to Solis that the insurgents had subverted their natural identities as subjects of the Spanish monarch in the name of mere mercenary self-interest. One of these men, Ramón Ruiz, was accused of telling colleagues that he had joined MacGregor because 'the general has seen me right'.[33] Others were said to enjoy 'ostentatious friendship with MacGregor's men'.[34] Miguel Gómez, a loyalist who led the defence forces of Goajira Indians, expressed his dismay that 'those who call themselves whites' were involved in intrigue with MacGregor. The alliance of Riohacheros with foreign rebels like MacGregor disorientated collective identities, with the Indians of Goajira showing more loyalty to the king than the whites of Riohacha. Gómez lamented that the enemy was not 'the one that comes from outside', as it should be, and that order had been reduced to chaos.[35]

MacGregor, however, was not tied to any fixed loyalty to a particular king or nation. His allegiance switched throughout his career. Those who supported MacGregor in Riohacha tended to be associated with Caribbean commerce in some way, either as merchants or traders.[36] One

---

[30] L. de Clemente, M. Thompson and P. Gual, 'Copia del diploma desp to al General MacGregor', 31 March 1817, Philadelphia, AGI Estado Legajo 69 No. 48, fo. 9.v.

[31] L. de Clemente to Bolívar, 28 July 1817, Philadelphia, AGI Estado Legajo 69 No. 48, fo. 8.v.

[32] I have explored the situation in Riohacha in 1818–1821 in some detail in M. Brown, 'Rebellion at Riohacha, 1820: Local and International Networks of Revolution, Cowardice and Masculinity', in *Jahrbuch für Geschichte von Staat, Wirtschaft und Gesellschaft Lateinamerikas*, 42 (2005), pp. 77–98.

[33] 'Declaración de Mateo Bermúdez', 22 January 1820, Riohacha, AGI Cuba, Legajo 745.

[34] 'Contra Felipe Rosado', 26 January 1820, Riohacha, AGI Cuba, Legajo 745.

[35] 'Declaración de Miguel José Gómez', 1 March 1820, Riohacha, AGI Cuba, Legajo 745. See also 'Declaración de Jacinto Amaya', 3 March 1820, Riohacha, AGI Cuba, Legajo 745, speaking of 'those who call themselves whites who were the only ones to unite with MacGregor'.

[36] For example 'Declaración de Ramón Ruiz', 14 April 1820, Cartagena, AGI Cuba Legajo 745.

witness claimed that MacGregor would not have travelled to Riohacha at all were it not for the Riohacha merchants based in Haiti who financed the expedition.[37] When MacGregor escaped from Riohacha, many of his men and officers were not so fortunate. They were taken captive by the local forces, interrogated and then executed on the beach. Their surviving testimonies reveal much about the way that MacGregor traded and exploited his Scottish identity when recruiting and motivating expeditions in this period. The prisoners claimed that they had been persuaded that 'the Main Object they were to be employed upon, was the Establishment of a Colony in the Bay of Caledonia; on the Isthmus of Darien; which territory General MacGregor claimed, and which was said to have been ceded to him'.[38] MacGregor told them that:

there was formerly a Company established by the Scotch on the Isthmus of Darien; in the Vicinity of the Bay of Caledonia, under the Title of the Scotch Darien Company, whose Object was to open a Communication between the Atlantic, and the Pacific Oceans. It is further asserted by General Macgregor, that one of his Ancestors was the Chief of the said Company; that the said Ancestor married the Daughter of the then Inca of the said Isthmus; at whose Marriage the aforesaid territory was ceded to the Ancestor of MacGregor ... and that upon this ground he founds his claim to the Title, and the territory of the Inca of the Isthmus of Darien.[39]

In a succinct summary, the doomed officers recalled that MacGregor claimed that his great object was 'the Completion of the Intentions of his Ancestors'. However, they noted that whereas they had expected 'to be received as friends' in Riohacha they had instead been captured, 'the victims of their own credulity, and the Machinations of designing Men, under whom they could reap neither Honor or Glory'. Those mercenaries who had followed MacGregor ended up rejecting his appeal to a common Scottish identity as fraudulent. Similarly, the Riohacheros who had conspired with MacGregor to overthrow the colonial regime accused him of being a 'traitor' to the cause of their freedom.[40] Several Riohachera women lambasted the 'perfidious English adventurer' with whom their

---

[37] H. Gummings, Interrogation, 23 October 1819, Riohacha, AGI Cuba Legajo 745.

[38] R. A. O'Daly and fourteen others to Solis, 24 October 1819, Riohacha, AGI Cuba Legajo 745. Different transcriptions and translations of this document can be found in S. E. Ortiz, ed., *Colección de documentos para la Historia de Colombia (Epoca de la Independencia), III Serie*, (Bogotá: Editorial el Voto Nacional, 1966), pp. 279–80, and Friede, 'La expedición de MacGregor a Riohacha – Año 1819', *Boletín cultural y bibliográfico* (1969), pp. 74–5.

[39] See also R. A. O'Daly, Interrogation, 20 October 1819, Riohacha, AGI Cuba Legajo 745.

[40] M. Llorens and F. de Paula Orite to Samano, Riohacha 11 October 1819, Riohacha, AGI Cuba Legajo 745.

husbands were accused of conspiring.[41] The failure of the attack on Riohacha led to all groups involved accusing MacGregor of having falsely assumed identities – as Scottish patriot or as Colombian liberator – in order to seek his own fortune.

THE 1820S: POYAIS

The charge of dissimulation followed MacGregor to Poyais. Historians continue to ridicule the crazed imagination or deliberate fraud of 'the land that never was'.[42] Detailed analysis of the correspondence and documentation triggered by the plan to colonise part of the Mosquito Coast reveals much about the way that MacGregor's successes, failures and frustrations in the Colombian Wars of Independence led him to actively seek out a new identity for himself on the frontiers between the British and Spanish empires.

The decision of George Frederick, recognised by the British as king of the Mosquito Coast Indians, to cede some of his territory to MacGregor in 1820, was one of several similar agreements signed in these years in an attempt to play off external actors against each other.[43] Local actors such as George Frederick attempted to carve out space for their own polities by using adventurers such as MacGregor to thwart possible formal Spanish, British and French colonial ambitions. Rather than representing any partisan cause or national power, MacGregor presented himself as the disinterested representative of the universalist, civilising cause of emancipation, happy to govern alongside a benign local representative.[44] When George Frederick later proclaimed the agreement null and void, it was because he believed MacGregor had broken their agreement by 'assuming to himself the title of Cazique of Poyais'.[45]

This was a fundamental change. At the beginning of the 1820s, MacGregor increasingly came to view himself as a key power broker in the turmoil surrounding the disintegration of the Spanish empire. While British commerce was heralded as one of the major factors that had

[41] A. M. Wila and others to Samano, 18 December 1819, Riohacha, AGI Cuba Legajo 745.
[42] Most recently, Sinclair, *Sir Gregor MacGregor and the land that never was.*
[43] See R. Naylor, *Penny ante imperialism: the Mosquito Shore and the Bay of Honduras 1600–1914. A case study in British informal Empire* (Rutherford, NJ: Fairleigh Dickinson University Press, 1989), pp. 78–82.
[44] 'Grant by George Frederick II, D. G. King of the Mosquito Shore and Nation, to H. E. General Sir Gregor MacGregor', Copy in James Towers English Papers, Suffolk County Record Office, Ipswich, HA 157/6/79.
[45] Copy of the 'Proclamation of the King of the Mosquito Shore', NAS, GD50/184/104/8.

undermined the Spanish imperial trade system, MacGregor flattered himself that he could act as a broker between the sides. In his attempts to fulfil this role MacGregor was indeed often pretentious and obsessed with status. By 1823 he was signing himself 'Gregor P' as an abbreviation of 'Gregor Prince'.[46] Yet he aimed to establish Poyais – or 'Indiada' or 'Indialand' as he came to call it – as an autonomous region within a Hispanic commonwealth, a bulwark against foreign pirates and against North American expansionism in the region.[47] Poyais would be populated by local Indians and by emigrants from the Scottish Highlands: this earned him a reputation as the paternalist provider of an escape route for the needy:

> Prince Gregor M'Gregor
> He's the Grand Seignior
> Who carves out a dinner
> For many a sinner.[48]

The symbolism MacGregor chose for his Poyais project demonstrates how his youthful radicalism and idealism were reformulated in the Caribbean. Rather than seeking to free colonial subjects from Spanish rule, he now became a colonial ruler himself. The Poyais crest, found on the constitution, bank notes, and loans, featured two strong, male, muscular Indians holding aloft the flags of St George and St Andrew, and between them a laurel for their king.[49] Cutting out the Spanish and even the creoles from the history of the region, and returning to a distant Indian past with which he personally had no connection, MacGregor was symbolically seeking a new land upon which to imprint his personality.[50]

---

[46] MacGregor to Count de la Cruz, 18 October 1823, Paris, NAS, GD50/184/104/11 and MacGregor to Count de la Cruz, 20 October 1823, Paris, NAS GD 50/184/84/30.

[47] The Poyais Constitution can be found in the National Library of Scotland, *Plan of a constitution for the inhabitants of the Indian Coast, in Central America, commonly called the Mosquito Shore*, Edinburgh: Balfour and Jack, 1836. Although printed in 1836, it seems that it was first written in 1825, and published in French. It is not known whether such an original still exists; in any case, it probably did not find its way to the Mosquito Coast.

[48] M. A. Lloyd, *To the gentlemen of the Stock Exchange. Lines on the Poyais Bonds, August 12 1823. Being His Majesty's natal day* (London, 1823).

[49] MacGregor, *Loan of two hundred thousand pounds stirling for the service of the state & government of Poyais*, countersigned by W. J. Richardson and dated 6 October 1823, London, British Library Political Pamphlets, 1881.c.16(7). See also 'Poyais loan bond note', NAS GD50/184/2. MacGregor's use of two men is suggestive, as in most cases of creole patriotism appropriating the image of the Indian for their own means in this period, submissive female Indians were used. See for example, T. Platt, 'Simon Bolivar, the sun of justice and the Amerindian virgin – Andean conceptions of the patria in nineteenth-century Potosi', *Journal of Latin American Studies* **25**, 1 (1993), p. 170.

[50] For an astute examination of the use of Indian symbolism by republican élites in the post-war period see R. Earle, 'Creole patriotism and the myth of the loyal Indian', *Past and Present* **172** (August 2001), pp. 125–45.

MacGregor's intention was not to create a republic only for the indigenous inhabitants. They would merely wave the flags to welcome the new immigrants. While he did try to secure local support for his rule, his emphasis on religious tolerance, secular marriage, a second chance for those accused of fraud or debt, and recognition to children born outside of wedlock, all indicate that MacGregor's vision of the American *patria* held potential European emigrants as an integral part of the nation. However, the distinctions made between inhabitants, men, and freemen in his constitution were imprecise and imply that he did not intend to completely exclude the Indians from Indialand. The preamble to the constitution declared that

we, the Representatives of the Freemen of the Mosquito territories, in General Convention met, resolve, that these territories shall henceforth be called Indialand; and further, embracing all men as brothers, of whatever clime, of whatever complexion, of whatever religious opinions they may be.[51]

In this Poyais stage of his career, MacGregor and his supporters backtracked considerably from their previous republican and revolutionary positions. Now they contrasted their support for the hereditary King of the Mosquito Indians with the lowly and unworthy characters of 'King Tom or King Jack in Africa'.[52] They stressed that 'the flame of the revolution [in South America] is far distant from Poyais'.[53]

In 1822, MacGregor's agent at the Spanish court proposed a series of plans that were notable for the dramatic reconciliation – in MacGregor's heart at least – with Spanish rule in the Americas. He presented the plans for Poyais as 'extremely favourable to the cause of the Spanish nation'.[54] MacGregor offered to pay 200,000 pesos for the islands of Ruatan and Guanaya in the Bay of Honduras, arguing that only he could prevent them from falling into the hands of 'pirates or the Guatemalan Insurgents'.[55] This was a time of chaos for the Spanish empire, in which Venezuela, New Granada, Mexico, Chile and the River Plate had definitively slipped from its grasp, and central America and Peru tottered on the brink. MacGregor exploited the uncertainty to gain a foothold in Poyais while his diplomatic missives were repeatedly shuffled from

---

[51] MacGregor, *Plan of a constitution*, p. 5.
[52] Verax, *A letter to the editor of the Quarterly Review for February 1823, on a review of Captain Strangeway's sketch of the Mosquito Shore* (London: C. and J. Rivington, 1823), pp. 4–5.
[53] Verax, *A letter to the editor*, p. 6.
[54] T. Irving to Spanish Secretary of State, 14 October 1822, Madrid, AGI Estado Legajo 50 No. 52, fo. 3.a.
[55] Irving to Spanish Secretary of State, 14 October 1822, Madrid, AGI Estado Legajo 50 No. 52, fo. 3.b.

ministry to ministry, with no particular office willing to take responsibility for dealing with him.

Faced with such indifference, MacGregor changed tack in 1823. He offered Spain 50,000 dollars per year in exchange for recognition of Poyais.[56] Spanish subjects would have the same rights as Poyaisian citizens. France would verify the treaty and would provide an army to annex the Guatemalan town of Trujillo to Poyais.[57] Later that year MacGregor addressed the Spanish secretary of state with plans for the reconfiguration of the Spanish empire, which was still apparently in the balance in Peru.[58] MacGregor proposed a 'general suspension of hostilities' while a great expedition was sent to Peru. He argued for the creation of 'four new Kingdoms in America, and naming for sovereigns of the same, four princes of His Catholic Majesty's Royal House'. To ensure loyalty to these new princes, MacGregor's solution was 'the liberal offer of honours'. He suggested that 'it might perhaps be of advantage, were His Catholic Majesty to assume either the title of "Emperor of the Indies" or that of "Sovereign Protector of the Indies"; and further to stipulate that the new sovereigns should pay a certain annual subsidy to Spain, for say a period of twenty years'. As part of this plan he proposed that Poyais, 'on account of the hostile disposition of the Indians of those parts towards the Spaniards' be 'erected into a principality, subject to the immediate authority of [MacGregor], but tributary, and under the protection of the crown of Spain'.[59] Increasingly confident of his position, in March 1824 he offered to use his base in Poyais to conquer Guatemala for Spain 'with the assistance of five hundred Spanish troops'.[60]

During this period, MacGregor continued to emphasise his Scottish identity and his noble ancestry when he felt it suited him. One of his supporters stressed MacGregor's noble lineage rather than his revolutionary credentials, noting that he was 'one of the chiefs of the most ancient clans, distinguished for its suffering from a loyal principle, and descended from royal blood'.[61] In 1824, MacGregor wrote to Ferdinand VII from Paris, describing himself as 'descendent of the ancient Kings of

---

[56] W. J. Richardson [MacGregor's Secretary] to Irving, 7 July 1823, London, AGI Estado Legajo 50 No. 52, fo. 12.a.

[57] Richardson to Irving, 7 July 1823, London, AGI Estado Legajo 50 No. 52, fo. 12.a.

[58] MacGregor to V. D. Sanz, 25 November 1823, Paris, AGI Estado Legajo 50 No. 52 fo. 19. The fate of Peru was effectively settled by the victory of Simón Bolívar's army over the massed royalist army at Ayacucho, in the Peruvian highlands, on 9 December 1824.

[59] MacGregor to Sanz, 25 November 1823, Paris, AGI Estado Legajo 50 No. 52, fo. 19.

[60] Irving to Secretary of State, 8 March 1824, Paris, AGI Estado Legajo 50 No. 52, fo. 21.f.

[61] Verax, A letter to the editor, p. 6.

Scotland'.[62] He proposed that by 'recognising the King of Spain as the Protector of the Country of Poyais, Gregor MacGregor will confirm the principle of sovereignty across the whole American continent, since Poyais was never a province of any of the possessions of the King of Spain'.[63] As such he tried to situate himself amongst a community of rulers, equal to Ferdinand in status and honour. In retrospect this was his moment of greatest hubris. The Spanish authorities used MacGregor and his agents as an important source of news but never acted on his suggestions or requests. MacGregor had little if any direct influence on events in this period. By the mid-1820s he was increasingly entangled in debt and mistrust, unable to muster funds to leave Europe, and hence ever-more distant from his recently assumed identity as a colonial ruler in Central America.[64]

One of MacGregor's defenders saw Poyais as an archetypal colonising project and an extension of the British imperial mission. In a piece of poetic propaganda, Mary Anne Lloyd compared Poyais to Lanark and asked God to bless the project:

> Father Supreme! Sovereign Lord of all,
> Hear my petition, when to Thee I call
> Give thy servant's help, when in distress,
> Succour thy People, and the land of Poyais:
> Where there's too much swamp, drain away;
> By thy all searching heat the healing ray,
> Where there is too much heat, send rain,
> To inculcate the manor into perfect grain.[65]

The 'Prospectus' to attract investors to Poyais promoted it as an agricultural colony aimed at producing gold, indigo, sugar and tobacco.[66] Poyais would 'form within itself a free and independent principality, under a Constitutional Government'. The valleys were said to be 'extremely rich and fertile', the climate was 'mild and salubrious, being

---

[62] MacGregor to Ferdinand VII, 4 December 1824, Paris, AGI Estado Legajo 50 No. 52, fo. 17 translation to Spanish from French.

[63] *Ibid.*

[64] While in the long run MacGregor's reputation was tarred by this financial mismanagement, at the time most anger about Poyais was focused on the unscrupulous speculators of South American loans rather than MacGregor himself. See, for example, a pamphlet written in July 1827 which made no mention of MacGregor at all: Anon, *Take care of your pockets – another Poyais humbug*, Handwritten manuscript copy, dated 10 July 1827, British Library Political Pamphlets, 1881.c.18.

[65] M. A. Lloyd, *A poetical prayer for relief to myself and the Poyais land and people. Also elegaic verses on departed plants by Mary Anne Lloyd, authoress of a defence of the Bible, lines on the Passions, Good Friday, on the funds foreign and English, &c &c* (London, 1823).

[66] [MacGregor], *Prospectus of a Poyais loan* (London, 1825).

greatly superior to that of most other parts of the same vast portion of the Globe'. The soil was 'extremely fertile and produces almost without labour, the necessaries of life in great profusion'.[67]

Preparing the way for the process of colonisation, the inhabitants of the land now to be known as Poyais were described as 'a brave and generous race of people' who were 'extremely fond of the English, whom they have at all time considered their friends and protectors'.[68] MacGregor stressed that the territory had never 'actually been under the power of Spain' because 'the courage of its native inhabitants [had] in all periods preserved its Independence'.[69] While such resistance to previous colonising projects was handy for MacGregor's claim to sovereignty, they needed to be undermined in order to legitimate his own rule. For this reason he promised only to introduce 'mild and beneficent laws . . . founded on the most rational principles of Civilised Society' which would 'ensure to the People the real blessings of true liberty'.[70]

Moreover, MacGregor had to reinterpret his own part in the revolutionary movements in South America. In jail in Paris in January 1826 he claimed that he was being persecuted 'as one of the founders of independence in the New World' but that he was now a responsible head of government.[71] One of his supporters argued that MacGregor's 'present intentions' were misunderstood: although 'he was indeed in the service of the Colombian Government; [he] has broken off all connection with it; whatever his political prepossessions may have been in early life, he has no views with respect to Poyais, but such as are consistent with the established state of things'.[72] MacGregor reinvented himself as a colonial ruler, offering subservience to the King of Spain, keen to provide the British West Indian colonies with maize rather than to threaten their markets or liberate their slaves.[73] He dismissed his old image as a revolutionary, claiming that 'whatever the views may have been of those with whom he formerly associated himself' he was now 'devoted to the arduous task of

---

[67] Ibid.

[68] Ibid.

[69] Ibid.

[70] Ibid.

[71] MacGregor to the Congress at Panama, 10 January 1826, in G. B. Hippisley, Acts of oppression committed under the administration of M. De Villèle, Prime Minister of Charles X, in the Years 1825–6. In a series of letters (London, 1831), quoted in Sinclair, Gregor MacGregor and the land that never was, p. 273. The British Library has mislaid its copy of Hippisley's rare work.

[72] Verax, A letter to the editor, p. 3.

[73] As described in Verax, A letter to the editor, p. 7.

colonizing a new country, one untrodden for years by any European foot'.[74]

Despite the amorphous nature of MacGregor's identity, one constant theme was as someone set apart from British history. His supporters argued that highlanders could not be blamed for seeking a new life in Poyais seeing as they had 'fought [Britain's] battles with distinguished courage' and expressed 'repugnance...to emigrate to the British colonies'.[75] In his retirement in Edinburgh in the 1830s, MacGregor found comfort in this vision of himself as the permanent outcast, destined from birth to operate subversively on the fringes of British life.

SCOTTISH RETIREMENT AND AUTOBIOGRAPHY

By the early 1830s MacGregor was no longer pursued by admirers, detractors or creditors. The Hispanic American republics were liberated and their internal conflicts were no longer a fashionable international cause. MacGregor's name disappeared from the newspapers and his correspondence was no longer preserved. Although his Poyais constitution was republished in Edinburgh in 1836 it was a last attempt to regain the public attention which had long since moved on. MacGregor's adventures were over and he lived in retirement in Edinburgh with his wife and children. In the early 1830s MacGregor began to assess his career and to reflect upon his experiences with the aim of writing his autobiography. Already several unauthorised biographies had been published and it seems that he wished to set the record straight, positioning his activities in the Americas as part of a lifelong pattern of travel, adventure and rebellion. Only the first chapter survives. In this section the remaining fragment is used to reconstruct MacGregor's state of mind in this period of Scottish retirement.[76]

In this text it was extremely important for MacGregor to stress his encounters with rebellious relations and ancestors. He recalled a visit as a child to see an uncle, the 'Chevalier John MacGregor, who had emigrated

[74] Verax, *A letter to the editor*, p. 8. Reporting MacGregor's difficulties with the Parisian Correctional Police, *The Times* mocked 'the famous Cacique of Poyais' for the situation in which his 'swindling' of 'dupes' had left him. See *The Times*, 10 April 1826.

[75] Verax, *A letter to the editor*, p. 12.

[76] MacGregor, 'Autobiographical segment', National Archives of Scotland, GD/50/112. Reproduced in the original English in M. Brown and M. Roa Celis, eds., *Militares extranjeras en la independenica de Colombia – nuevas perspectivas* (Bogotá: Museo Nacional de Colombia, 2005), pp. 294–310. Circumstantial evidence suggests that this was written in the mid-to-late-1830s. Folio numbers are from the original manuscript. Chapter 2, for which one sheet of vaguely legible notes remains, detailed MacGregor's enlistment in the British Army until his marriage and departure for Portugal in 1808.

to France after the unsuccessful attempt of Charles Edward to place his father on the throne of Great Britain; the Chevalier was an officer in the French service, and generally resided at Avignon'.[77] MacGregor recollected the occasion on which Lord Sempill – a cousin of his mother – dined with them in Queen Street. This 'stranger in the glazed hat' 'excited my infantine curiosity'. Sempill was a 'liberal man in every sense of the word and was so great an admirer of the French Revolution that he had sent over as a present to the French Republican army 30,000 pairs of shoes' and 'dissipated all his ready money'.[78] Right from the beginning MacGregor situated himself within a family tradition of service outside of Britain's armed forces and of sympathy with revolutionary causes.

His father died when Gregor MacGregor was in his early teens.[79] The family fortune had already been spent, wrote MacGregor, by his grandfather 'Gregor Boidach'

in assisting his brother the Chevalier MacGregor in fitting out his sons in the East India Company service, in the education of his daughters at Convents in France, and in heavy expenses attending an Act of Parliament, which was passed in 1744–5, authorising him (therein designated Gregor Drummond) and the Clan Gregor, to resume once more the ancient name of MacGregor of which they had long been deprived by different Acts of Parliament of Scotland and of Great Britain.[80]

The constant themes were service overseas and the hostility of the British establishment towards his family. Another was the shadow of financial failure that hung over the MacGregors' adventures overseas. Gregor MacGregor's father had been in colonial service in India before returning to Scotland to marry. Upon return he remitted part of his fortune in respondent bonds to a house in Lisbon which subsequently went bankrupt. Gregor MacGregor's mother thereafter refused to travel to India 'where she had lost an only brother', and subsequently her husband resigned his commission and died soon after. MacGregor wrote that '[m]y father's fortune, therefore, only consisted of a handsome house in Edinburgh, the small estate of Inverarderan in Perthshire, and a few thousand pounds in the funds'.[81]

The experiences of his family in relation to India can be seen to have influenced his own decision to travel west rather than east. They also

---

[77] MacGregor, 'Autobiographical segment', fo. 1.
[78] Ibid., fos. 8–9.
[79] Ibid., fo. 2.
[80] Ibid., fos. 2–3.
[81] Ibid., fo. 3.

informed the way he interpreted his own adventures. MacGregor recalled that his mother's brother, Hugh Austin, was a relation of Lord Clive, governor general of India. Austin was appointed a judge in India at the age of twenty-one, but gave

great offence to his colleagues by refusing to accept the presents which it was the established custom to present to the Judges. One morning, he was going out to pay a visit at some short distance, I believe to my father; the carriage was at the door to take him, but he changed his mind, and embarked with his secretary on board of a pleasure boat that he had; he was never heard of more, but the body of the secretary was found near the walls of his garden. It was supposed that the sailors had been bribed, and had thrown them out of the cabin windows. Such is the story of my uncle's death, if my memory serves me, as I have heard my mother frequently repeat it.[82]

Implicit in this story was the understanding that Gregor MacGregor had himself learned the lessons of misunderstanding or ignoring 'established customs' in the colonies. The alternative was harsh or savage reprisals from local populations.

Resident in Edinburgh as he wrote his memoirs, MacGregor dedicated much attention to his schooling in the city. He recalled spending much time in the recently completed New Town with his grandaunt, the Honourable Miss Rebecca Sempill who was 'very prim and antiquated in her manners', but who nevertheless gave him a daily 'piece of gingerbread and a glass of port wine, which latter I was very fond of'.[83] MacGregor recalled that as a youth he spent a few months every summer with his uncle General Robertson of Lawers. Robertson had served in the British army in the American War of Independence and 'consequently he was an ultra-royalist'.[84] At this summer home MacGregor spent much time with horses, being trained by the estate's groom Peter who 'had been a soldier with my uncle in America'.[85] General Robertson occupied the position of chief engineer in the Seven Years War when British troops occupied Havana in 1763 and MacGregor related the following anecdote often told by his uncle about his time in Havana:

The English officers had given a great many entertainments to the principal inhabitants, who resolving not to be outdone, invited the greater part of the British officers to a grand-dinner on a certain day. Whilst the preparations of the feast were going on an English vessel arrived at the Habana, and a part of

---

[82] *Ibid.*, fos. 3–4.
[83] *Ibid.*, fo. 6.
[84] *Ibid.*, fo. 10.
[85] *Ibid.*, fo. 12.

her cargo consisting of common crockery was bought up by the Committee appointed to conduct the entertainment. Amongst these were several hundreds of a very useful article, indispensable in every English bedchamber, although its use was at that time unknown in the Habana. The day of the feast at last arrived; the entertainment was sumptuous; at the conclusion of the dinner one of the articles in question filled with punch with large slices of Seville oranges swimming on its top, was placed before each of the guests. It is impossible to describe the surprise and astonishment of the guests at this sight, or the consternation of their hosts upon being informed of the use to which these new punch bowls are appropriated to [sic] in England. I do not remember how the feast terminated, but take it for granted that the Seville punch was not thrown away.[86]

The re-remembering of this story revealed how MacGregor portrayed cultural confusion between British and Hispanic élites as an integral part of his education and preparations for his own adventures in South America. The mistaken misuse of a toilet bowl was a way of ridiculing the pretensions of the creole élites he had often fought alongside during the Wars of Independence, but it was also symbolic of the way in which cultural differences could be overcome with good humour in the pursuit of entertainment.

The longest section of the autobiographical chapter detailed a prolonged period of truancy, an 'evasion both from school and from home', an adventure which began by MacGregor setting out on foot from Edinburgh for Stirling, a distance of thirty-five miles.[87] By putting such emphasis on his youthful misdemeanours MacGregor was clearly setting the scene for the rest of his memoirs, in which he would present himself as a lifelong rebel and adventurer. He claimed to have been around ten years old, 'and it must be admitted that it was rather a bold undertaking in a youth of that age'.[88] This 'jaunt to the Highlands' and to 'what is or was called the MacGregor Country' was an early opportunity to independently explore the land of his forefathers.[89] He remembered stopping in 'the common room[s] allotted to travellers' and chatting with 'a great number of Highland drovers'.[90] When the drovers were

informed that I was the grandson of the celebrated Grighair Boidach [they] treated me with the greatest attention, and amused me with numerous anecdotes of my family and particularly of my grandfather, whose memory was held in

[86] *Ibid.*, fos. 10–11.
[87] *Ibid.*, fos. 13–25.
[88] *Ibid.*, fo. 13.
[89] *Ibid.*, fo. 17.
[90] *Ibid.*, fo. 18.

great respect all over the country. Large draughts of whisky were swallowed to the success of the MacGregor.[91]

Invented or not, this story and its many details – such as when he played alongside 'little Highland ragamuffins'[92] or insisted on breaking social barriers by dining with his coachman[93] – contributed to setting a scene of insubordination and rebellion.

MacGregor's 'first youthful campaign' was ended when his mother and aunt contrived an elaborate scheme to recapture him and to send him back to Edinburgh.[94] Back at school he recalled 'nocturnal parties' and unofficial 'excursions' from school. In these anecdotes it was generally MacGregor himself who 'boldly proposed' escape.[95] For these sorties he generally received 'a most confounded flogging'.[96]

MacGregor's upbringing was also seen, with hindsight, to have had a profound West Indian connection. He was sent to Mr Taylor's boarding school at Musselburgh where he roomed with the son of the Earl of Balcharas, at the time Governor of Jamaica.[97] The last surviving para-graph recalled a visit paid to the estate of the Beveridge family (which was 'also the proprietor of an estate in the West Indies') in 'the ancient town of Falkland' in 'Fifeshire'. He 'often wandered ... through the old ruined palace of Falkland, once a residence of the Kings of Scotland, but now converted into a granary'. In this uncompleted memory, MacGregor combined the themes of his narrative – links to the Car-ibbean, independent wanderings, and a vague sense of the lost greatness of Scotland. His subsequent career would be seen in the light of these influences in order to portray MacGregor as a man fulfilling his destiny in the world.

Nevertheless, one thing missing from these autobiographical musings was any mention of Poyais or South America. No doubt these were intended for later and unwritten chapters and the reason for the abrupt break in the narrative is unknown. What is certain is that the period of retirement in Edinburgh in the 1830s focused MacGregor's thoughts for the first time on the land of his birth. In his autobiographical writings he explored the influence of his youthful adventures and his links to the

---

[91] *Ibid.*, fos. 18–19.
[92] *Ibid.*, fo. 21.
[93] *Ibid.*, fo. 24.
[94] *Ibid.*, fo. 25.
[95] *Ibid.*, fos. 26–8.
[96] *Ibid.*, fo. 30.
[97] *Ibid.*, fo. 26.

Highlands upon his later activities. However, when his Venezuelan wife Josefa died at Boroughmuirhead near Edinburgh on 4 May 1838, he did not return to his roots.[98] Instead, he left Scotland for Venezuela almost immediately.

VENEZUELAN RETIREMENT

Returning to Caracas after an absence of over twenty-five years MacGregor had to reassess the way he understood his career. Rather than the private reminiscences of his autobiography written in Scotland, focusing on his adventuring lifestyle from an early age and pointing out his links to prominent Scottish rebels, in Venezuela he had to publicly petition the state and convince the authorities that he had been a loyal and heroic commander. He encountered robust state authorities that had survived political rebellions, civil wars and the threat of foreign (British) intervention.[99] As such, he stressed his military exploits in the name of the Venezuelan nation. As part of his application to the authorities MacGregor set down on paper 'some of the key events of my political existence'.[100] He described all of the military engagements he was involved in, noting each time that he personally used (and lost) his own money or possessions. The front illustration of this published appeal to the Venezuelan government was a far cry from the optimistic symbolism of his Poyais project. Stressing his military exploits, it featured a metal helmet, a battleaxe, a sword, a shield, and heraldic plumage.[101] He stayed firm to his interpretation of an adventurous life but now emphasised Venezuela as both his proving ground and his end point. 'After a long series of adversities, I have returned to my adoptive *patria* trusting that I will receive the same hospitality and even greater protection than on my first arrival'.[102]

MacGregor presented his final departure from Venezuela in 1821 as the result of a personally motivated order from Bolívar that he should be expelled from the territory, rather than as part of an ongoing quest for more adventure as a mercenary.[103] He claimed that in response to

---

[98] *Edinburgh Evening Courant*, 10 May 1838, cutting in NAS GD50/184/104/17.
[99] A splendid source for the period during which MacGregor was absent from Venezuela is Sir R. Ker Porter, *Diario de un diplomático británico en Venezuela* (Caracas: Fundación Polar, 1997).
[100] MacGregor, *Exposición documentada*, p. 1.
[101] *Ibid.*, frontispiece.
[102] *Ibid.*, p. 1. MacGregor's introduction to the documents was dated 6 October 1838, Caracas.
[103] *Ibid.*, p. 5.

Bolívar's belief that his prolonged presence in the region 'could destabilise order and the new system' he returned to Europe 'sacrificing my rights and my desires' until time had the opportunity to clarify matters. He claimed that he repeatedly asked to be allowed to return, requests that were continually refused. 'I did not choose to remain outside the Republic, but rather I was forced to, by causes and obstacles out of my control'.[104] In the long struggle to return he claimed to have lost 'the best years of my life and all my fortune', along with two children and a wife.[105] As such, by returning to Venezuela MacGregor recognised the overall failure of his Scottish retirement and the vision of his 'adventures' that this entailed. Unable to guarantee himself a comfortable income and having lost the backup of his previously wide network of friends and supporters, he reassessed his career and claimed that Venezuela was where he had been most accepted and most valued. It was the land of birth of his recently deceased wife, and he pleaded to be allowed to 'dedicate my last years to the *patria* of my choice'.[106]

MacGregor's long absence from the Venezuelan scene had meant that he lacked active political networks to lobby for his protection but some of his old comrades were still in power. In 1839, the minister of war Rafael Urdaneta – an old colleague of MacGregor's from the 1816 Aux Cayes expedition – recommended that the rules be bent a little to accommodate MacGregor.[107] Urdaneta was effusive in his praise: 'MacGregor enlisted in our ranks from the very start of the War of Independence, and ran the same risks as all the patriots of that disastrous time, meriting promotions and respect because of his excellent personal conduct'.[108] His service at Ocumare was 'heroic with immense results'.[109] The decision was approved by President José Antonio Páez, another veteran of the early stages of the Wars of Independence.[110]

Urging the Venezuelan Congress to ratify the decision, MacGregor pleaded with them to consider 'the characteristics that are recognised by the civilised world: my honour and the paternal affection I owe to my

---

[104] *Ibid.*, p. 7. The rest of the collection reproduces letters sent to this effect throughout the 1820s and 1830s.
[105] *Ibid.*, p. 7.
[106] *Ibid.*, p. 8. The phrase used was '*patria de mi elección*'.
[107] R. Urdaneta to Leader of the Venezuelan Senate, 23 January 1839, Caracas, reproduced in MacGregor, *Exposición documentada*, document 12.
[108] Urdaneta to Leader of the Venezuelan Senate, 23 January 1839, Caracas.
[109] *Ibid.*.
[110] 'Decreto', 8 March 1839, Caracas, reproduced in *Exposición documentada*, p. 23.

three Venezuelan children'.[111] In stressing the kinship ties that bound him to Venezuela MacGregor hoped to position himself as a *padre de familia*, the most honourable type of masculinity for men in Venezuela in this period, and one which other veterans aspired to with its connotations of dominance over women, children and (often) slaves.[112] The fact that his children had not been born in Venezuela was immaterial: they traced their Venezuelan heritage through the lineage of their mother and the heroic feats of their father.

MacGregor was henceforth recognised as a naturalised Venezuelan citizen. He was reinstated into the Venezuelan army with the ceremonial rank of general and allowed to claim a pension of one-third salary.[113] Because of his 'glorious days of action' in the Ocumare retreat back in 1816, in which he led to safety many officers who later went on to occupy prestigious positions of political and military authority, MacGregor was considered to be a Venezuelan hero.

CONCLUSIONS

The four sites of Gregor MacGregor's career demonstrate how imperial discourses and practices were translated and transformed across space in the interstices between the British and Spanish empires in the first half of the nineteenth century. MacGregor freed slaves in Florida, sold them in Jamaica and abolished slavery in Poyais. In Scotland he emphasised his links to rebels against the British state and in Paris he presented himself as 'descendent of the Scottish Kings'. In the Hispanic Caribbean he was regarded as a 'perfidious English adventurer' and compared to pirates like Sir Francis Drake.

It could be argued that MacGregor was simply seizing upon whichever identity was most expedient to him at each stage of his career, for his own material gain or to enhance his reputation. Yet the evidence presented and discussed in this chapter, in particular the autobiographical writings discussed in the final two sections, suggests that he did genuinely reimagine his own subjectivity at each stage as he gained more experience and got older. MacGregor is a prime example of how armed forces could be much more than the 'military melting pot' that many excellent historical

---

[111] MacGregor to Congress of Venezuela, 4 February 1839, Caracas, reproduced in *Exposición documentada*, p. 19.

[112] See A. Díaz, *Female citizens, patriarchs, and the law in Venezuela, 1786–1904* (Lincoln, NE: University of Nebraska Press, 2004).

[113] 'Informe de la Comisión', reproduced in *Exposición documentada*, p. 21.

studies of the British Army have shown them to be.[114] The identities of soldiers, sailors and officers were not only given space and time to coalesce in the 'melting pot', but they were formulated and reformulated as the armed forces (and the 'melting pot' with them) moved through and across imperial spaces. MacGregor's particular experience of dwelling in imperial spaces, marrying and fathering children across the empire (his three children were born in Nassau, Dublin and Kingston) had especial influence on the changes in his subjectivity. He constructed kinship and friendship networks that elevated him to a position of some authority in 1817 in Venezuela but which had deteriorated by the late 1820s to plunge him into retirement and retrospective contemplation. Ironically, when he returned to Venezuela upon the death of his wife in 1838 it was the last vestiges of these networks – his old military comrades now occupying positions of influence – which granted him a pension and enabled him to live out his last days in Caracas.

No documents have yet been found to record MacGregor's last years in Venezuela, 1840–5. He did not dine with the British representative and seems to have lived an independent and relatively solitary existence. The official newspaper of the Venezuelan state, *La Gaceta de Venezuela*, noted his previously precarious health and lamented 'the death of a warrior who contributed to the triumph of the cause of justice, reason and philosophy'.[115] *El Liberal* called him 'this valiant champion of Venezuelan independence [who ...] came back to live amongst us and enjoy his pension, but now attacked by illness he has left us forever'.[116] Perhaps during these final years of illness and solitude MacGregor was able to continue his reflections and even finish writing his autobiography. The existence of such a document would provide a further insight into the ways that diverse imperial experience affected colonial biographies. The distinction between home and abroad was never fixed and always challenged. Repeated departure from homes and friends was often the only constant.

---

[114] For the 'military melting pot' in the British Army in the late-eighteenth century see S. Conway, *The British Isles and the War of American Independence* (Oxford: Oxford University Press, 2000), Chapter 5.
[115] *La Gaceta Oficial*, 14 December 1845.
[116] *El Liberal*, 14 December 1845.

CHAPTER 2

A blister on the imperial antipodes: Lancelot Edward Threlkeld in Polynesia and Australia

Anna Johnston

In February 1832, George Bennet complained to William Ellis, foreign secretary of the London Missionary Society (LMS), of the 'perpetual blisters' that the society 'seem[ed] destined to carry'. From his experience as a director of the LMS and as the surviving member of a deputation that had travelled to the mission stations in the Pacific, India, and Africa, Bennet nominated nine missionaries as key troublemakers:

Mr *Thorn* – Mr *Threlkeld* – Mr J. *Adams* – Msrrs *Laidler* and *Massic* – Mr *Thomsen*, and Mr *Tomlin* ... The least efficient (not in capability as to talents but in disposition and in fact) we ever found were the most troublesome and dangerous to the welfare of the Society, and the cause.[1]

That the problems of the LMS could be attributed to its own missionaries – rather than, say, white colonial resistance to evangelical activity (as in the West Indies), imperial policies that hindered missionary expansion (as in India), or native resistance to Christianity (common in many of the LMS's sites of operation) – reveals the significance of individual missionary figures within a large and influential institution. This chapter focuses on just one of these troublesome missionaries: Lancelot Edward Threlkeld (Fig. 2.1). Bennet and others within the LMS had found their dealings with Threlkeld difficult from the moment of his appointment, but they were not the only members of metropolitan or colonial élites to be exasperated by Threlkeld and his behaviour. Around the British empire, Threlkeld agitated, frustrated, and provoked imperial élites.

Deeply pious, profoundly opinioned, and blithely indifferent to public opinion, Threlkeld and his service for the LMS (from 1815–28) were characterised by controversy. Ordained in 1815, Threlkeld worked

---

[1] George Bennet, 13 February 1832, Home Odds Box 12; Folder 5, Council for World Mission (hereafter CWM), School of Oriental and African Studies, London.

Fig. 2.1 Portrait of Lancelot Edward Threlkeld, made from a drawing shortly before he went to the South Seas, from his papers (ML MSS 2111/1:CY Reel 341), from a copy held in the Mitchell Library, State Library of New South Wales.

for the LMS as a missionary in Rio de Janeiro (1816–17), on various Polynesian islands (1817–24), and in New South Wales (1824–8 – see Map 2.1). After fifteen years of service, he was effectively dismissed by the LMS. They accused him of accruing 'enormous expenses without any warrant from us' in the establishment of the Lake Macquarie mission in New South Wales, of resisting and disobeying society regulations, and of 'plac[ing] yourself in an attitude of hostility and defiance'.[2] From 1829, Threlkeld was funded by the colonial government to run the Lake Macquarie mission; when that funding ceased in 1841, he served first as

---

[2] W. Alers. Hankey, 30 May 1828, South Seas and West Indies western outgoing letters 1822–1830, Box 1, CWM.

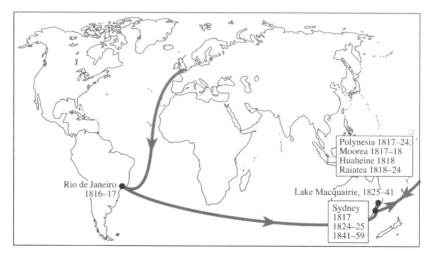

Map 2.1 Lancelot Edward Threlkeld's imperial career.

pastor of the South Head Congregational Church, and then as chaplain of seamen, appointed by the Sydney Bethel Union, until his death in 1859. Fuelled by evangelical zeal and a strong sense of righteousness, Threlkeld disturbed each of the colonial spaces in which he operated, calling into question imperial philosophies as he did so.

THRELKELD AND THE LMS

From the moment that the LMS appointed Threlkeld, he sought to undermine the hierarchical relationship that existed between the society and their missionary representatives. Specifically, he sought to position himself quite carefully within the imperial realm in which the society operated. Initially proposed to go to Africa, Threlkeld never truly accepted his subsequent posting to Polynesia. Despite agreeing to LMS appointment regulations in 1814 – assuring the society that he and his wife Martha were 'not prepossessed in favour of any part of the World, wherever we may be thought most useful to Immortal Souls there may the Lord incline the Directors to send us'[3] – by 1815 Threlkeld sought to convince the Directors that he would be more gainfully employed in their new mission 'to the Afghans and to the Tartars' than their established Polynesian mission because of 'the smallness of the Islands, the inconsiderable

---

[3] L. E. Threlkeld, 6 September 1814, Home candidates papers 1797–1899, Box 16, CWM.

number of their respective Inhabitants and the large number of Missionaries at that Station ... being already there'.[4] Besides, he suggested, 'It is the most earnest desire of my Soul to preach Christ crucified, and to do it not upon another Man's foundation would be inexpressibly delightful.' Threlkeld's desire to find an originary colonial landscape on which to make his mark ensured that when he stopped at South America on the way to Polynesia (having found no relaxation of the Society's directives to go to the islands), here too he petitioned the society. Choosing to break the voyage in Rio de Janeiro to ameliorate his wife and child's health (Martha had given birth to a sickly child on the voyage from England, and the child died in Rio soon after their arrival), Threlkeld found troubling signs of competing empires, both religious and economic in nature. 'There are swarms of monks &c. but no Inquisition,' he reported: 'It is very shocking to our feelings to see the shiploads of slaves bought and sold at this place. When will that abominable traffic cease.'[5] Discovering that the English settlers there were keen to retain a Protestant minister, soon a temporary stop *en route* seemed to provide him with a 'providential' opportunity of 'improving this Harvest which is fully ripe'.[6] The LMS disagreed. After their third letter insisting that Threlkeld continue to Polynesia, he finally acquiesced, albeit ungraciously:

it is solely from your peremptory order accompanied with the threats of disgracing my character as a Missionary and of withholding your support by which means the most effectual Method is taken to prevent the entrance of the Gospel in S. America that I leave this place.[7]

Travelling to Polynesia via New Zealand – where he reported of the Church Missionary Society station that 'the management of the affairs of this Mission ... is very improperly done by a Majority'[8] – and the Australian colonies, Threlkeld finally arrived at the island of Moorea in 1817. His first letter from here to the Reverend Samuel Marsden, the society's only southern-hemisphere director, reported on the behaviour of his fellow missionaries:

I am glad to find Mr Ellis has behaved with the greatest propriety since his arrival, not so with Mr Orsmond who has I am informed by the Old Missionaries been in the habit of getting frequently intoxicated you may judge how far this is correct or at least a probability of the truth of it when you are informed

---

[4] L. E. Threlkeld, 27 September 1815, Home candidates papers 1797–1899, Box 16, CWM.
[5] L. E. Threlkeld, 1 April 1816, South Seas incoming correspondence 1812–1818, Box 2, CWM.
[6] *Ibid.*   [7] *Ibid.*
[8] L. E. Threlkeld, 29 September 1818, South Seas incoming correspondence 1812–1818, Box 2, CWM.

that all their abundant supply of wine &c. is consumed by them already, such things ought not to be!⁹

Threlkeld's elongated and argumentative passage from Britain to his mission station clearly demonstrates his difficult personality, characterised by a high self-regard and a pompous and self-righteous sense of moral and intellectual superiority. It also demonstrates his tendency to put in writing matters that more prudent men might have withheld. It is evident, then, that the controversy that almost continually surrounded Threlkeld was in some regard a result of what many saw as his infuriating character. Yet these personal traits ensured that he identified strongly with the marginalised and dispossessed, and that he invested fully in the complex colonial politics of each location he inhabited. What for some missionaries might have been local issues of little significance to their greater commitment to God became highly personal crusades for Threlkeld and, arguably, key modes through which he negotiated his identity and authority. One of the new breed of missionaries sent to reinvigorate the LMS Pacific missions after 1815, Threlkeld and his companions were 'supposedly better trained than their predecessors, more practical and less pietistic, more appreciative of knowledge for its own sake, more imbued with a sense of their own destiny'.¹⁰ In his clashes with earlier missionaries and their evangelical processes in Polynesia, Threlkeld demonstrates the reinvention of missionary subjectivities in particularly modern terms.

THRELKELD IN THE PACIFIC

Even after his eventual arrival in the Society Island group, Threlkeld did not settle down. He spent time on Moorea, before moving to Huaheine in 1818, then moving again to Raiatea, where he remained from 1818 to 1824. At no point did Threlkeld accept his position within the mission community, for he regularly criticised the practices of the first generation of LMS missionaries and continually asked to leave Polynesia. From Raiatea in 1818, he wrote to the directors, describing the difficulties of the mission and the wickedness of the islanders. He concluded: 'such are the abominations in these Islands and such are the oppositions of one

⁹ L. E. Threlkeld, 4 December 1817, South Seas incoming correspondence 1812–1818, Box 2, CWM.
¹⁰ N. Gunson, 'Preface', in *Australian reminiscences and papers of L. E. Threlkeld, missionary to the Aborigines, 1824–1859, Australian aboriginal studies, No. 40 Ethnohistory Ser. No. 2* (Canberra: AIAS, 1974), p. v.

and another and such is the confusion that exists among us that it is no disgrace not to belong to this society and do implore the Directors to change my station'.[11] By 1820, his pleas for removal focused on the inadequate support for missionaries with families, writing to the directors:

Feeling confident of the utter impossibility of remaining in these Islands without a considerable augmentation of expenditure in proportion as families increase, and numberless other circumstances, all tending to increase the expences [sic] of this mission I humbly submit my request to your kind attention and commiseration namely, that you will be pleased to remove me from these Islands.

The food, he said, 'does not suit my constitution, nor is it possible for me to remain without a *continuance* of supplies both for myself and family'. Concern for his children became a prime motivation for wanting to move on – 'the dread of my children becoming vagabonds, and my own life becoming a life of comparative uselessness in the Saviour's cause' – and he volunteered that he would have no objection to missionary service in Asia.[12]

Other missionaries similarly fulminated against 'heathen abominations'. Indeed, this was a standard feature of missionary discourse. Yet Threlkeld reserved his strongest criticism for his fellow evangelists. He told the LMS that he deeply regretted leaving Rio for this missionary community typified by 'furious strife envy and every evil work'. In 1819, he felt compelled to notify the directors of 'a circumstance that however much it may pain your or my mind is absolutely necessary to be investigated not only for the honor of the Society but also for the honor of the Gospel': a 'bare outline of an enquiry into the conduct of Mr Davies with the Native Females'.[13] An islander had testified that he 'saw Mr D [sic] in criminal connection with a native woman', other leading islander men confirmed that they forbade women from talking with the missionaries because Davies was 'throwing them on his bed and taking improper liberties with them', and, when the Tahitian brethren conducted an enquiry, 'more shocking things were discovered'. Davies had vigorously defended himself,[14] the missionaries at Tahiti had recanted their former confirmation of Davies' guilt, and Threlkeld's fellow labourers Reverends

[11] L. E. Threlkeld and John Williams, 30 October 1818, South Seas incoming correspondence, 1812–1818, Box 2, CWM.
[12] L. E. Threlkeld, 1 June 1820, South Seas incoming correspondence 1812–1818, Box 3, CWM.
[13] L. E. Threlkeld, 1819, South Seas incoming correspondence 1812–1818, Box 3, CWM.
[14] Davies protested his utter innocence: 'I do boldly declare that I am no *adulterer*, no *fornicator*, no abettor of *immorality*, neither in *doctrine* nor in *practice*': J. Davies, 24 February 1821, South Seas incoming correspondence 1812–1818, Box 3, CWM.

Orsmond and Williams were 'rather averse' to bringing the matter to the attention of the directors back in London. The incidents had occurred in March, yet, in August 1819, Threlkeld felt the need to write to London with the full particulars, and to 'strongly urge the necessity of a deputation being sent out to visit this unhappy mission. This measure would I think not only satisfy your minds but it would satisfy the mind of the Publick and give great joy to every upright Missionary.' Pacific historians have concluded that Davies was probably not guilty of the main charge against him,[15] yet Threlkeld's obsessive interest in this affair reveals more, I think, than merely his crusading and moralistic nature.

A focus on the precariousness of white identities typifies Threlkeld's writing from this period of his imperial career. His letters provide repeated evidence of missionary misbehaviour, or suspected misbehaviour, but details of religious ministry are rare. Threlkeld clearly undertook his religious duties with diligence and skill,[16] though one wonders how he found the time amongst his voluminous correspondence and various campaigns against pre-existing missionaries and missionary practices. His home correspondents noticed this peculiar bias in his letters. William Burd, an itinerating preacher in Devon, wrote to Threlkeld:

I am glad that your allowance is at last made certain; now you can go on more easily. I am glad that you opposed the wicked conduct of Mr Davies; and trust the Lord had this design among others in sending you where you are. But your main concern is to save souls ... Think of the value of 1000 souls.[17]

Burd's admonition to Threlkeld to focus on 'the individual success of your own labours' rather than the failures of other missionaries and the immorality of islanders made no difference to Threlkeld's *modus operandi*.

Threlkeld's determination to prosecute Davies for his suspected immorality mirrors his intention to remove his children from a colonial place in which white authority and morality appeared vulnerable. Part of his 1820 appeal included thinly disguised criticism of other missionary children: 'looking back to the past, with regret I see children, ignorant,

---

[15] N. Gunson, *Messengers of grace: evangelical missionaries in the South Seas 1797–1860* (Melbourne: Oxford University Press, 1978).

[16] George Bennet praised missionary efforts at Raiatea: 'Religion and Civilization are also here going hand in hand, aiding and adorning each other, and confounding all opposition. The Kings and Chiefs are the foremost in supporting the best of causes – this is one of the singular and extraordinary characteristics of this mighty work': Bennet, 12 November 1822, Home Odds Tyerman and Bennet's deputations 1821–1828, Box 10, CWM.

[17] William Burd, 20 April 1822, MSS 2111, Mitchell Library, Sydney (hereafter ML).

debauched, ruined: looking forward, we can only expect, melancholy prospect, our sons to become sailors and our daughters to become women a disgrace to their sex, without the means for usefulness, or support'.[18] Here Threlkeld was explicitly condemning the children of older missionaries, with whom he was in a constant power struggle, and clearly his letter sought to circulate gossip in order to discredit his rivals in evangelical spheres. Perhaps through such means he sought to continue his campaign to get an independent mission, free from the company of other evangelists. Yet his concern for the degradation of missionary children reverberates on another plane too. Here, in the Pacific, the most successful site of colonial evangelisation in the early nineteenth century, Threlkeld's concern was not with indigenous idolatry and conversion: instead he was most focused on the provisional and precarious status of white moral authority in a colonial environment. This authority could be invoked, and challenged, in a variety of ways, and at a number of key cultural locations. Threlkeld's condemnation of Davies reveals one of the most potent sites of cross-cultural contact in the nineteenth-century Pacific – the body, and especially sexualised encounters across cultures – and his concern with missionary children in part repeats this preoccupation. A specific fear of racial degeneration always haunts laments about the fate of white children in a colonial environment, and Threlkeld's claims are no different. Both of these highly charged sites of cross-cultural contact reveal concerns with the maintenance of imperial bodies and subjectivities in colonial spaces, and both of these sites suggest that the boundaries between imperial subjects and their heathen others were rather more permeable than missionaries would have hoped.

Issues of bodily intimacy, sexuality, and the influence of colonial environments (both physical and cultural) had troubled and/or attracted Europeans from the first voyages of 'discovery', of course, for Polynesia in particular had been constructed as a site for voyeuristic European delight, a new 'Garden of Eden' which offered sensual opportunities of which moralists and missionaries strictly disapproved. Threlkeld's narratives of debauchery amongst the older missionaries, and the racial degeneration of their children, thus play directly into Pacific stereotypes that the LMS knew well, images of the exotic and erotic others whom missionaries were specifically sent to reform. Threlkeld's challenges to the authority of his fellow missionaries in these ways were highly effective, for they attacked the foundation of missionary identities in the Pacific and positioned his

---

[18] L. E. Threlkeld, 1 June 1820, South Seas incoming correspondence 1812–1818, Box 3, CWM.

morality and authority as superior to many of his fellow evangelists. But Threlkeld's challenge to the established missionary practice in another sphere was perhaps less conventional.

EVANGELICAL TIME AND THE POLYNESIAN OTHER

Back in Britain, the LMS was deeply concerned about the conflicting (and conflictual) accounts of Pacific missions that they received from Threlkeld and his fellow missionaries. James Hayward, one of the first evangelists in the Pacific and typical of the less-educated 'mechanic' missionaries the LMS first appointed, returned to Britain on furlough and was interviewed at length by the society's directors. One of the key elements he identified as lacking in islanders was a sense of time and a desire for labour: 'The Natives feel but very few wants which we can supply, Hard Labour they will not persevere in. They have not as yet any conception of the virtue of time, weeks and months they will thoughtlessly squander away.'[19] Elsewhere I have argued that central to this recurrent missionary discourse about time and labour was the attempt to transform native communities into models of British Protestant lower- and middle-class communities,[20] and Hayward's linking of the two concepts, 'Hard Labour' and time, makes this connection evident. Here, though, I want to consider the question of time more abstractly, and particularly the ways in which Threlkeld's interventions into the calendar challenged the missionary order in Polynesia.

Key to an evangelical conversion (the essential selection criterion for an aspiring missionary candidate) was an adherence to doctrine which insisted on living one's life in fear of damnation, and a central characteristic of a virtuous life was the strict observance of Sabbath.[21] One of the first challenges for missionaries sent out in the world, then, was to establish amongst the community of potential converts a specifically religious (and also specifically cultural) calendar. More than anything, getting a community to adhere to Christian protocols on a period of time marked off as Sunday was central to efforts to evangelise non-Christians. Hayward's complaint at his interview back in London, that islanders had

[19] J Hayward, 'Substance of Mr Hayward's communications in answer to queries &C.' no date 1819–20, South Seas incoming correspondence 1812–1818, Box 3, CWM.

[20] A. Johnston, *Missionary writing and empire, 1800–1860*, Cambridge Studies in Nineteenth-Century Literature and Culture (Cambridge: Cambridge University Press, 2003), pp. 120–4.

[21] See also A. Lester and D. Lambert on the missionary Reverend Shrewsbury, Chapter 3 in this volume.

no sense of 'the virtue of time', shows his ignorance of the system of time measurement that was specific to those communities. His comment reveals, however, the difficulties that missionaries faced first in explaining abstract ideas about time (more often than not, in an imperfect translation across at least two linguistic systems) and then in imbuing that idea of time with the moralistic meanings that seemed natural to hard-working and god-fearing evangelicals of the early nineteenth century. Exactly what islanders made of the first missionary efforts to observe the Sabbath is the subject for another study, yet the disruption that Threlkeld caused through his intervention in the Polynesian Christian calendar makes evident the tenuous nature of this cultural practice in the early Pacific missions.

In May 1822, the Raiatean government changed the day on which the Sabbath was celebrated, moving it a day forward.[22] They did so on Threlkeld's instigation, for he had calculated that the ship's company carrying the first group of LMS missionaries, led by Captain Wilson, had made an error in their nautical reckoning.[23] Such a fundamental error in the establishment of a new evangelical regime provided Threlkeld with further evidence of his superiority – in this instance, in intellectual and scientific terms, overlaid with moral righteousness – over older evangelists and their missionary practices. It was an error that he could not leave uncorrected. Hayward wrote to the LMS from Matavai condemning Threlkeld's actions:

It ought to be a matter of serious grief to every Missionary here that such disunion should exist among them. Mr T [*sic*] never reflected, probably, on the objection the Devil by and by, may raise in the Sceptic Natives mind, against the sacredness, and morality of the Sabbath day, by the unadvised step he has taken in this affair.[24]

Reverend William Henry, one of the original missionaries based at Eimeo (Moorea), wrote in much stronger terms, claiming that the change of date

[22] Gunson notes that the change was almost certainly also a political 'act of defiance against the new Tahitian government', although Threlkeld's reckoning was correct. It took the French administration another twenty years to correct the calender: Gunson, *Messengers*, p. 125.

[23] Threlkeld's version is as follows: 'It is an indisputed fact by all, but a few of the Missionaries in these Islands, that the Style of reckoning time at Pitcairns Island Tahiti Moorea &c. &c. does not agree either with English time or with the time observed in the Sandwich Islands. Another still more inexcusable blunder is universal in the Georgian and Society Islands [where they call Monday the first day, rather than Sunday] ... So that to be correct with this most erroneous mode of reckoning we ought to say Christ died on a Saturday and rose on the Monday the first day of the week, according to Tahitian reckoning': 24 December 1823, Home Odds Box 10, CWM.

[24] J Hayward, 16 August 1822, South Seas incoming correspondence 1812–1818, Box 3, CWM.

has occasioned much confusion and discord between its inhabitants and the people of these Islands, and still more between them and the people of the islands adjacent to it . . . Surely our Directors and the Christian world at large must disapprove of that very rash, inconsiderate and injudicious subversion of the long established order of things there by a single individual, and he comparitively [*sic*] but a new comer. Such an alteration is not a little calculated to stagger the people in general respecting the observance of the Sabbath, and upon their veneration for that sacred day, which effects I fear have in too inconsiderable a degree been already produced.[25]

A flurry of letters concerning the change of calendar circulated between the missionaries at different islands, and between the men in the Pacific and LMS directors in London. These were vituperative, argumentative letters and they threatened to break the already strained social contract between this community of religious men isolated from Britain in the antipodes. Threlkeld defended his actions by insisting that he had heard from several sources including a ship's captain that the older missionaries at the Windward Islands had considered changing the day first, and that he was merely following their example. To Henry's pious suggestion that if time should be reckoned from anywhere, it should be from Jerusalem, Threlkeld suggested sarcastically that 'the board of Longitude will not perhaps readily fall into your views'.[26] Henry wrote back, recommending to Threlkeld 'a spirit of humility and becoming diffidence in your own judgement, and deference to the judgement of your brethren, especially that of your senior brethren'. He noted with forbearance Threlkeld's 'taunting observations' and '*sneering sarcastic retort*'.[27] Fortunately for the missionary community, the LMS had sent a deputation of two religious men to survey the society's mission stations around the world, and the Sabbath debate in the Pacific coincided with Reverend Daniel Tyerman and George Bennet's tour of the region. Both parties placed the debate in the deputation's hands, each confident that their decision would be upheld.

Tyerman and Bennet met with the aggrieved missionaries, their respective island communities, and others in the region. After much debate, and many attempts at a negotiated settlement, in May 1822 Tyerman wrote to Threlkeld that opposition to the changed date 'was so determined, that we saw it was in vain to push the subject further', and recommended, 'unless there should be some reasons of a very peculiar

[25] Quoted in L. E. Threlkeld, 21 July 1823, Home Odds Box 10, CWM.
[26] L. E. Threlkeld, 3 April 1823, Home Odds Box 10, CWM.
[27] William Henry, 3 June 1823, Home Odds Box 10, CWM.

force to the contrary', that they return to the original date reckoning.[28] Somehow Threlkeld misread the letter – perhaps deliberately – and continued a letter-writing campaign which explained 'most cheerfully ... the occasion of the Style being altered here at Raiatea'.[29] When, a year later, he received the deputation's public letter to the church and congregation at Raiatea stating that 'we cannot be but most deeply concerned that any difference should exist between you and your Neighbours on any subject of a religious nature, and especially when that difference involves the Glory of God, the sanctity of the Lord's Day, and your own respectability in the opinions of your fellow Christians',[30] Threlkeld was furious.

> You have charged me and the church with being in error so gross that it destroys everything that is good, a sin so heinous that it involves the Glory of God. This I deny in any sense of the term error whether as a mistake, blunder, sin, crime, or offence.[31]

Time, as Johannes Fabian has argued, 'is a carrier of significance, a form through which we define the content of relations between the Self and the Other'.[32] The European relegation of non-Europeans to a prior time, usually figured as primordial savagery, is a familiar feature of imperial discourse, a representational manoeuvre that naturalises modern imperial domination over lands and peoples designated as archaic. Hayward's condemnation of Polynesian ignorance of European time confirms such hierarchical relationships, and positions the LMS missionaries as harbingers of modernity. In religious terms, time is crucial as the 'medium of a sacred history ... a sequence of specific events that befall a chosen people'. Christian valorisation of the knowledge of time was consolidated by Enlightenment attempts to 'secularize Judeo-Christian Time by generalizing and universalizing it'.[33] Nineteenth-century theories challenged older Christian notions, because biblical time did not provide enough time for natural history. Neither was it, Fabian argues, the *'right kind of Time* ... It was Time relaying significant events, mythical and historical, and as such it was chronicle as well as chronology ... it did not allow for Time to be a variable independent of the

---

[28] Daniel Tyerman, 22 May 1822, MSS 2111, ML.
[29] L. E. Threlkeld, 24 December 1823, Home Odds Box 10, CWM.
[30] Daniel Tyerman, and George Bennet, 17 November 1823, Home Odds Box 10, CWM.
[31] L. E. Threlkeld, 29 December 1823, Home Odds Box 10, CWM.
[32] J. Fabian, *Time and the other: how anthropology makes its object* (New York: Columbia University Press, 1983), p. ix.
[33] *Ibid.*, p. 2.

events it marks'.[34] Remarkably, these complex negotiations about the meaning and measurement of time were played out explicitly in the Polynesian calendar debate, against the backdrop of colonial evangelisation.

Henry's argument for Jerusalem as the ultimate site of temporal authority marks his adherence to an older, pre-Enlightenment notion of time, a time grounded in the bible and a specific geographical and cultural landscape: 'it appears to me that *Jerusalem* is that place above all other places upon the Earth, and if we reckon from thence the Old Sabbath so long observed among these Islands is nearer the *proper* time than the *innovation* of *Raiatea*'.[35] As Henry's letter makes clear, this is a debate that resonates with anxieties about modernity – 'innovation' – and the threats that it appeared to pose to older forms of religion. Threlkeld's brisk and scientific revision of the hard-won recognition of the Sabbath threatened Henry's sense of religious time and thus his religious authority. The authorities by which Threlkeld justified his reckoning – which included modernising institutions such as the Longitude Board, 'several nautical Gentlemen in His Majesty's service',[36] and the 1822 alteration of the style in Britain[37] – mark his identification with a modernising evangelism quite different to Henry's older form of piety. As Gunson suggests of the younger Pacific missionaries, 'To discover the writings of these men is to discover, as it were, the birth of new principles in the human sciences.'[38] In this way, Threlkeld challenged the very basis of the initial missionary community in Polynesia, and the modes by which those first missionaries constructed and maintained their identities.

Crucial to both men was their standing at the head of a watchful community of Polynesian converts (and non-converts, Hayward's 'Sceptic Natives'). The calendar change contested Henry's authority with his congregation – he stridently asserted that the Windward Islanders would not be 'relinquishing the order of things established among them by their Old Teachers who have long borne the burthen and heat of the day for their good'.[39] The grounds on which Henry bases this part of his argument are revealing. It is the 'order of things' established by the first missionaries which structures the Windward Islanders into a community of Christians. Michel Foucault reminds us that order is, simultaneously, 'that which is given in things as their inner law' and 'that which has no existence except in the grid created by a glance, an examination, a

---

[34] *Ibid.*, p. 13.   [35] L. E. Threlkeld, 21 July 1823, Home Odds Box 10, CWM.
[36] L. E. Threlkeld, 3 April 1823, Home Odds Box 10, CWM.
[37] L. E. Threlkeld, 29 December 1823, Home Odds Box 10, CWM.   [38] Gunson, *Messengers*, p. v.
[39] L. E. Threlkeld, 29 December 1823, Home Odds Box 10, CWM.

language'. 'The order of things', for Foucault, is made up of the fundamental codes of a culture, which govern its language, modes of perception, values, and hierarchies of its practices (amongst others), but also the scientific or philosophical theories which explain 'why order exists in general, what universal law it obeys, what principle can account for it, and why this particular order has been established and not some other'.[40] Time and a religious calendar were central to the missionary 'order of things' in nineteenth-century Polynesia, as Henry suggests, for these elements were fundamental to evangelical understandings of cultural and religious practices. The threat that Threlkeld posed to Henry was his suggestion that the original missionary calendar was not omniscient and omnipresent but instead a cultural order that could be challenged as but one of a variety of different kinds of ordering that could be chosen. Henry's calendar was not transparent and overarching but rather a constructed system of social organisation. In this way, Threlkeld's intervention represents precisely the shift Foucault identifies with (late eighteenth- and early nineteenth-century) modernity, when 'the mode of being of things, and of the order that divided them up before presenting them to the understanding, was profoundly altered'.

Henry claims no superior reckoning for the maintenance of the Polynesian calender. It is the physical suffering of the older missionaries – their long-term endurance of 'the burthen and heat of the day' – which demands the islanders' respect, both for the men and for the cultural practices they have instituted. This is an authoritarian model of social relations, and it demands the islanders' unquestioning obedience to the authorities upheld by the longest period of residence in the region. Here again Threlkeld's 'new principles' sought to institute a different model of social relations. Threlkeld questioned Henry's capacity to transform islanders into modern Christian subjects, expressing his hope that Henry and his supporters would 'let the natives act as men, as free men, as Christians taught by Englishmen, who, if their boasting is not vain, find themselves in their own country on their religious liberty and freedom of discussion on all subjects'.[41] The language here is redolent with the revolutionary zeal that had transformed some nations, most obviously France and America, and had restructured social relations through an emphasis of egalitarianism and freedom of debate. Crucially, Threlkeld

---

[40] M. Foucault, *The order of things: an archaeology of the human sciences* (London and New York: Tavistock Publications, 1970), p. xx.
[41] L. E. Threlteld, 29 December 1823, Home Odds Box 10, CWM.

locates Polynesian masculinity in this sphere. He emphasises their freedom – for Polynesia was not a formal British possession, even if
missionary stations often gave this impression – and situates that freedom
in terms of citizenship, religious liberty, and freedom of debate. These
distinctly modern markers of masculine subjectivity and citizenship are
here grafted onto his argument for modern forms of reckoning. Har-
nessing contemporary theories of time to modern subjectivities in this
manner, Threlkeld condemns older forms of missionary authority for
seeking to produce obedient and subservient converts, akin to feudal
social systems. He suggests that, in letting Windward Islanders choose as
their Raiatean brethren had, modernising the calender would empower
Christian islanders and give them access to progressive European subjectivities. Fabian suggests that 'for human communication to occur,
coevalness has to be *created*. Communication is, ultimately, about
creating shared Time.'[42] Threlkeld's insistence on modernising Pacific
mission communities – by restructuring the religious calendar and by
restructuring modes of converted subjectivity – tested the complex cultural politics of early LMS mission stations, for his challenges undermined the authority assumed to rest in white, imperial subjects (such as
Henry) and raised the possibility of a coevalness and an equality for which
the first missionaries were not prepared.

Forced to capitulate to the authority of his missionary elders, Threlkeld
continued to chafe under the structures of Pacific mission stations. But in
early 1824, Martha Threlkeld died, after a short illness, and her death
provided him with an opportunity to leave Polynesia with dignity: 'In
consequence of the late afflicting dispensation of God's providence
towards me, I feel it a duty to visit my native country, for a season, with
the intention of returning to these Islands as speedily as circumstances
will admit.'[43] In joining the LMS deputation on their voyage to the
Australian colonies, Threlkeld managed finally to assume the originary
mission that he had so long wished for. In Sydney, Tyerman and Bennet
found 'a party of the natives . . . surely, there never trod on the face of
this earth more abject creatures'. Yet 'All attempts to civilize the savage
occupants have been fruitless; – it must be confessed, however, that those
attempts have been few and feeble.'[44] By October, the deputation had

---

[42] Fabian, *Time and the other*, pp. 30–1.
[43] L. E. Threlkeld, 10 May 1824, Home Odds Box 10, CWM.
[44] Rev. Daniel Tyerman and George Bennet, Esq., *Journal of voyages and travels by the Rev.
Daniel and George Bennet, Esq. deputed from the London Missionary Society, to visit their various
stations in the South Sea Islands, China, India, &C., between the years 1821 and 1829. Compiled from*

negotiated with Sir Thomas Brisbane, the Governor of New South Wales, for a land grant of 10,000 acres on which to institute a new mission station, with Threlkeld as the sole missionary.

THRELKELD IN AUSTRALIA

Threlkeld ran the only LMS mission in Australia in the nineteenth century, established in 1824–5. Threlkeld's Lake Macquarie mission, near Newcastle, was a dramatic failure, and it affected colonial culture in complex ways. For the LMS, the Australian mission was one of the least successful and most publicly embarrassing of their many colonial ventures. Its uniqueness in Australian history, and its ignoble place in the history of the LMS, means that it functions both as an exemplary case study of missionary effort in Australia and a limit case for colonial missionary activity in comparative contexts.

From the beginning, the mission was positioned in opposition to mainstream colonial practices and policies. Humanitarian interests were directly opposed to the explicitly genocidal alternatives to cross-cultural conflict endorsed by many Australian settlers. In addition, Threlkeld's appointment ensured that the mission would be controversial, given his history of antagonising his fellow missionaries. Reverend Samuel Marsden, the colonial chaplain, magistrate, and highly influential player in the colonial politics of both church and state, had had considerable experience with Threlkeld in his role as the designated LMS agent in the southern hemisphere. His scepticism about the likelihood of a successful Aboriginal mission and his role representing the LMS (approving bills, providing [often unsolicited] advice, and protecting the institution's interests and image) inevitably put Marsden and Threlkeld on a collision course. Threlkeld came to New South Wales with expectations that evangelical achievements in Polynesia – where, partly for local political reasons, entire communities had converted to Christianity when their leaders did – would be replicated in Australia. Early failures to convert Aborigines, which had thwarted religious men and humanitarian-influenced settlers such as Marsden, did not register with Threlkeld, who had finally been granted the virgin mission field to which he had aspired. New South Wales, Polynesia, and the metropolitan centre were closely linked through shipping routes and the continual traffic of missionary and other colonial travellers, and

original documents by James Montgomery, 2 vols. Vol. II (London: Frederick Westley and A. H. Davis, 1831), p. 152.

Threlkeld's reputation preceded him.[45] In New South Wales, there were few other missionaries for Threlkeld to clash with, but there were alternative forms of authority, particularly the colonial clergy, the courts, and the press, which predictably drew his ire.

As a frequent visitor to the law courts, particularly as translator for Aboriginal defendants in criminal cases, Threlkeld was acutely conscious of the value of public testimony. Across a range of issues, Threlkeld both contributed to and critiqued what he called the 'paper war'[46] plaguing the colony: the rancorous, heated, and conflicted writings that appeared in contemporary newspapers, pamphlets, and other published reports, which debated the ethics of settler invasion, the appropriate mode of black and white relationships, the dispossession of aboriginal peoples, and the responsibilities of white settlers. In New South Wales, Threlkeld constructed (and vigorously defended) a public role for himself, based on his moral authority and his unprecedented engagement with Aboriginal culture, which both augmented and at times compromised his status as a missionary.

Threlkeld's position within early Australian colonial culture makes him a particularly interesting figure. His aggressive individuality, high moral stance, and righteous indignation at white colonial attitudes towards, and actions against, the Aborigines ensured that he challenged celebratory narratives of settler expansion. Threlkeld's preparedness to witness, report, and circulate instances of cross-cultural violence rapidly alienated him from the majority of white settlers. By 1826, when he was about to take up residence in the bush, Threlkeld's letters reverberated with the shock of colonial violence: 'I do not mention half of what I know of cruelties to the Aborigines, only what comes under my own cognizance and then I can face anyone that dares to contradict ... No man, who comes to this Colony and has ground and cattle and Corn, can dispassionately view the subject of the blacks, their interest says annihilate the race.'[47] Few in the colony would make such controversial statements publicly, and Threlkeld's claims were rarely investigated with the rigour he wished. This was especially the case when Threlkeld's information came from Aboriginal witnesses, who were effectively ignored by the nascent law courts. Threlkeld, however, gave credence to accounts that he

---

[45] Indeed, Threlkeld had spent some time in Sydney in early 1817 *en route* between Rio de Janeiro and Polynesia and, in attending the founding of the 'New South Wales Auxiliary Missionary Society', had met many of those settlers interested in religious matters.

[46] L. E. Threlkeld, 10 October 1825, Australia Box 2, CWM.

[47] L. E. Threlkeld, 10 August 1826, Australia Box 2, CWM.

investigated or those provided by witnesses (either black or white) in whom he had confidence. Sending his second half-yearly report from Lake Macquarie to the directors of the LMS, he advised them that 'M'gill, the Black who instructs me in the language, told me the other day that he remembers a white settler (one I know, and I believe the fact) shot a native who was stealing indian corn out of the field as it grew, he then hung him upon a tree with a cob of corn stuck between his teeth!'[48] In 1838, however, the testimony of Threlkeld and many others ensured that the Myall Creek massacres of Aborigines were brought to public attention and resulted in highly controversial court cases. Threlkeld claimed to have explicit evidence about the massacre, giving graphic evidence of the physical and sexual violence against Aboriginal women and children, in particular, that the stockmen were accused of perpetrating.[49] Roger Milliss has noted that Threlkeld's evidence for the trials surrounding Myall Creek was crucial, though contradictory, and fomented much debate at the time. The Myall Creek massacres are probably the most infamous in Australian history, particularly because of the execution of white men for the murder of Aborigines. As in this instance, throughout his residence in New South Wales Threlkeld produced a stream of texts attesting to his colonial observations, and circulated these widely and strategically.

Threlkeld situated himself on the borders of state governmentalities and evangelical concerns, both a 'man of god' and a man who frequented the colonial law courts, newspapers, and public forums. Threlkeld's liminality, arguably, led to his estrangement from more conservative religious institutions and individuals, such as Marsden and the first Presbyterian minister Reverend John Dunmore Lang. It meant that he constantly challenged the colonial order in Australia. His voluminous correspondence and strategic publications displayed this challenge repeatedly, as did his commitment to translating for Aboriginal witnesses in court. Threlkeld deliberately and strategically used private and public correspondence to publicise his opinions and causes. In the textual debates between Threlkeld and other religious men, the highly provisional nature of humanitarian ideas in the colonies was played out explicitly.

Threlkeld's public role ensured that he became a target for criticism, from settlers who virulently disagreed with his activism on behalf of

[48] *Ibid.*
[49] L. E. Threlkeld, 'Report of the Mission to the Aborigines at Lake Macquarie, New South Wales', 1837.

Aborigines, and from fellow religious men who castigated his missionary methods or his political interventions. In 1835, John Dunmore Lang published a series of articles, 'Missions to Aborigines', in his *Colonist* newspaper. These three lengthy and vitriolic essays surveyed white efforts to evangelise indigenous populations, but were particularly focused on condemning Threlkeld. The supposedly anonymous author, who all in the colony knew to be Lang (just as the *Colonist* was supposedly edited by Kenneth Munro although Lang was widely known to be the financial and editorial controller),[50] publicised the split between the LMS and Threlkeld, very much supporting the former. He criticised the choice of the Lake Macquarie site as 'a piece of downright folly', and represented Threlkeld as incompetent and 'utterly unfit for the office assigned him'. Worse, Lang suggested, Threlkeld had set back the unpopular mission cause in New South Wales: 'The loss which the whole Protestant community of all denominations in this colony have thus sustained, through the incompetency (to use the very mildest phrase which the case warrants,) of a single individual, is quite incalculable.'[51] Unsurprisingly, Threlkeld sought redress, ultimately suing Lang for libel. In 1836, the unedifying sight of two of the colonies' leading religious figures attacking each other in court attracted crowds of onlookers for the two days of the trial, and the case was widely reported in the newspapers. Unfortunately for Threlkeld, Lang represented himself, and put a defence of justification. The almost five-hour speech that Lang gave in his defence provided further opportunity to deride Threlkeld and condemn his mission as a failure. The solicitor general Richard Windeyer, appearing for Threlkeld, claimed that Lang's plea of justification 'heaped injury upon injury', whereby he 'iterated the truth of the libels, came into Court to justify them, and then talked of character and the freedom of the press, and the privileges of a public writer'.[52] Ultimately, the jury found in Threlkeld's favour, but the paltry damages – one farthing – clearly indicates that their sympathy lay with Lang. This case sought to prove the credibility of a particular missionary, but it reveals the intense contest between religious men in the colonies to claim the authoritative moral ground and the extraordinarily public and textual nature of these claims for authority.

---

[50] R. B. Walker, *The newspaper press in New South Wales, 1803–1920* (Sydney: Sydney University Press), 1976, p. 146.

[51] Lang, 'Missions to Aborigines 2', p. 361.

[52] Threlkeld v. Lang. Decisions of the Superior Courts of New South Wales, 1788–1899. *Sydney Herald* 28 March 1836. Supreme Court of New South Wales 1836: http://www.law.mq.edu.au/scnsw/cases1835–36/html/threlkeld_v_lang__1836.htm, accessed 12 May 2005.

Religious men, such as Threlkeld, Marsden and Lang, produced the extensive array of texts expected of pious nineteenth-century public figures. These texts are curious artefacts: both personal and institutional, private and public. They resound with extraordinarily colourful, impassioned language and forceful political opinion. In an important sense, it was in the field of textuality that the real disintegration of the Lake Macquarie mission occurred, because it was in written records that the battles of the morality of colonisation were fought. These authors corresponded with key colonial figures, from governors to newspaper editors, in Australia and in Britain, and they made many recommendations about progressing humanitarian cross-cultural relationships. Despite their well-intentioned Christian sentiments, however, their texts reverberate with the Eurocentric rhetoric of the early nineteenth-century British empire. More specifically, they simultaneously participate in and critique the discursive violence of colonialism.

THE DISCURSIVE VIOLENCE OF COLONIALISM: THE STORY
OF WILLIAM COX

I want to trace here one particular instance of Threlkeld's disruptive witnessing. In February 1825, he wrote to the LMS from Sydney:

In some parts of this Colony there is quite a hostile feeling against the Blacks. And those who ought to be their champions are silent on the subject. A Gentleman (Mr Cox) of a large property recommended at a public meeting in this Colony that the best measure towards the Blacks would be to 'Shoot them all and manure the ground with them!!!'[53]

This anecdote operates as what Ian Duffield calls a micronarrative – 'brief, super-charged narratives'[54] – and, as Niel Gunson suggests, this particular micronarrative 'was to haunt Threlkeld in his long appeal for Aboriginal rights'.[55] The story was told to Threlkeld by Saxe Bannister, the attorney general in the late 1820s and a fellow evangelical humanitarian. The two parts of this micronarrative were equally important for Threlkeld: it served simultaneously as a paradigmatic narrative about the excesses of settler violence towards Aborigines, and the complacency of Threlkeld's fellow religious men. He included the narrative in subsequent

---

[53] L. E. Threlkeld, 2 February 1825, Australia Box 2, CWM.
[54] I. Duffield, '"Stated this offence": High-density convict micro-narratives', in L. Frost and H. Maxwell-Stewart (eds.), *Chain letters: narrating convict lives* (Carlton South, Vic.: Melbourne University Press, 2001), p. 135.
[55] N. Gunson, 'Introduction', in *Australian reminiscences*, p. 14.

accounts of his battles with cynical settlers in New South Wales. In 1838
Threlkeld produced a copy of his (then unpublished) *Memorandum
selected from twenty four years of missionary engagements in the South Seas
and Australia* for William Westbrooke Burton, a Supreme Court judge
who had previously served at the Cape of Good Hope, and who was
keenly interested in humanitarian efforts on behalf of the Aborigines.
Here, Threlkeld repeated the Cox micronarrative.[56] His 'Reminiscences
of the Aborigines of New South Wales: traits of the Aborigines of New
South Wales' was serialised in a Sydney-based Presbyterian newspaper
The Christian Herald, and Record of Missionary and Religious Intelligence
between 1853 and 1855,[57] and the micronarrative reappears there, showing
some discretion by keeping Cox's name out of the story but effectively
identifying him through a description of 'One of the largest holders of
sheep in the Colony', based in Bathurst.[58] George Bennet circulated the
micronarrative about Cox: in writing to his friend James Montgomery, a
minor evangelical poet, he repeated the story, adding

You need not hesitate to mention this leaving out the name tho' everybody
knows it here as well as the fact of his using such *language* – perhaps nothing in
the West Indies has surpassed this *language* and the Gentleman has also acted
upon it for his people have killed many.[59]

For both men, bearing witness to such sentiments and refusing to remain
silent about them was crucial.

   Bennet's connection between the treatment of indigenous peoples in
settler colonies and slaves in the West Indian colonies is significant, for it
draws together British humanitarian concerns about slavery and the
impact on indigenous populations of settler colonisation. Yoking together
these two kinds of colonial disturbance was popular among missionaries,
and after 1833 humanitarian activists were motivated to extend their
reforms.[60] Importantly, evangelical activists mobilised both the communication networks and the discursive regimes that emerged from
abolition debates. As Alan Lester describes it, individual instances of
missionary conflict with settlers formed an integral part of a broader

---

[56] Gunson notes that Burton's imperial career continued to expose him to new colonial locations and
roles: after serving twelve years in Sydney, he was appointed to Madras, although he returned to
Sydney in 1857, serving as president of the Legislative Council in 1858: *Australian reminiscences*,
p. 320.

[57] *Ibid.*, p. 2.   [58] *Ibid.*, p. 49.

[59] Emphasis added, George Bennet, 25 December 1824, pp. 36–528, Sheffield Literary and
Philosophical Society, Sheffield Archives, Sheffield.

[60] The 1837 Select Committee on Aborigines (British Settlement) was the most public result of this
transfer of political interests.

'propaganda war' throughout the 1820s and 30s, one that was 'fought out across trans-imperial networks of communication'. What was at stake in this war 'was the definition and determination of "proper" relations between British colonists and their others'.[61] Bennet's second emphasis, on the nature of the *language* of cross-cultural violence, is equally important, for it reveals the way in which nineteenth-century humanitarians privileged language and the political effectiveness of discursive interventions into imperial affairs. If we understand that discursive regimes regulate 'who can speak about what in what way ... and with what authority', then we can begin to understand the subversive potential of evangelical critiques of settler colonisation. As Bob Hodge and Vijay Mishra note, discursive regimes produce 'political and social facts which profoundly affect what is commonly said or communicated, and what is recognised to be a legitimate meaning'.[62] Bearing public witness to colonial atrocities was thus embedded in two authorising systems for religious humanitarians: the first, the Christian valorisation of 'witnessing', was consolidated by the second, the political value of testifying on behalf of the dispossessed and colonised.

Threlkeld's micronarrative about Cox ricocheted through evangelical imperial networks, finding its target back in Britain. In 1835, ten years later, George Bennet would write to Samuel Marsden from London, seeking information specifically about 'the person near the river Hawkesbury [who] proposed manuring the ground with the carcases of the Aborigines'.[63] In 1836, the former attorney general Saxe Bannister gave evidence to the British Parliament's Select Committee on Aborigines (British Settlements), chaired by the leading metropolitan humanitarian campaigner, Thomas Fowell Buxton. More discreet than Threlkeld and Bennet, Bannister did not mention Cox by name, but testified to the 'cold-blooded murder' of Aborigines by settlers, noting that the 'natives are peculiarly helpless when in conflict with powerful men, and ought to be protected, most especially against the highest oppressors'.[64] The committee's report condemns the 'Many deeds of murder and violence [that] have undoubtedly been committed by the stock-keepers ... by

---

[61] A. Lester, 'Humanitarians and white settlers in the nineteenth century', in N. Etherington (ed.), *Missions and empire*, Oxford History of the British Empire Companion Series (Oxford: Oxford University Press, 2005), p. 64.

[62] R. Hodge and V. Mishra, *Dark side of the dream: Australian literature and the postcolonial mind* (North Sydney: Allen & Unwin, 1990), p. 26.

[63] George Bennet, 5 Nov. 1835, copied from CY 229, Vol. IV, A1995, ML.

[64] 'Report and evidence of the select committee on Aborigines in the British Settlements' (British Parliamentary Papers, 1837), p. 21.

the cedar-cutters, and by other remote free settlers' and noted that 'many natives have perished by the various military parties sent against them'.[65] Bannister may have regretted his discretion, for he soon after expressed his dissatisfaction with the committee's response. Highly critical of many who gave evidence to the hearing,[66] he declared that the committee's report 'when good, is almost a dead letter; and its bad passages, grossly inconsistent wit [sic] its evidence, are of a most dangerous tendency'.[67]

In 1836, then, the narrative that Threlkeld deliberately circulated as evidence of violent settler colonialism and the depravity of certain British subjects in colonial situations informed authoritative testimony back in the imperial centre. The ultimate failure of the progressive social activism that the British select committee represented is encapsulated in this particular convergence of events. Under siege from more aggressive colonial interests, and undermined by its internal conflicts, this moment in the history of imperial ideas about race was doomed to fail.

THE 'PAPER WAR' IN CONTEMPORARY AUSTRALIA

This chapter has thus far presented a reading of a part of the colonial archives, drawing connections between documents that are usually examined in the context of colonial history. The final section examines this practice of reading more theoretically, and locates Threlkeld's career in both national and international contexts. Margarita Zamora reminds us that 'Reading is a contentious practice ... [T]he act of reading is never perfectly smooth; it is usually carried out in tension with the text as well as with other readings.'[68] My reading of the LMS archive is carried out in tension with at least two other readings – those by Henry Reynolds and Keith Windschuttle – and in the context of contemporary cultural debates about the morality of colonisation in Australia, or more specifically the lack of it.

In *This whispering in our hearts*, Henry Reynolds uses Threlkeld's writings as evidence of nineteenth-century challenges to 'the ethics of colonial progress'.[69] Threlkeld's annual reports provide Reynolds with

---

[65] *Ibid.*, p. 10.
[66] Specifically, Major Dundas, acting Governor Wade, and Governor D'Urban: men, Bannister declared, 'with memories as infirm as their judgments, to whom the colonial-office is in the habit of confiding the interests of our remote possessions, and the fate of the coloured people': S. Bannister, *British colonization and coloured tribes* (London: William Ball, 1838), p. 244.
[67] *Ibid.*, p. 253.
[68] M. Zamora, *Reading Columbus, Latin American literature and culture* (Berkeley: University of California Press, 1993), p. 2.
[69] Henry Reynolds, *This whispering in our hearts* (St Leonards, NSW: Allen & Unwin, 1998), p. xv.

evidence about border wars, official and private punitive expeditions by white colonials, European attitudes towards Aborigines, and colonial atrocities. Reynolds is arguably Australia's highest profile historian, having built his career since the 1970s on groundbreaking, revisionist, and popular accounts of Australia's colonial past. Reynolds represents the vanguard of politicised reimaginings of Australia's past, reacting against earlier histories that had effectively elided white-colonial violence and indigenous resistance to colonial invasion.[70] Widely read and lauded particularly during the late 1980s and 1990s, these revisionist histories at the same time stimulated a concerted conservative campaign to discredit what the historian Geoffrey Blainey (and subsequently the Australian prime minister) called 'black armband history'.[71] The notoriously partisan magazine *Quadrant* was central in encouraging the counter-revisionist campaign, specifically in publishing and promoting the work of Keith Windschuttle, a former media-studies academic. After a series of tendentious articles on 'The myths of frontier massacres in Australian history' in *Quadrant* from 2000 onwards, Windschuttle self-published *The fabrication of Aboriginal history* (2002), a book which has come to represent the epitome of the 'history wars' as they are being played out in Australia.[72]

Because Reynolds uses Threlkeld as a case study, Threlkeld himself becomes a target for Windschuttle's own revisionism. Their debate is, in part, about the reliability of Threlkeld's archival testimony as historical fact – an argument that is unsolvable in empirical terms, based as it is on subjective assessments of Threlkeld's authority and character. For Reynolds, Threlkeld is one of a number of 'disturbing and even dangerous agitators',[73] whose conviction and faith made them secure in their virtue and righteousness: 'tenacious, determined and often fearless opponents',[74] who, for their efforts, 'were seen as self-righteous, disturbing, dangerous, obsessive or mad'.[75] For Windschuttle, Threlkeld had

---

[70] Attwood and Foster describe this as 'a myth about Australia that celebrated British colonisation of the continent as a peaceful act of discovery and settlement, whereby a progressive people and their venerable institutions were successfully transplanted and the land was transformed, thus resulting in the new nation of Australia' (B. Attwood and S. G. Foster, 'Introduction', in B. Attwood and S. G. Foster (eds.), *Frontier conflict: the Australian experience* (Canberra: National Museum of Australia, 2003), p. 11). See Attwood and Foster's excellent introduction for a more detailed account of Australian debates about frontier/colonial history than space allows here.

[71] G. Blainey, 'Drawing up a balance sheet of our history', *Quadrant* **37**, 7–8 (1993), p. 15.

[72] K. Windschuttle, *The fabrication of Aboriginal history: Vol. I: Van Dieman's Land 1803–1847* (Sydney: Macleay Press, 2002).

[73] Reynolds, *This whispering in our hearts*, p. 30.   [74] *Ibid.*, p. 31.

[75] *Ibid.*, p. xiv.

'an obsessive desire' to exaggerate colonial violence so as to ensure his continued employment: he was imaginative and may have 'intentionally exaggerated' the size of the pre-contact Aboriginal population to emphasise the decline after colonisation. He 'not only invented the notion of a "state of war" and "a war of extirpation" but was "actually caught lying"'. Windschuttle opines that Threlkeld's conscience 'must have been troubled at times by some of the gruesome details and inflated numbers he could not help himself adding to his tales'. 'The works of his imagination', Windschuttle complains, 'have coloured the whole record of Aboriginal–European relations in our early colonial history.'[76]

This is not the place to analyse the debates between Reynolds and Windschuttle in the painstaking detail they require. Suffice to say, Windschuttle's methodology of unverified impugning of character and attribution of deceit hardly promises to advance the debate. Yet the dispute about Threlkeld (and others) makes clear the extent to which colonial texts continue to have essential cultural valency in postcolonial cultures such as Australia. It also throws into relief the nature of the 'paper war' between Reynolds and Windschuttle, one that directly mirrors the 'paper war' of the early nineteenth century. The nature of these debates is uncannily similar: they focus on the dubious morality of colonisation, on the reliability or otherwise of testimony, and on the dangerously unstable nature of strategic textuality.

The kinds of narratives about Australia that Threlkeld circulated in the nineteenth century are those which W. E. H. Stanner described as falling into a 'cult of forgetfulness on a national scale'.[77] Threlkeld's writing repeatedly tells shocking stories of the violence of settler colonisation. His allegations about William Cox and his testimony for the Myall Creek trials represented only some of the controversial and lurid accounts that Threlkeld made public in New South Wales. These are typical of a kind of story that circulated in the early nineteenth century with distinct generic links to stories about the violence of slavery familiar to religious readers, which similarly provided graphic representations of white cruelties against black peoples, with added emphasis on victims who were women or children, and which sought to shock and then to galvanise sympathetic white readers into action. In both variants of the genre, at the time, such stories were subject to outraged denial in some quarters,

[76] K. Windschuttle, 'The myths of frontier massacres in Australian history: part 3, Massacre stories and the policy of separatism', *Quadrant* **44**, 12 (2000).
[77] B. Smith, *The spectre of Truganini: 1980 Boyer lectures* (Sydney: Australian Broadcasting Commission, no date), p. 23.

and their authors accused of possessing over-active imaginations and overly ambitious political or moral agendas. But others took these stories seriously, and were convinced of the credibility of the eyewitness and the informant. Still, such stories gradually slipped out of the public historical record, even if they remained visible in the colonial archives. In Australia, such narratives of colonisation were submerged beneath more straight-forward and celebratory narratives of white nationhood.

Revisionist historians such as Reynolds have ensured that lurid stories such as Threlkeld's were returned to the foreground of historical accounts of the colonial frontier. As a consequence, as Haydie Gooder and Jane Jacobs note, 'Settler Australians have ... had to come to terms with a new understanding of the nation, one in which settler heroics has been replaced with colonial brutalities and injustices.'[78] It is precisely this kind of new national fiction, of course, that Windschuttle is reacting against. But Windschuttle's *ad hominem* arguments totally miss the point, for he plays the man, not the text. His attempts to assign intent to Threlkeld's actions – the accusations of obsession, deliberate and politically strategic deception, and speculation as to how Threlkeld 'must' have felt, cited above – demonstrate this slippage, the laziest and least convincing kind of historical revisionism. One of Windschuttle's central rhetorical moves is to construct Threlkeld as a 'story teller' rather than an historically reliable archival source. Of the 1838 Lake Macquarie Report, he declares that 'It does not require much scepticism to decide that this passage does not ring true. Bellies ripped open, blacks roasted alive, babies dashed upon stones, all speak of a storyteller who deserves to be taken with a large dose of salt.'[79] Yet his critique of Reynolds' representation of humanitarians – Reynolds 'portrays his subjects in only one dimension ... Most of his characters had far more ambitious motives than he has given them' – is instructive, for Windschuttle's language of 'characters' and the historian's agency in 'giving' motive to historical agents reveals the constructed nature of his own historiography. Windschuttle seeks to rewrite Threlkeld as a different kind of 'character' and, as is the fictional author's pre-rogative, to recast this character's motives. That such modes of argument have any purchase whatsoever within public debates about history is

---

[78] H. Gooder, and J. M. Jacobs, ' "On the border of the unsayable": the apology in postcolonizing Australia', *Interventions* **2**, 2 (2000), p. 235.

[79] Windschuttle, 'Myths'. This is the extent of argumentation in the article: no evidence, no analysis, but merely Windschuttle's (overly) confident assertion that something 'does not ring true'. For Windschuttle, the fact that Threlkeld's evidence came from an Aboriginal man who subsequently disappeared – according to Windschuttle, 'probably with his throat cut' – is sufficient to exclude the story.

extraordinary, yet the political climate ensures that media pundits and politicians, seeking to construct a palatable understanding of the national past, claim that Windschuttle's publications 'have struck at the heart of the accepted view of Australian colonial history in the past 30 years'.[80] Literary scholarship and contemporary forms of historiography suggest that ascertaining intent is always problematic: difficult enough to verify the author's intention in the fictional works, but almost impossible to reconstruct a single figure's internal motivations from historical sources, and particularly so from those emanating from the fluid and improvisational colonial cultures of the southern hemisphere in the early nineteenth century. We can map the trajectory of Threlkeld's travels as he worked in the service of the LMS (and, by extension, in the service of Empire); we can trace the points at which he appears in the official records of institutions such as the law courts and missionary societies; and we can read his version of the events of his extraordinarily public and controversial career, and the accounts of others who witnessed that career. But I remain sceptical about our ability to decide which 'character' – Reynolds' or Windschuttle's – in Australian historiography more appropriately approximates the historical figure of Lancelot Threlkeld. Representation, even (or perhaps especially) historical representation, is asymptotic: it approaches, but can never reach, the curve of a real human life. It is at this point that interdisciplinary studies can make a genuine intervention.

Mary Poovey suggests that 'it makes a difference to treat history-writing and textual analysis as facets of a single enterprise'.[81] In this debate Poovey's analysis is suggestive, precisely because neither Reynolds nor Windschuttle engage with textual analysis or consider the practices of reading. Zamora reminds us that

just as every text arises in a particular context ... so do readings of that text. And although we cannot reconstruct those contexts in all their complexity and specificity nor approach writing and reading as if they were only responses to circumstances, to disregard the contexts within which texts become meaningful is to ignore an important aspect of how writing and reading help make history.[82]

Windschuttle's recent work returns to the colonial archives to refute revisionist histories of frontier conflict, and in doing so he politicises the

---

[80] E. Higgins, 'Who's still afraid of Keith Windschuttle', *The Australian*, 22 July 2004: http://hnn.us/roundup/entries/6905.html, accessed 21 February 2005.

[81] M. Poovey, *Making a social body: British cultural formation, 1830–1864* (Chicago and London: University of Chicago Press, 1995), p. 1.

[82] *Ibid.*, p. 3.

archive in complex and contradictory ways. Windschuttle wants to have it both ways: he wants to insist that if the colonial archive does not contain irrefutable proof of Tasmanian Aboriginal deaths, for example, then they did not happen. On the other hand, he wants to de-contextualise the archive by refusing to deal with it as a constructed system of colonial knowledges; and by personally impugning archival voices that provide evidence that he does not want to credit.

Windschuttle's de-contextualisation of the colonial Australian archives refuses to acknowledge what Antoinette Burton describes as the condition of all primary sources: that 'the experiences these materials give us access to are partial representations of complex historical realities, and the voices they permit us to hear require us ask under what material conditions they have been made available, and for what purposes'.[83] Instead, Windschuttle and, to a lesser extent, Reynolds construct the colonial archive as the ultimate site of authority, a stable and fixed collection of documentary evidence.

Such a notion of the colonial archive belies not only the complexity of the narratives that it contains, but also the very nature of archives themselves. Jacques Derrida has suggested that 'Nothing is less reliable, nothing is less clear today than the word "archive".'[84] He defines the current times as experiencing 'archive fever or disorder ... concerning its lightest symptoms or the great holocaustic tragedies of our modern history and historiography: concerning all the detestable revisionisms, as well as the most legitimate, necessary, and courageous rewritings of history'.[85] Archive fever, though, takes on a double meaning in French: '*en mal d'archive*: in need of archives': 'It is to have a compulsive, repetitive, and nostalgic desire for the archive, an irrepressible desire to return to the origin, a homesickness, a nostalgia for the return to the most archaic place of absolute commencement'. I speak as a fellow sufferer, of course, as a secular researcher who gets obsessed with missionary archives. But Derrida reminds me that I am not the only one struck down in such a way, and reminds us of the conservative nostalgic desires that archives can induce.

Settler colonies such as Australia have always felt the lure of the *tabula rasa* – its promise of a new beginning (with the pleasurable shedding of

---

[83] A. Burton, *At the heart of empire: Indians and the colonial encounter in late-Victorian Britain* (Berkeley, Los Angeles, London: University of California Press, 1999), p. 13.
[84] J. Derrida, *Archive fever: a Freudian impression*, trans. Eric Prenowitz (Chicago and London: University of Chicago Press, 1997), p. 90.
[85] *Ibid.*

old subjectivities, histories, and difficulties), the allure of being the first author on the page of a new story, and the appeal of becoming self-made. Settler colonies always inevitably find, however, that *tabula rasa* is a palimpsest. Old stories have been scraped off the surface, in order to provide the 'clean slate,' but these pre-existing narratives have permeated the base material, and their lettering ghosts all subsequent writing. One of the problems with Windschuttle's return to the archives is that he seems to assume that in doing so he can clear the slate entirely. What he does not acknowledge is that the archive to which he returns is itself already multilayered and contested.

Relocating Threlkeld's narrative about William Cox within its original context of writing and reading reveals neither the (disputed) truth of this story, nor its use value for contemporary polemical history. What it does reveal is the context of such a narrative – not simply an historical context, but a discursive one. If we see this utterance within the context of abolition narratives, and as part of a broader international network of humanitarian activism, we understand that the anecdote operates only in a limited sense as local. It does not operate, as Windschuttle claims, as a 'massacre story' 'to justify separating Aboriginal people from the European population'. Rather, it serves to connect Australian colonial politics with an international debate about the ethics of colonisation, as a story that would have resonated at the time with similar stories emanating from Britain's other colonial projects, connecting Australia to Polynesia to the Caribbean. This makes the Cox anecdote no less truthful (equally, no more verifiable), but it situates it within a genre of public utterances that made complex cultural meaning in Britain's second empire. It serves, as Barry Morris suggests, to reveal 'a sense of the social chaos that resulted from British imperialism and the conflict it unleashed'.[86]

Threlkeld's circulation around LMS stations in the Pacific and Australia enabled his peculiar view of this 'social chaos'. As a committed missionary, his work promised to introduce evangelical Christianity as a panacea to the cultural disruption that resulted in the aftermath of both official (as in Australia) and unofficial (as in Polynesia) imperial incursions. Well placed to observe the multiple and varying ways in which different kinds of imperial projects affected and effected local populations, Threlkeld's advocacy on behalf of Aboriginal and islander communities was not only based in his tendency to focus on white imperial

---

[86] B. Morris, 'Frontier colonialism as a culture of terror', in B. Attwood and J. Arnold (eds.), *Power, knowledge and Aborigines* (Bundoora, Vic.: La Trobe University Press, 1992), p. 75.

disorder in colonial environments. In both mission regions, Threlkeld sought to protect communities from what he perceived as the immoral conduct of other white men, conduct that he saw was unbecoming to the role of LMS missionary, in Polynesia, or the role of white settler, in Australia. His advocacy on behalf of indigenous peoples might now seem mired in the patriarchal practices of the imperial protector, and his strategic manipulations of colonial politics as using imperialism's 'social chaos' for his own advancement. But understanding Threlkeld's involvement in a series of improvisational and controversial colonial enterprises, in Polynesia and New South Wales, enables an integrated analysis of his diverse and at times contradictory career. Whether because of his engrained restlessness and ambition, or because of a more strategic political sense, Threlkeld acted throughout his career at both a local and an international level. His actions were designed for an effect both in the southern hemisphere, and back 'at home'. His letters connected the mundane affairs of colonial missions with the visionary schemes of both modern British evangelism and imperialism, and constructed an identity for himself as an actor on that larger stage. Perhaps this willed subjectivity reveals as much about his difficult character and his grandiose self-perception as about his significance in nineteenth-century colonial affairs. Yet, because of the geographical mobility and the access to evangelical textual networks that missionary work offered, Threlkeld's imperial career had, and continues to have, significance beyond the narrative of a single missionary life. His strident condemnation of other imperial actors, his willingness to circulate controversial issues in public forums both in the colonies and back in Britain, and his wilful disregard of the tacit social niceties that maintained religious communities in these often unwelcoming antipodean contexts ensure that Threlkeld and his writing continue to challenge our understandings of early colonial cultures in the southern hemisphere.

CHAPTER 3

Missionary politics and the captive audience: William Shrewsbury in the Caribbean and the Cape colony

Alan Lester and David Lambert

INTRODUCTION

William James Shrewsbury (Fig. 3.1) was born in Deal, Kent, in 1795. He came from the kind of improving lower-middle class background that was common among British missionaries in the early nineteenth century: his father was a grocer and tailor, his mother a former servant and his grandfather a Deal harbour pilot. Shrewsbury's son later noted that the young William had inherited his mother's nature, which was pensive and melancholy, in contrast to the 'irrepressible light-heartedness' of his father.[1]

Even by the standards of the British evangelical revival, the young Shrewsbury was pious. When only nine, he 'very often continued awake some time, and lay thinking on divine subjects, and breathing out [his] desires to God, till [his] eyes overflowed with tears'.[2] He had read all of John Wesley's works and begun preaching at the age of sixteen. Around the same time, Shrewsbury succeeded in converting his own parents to Methodism.[3] By the age of nineteen, he felt assured of his calling to secure the redemption of distant strangers too, in the Wesleyan overseas mission, despite the fact that this would mean breaking off with the young woman to whom he had formed a 'hasty attachment'.[4] Shrewsbury began his missionary career with a posting to Tortola in the West Indies in 1815. He would remain in the Caribbean for a further nine years, serving in Grenada and then Barbados. Returning briefly to Brighton in England, he was sent to the Cape Colony in southern Africa in 1825, where he remained, on different mission stations, until his passage to England in 1835 (see Map 3.1).

---

[1] J. V. B. Shrewsbury, *Memorials of the Rev. William Shrewsbury* (London: Hamilton Adams and Co., 1868), p. 15.
[2] *Ibid.*, p. 3.   [3] *Ibid.*, p. 6.   [4] *Ibid.*, p. 29.

Fig. 3.1 Portrait of Reverend William James Shrewsbury, 4454.h.12 F, from frontispiece of W. J. Shrewsbury, *Sermons preached on several occasions, in the Island of Barbadoes* (London, 1825), by permission of the British Library.

Shrewsbury is best known to historians for the central roles that he played in two controversial episodes. The first took place during his spell in Barbados, when his chapel was demolished and he was forced to flee the island by a 'mob' of local whites, who believed that he was an agent of the antislavery campaign. Such was the publicity generated by this episode that Shrewsbury became the subject of a parliamentary debate in 1825. The second controversy seems to represent something of a contrast, although it too led to Shrewsbury's name appearing in the parliamentary record. This time, Shrewsbury aligned himself with British colonists, against Africans and British humanitarians. Shrewsbury's draconian thoughts on how the Xhosa should be dealt with by the Cape colony's authorities led to his appearance in testimony gathered by a House of Commons select committee. This second appearance in the parliamentary record culminated in Shrewsbury being roundly condemned by humanitarians, disowned by the Wesleyan Methodist Missionary Society (WMMS) Committee, and proclaimed the 'Kafir-hating Methodist missionary' in the British provincial press.

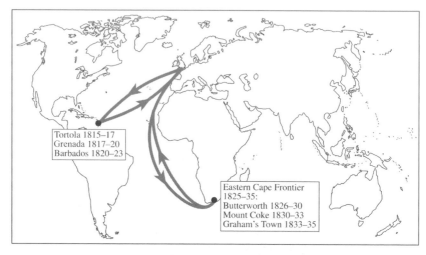

Map 3.1 William James Shrewsbury's imperial career.

Despite the notoriety of each of these episodes in Shrewsbury's colonial career, there are very few accounts which link them together. The controversy in Barbados is well known to historians of Caribbean slavery, missions and the antislavery movement,[5] and the controversy in the Cape is well known to historians of colonial South Africa.[6] But where the focus is on the Caribbean, or on antislavery, Shrewsbury disappears from the narrative as soon as he flees the wrath of the Barbadian slaveholders. Where Shrewsbury's recommendations concerning the Xhosa feature in the South African historiography, he appears on the Cape frontier, as if from nowhere, in 1834. There is thus no account which treats Shrewsbury's colonial career as one among many threads connecting the colonial histories of the Caribbean, southern Africa and Britain.[7] In tracing this

---

[5] N. Titus, *The development of Methodism in Barbados, 1823–1833* (New York: Peter Lang, 1994); F. Blackman, *Methodism: 200 years in Barbados* (Bridgetown: Caribbean Contact, 1988).

[6] R. Davenport, 'Settlement, conquest, and theological controversy: the churches of nineteenth-century European immigrants', in R. Elphick and R. Davenport (eds.), *Christianity in South Africa: a political, social and cultural history* (Oxford and Cape Town: James Currey and David Philip, 1997), pp. 51–67; N. Mostert, *Frontiers: the epic of South Africa's creation and the tragedy of the Xhosa people* (London: Jonathan Cape, 1992), p. 359.

[7] Although, see A. G. Cobley, 'Forgotten connections, unconsidered parallels: a new agenda for comparative research in southern Africa and the Caribbean', *African Studies* **58**, 2 (1999), pp. 133–55 and A. Porter, *Religion versus empire? British Protestant missionaries and overseas expansion, 1700–1914* (Manchester: Manchester University Press, 2004), pp. 114–15 and 136–9, which do draw attention to Shrewsbury's experiences in both the West Indies and the Cape.

thread, we suggest that Shrewsbury's apparent political shift was not in fact so great, and that his story tells us much about the contingent deployment, reception and appropriation of the universalising missionary project in different places.

In the course of attempting to explain Shrewsbury's involvement in colonial politics, we are also conscious that the political is never far from the personal. Shrewsbury's relation to his intended converts, as well as to the community of colonists, was always configured through the prism of his family life. In the inside cover of the bound quarto journal that he kept while in southern Africa, in which he indicated what really mattered to him, Shrewsbury not only wrote out the questions that Methodists were to ask themselves every day ('Hast thou lost a moment? What hinders thee from being more holy?'), but also the names of his children and the prayers that he had offered on their behalf.[8] At the same time that this chapter seeks to shed light on the particular set of linkages between the Caribbean, southern Africa and Britain, at its most intimate level, it also seeks to situate Shrewsbury within an increasingly difficult and even traumatic set of familial relations, which came to problematise his missionary zeal.

FIRST MISSIONS: THE BRITISH CARIBBEAN

The dominance of plantation economies across the British Caribbean and the monetary value attached to life meant that the spiritual well-being of the enslaved workers was not a priority for most white colonials. Many feared that the religious instruction of slaves would undermine slavery and the racial ideologies that supported it.[9] The local established churches were dominated by planter interests and it was largely left to the missionary churches, which had arisen out of the evangelical revival, to undertake work among the enslaved populations of the region. Given the entrenched power of slaveholders, however, the slave societies of the British Caribbean 'presented missions with some of their most difficult challenges'.[10] Indeed, much of that which was seen as threatening by West Indian slaveholders 'became condensed into the hated figure of the missionary', and especially the Wesleyan missionary, since in both

---

[8] W. J. Shrewsbury, *The journal and selected letters of Rev. William J. Shrewsbury, 1826–35*, ed. H. Fast (Johannesburg: Witwatersrand University Press, 1994), p. xii.

[9] C. Hall, *Civilising subjects: metropole and colony in the English imagination, 1830–1867* (Cambridge: Polity, 2002), pp. 104–5.

[10] Porter, *Religion versus empire?* p. 85; Blackman, *Methodism*.

England and the Caribbean, Methodism had come to be associated with radicalism.[11]

While the twenty-one year-old Shrewsbury was establishing himself in Tortola, slaveholders across the region were thrown into panic by the 1816 revolt in Barbados, and anti-Methodist feelings intensified.[12] Even though it had no missionaries in Barbados at the time, the WMMS still felt the need to respond to accusations of involvement, and all the missionaries in the Caribbean were warned 'against meddling with political parties, or secular disputes'.[13] The increasingly difficult position of missionaries was apparent during Shrewsbury's second posting to Grenada from 1818.[14] There, he faced restrictions on when he could preach to enslaved people.[15] Shrewsbury came to resent the local slaveowners, especially for their failure to lead the slaves by example when it came to observance of the Sabbath – something which, as we will see, would preoccupy him and serve as a focal point for both his self-belief and his self-doubt as a missionary. Increasingly, slaveowners expected their slaves to work on the Sabbath, cultivating food for themselves on provision grounds.[16] Shrewsbury lamented the white economic self-interest that enforced this Sabbath-breaking: 'O! the depth of the piety there is in the West India Planters! How can they escape the damnation of Hell?'[17]

However, Shrewsbury's disappointment was not confined to the owners of slaves. In general, he found the slaves themselves to be ignorant and, in this former French colony, mired in 'popish' ways. He was

[11] D. B. Davis, *Slavery and human progress* (New York: Oxford University Press, 1986), p. 195; D. Hempton, *Methodism and politics in British society, 1750–1850* (London: Hutchinson, 1984); M. F. Snape, 'Anti-Methodism in eighteenth-century England: the Pendle Forest riots of 1748', *Journal of Ecclesiastical History* **49** (1998), pp. 257–81.

[12] See D. Lambert, *White creole culture, politics and identity during the age of abolition* (Cambridge: Cambridge University Press, 2005).

[13] See W. Peirce, *The ecclesiastical principles and polity of the Wesleyan Methodists* (London: Wesleyan Conference Office, 1873), p. 747.

[14] Shrewsbury's efforts in Tortola had been undermined by the effects of emigration from the islands: G. G. Findlay and W. W. Holdsworth, *The history of the Wesleyan Methodist Missionary Society*, Vol. II (London: The Epworth Press, 1921, 1st edition), p. 146; *Minutes of the Methodist Conferences, 1814–18*, Vol. IV (London: Thomas Cordeux, 1818), pp. 32, 223. On Grenada, see B. A. Steele, *Grenada: a history of its people* (Oxford: Macmillan Education, 2003); Shrewsbury to WWMS, incomplete journal, starting 6 January 1818, West Indian Correspondence Fiche Box No. 2, Sheet 61, Methodist Missionary Society Archives (henceforth MMS). All MMS references are to microfiche in the Special Reading Collection at the School of Oriental and African Studies, London.

[15] Findlay and Holdsworth, *The history of the Wesleyan Methodist Missionary Society*, p. 184.

[16] R. Sheridan, *Doctors and slaves: a medical and demographic history of slavery in the British West Indies, 1680–1834* (Cambridge: Cambridge University Press, 1985), p. 174.

[17] Shrewsbury to WWMS, incomplete journal, starting 6 January 1818, West Indian Correspondence Fiche Box No. 2, Sheet 61.

particularly concerned about their own custom of meeting on the evening of the Sabbath for feasting and dancing:

The noise of the tom-tom, and the sight of the people at that place of amusement is exceedingly grievous and I resolved to go and warn them of the evil of their ways. When I came to the spot, I saw a large circle formed and within were the dancers decked in the most gaudy and indecent manner.[18]

On this occasion, Shrewsbury attempted to stop the activities by entering the circle and urging his audience to turn from their sin in an impromptu sermon. Yet, '[s]ome scoffed, and others gave me a contemptuous grin, especially the ladies ... During the sermon, first one man and then another took up his drum, and sneaked out of the ring.'[19]

The practice of keeping the Sabbath brought Shrewsbury's missionary impulses up against the realities of the British Caribbean. Music and dancing at weekends was an integral and customary part of the slave culture. Despite slaveowners' pressure, Sunday was still a day largely free from labour for many slaves and they sought to enjoy themselves, irrespective of disparaging comments from missionaries about their 'misuse' of it.

THE FIRST CONTROVERSY

The Barbados mission, to which Shrewsbury was appointed from 1820, represented Methodism's only real failure in the region, with local membership remaining under fifty – mostly free people of colour.[20] Because of the island's pronounced culture of anti-Methodism, Shrewsbury was permitted to preach on only four estates, which belonged to sympathetic planters.[21] In his journal, he admitted feeling 'alone, desolate

---

[18] Shrewsbury to WWMS, incomplete journal, starting 6 January 1818, West Indian Correspondence Fiche Box No. 2, Sheet 61. On the role of dance and self-expression in resistance to slave order, see M. Craton, 'Forms of resistance to slavery', in F. W. Knight (ed.), *The slave societies of the Caribbean*, vol. III of *General history of the Caribbean* (London: UNESCO Publishing, 1997), pp. 233–6.

[19] *Ibid.*

[20] This term is usually used to refer to formerly enslaved people who had been freed or to the children of women of this status. It denotes *both* black and mixed-race people. In late eighteenth- and early nineteenth-century Barbados, the terms 'free coloured', 'free mulatto' and 'free black' were used almost interchangeably. Despite their free status, they were a marginalised group occupying a liminal position in society. See Lambert, *White creole culture*, chapter 3; Titus, *Development of Methodism*, p. 16.

[21] *WMMS Society Reports*, Vol. II, 1821–24, 1822 – Barbados, p. lxvii; Blackman, *Methodism*, p. 26. On hostility to Methodist missionaries, see K. Davis, *Crown and cross in Barbados: Caribbean political religion in the late nineteenth century* (Frankfurt: Peter Lang, 1983) and J. Gilmore, 'Church and

and solitary'.[22] It was thus of great joy and comfort to him when he married a Methodist convert, Hilaria King. She came from a well-known and respected local family – her father an architect and her brother a physician.[23] She had discovered Christ through Shrewsbury's ministry, though her parents, who were Anglicans, did not approve of her joining a society associated with the antislavery cause and dominated by free people of colour. Despite this opposition, William and Hilaria were married in 1823.

As well as providing Shrewsbury with companionship, the marriage also prompted Shrewsbury to reveal his personal attitude to slavery:

as my father-in-law's property had been accumulated, though not by slave-dealing, yet by slave-labour, my wife agreed with me, after our marriage, to renounce our expectation of our share in it; and, accordingly, we expressed our desire to be excluded altogether from his will.[24]

Yet Shrewsbury saw this as a private matter and not a public expression of opposition to slavery in general. The couple retained friendly relations with Hilaria's family,[25] and he continued to try and follow the directions of the WMMS in not 'meddling with political parties, or secular disputes'.

Shrewsbury, then, was far from being an outspoken critic of slavery in Barbados, but this did not prevent him from being viewed as such by white society. As the British antislavery campaign underwent a resurgence in the 1820s, and the imperial authorities began to seek colonial reforms, Shrewsbury became the target of intensified public hostility. Extracts of a letter that he had written in 1820 were reprinted in the local press as 'evidence' of his antislavery sentiments. The letter had been written within weeks of his arrival in Barbados and described the moral condition of the island's population in unflattering terms, although it actually said nothing against slavery.[26] In an attempt to silence his critics, Shrewsbury made a complete copy of the letter available to the public, but this only served to inflame his opponents. Some accused him of arrogant incitement, others said that the letter was 'a sham' to 'blind our eyes' and

society in Barbados, 1824–1881', in W. Marshall (ed.), *Emancipation II: a series of lectures to commemorate the 150th anniversary of emancipation* (Bridgetown: Cedar Press, 1987), pp. 1–22.

[22] Shrewsbury, *Memorials*, pp. 105–7, 114.

[23] Shrewsbury, *Memorials*. The date of Shrewsbury's wedding given in Findlay and Holdsworth, *The history of the Wesleyan Methodist Missionary Society*, is incorrect.

[24] Shrewsbury, *Memorials*, p. 151.

[25] Findlay and Holdsworth, *The history of the Wesleyan Methodist Missionary Society*, p. 197.

[26] Titus, *Development of Methodism*, p. 30; W. Shrewsbury and W. Larcom to WMMS, 28 March 1820, Box 3, MMS. The letter was published in *The Missionary Notices* of October 1820.

rumours circulated that Shrewsbury maintained a secret correspondence with antislavery campaigners.[27]

Events took a turn for the worse in August 1823, after news reached Barbados of a major slave revolt in Demerara. Most white West Indians attributed it to the upsurge in antislavery campaigning in Britain and the local activities of the Reverend John Smith of the London Missionary Society. Arrested for allegedly encouraging the revolt through his preaching, he was convicted of treason and sentenced to death.[28] The 1823 revolt also focused suspicions in Barbados on Shrewsbury, especially given that he was personally acquainted with Smith.[29] Shrewsbury's religious services were disrupted and two masked horsemen fired upon the chapel. He tried to have his enemies prosecuted but was himself abused by the island's constables and magistrates.[30] Shrewsbury sought protection from Barbados' colonial governor, Henry Warde, only to be told that he would have to rely on the very authorities that were harassing him.[31]

At the same time that Shrewsbury was trying to secure Warde's help, an anonymous handbill was circulated that called for the destruction of the Bridgetown Methodist chapel.[32] Shrewsbury received warning of the plot and fled to the neighbouring island of St Vincent and whilst at sea Hilaria gave birth to their first child, Jeremiah. Meanwhile, a crowd of up to two hundred white Barbadians began the demolition of the chapel. They set out their motives in a handbill:

in consequence of the unmerited and unprovoked attacks which have repeatedly been made upon the Community by the Methodist Missionaries (otherwise known as agents to the villainous African Society), a party of respectable Gentlemen formed the resolution of closing the Methodist Concern altogether: with this view they commenced their labours on Sunday Evening; and they have the greatest satisfaction in announcing that by 12 o'clock last night they effected the TOTAL DESTRUCTION OF THE CHAPEL.[33]

---

[27] Shrewsbury to WMMS, 3 July 1823, MMS, Box 4, No. 192; Shrewsbury, *Memorials*, p. 135.
[28] M. Craton, *Testing the chains: resistance to slavery in the British West Indies* (London: Cornell University Press, 1982), pp. 267–90; M. St. Pierre, *Anatomy of resistance: anti-colonialism in Guyana, 1823–1966* (London: Macmillan Education, 1999); E. V. da Costa, *Crowns of glory, tears of blood: the Demerara slave rebellion of 1823* (Oxford: Oxford University Press, 1994).
[29] Findlay and Holdsworth, *History of the Wesleyan Methodist Missionary Society*.
[30] Shrewsbury to WMMS, 20 June 1820, Box 3, No. 121, MMS.
[31] Warde to Barbados Council, 21 October 1823, CO 28/92, fo. 244, PRO.
[32] 'Spirit of West Indian society – outrage at Barbadoes', *Edinburgh Review* (August 1825), pp. 479–99, Foreign and Commonwealth Office Library, London.
[33] CO 28/92, fo. 244, PRO; reproduced by the Methodist Missionary Society as *The late insurrection in Demerara, and riot in Barbados* (London: WMMS, 1823).

While his opponents were celebrating, Shrewsbury, his wife and their new son reached St Vincent. Concerned that the missionary might be the incendiary preacher alleged in Barbados, the authorities there required him to provide testimonials before allowing him to preach on the island. Despite being given twenty-four hours to leave the island, another Methodist missionary, Moses Rayner, gathered these testimonials from Shrewsbury's few friends among the planters on Barbados. The testimonials complimented Shrewsbury on the spirit of duty he sought to inculcate in the enslaved people to whom he had preached and were later used to great effect by Shrewsbury's supporters in Britain.[34] Shrewsbury himself was ordered to return to Grenada to resume his duties there, but was soon caught up in further controversy after publicly defending John Smith, who had died in prison in Demerara in February 1824. After being barred from preaching on a number of estates, and, given the hostility he was attracting across the West Indies, the local Methodists judged that Shrewsbury's presence was counterproductive to the broader missionary project and he was ordered to return to Britain.[35]

BACK IN BRITAIN

On return in June 1824, Shrewsbury preached in his home town of Deal and continued to defend Smith. He was much more reticent about his own treatment, however, and resisted the renown that was growing up around him in Methodist circles, agreeing only to put out a collection of sermons he had preached in Barbados in order to vindicate himself.[36] Years later, Shrewsbury wrote of his time in Barbados:

It was firmly believed by most persons that I was an agent of the Society established in England for the extinction of colonial slavery. This was altogether a mistaken opinion; for I never wrote a single line to any public political man on the subject; nor in my correspondence with my private friends did I ever mention one single fact prejudicial to the interests of that or any other colony in which I resided.[37]

---

[34] Testimonials for Shrewsbury, 10–11 November 1823, MMS, Box 5, No. 206.
[35] Findlay and Holdsworth, *The history of the Wesleyan Methodist Missionary Society*, p. 204.
[36] W. J. Shrewsbury, *Sermons preached on several occasions in the island of Barbados* (London: No publisher, 1825). The sermons were not published until after the excitement about the incident in Barbados had subsided and Shrewsbury was saddled with debt for some time afterwards: Shrewsbury, *Memorials*, p. 396.
[37] Shrewsbury, *Memorials*, p. 483.

Shrewsbury's denials, however, could not prevent his opponents in the Caribbean naming him among the 'agents to the villainous African Society'.[38] His unwilling association with the antislavery campaign was further reinforced by the response of the Antislavery Society itself to the events in Barbados. John Smith had already been hailed a martyr and the treatment of Shrewsbury also attracted considerable public interest.[39] In June 1825, Thomas Fowell Buxton, leader of the Antislavery Society, who denied any previous knowledge of Shrewsbury, introduced a Commons motion calling for the condemnation of Shrewsbury's persecution, the chapel's reconstruction at local expense and the protection of religious freedom in Barbados.[40] Drawing on correspondence about Shrewsbury's time in Tortola and Grenada, and the testimonials gathered by Moses Rayner, Buxton and other antislavery members of parliament portrayed Shrewsbury as a well-respected missionary who had faced an intolerant and prejudiced colonial culture.[41] At the end of the debate, although Buxton's original motion was amended, the tone of censure remained and Parliament was united in its denunciation of Shrewsbury's persecutors.[42] The motion was given particular coverage in the antislavery and missionary press, and the persecution of Shrewsbury, like Smith before him, made him a humanitarian *cause célèbre*, whether he liked it or not.

Even as Shrewsbury's imperial career was becoming the subject of parliamentary debate for the first time, however, he was back where he wanted to be – on the edge of empire. Throughout his time in England, his stated desire had been to return to missionary duties, this time in Africa. He wrote to his former congregation in Barbados that

Missionary sufferings have not made us weary of missionary work. On the contrary, we love it more than ever ... My heart is set on Africa, and my soul rejoices in the hope of the more glorious accomplishment of this promise, – 'Ethiopia shall stretch out her hands into God;' 'stretch out' in supplication, earnestly longing for teachers, and instruction, and the knowledge of salvation.[43]

---

[38] CO 28/92, fo. 244, PRO.

[39] J. Walvin, *Black ivory: a history of British slavery* (London: HarperCollins, 1992); Findlay and Holdsworth, *History of the Wesleyan Methodist Missionary Society*, p. 202.

[40] Methodist Missionary Society, *An authentic report of the debate in the House of Commons, June the 23rd, 1825, on Mr Buxton's motion relative to the demolition of the Methodist chapel and mission house in Barbadoes, and the expulsion of Mr Shrewsbury, a Wesleyan missionary, from that island* (London: J. Hatchard and Son, 1825).

[41] Hall, *Civilising subjects*, p. 114.

[42] Speech of George Canning, in *Authentic report*, p. 76.

[43] Shrewsbury to Gill (in Barbados), Brighton, 11 September 1824 in *Memorials*, p. 211.

After a brief posting to Brighton, Shrewsbury was offered a post in Ceylon, Sierra Leone or Madagascar. He elected for Madagascar, but was diverted to the Cape in response to an appeal by the frontier Albany district's Wesleyan superintendent, William Shaw. Shrewsbury was disappointed at this turn of events, but nevertheless sailed for the Cape in 1824 with Hilaria, who was pregnant with their third child, his son Jeremiah and baby daughter Julia. He arrived in Cape Town knowing next to nothing about the social and political environment of the contested frontier region, some 600 miles to the east, for which he was destined.

BUTTERWORTH: THE FAILURE OF THE MESSAGE

Even the four thousand British settlers, who had been encouraged by the Colonial Office to emigrate to this frontier zone only six years previously, had known little about it. They did not know, for instance, that they were to be settled on land forcibly appropriated from the Ndlambe Xhosa chiefdom in 1812, nor that fighters from that chiefdom had launched an attack on the frontier garrison at Graham's Town only a year before their arrival. They certainly did not know that their settlement had been requested by the colony's governor in order to help defend the colonial border against continuing Xhosa raiding.

The British settlers who had taken part in the well-publicised emigration scheme were very different from the planter classes of the West Indies. They were comprised mainly of artisans or professionals and their families.[44] Many of them were nonconformists. Hezekiah Sephton's emigrant party from London, in fact, was defined and recruited as a Methodist party, and William Shaw himself had arrived in the colony as its chaplain.[45] Having been accustomed in the Caribbean to being a member of a persecuted, minority sect, treated with hostility by the dominant planter class, Shrewsbury found in the Cape a community of colonists comprised in large part of men and women who shared his socioeconomic background and, for many, even his religious convictions. Indeed, alongside the money sent out from their co-religionists in Britain, it was the financial contributions of the Methodists among the settlers that helped sustain Shrewsbury's and the other Wesleyan missions in the

---

[44] See A. Lester, *Imperial networks: creating identities in nineteenth century South Africa and Britain* (London: Routledge, 2001), pp. 48–54.
[45] W. Hammond-Tooke (ed.), *The journal of William Shaw* (Cape Town: A. A. Balkema, 1972), p. 40.

colony.[46] Shrewsbury never seems to have commented on the way that these settlers utilised the colony's labour regulations to exploit a colonised Khoesan workforce in a manner akin to slavery.

Shrewsbury's first encounter with uncolonised Xhosa people on the other side of the colonial frontier occurred when his mentor, Shaw, took him to his own mission station at Wesleyville. Shrewsbury's first impressions were not encouraging. He wrote,

> there are several comfortable little dwellings on this station, but most of the natives still reside in their little smoky habitations and without much clothing. Their appearance, except on the Sabbath-day, is in no sense consistent with decency, nor do they seem to have any sense of shame.[47]

Nevertheless, Shrewsbury was keen to make an impression and he chose to establish a new mission in independent Xhosa territory rather than minister to the settlers of Albany. Together with Shaw, he set about persuading the paramount chief of the senior Gcaleka branch of the Xhosa, Hintsa, to host him. This would mean a location some one hundred miles to the east of the colonial frontier, further into independent African territory than any other mission outpost at the time. Shrewsbury would thus be a southern African pioneer. He was certainly represented as such by the Wesleyan missionary press.[48]

Hintsa was ambivalent about Shrewsbury's mission. He maintained a steady flow of communication with those chiefs to the west whose people were most affected by the colony. He knew that missionaries could be problematic, acting as informants for the colonial authorities. But he also knew of their potential political utility, since they could serve as channels of communication with the colony that chiefs themselves could manipulate. They could also provide chiefs with commodities, which enhanced their power over commoners.[49] Shaw himself was well aware of the motivations of those Xhosa who chose to accept missionaries:

> Let no one imagine for a single moment that, because a Chief or his Council favourably receive the Christian missionary, they arc therefore earnestly desirous of heartily embracing the Gospel ... worldly policy is yet the grand and most influential motive, by which rulers of Kaffraria are, in general, actuated.[50]

---

[46] W. Eveleigh, *The settlers and Methodism, 1820–1920* (Cape Town: A. A. Balkema, 1920), p. 54.

[47] Shrewsbury, *Journal*, p. 29.

[48] *WMMS Reports*, Vol. III, 1825–27, 1825 – Report from W. Shaw, pp. 42–3.

[49] J. B. Peires, *The House of Phalo: a history of the Xhosa people in the days of their independence* (Berkeley, Los Angeles and London: University of California Press, 1981), pp. 74–8, 106–8.

[50] Quoted Shrewsbury, *Journal*, fn. 234, pp. 203–4. See also Porter, *Religion versus Empire?* p. 110.

Hintsa was still consulting with the frontier chiefs while an impatient Shrewsbury selected a site about a mile from Hintsa's kraal, named it Butterworth after the WMMS Treasurer and started building his chapel.[51]

It was during this period of establishment that Hilaria suffered her first bout of serious illness, as rheumatoid arthritis and opthalmia rendered her eyes inflamed and her health permanently weakened. It did not help that Shrewsbury concentrated on building the chapel before he turned his attention to the family's accommodation. Eventually, after securing assurances from Shrewsbury that he would not challenge his secular authority, Hintsa did decide to tolerate the mission, but he remained wary of it throughout.

It was not only the chiefs who were ambivalent towards the missionaries. Shrewsbury himself reported that 'Nothing, I find, appears more inexplicable to the unenlightened heathen than the motives by which a missionary is actuated'. The ambiguity of these motives 'sometimes gives rise to a suspicion that we must have some secret, deep designs which are not yet discovered.'[52] Nevertheless, in the early months of the mission, Shrewsbury was appreciative of the protection that the chief offered him, and of the tolerance shown by his followers. At least it made a change from the reception of the 'host' society that he was used to in the Caribbean:

The work in this country is widely different from that to which I have been accustomed in the West Indies, and the state of society exactly the reverse. There white men bear the rule, here black men have the authority and power, and I must say they are far less disposed to be tyrannical towards us, than we are towards them in the West Indies.[53]

Shrewsbury brought with him from the West Indies his, so far unassailed, belief in universal humanity and fundamental human equality. He took Hintsa to task, for instance, for employing the Xhosa idiom by which chiefs referred to their followers as their 'dogs'. Through his Khoesan translator, he endeavoured to persuade the chief 'that all considerations of relative dignity apart, the expression was too degrading to be used ... in reference to any human being; that the ... meanest slave was a man, equal *in his nature* and *in his natural rights* to Hintsa, or to the greatest prince upon the earth'.[54] A few weeks later, Shrewsbury expressed his desire 'to help as much as in us lies to abolish from the face of the

[51] *WMMS Reports*, vol. 3, 1825–27, 1825 – Report from W. Shaw, pp. 42–3.
[52] Shrewsbury, *Journal*, p. 55.   [53] *Ibid.*, p. 6.
[54] *WMMS Reports*, Vol. III, 1825–27, 1827 – Extract from a letter from Mr Shrewsbury, 12 July 1827, p. 45; Shrewsbury, *Journal*, p. 67.

earth those vile distinctions arising from caste or the colour of the skin, and which ought to have no existence in the Church of Christ'.[55]

Shrewsbury's language of universal humanity was not, however, to be enduring. Once he found that his redemptive message was of little use or interest to the Xhosa, the rhetoric of their fundamental equality would be replaced by that of their multiple failures as a 'nation'.

Shrewsbury's experience of gaining only a very few converts was not unusual. It was well known that the mission stations attracted mostly people who were in some way discriminated against in Xhosa society. Many converts were people with disabilities, the aged or those accused of witchcraft.[56] By 1828, Shrewsbury had baptised only four people, one of them a seventy-year-old former slave from the colony and another an elderly Namacqua woman who was devoid of kin to care for her. A young Xhosa man who had come to Shrewsbury to seek admittance into the community of converts had been roundly condemned as a 'madman' by his fellow Xhosa.[57]

In December 1826, Shrewsbury wrote with some puzzlement that the Xhosa were

much more ready at raising objections against divine truth than at receiving it with a meek and lowly mind ... it will be of all things important to *their* salvation to insist on the absolute necessity of making the reasonings of a carnal mind bow to the high and holy authority of the unerring Word of God.[58]

For four years, between 1826 and 1830, he laboured in vain to render the Butterworth mission a transformative agent within Gcaleka Xhosa society. While he was thus engaged, one hundred miles to the west, relations between the frontier Xhosa chiefdoms and the colonial authorities were deteriorating. In part this was due to widespread drought, which intensified Xhosa attempts to reclaim grazing land or simply raid colonial farms. But it was also, in part, the result of arbitrary and brutal colonial responses, including the expulsion of chiefdoms from their lands, the shooting of resistant chiefs and the raiding of homesteads, supposedly

[55] Shrewsbury, *Journal*, p. 67.
[56] D. Williams, 'The missionaries on the eastern frontier of the Cape Colony, 1799–1853', unpublished Ph.D. thesis, University of the Witwatersrand (1959), p. 276; N. Etherington, *Preachers, peasants and politics in southeast Africa, 1835–1880* (London: Royal Historical Society, 1978), pp. 67–8, 90–9; N. Erlank, 'Re-examining initial encounters between Christian missionaries and the Xhosa, 1820–1850: the Scottish case', *Kleio* **31** (1999), pp. 6–32.
[57] Shrewsbury, *Journal*, p. 70; see also pp. 104–5.
[58] *Ibid.*, p. 35.

in pursuit of stolen cattle, under the notorious 'spoor law'.[59] Shrewsbury moved from the relative calm of Butterworth to the Mount Coke mission station, in the midst of the area of greatest frontier tension, in January 1830.

MOUNT COKE: DISILLUSIONMENT

Shrewsbury's mission was now with the Ndlambe Xhosa. This was the chiefdom that had been expelled from what became the settlers' Albany District in 1812, and men from this chiefdom were some of the most prolific raiders of farms there. The homesteads around Mount Coke were also some of the most vulnerable to colonial patrols acting under the 'spoor law'. It was whilst he was at Mount Coke that Shrewsbury encountered the fiercest resistance to his prescriptions for Xhosa transformation. The disillusionment that ensued, however, was not with the effects of colonial policy, nor with the evangelical imperative *per se*, but instead with the Xhosa's apparent incapacity to 'improve'.

During the three years that Shrewsbury spent at Mount Coke, he had a series of difficult encounters with Xhosa men and women who associated him with the colonial presence in general (just as he had been associated by others before with the antislavery movement), and for whom he promised little utility. In an itineration visit in May 1831, for instance, Mnyaluza, a significant chief 'would neither hear himself nor collect his people together'. When Shrewsbury persisted, entering the chief's hut and preaching on regardless, the chief 'at length became furiously angry', so that Shrewsbury was 'obliged to desist, after [he] had warned him to prepare to meet his God'.[60] Shrewsbury's account of a visit to a nearby kraal the following year is further indication of the decline in his ability to secure a hearing:

The men were absent, but several women were there in a hut, two of whom were sick. As they would not come out to hear us, I sat by the doorway and began to address them. First one and then another said, 'let me come out', and departed, till only two were left, and as they would not hear, it was useless tarrying longer with them.[61]

We could go on with many more such examples of mundane resistance and rejection, and not only by those living in homesteads on Shrewsbury's circuit, but even by those who had chosen to live on the mission

---

[59] See Lester, *Imperial networks*, pp. 42–3, 62–3.   [60] Shrewsbury, *Journal*, p. 141.
[61] *Ibid.*, p. 156.

station itself as converts. Some of these insisted on sleeping during his sermons, while others persisted in attending dances and refused to humble themselves in repentance before the congregation as Shrewsbury demanded.[62] By 1831, Shrewsbury was lamenting that 'numbers' of his own converts, 'who are but little the better themselves for the Christianity they possess, are frequently remarking missionaries have done no good, nothing will ever make the kafirs to become Christians'.[63]

Two of the Xhosa's 'failings' in particular preoccupied Shrewsbury. Although he participated in the same struggles against polygamy and what he called 'witchdoctors' as did his missionary colleagues elsewhere in Xhosaland, Shrewsbury was especially provoked first by the Xhosa's 'nakedness' and secondly, by their disregarding of the Sabbath. His notion of proper clothing first prompted Shrewsbury to express his disapprobation of the Xhosa in general terms. He wrote,

the *most discouraging* fact is the *licentiousness* of the people. It *exceeds all description* ... The men are all naked without the least sense of shame, for the kaross that is occasionally worn is thrown around the body like a mantle *only as a defence from the cold*; at other seasons, old men and young men are alike without covering, and fathers sit before their children without a single rag upon their bodies. This is an *universal* custom, except on mission stations; nor will anything sooner excite laughter and merriment in a Kafir, than to be reminded by a missionary that while hearing the word of God, it is expected that he will decently draw his kaross around his person. This shocking practice, to which I am so far from being reconciled by habitually beholding it, that it fills me with greater loathing and disgust every day, may be regarded as a principal source of all the abominations that pollute the land. Were it not that I desire to promote the salvation of their souls, I would not dwell amongst such a wretched people another hour, and much less bring up my family amongst them.[64]

Shrewsbury's especially fierce adherence to the keeping of the Sabbath seems to have been bound up with nostalgic memories of the Methodist community to which he had belonged in his youth, and thereby of Englishness, and of 'home'. 'On Sabbath Day', he wrote, 'we cannot help thinking on happy England, and on British Christians, and on ... the elevated devotion we have witnessed in the multitudes that there keep that holy day. With them we have eaten the fruits of Paradise; but here we plough up a wilderness. The heart would sometimes mourn, were not its grief suppressed.'[65] It was his reflection on the Xhosa's reluctance to observe the Sabbath that prompted him to write that 'discouraging circumstances *should only add vigour to [my] soul* and excite [me] to

[62] *Ibid.*, p. 153.   [63] *Ibid.*, p. 125.   [64] *Ibid.*, p. 75. See also p. 13.   [65] *Ibid.*, p. 74.

greater and more persevering effort'. But, he continued, 'I find myself unable at all times practically to adhere' to such maxims.[66]

It would be telling only half the story of the disillusionment that Shrewsbury expressed, though, if we focused solely on his relationship with the Xhosa who lived at, or around Mount Coke. The 'discouraging circumstances' that Shrewsbury mentions were as much to do with the intimate, familial relationships in which he was embedded. At first, Shrewsbury's move to Mount Coke had promised a more fulfilling family life. For the last two years of Shrewsbury's tenure at Butterworth, Hilaria and the children had been living in the colony, where the children could receive schooling, and he had rarely seen them. Shrewsbury wrote that 'To part with them so long at so early an age was no small sacrifice.'[67] But at Mount Coke, he was in greater proximity to them and they could stay with him for extended periods. It was during the first reunion, however, that, as his son later put it, 'an affliction suddenly came, which deepened into an abiding sorrow'.[68] Shrewsbury's six year old daughter Julia set herself on fire whilst in the kitchen of the mission house. Although Shrewsbury saved her life by extinguishing the flames with a towel, the trauma affected her for the rest of her life. Seven years after the family's return to England, a fire broke out in a house opposite her bedroom, triggering night terrors from which she never escaped. As her brother wrote, 'Ultimately, under urgent medical advice, she was removed to a retreat for afflicted minds, and despite all that science and skill could do, confirmed dementia ensued'.[69]

Further family trauma soon followed. Hilaria was taken ill again with rheumatism in January 1831.[70] Shrewsbury was undoubtedly at his most dispirited at this time, reporting that on the Sabbath day especially his 'soul was exceedingly lifeless and dull'.[71] Although Shrewsbury himself had developed asthma and rheumatism, Hilaria suffered much worse. Constant childbearing and heavy physical labour left many of the missionaries' wives in the region susceptible to illness and three of the five missionary wives in Xhosaland died during Shrewsbury's ministry, while all of their husbands survived to ripe old ages.[72] After giving birth to another daughter, Hilaria had a third attack of rheumatism in 1832. For a long time after this, she was completely immobile, with every joint in her hands and feet distorted.[73]

[66] *Ibid.*, p. 130.   [67] *Ibid.*, p. 133.   [68] Shrewsbury, *Memorials*, p. 394.
[69] *Ibid.*, p. 394.   [70] Shrewsbury, *Journal*, p. 134.   [71] *Ibid.*, p. 133.
[72] *Ibid.*, p. 14.   [73] *Ibid.*

The one comfort that Shrewsbury found during his time at Mount Coke was the society of the British settlers in Graham's Town. Shrewsbury wrote that whilst in the town 'it almost seemed a reverie to conclude that I was in Africa. It certainly is pleasing to think that from my circuit in the heart of Caffraria, I can at any time ride on horseback in the short space of 5 days to Graham's Town, and behold England in the miniature'.[74] In fact, the missionary was aware that he perhaps enjoyed his occasional visits to Graham's Town a little too much. In retrospect, he felt that one such visit, conducted while he was still at Butterworth, to attend a District Meeting in 1829,

was very unprofitable to my soul … And I do resolve at every future visit to the Colony … To spend more time in early morning devotion; … To retire for prayer more frequently in the day; [and] To suffer neither company nor visiting to prevent my usual season of retirement for self-examination.[75]

In view of Hilaria's poor health and the impending absence of Shaw, who was returning to England, the Wesleyan District Meeting decided to transfer Shrewsbury to Graham's Town itself in 1833.[76] Hilaria, however, was by now gravely ill (although still able to give birth again in November 1833), and Shrewsbury was busier than ever with the entire Albany District circuit to administer. Shrewsbury wrote little during 1834–5, but it was the one substantial thing that he did write which sparked the second great controversy of his career.

THE SECOND CONTROVERSY

For the first time since 1819, a number of Xhosa chiefs came together in 1834 to sanction an attack across the colonial frontier. Many of the Ndlambe joined in a coordinated onslaught on the colony in December. Albany in particular was singled out for retribution and twenty-four British settlers were killed in the first attack.[77] Shrewsbury described his reaction to the WMMS Committee:

Throughout the entire line of our frontier, a more wanton aggression upon a peaceful people – who were desirous of promoting their best interests – has never been committed … The hordes of Kafirs are murdering the scattered settlers in their solitary habitations daily, plundering them of all their property and taking their flocks of sheep and herds of cattle without any resistance.[78]

[74] *Ibid.*, p. 27.   [75] *Ibid.*, p. 97.   [76] *Ibid.*, p. 161.
[77] The best account of the Xhosa attack is Mostert, *Frontiers*, pp. 664–82.
[78] Shrewsbury, *Journal*, p. 166.

The experience of the war prompted most of the settlers to forge an unprecedentedly clear and embattled political identity, defined in vehement opposition to both the Xhosa and the British humanitarians who blamed their attack on colonial provocation. Prominent settlers declared themselves convinced that 'many of the [humanitarian] missionaries have been labouring under the greatest delusion and although living for years amongst the Kafirs, they have not been able to form anything like a correct estimate of the character of the people around them'.[79] Shrewsbury, whose family was at this time obliged to sleep each night in the barricaded part of the town, now subscribed to this settler political identity more explicitly and publicly. For the first time, he expressed his opposition to his fellow missionaries from the London Missionary Society, who supplied metropolitan humanitarians, and Buxton in particular, with testimony. He told his superiors in England that

although not a few have accused the colonists of cruelty towards the kafirs, from a thorough knowledge of most transactions connected with Albany, we are bold to maintain that such accusations are generally unjust. To a great extent true philanthropy prevails amongst the people [settlers] here, without that ostentatious boast thereof, which is found in some who excel therein more in word than in deed.

Shrewsbury determined to keep sending the WMMS committee copies of the settlers' *Graham's Town Journal*, stating that this paper alone 'contains a correct narrative of events as they occur'.[80]

After the initial attack, the commander of the colonial forces, Lieutenant Colonel Harry Smith, asked a number of the missionaries who had lived among the Xhosa for their advice on how to deal with them. By this time, Shrewsbury had already written to the WMMS asking for permission to return to England in view of Hilaria's health and the need to secure his children's future, but he prepared a response for Smith nonetheless. Privately, he wrote, 'I want to be spiritual [but] converse about Kaffir wars not constantly connected with thoughts of a heavenly kind'.[81]

[79] *Graham's Town Journal* (hereafter *GTJ*), 23 Jan. 1835.
[80] Shrewsbury, *Memorials*, p. 398; Shrewsbury, *Journal*, p. 167. See also *WMMS Reports*, Vol. VI, 1835–37, 1835, p. 40.
[81] Shrewsbury, *Memorials*, p. 405.

Shrewsbury's primary suggestions, headed 'Thoughts on the principles to be adopted in reference to the Kafir tribes' (henceforth 'Thoughts'), were:

The chiefs who have invaded the colony to forfeit their chieftainships, and their people to forfeit their country, their arms and their property; the actual murderers of British subjects to be everywhere demanded, and when obtained, executed on the spot, that the Kafirs may *see* that *murder*, with Britons is an *unpardonable crime*.

He continued to suggest that Xhosa 'offenders' during the war whose lives may be spared should be put to work making roads 'in every part of Kafirland, if necessary even to Natal: –their labour as convicts being a visible proof of the punishment mercifully inflicted on those who might have lost their lives'. In addition,

An universal registration of Kafirs to be effected; every man wearing on his neck a thin plate of tin containing his name, and the name of his chief, which will be to him a passport of peace, and the absence of it, the token of enmity. This will both serve to identify offenders and enable the British Government at once to know the number and strength of the Frontier tribes.[82]

While the war was continuing, Governor D'Urban announced that some 7,000 square miles of Xhosa territory would be annexed by the colony, with the intention of driving the 'hostile' Xhosa from this territory once the fighting was over. In support of his decision, he enclosed Shrewsbury's 'Thoughts' in a despatch to the sceptical humanitarian colonial secretary, Lord Glenelg. The governor intended to show that his own treatment of the Xhosa was actually more lenient than that which even a missionary had advocated. Whether Shrewsbury was consulted about this employment of his 'Thoughts' is unclear, but it certainly brought him unwelcome attention upon his return to England.

With Hilaria pregnant again, and her health deteriorating rapidly, Shrewsbury booked passage for England soon after writing his 'Thoughts'. But Hilaria died, apparently as a result of a miscarriage, just a week before they were to set sail. She was only 33 years old.[83] Shrewsbury and his seven children left for England ten days after her funeral. Shrewsbury wrote to the WMMS that he 'had desired of the Lord that

---

[82] D'Urban to Glenelg, 19 June 1835, 'Shrewsbury's "Thoughts on the Principles to be Adopted in Reference to the Kafir Tribes"', dated 10 January 1835, enclosure no. 14, GH 28/12/1, Cape Archives, Cape Town.

[83] For the briefest glimpses of Hilaria's colonial experiences, as rendered by her husband (the only archival traces of her that we have found), see Reverend William J. Shrewsbury, 'Memorial of Mrs Hilaria Shrewsbury', *Wesleyan Methodist Magazine* **18**, 3 (1838), pp. 485–6.

she might be spared to reach England, as it would have been some alleviation of my sorrow to have been enabled occasionally to visit her grave, and to have led much of her West India friends, as may now or hereafter be in England, to the place'.[84] Soon after Shrewsbury and the children arrived at Deal, Shrewsbury's youngest daughter also died. It was exactly at this time, some two months after his return to England, that the controversy prompted by his 'Thoughts' broke out.

The directors of the WMMS were placed in a difficult situation due to the publicity that Shrewsbury's remarks, and the governor's despatch containing them, had gained once Buxton started to agitate for a parliamentary enquiry into the causes of the war in the Cape.[85] Their position became even more difficult when the colonial secretary specifically denounced the Wesleyan missionaries' role in the war, stating that he could not 'attach the slightest value to [Shrewsbury's] judgement'.[86] This denunciation 'made the decision of the Wesleyan Missionary Committee inevitable, when it met four days later' in December 1835.[87] The committee recorded its 'most entire and unqualified disapprobation' of Shrewsbury's action, and judged 'that the advice given by him to the commander of the forces ... was ... most unwarrantable and revolting to the principles and feelings of humanity and religion'. Furthermore, the committee resolved to forward its resolution of censure to the colonial secretary.[88] The fact that Shrewsbury was vocally supported by his fellow Wesleyan missionaries in the Cape, as well as by the *Graham's Town Journal*, was little consolation for him in the light of this condemnation.[89]

AFTERMATH AND AFTERLIFE

The WMMS committee assigned Shrewsbury to a British congregation across the English Channel in Boulogne until the furore prompted by his 'Thoughts' had died down. According to his son, by the end of 1835, Shrewsbury was 'thoroughly wounded and crushed'.[90] '[S]hut out from all society, my deceased wife in Africa, my children widely separated in

---

[84] Shrewsbury, *Journal*, p. 173.
[85] See Lester, *Imperial networks*, pp. 105–24; E. Elbourne, *Blood ground: colonialism, missions, and the contest for Christianity in the Cape Colony and Britain, 1799–1853* (Montreal: McGill-Queen's University Press, 2002).
[86] Glenelg to D'Urban, 26 December 1835, GH 1/107, Cape Archives, Cape Town.
[87] Porter, *Religion versus empire?* p. 137.
[88] WMMS Incoming Correspondence, extracted in Shrewsbury, *Journal*, pp. 215–16.
[89] *GTJ*, 25 February 1836.
[90] Shrewsbury, *Memorials*, p. 413.

England, and myself hunted with calumnies', he wrote, 'I had full leisure to sit in my room and weep from day to day over the extraordinary calamities which had come upon me.'[91] For a brief period, he considered returning to Graham's Town as a missionary helper in order to avoid the responsibility and expectations of being a missionary any longer himself.[92]

Nevertheless, Shrewsbury went back to England after a year in France, and actually remarried the following year. He had six more children, calling them his 'second family'. After the personal crisis of 1835, Shrewsbury himself seems to have recovered his authoritarian streak. Ministering in different circuits in the northern English counties, he continued to attract controversy. He was a key protagonist in the Methodist teetotal debate – on the side of total abstinence, of course – and more significantly, while ministering in Yeadon near Leeds in 1852, he managed once again to have his chapel and home attacked by an angry 'mob' of Methodist revivalists whom the conservative minister had barred from his chapel. It was during this episode that Shrewsbury was described by a newspaper as the 'Kafir-hating Methodist missionary'.[93]

After Shrewsbury's death in 1866 the WMMS chose to forget about the regrettable incident that closed the southern African chapter in his career. The obituary printed in the *Minutes of the Methodist conferences* dwelt rather on his more youthful experience of 'severe and unmerited persecution from interested upholders of slavery' in Barbados. His South African experiences were characterised perfunctorily as 'ten years of happy and successful toil'.[94] In the Cape itself, he remained something of a hero among the settlers for having spoken out against humanitarian 'interference'. John Shrewsbury published his father's *Memorials* in 1868, a time in which the dominant British discourse on the Cape's 'Kafir' Wars, as they were now known, had shifted significantly. Mid-Victorian readers were assured that it was the simple jealousy of savage nations when confronted by a superior civilisation that had prompted the Xhosa's attack in 1834. With this changed understanding of the South African situation, 'Time' had 'fully avenged the traduced missionary', such that Shrewsbury was 'publicly vindicated' by one of the WMMS secretaries.[95]

[91] *Ibid.*, p. 419.   [92] *Ibid.*, pp. 420–1.
[93] *Ibid.*, pp. 423–9. We have not been able to identify the newspaper in question.
[94] Minutes of the 123rd Methodist Conferences, 1866, Obituary of Rev. W. J. Shrewsbury, pp. 23–4, MMS.
[95] Shrewsbury, *Memorials*, p. 418.

CONCLUSION

This narrative of Shrewsbury's imperial career suggests that it was not any great shift in his personal politics that made him 'side' with enslaved people in Barbados during the first controversy and colonists in the Cape during the second. Although opposed in principle to slavery as an institution, he felt that the enslavement of Africans in the Caribbean had at least brought them under the improving influence of British rule and 'caused them to become acquainted with the knowledge of Letters, of the written word of God'.[96] He had never been an antislavery activist, and although he subscribed to a belief in the fundamental equality of 'men', neither had he ever been a public proponent of humanitarian discourse.

It was the configuration of relations between three parties, each of them dynamic in its own right, within each colonial space, which produced the impression that Shrewsbury had moved across the political spectrum during the course of his journey from Barbados to the Cape. The first of these parties in each space consisted of the community of British colonists, the second of Shrewsbury and his family, and the third of his potential African and black creole converts.

In Barbados, what was critical to Shrewsbury's apparent support of slaves against their masters was the suspicion with which Methodists, including Shrewsbury, were regarded by the dominant planters of the island, and precisely the enslaved congregation's lack of freedom. For Shrewsbury, enslaved Africans were literally a captive audience – one on whose behalf he felt himself entitled to speak, against an aberrant white planter class.[97] Shrewsbury was far from delighted with the reception that his enslaved congregation gave his 'message', because they appropriated it in ways of their own choosing, but he could at least feel that they had 'embraced the Gospel as the *only* source of consolation' in their enslaved state.[98] In the same passage, however, Shrewsbury wrote that people of African descent in the Caribbean had joined Christian societies 'to an extent which could never have been realized in their own country, where they indulged in wandering habits, & lived in a predatory manner, plundering and destroying one another'.[99] His stance against slavery, then, would not necessarily translate into a stance against the colonisation of independent Africans.

---

[96] Quoted in Porter, *Religion versus empire?* p. 138.
[97] Lambert, *White creole culture.*   [98] Quoted in Porter, *Religion versus empire?* p. 138.
[99] *Ibid.*

On the eastern Cape frontier, Shrewsbury encountered a very different, and much more amenable, community of British colonists. However, Shrewsbury's resiliently independent African audience on the other side of the frontier was far from captive. His intended Xhosa congregation, by and large, refused to be spoken for, and frequently refused even to be spoken to, by 'their' missionary. There was, Shrewsbury came to realise, a marked contrast in the reception given to an authoritarian missionary such as he was by a people seeking ways through, or routes out of, enslavement on the one hand, and a people fighting to avoid the initial imposition of colonial rule on the other. 'As a nation, or as tribes', Shrewsbury complained while in Xhosaland, 'we have to do with a haughty, fierce, proudly independent people, and they are too apt to consider themselves alike independent both of God and man.'[100]

The two colonial controversies that punctuated Shrewsbury's career thus marked, in part, the difference between the societies of the Caribbean and of southern Africa. They resulted from Shrewsbury's being positioned differently within the coordinates of colonial oppression in each case. Shrewsbury, like other colonial missionaries, posited an ambivalent set of relationships between 'freedom', 'civilisation' and subjectivity, but these relationships changed in each colonial space. In the Caribbean he could think of the legal freedom of enslaved people from their oppressive British masters as a precondition for their attainment of civilisation and full Christian personhood; in southern Africa, he came to think it necessary to restrict Africans' freedoms and promote the freedom of British settlers to pursue their own colonising projects, in order to bring about the same objectives.

Shrewsbury's disillusionment with indigenous subjects in the Cape, which mirrored that of other missionaries elsewhere in the mid-nineteenth century, was not just a product of wider political configurations, however.[101] It was also the outcome of the distress and trauma that his mission entailed for his wife and children, whom he clearly held very dear. Perhaps (although he never wrote as much), even with his remarkable faith and conviction, Shrewsbury developed a sense of guilt about their suffering, which contributed to his disillusionment.

In order to comprehend Shrewsbury's differential political engagements, we need, then (and despite the unfashionable terminology), to pay attention to both the 'structures' of each colonial society in which he and his family lived, and the 'agency' which he and his family themselves exercised

---

[100] Shrewsbury, *Journal*, p. 125.   [101] Hall, *Civilising subjects*.

in those societies. In turn, an understanding of Shrewsbury's political engagements helps us to reconsider the historical geographies of British colonialism more broadly. It enables us to appreciate that Shrewsbury was one among other figures who embodied certain connections between very different colonial sites and mediated between the universal discourses of colonialism and their specific outcomes in different places.

In Shrewsbury's case, an imperial career was based upon the most universal of notions – the pursuit of redemption for all humankind. However, that project's different reception, absorption, adaptation and redeployment by both colonists and colonial subjects in each of the spaces where he tried to carry it out, led to Shrewsbury's personal disillusionment and despair. As Catherine Hall has pointed out, colonial lives such as that of Shrewsbury consisted also of the entanglements, the attempted separations and the inevitable blurring between the private and the public, between duty to family and more public forms of duty within the British imperial enterprise.[102] The mounting contradictions between these obligations played as significant a role in engendering Shrewsbury's punitive recommendations for colonial policy in the Cape, as did his explicit rationalisations.

Towards the end of Shrewsbury's life, his son wrote,

on the mantel piece of Mr Shrewsbury's study ... might be seen two pieces of stone, each having its own history. The one was part of the first letter of the word 'Wesleyan', which had once belonged to the marble inscription upon the front of the Barbados chapel; the other was a stone weighing from three to four pounds, which had been thrown violently through the window of Mr Shrewsbury's house [in Yeadon], and had all but maimed one of his children.[103]

Although they left at least one significant and sorrowful gap in the story of his career, the two stones symbolised Shrewsbury's own rather idiosyncratic trajectory across imperial space.

---

[102] *Ibid.*   [103] Shrewsbury, *Memorials*, p. 422.

CHAPTER 4

Richard Bourke: Irish liberalism tempered by empire

Zoë Laidlaw

> When Governor Bourke stepped ashore in New South Wales in
> December 1831, he brought with him as an invisible, but none the
> less significant, item of his viceregal equipment, his past experience
> as a colonial administrator.[1]

Thus began Hazel King's 1964 article on Sir Richard Bourke's (Fig. 4.1)
two colonial administrations. King was concerned to emphasise the
similarities between the Cape colony and New South Wales; it was 'these
similar characteristics' that made Bourke's 'first colonial administration ...
of significance to his second'. This chapter returns to the question of what
Bourke carried with him, not only from colony to colony, but also
between Britain and each colony. While King's article, and her 1971
biography of Bourke, treated the British empire as a series of discrete
colonial sites, which could and should be compared and contrasted, this
chapter considers the empire as an interconnected whole. Bourke's
experiences travelled with him, but so did his reputation, and his ability
to connect to and to utilise complex personal networks. Moreover, these
networks and Bourke's reputation stretched across the empire, shaping
his ability to govern and his understanding of governance. In this analysis,
Bourke's Irish background, his liberal tenets and his understanding
of 'Britishness', are both illuminated by, and help to illuminate, his
imperial career. Examining Bourke's colonial experiences and policies –
on indigenous peoples, on juries and settler representation, and on
education and the colonial church – reveals how his identity as an 'Irish
Liberal' was articulated and altered over time and across distance. Consideration of Bourke's governance in this imperial context also encourages
an analysis that goes beyond nation-focused histories of Australia and
South Africa.

[1] H. King, 'Richard Bourke and his two colonial administrations: a comparative study of Cape
Colony and New South Wales', *Royal Australian Historical Society Journal* **49** (1964), pp. 360–75.

Fig. 4.1 Portrait of Richard Bourke (1829, lithograph) Bib ID: 707573,
by permission of the National Library of Australia.

Sir Richard Bourke was a distinguished soldier and colonial governor.
Born in Dublin in 1777, he was educated at Westminster School and
Oriel College, Oxford. Bourke joined the Grenadier Guards in
November 1798 and served in the Netherlands, South America and the
Iberian peninsula, rising to the rank of colonel in 1814. His colonial career
followed a further ten years resident on his Limerick estate, Thornfield.
Bourke served first as acting governor of the Cape of Good Hope (1826–8)
and then as governor of New South Wales (1831–7), before returning to
Limerick where he was appointed high sheriff in 1839 (see Map 4.1). He
died there in 1855.[2] Bourke's views of society, his approach to government, and the policies he attempted to implement, were shaped by his

---

[2] Bourke turned down both the government of Jamaica and the command-in-chief of the troops in
India in 1839. He remained resident in Ireland until his death. H. King, *Richard Bourke*
(Melbourne: Oxford University Press, 1971), pp. 244–54.

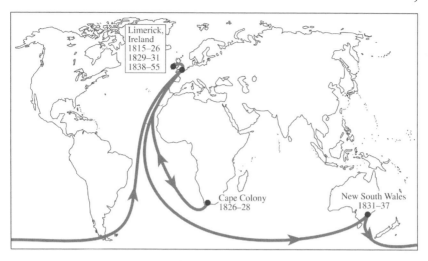

Map. 4.1 Portrait of Richard Bourke's imperial career.

experiences in each of these imperial locations. And, in turn, his ability to shape the colonies he governed was dependent largely on the connections he had made, and continued to exploit, in the army, Ireland and London.

Bourke identified himself variously as British, Irish, a Whig, a Liberal, an Anglican and a Christian. Among his closest friends he counted a Guernsey soldier and an Anglo-Irish Whig cabinet minister. A keen correspondent, Bourke maintained family, patronage and professional networks stemming from each period of his life. He was connected to senior figures in the British military establishment, including the Duke of Wellington and Sir Herbert Taylor (Wellington's military secretary at the Horse Guards and subsequently private secretary to two kings). Bourke was also a friend and correspondent of the evangelical bishop of Limerick, John Jebb; this connection was strengthened, despite religious differences between the two, when Bourke's daughter Frances married Jebb's nephew. Another of Bourke's daughters married Dudley Perceval, son of the assassinated Tory prime minister; while a third married Edward Deas Thomson, the colonial secretary of New South Wales, and the son of a confirmed English Tory. Richard Bourke's life cannot be fitted neatly into any pigeonhole, or set of relationships; a dilemma apparent not only to historians, but also to Bourke's contemporaries. Dudley Perceval, a self-described Orangeman, wrote in frustration that despite his father-in-law's 'many good and great qualities and principles', allowances had to be made 'for the misfortune of hereditary Whiggery, which somehow blinds men to true policy in all Church questions'.[3]

Certainly, to those he governed, Bourke was regarded as a Whig sympathiser and a man of '*liberal* principles'. His reputation in the press of the Eastern Cape colony, as a governor whose humanitarian attitudes towards the Khoi people left him unconcerned with settler rights, was picked up and reinforced by the New South Wales' newspapers even before Bourke arrived in that colony.[4] Bourke's perceived humanitarian stance towards one colony's indigenous peoples was easily translated into a hostile comment on his support for convicts and emancipated convicts in another. Bourke's Irishness was also a reason for hostile comment. In New South Wales, Bourke's advancement of Catholic lawmakers, like solicitor general Roger Therry and attorney general John Plunkett, and his plans for non-denominational schools, were attributed by Protestant élites to the governor's Irishness.[5]

Bourke has been the subject of numerous articles, as well as Hazel King's full-length biography. King's biography, while comprehensive and often perceptive, adopted a slightly hagiographic tone: certainly, of New South Wales' early governors, it was relatively easy to portray Bourke as a good, liberal and principled man.[6] A. G. L. Shaw disagreed with this portrayal of Bourke, which was not only advocated by King, but also triumphed in popular Australian memory. Shaw's 1966 lecture, 'Heroes and villains', drew attention to Bourke's attitude to convicts, and his management of the colony's public servants, to demonstrate that Bourke was as self-interested and inconsistent as his predecessor Ralph Darling. Bourke, argued Shaw, was simply better at manipulating public opinion than Darling.[7] Mark Francis' comparison of the careers of Bourke and Darling in *Governors and settlers* in turn challenged Shaw's interpretation. Francis argued convincingly that popular opinion, and the colonial construction of 'reality' to which it contributed, were just as important as

---

[3] Perceval to S. L. Giffard, private and confidential, [1831–33], fos. 11–12, Add 56369, British Library.

[4] A. Lester, 'British settler discourse and the circuits of empire', *History Workshop Journal* **54** (2002), pp. 33–4.

[5] J. Ridden, 'Making good citizens: national identity, religion and liberalism among the Irish élite, c.1800–1850', unpublished PhD thesis, Kings College London (1998), pp. 282–3.

[6] King, *Bourke*.

[7] A. G. L. Shaw, *Heroes and villains in history: Darling and Bourke in New South Wales* (Sydney: Sydney University Press, 1966). Shaw was responding to King's article 'The humanitarian leanings of Governor Bourke', *Historical Studies, Australia and New Zealand* **10** (1961), p. 19; and dissertation, 'Aspects of British colonial policy, 1825–1837, with particular reference to the administration of major general Sir Richard Bourke in Cape Colony and New South Wales', unpublished D.Phil. thesis, University of Oxford (1959).

whether or not Bourke's liberal reputation in New South Wales was deserved.[8]

Bourke's reputation as hero or villain has also been debated in South African historiography, although this debate has focused on Bourke's policies for the Cape's indigenous peoples. In particular, Bourke's role in the passage of Ordinances 49 and 50, which regulated respectively the lives of Africans entering the colony, and Khoi and other 'free persons of colour' already within it, has been interrogated extensively. In this discussion, Bourke's liberal reputation usually emerges intact. It is his role in authorising, or accepting, the massacre that accompanied the Battle of Mbholompo in 1828, which damaged his humanitarian reputation at the time, and continues to divide historians today.[9]

Jennifer Ridden has produced the most interesting recent work on Richard Bourke, in her study of Irish liberalism and the construction of a form of British identity which circumvented the problems of conflating 'Englishness' with 'Britishness'.[10] Ridden's work encompasses Richard Bourke's period in Australia, but focuses on his, and others', Irish experiences. As any assessment of how Bourke's experiences in the Cape Colony and New South Wales affected him must depend on an examination of the beliefs and attitudes that were formed earlier in his life, these are examined in some detail, before Bourke's colonial career is considered.

BOURKE AND IRISH LIBERALISM

Bourke spent the decade after the war in Limerick, where he was heavily involved with his family, his estate, and the local community.[11] Bourke had spent almost no time as an adult in Ireland until this period, and he busied himself with educating his children, making agricultural improvements and upgrading his tenants' physical and moral environment. Beyond the estate of Thornfield, Bourke sat as a magistrate, and chaired the Irish Relief Committee for Limerick. In this latter role he advanced plans for encouraging the manufacture of linen, as offering 'the fairest chance of immediate, as well as future benefit' for the people

---

[8] M. Francis, *Governors and settlers: images of authority in the British Colonies, 1820–1860* (Basingstoke: Macmillan, 1992), pp. 83–97.

[9] See the discussion on interpretations of Bourke's role and Ordinance 50 in J. Peires, 'Matiwane's road to Mbholompo: a reprieve for the Mfecane?', in C. Hamilton (ed.), *The Mfecane aftermath: reconstructive debates in Southern African history* (Johannesburg: Witwatersrand University Press, 1995), pp. 213–39.

[10] J. Ridden, 'Making good citizens'. [11] King, *Bourke*, pp. 53–60.

involved.[12] Bourke was also involved in party politics, managing the parliamentary campaigns of his neighbour and close friend, Thomas Spring Rice in the 1820s. Spring Rice, later Baron Monteagle, would go on to be secretary of state for the colonies and chancellor of the exchequer in the Whig administrations of the 1830s.[13]

Bourke was an important member of a group Jennifer Ridden describes as the 'Irish Liberals'. Her analysis highlights the interplay of religion, politics and identity in Richard Bourke's life. Of Bourke and his fellow Irish Liberal, Thomas Spring Rice, Ridden has argued:

They were Protestant but they also supported the extension of full civil and political participation to Catholics; they were Irish but were also important actors in Britain and the British empire ... they refused to accept that Irish and British identities were opposed ... and they were Irish Liberals.[14]

Bourke's 'Irish Liberal' understanding of a non-denominational Christian citizenship, and of what it meant to be British, affected fundamentally not only his attitude to Ireland, but also his colonial career. Here, it will be considered under three overlapping headings: religion, nation and empire.

Liberal religious views were fundamental to the Irish Liberals' political ideology. Bourke advocated Catholic emancipation and religious tolerance, and disapproved of the enthusiastic or bigoted pursuit of any Christian creed.[15] 'We should remember ... that the Roman Catholick [sic] is a Christian', wrote Bourke in 1820, criticising the Irish Protestant crusade which, 'instead of filling', sought 'to widen the unhappy breach' between Catholics and Protestants.[16] As will be seen, Bourke practised religious toleration in his political and personal lives: promoting the interests of Catholics, Quakers and other nonconformists in the pursuit of a cohesive society. Nevertheless, although distanced from evangelical crusaders, Bourke was sympathetic to the paternalistic and humanitarian actions of the moderate evangelicals of the Clapham Sect who campaigned not only on British issues, but also – perhaps because colonial outrages raised less difficult questions about British society than domestic matters – against slavery and for the better treatment of indigenous

---

[12] Richard Bourke (Chairman, County Limerick Committee) to the Irish Distress Committee, 8 August 1822, fo. 68, Peel Papers, Add 40351, British Library.

[13] Ridden, 'Making good citizens', pp. 167–90; King, *Bourke*, p. 55.

[14] Ridden, 'Making good citizens', p. 8.   [15] *Ibid.*, pp. 23–30, 54–8.

[16] Athamik [Richard Bourke], *Letter to the Right Hon. Charles Grant from an Irish layman of the established Church, on the subject of a charge lately published, and purporting to have been delivered to his clergy, by the Lord Bishop of Killaloe and Kilfenora* (Dublin, 1820), pp. 14, 16.

peoples in the empire. Bourke corresponded with several leading evangelical British humanitarians, including Thomas Fowell Buxton, Thomas Pringle and Saxe Bannister, and advocated both antislavery and missionary activity amongst non-Christian communities. Before he left for the Cape Colony in 1826, for example, Bourke was briefed by the London Missionary Society on indigenous affairs.[17]

While Bourke was determined to diminish suffering, he was concerned always that the beneficiaries of humanitarian efforts should develop as responsible individuals: enabled to look after themselves, rather than becoming dependent. Individual responsibility had both religious and moral connotations; when Bourke opposed the introduction of poor laws to Ireland, he emphasised that for the state to give 'gifts' to the poor would 'deteriorate their habits, and ... aggravate the evil it was intended to remedy'.[18] Creating a society with sustainable employment and the opportunity for individual advancement was much preferable in the eyes of Bourke and the other Irish Liberals. To this end, Bourke advocated the removal of Irish Catholics' religious disabilities; the introduction of industrial schools; and the reduction – through emigration and support for industry – of overpopulation and under-employment.[19]

Bourke's belief that social cohesion stemmed from religious toleration was central to his political views, not only in Ireland but also in the Cape Colony and New South Wales. Ridden's conclusion that the Irish Liberals' ideal nation rested on the moral responsibility of each individual is borne out by Bourke's writings and actions.[20] Although Bourke argued that appropriate mechanisms and institutions for representing 'the people' contributed to the creation of such a society, he was not a democrat. Rather than universal enfranchisement, he envisaged the development of a larger, morally responsible, Christian middle class. In Ireland, Bourke thought, the lack of a 'respectable middle-class' was 'much felt'.[21] Political responsibility should be extended to a society only gradually, when, in his

---

[17] T. Keegan, *Colonial South Africa and the origins of the racial order* (Cape Town and Johannesburg: David Philip, 1996), p. 103. See also Pringle to Bourke, 4 June 1834, pp. 216–17, A1737, Mitchell Library, Sydney (hereafter ML); Saxe Bannister to Richard Bourke, 26 July 1828, fo. 130, Mss. Afr t 7/7, Rhodes House Library, Oxford (hereafter RHL); Richard to Dick Bourke, 31 January 1836, fo. 184, Mss. Afr t 7/3, RHL; Dick to Richard Bourke, 4 July 1836, pp. 149–50, A1739, ML.

[18] *PP 1830*, vii (665), Third report of evidence from the Select Committee on the State of the Poor in Ireland, evidence of Bourke, pp. 505, 508, 510–11, 516.

[19] *PP 1825*, ix (181), Minutes of evidence taken before the Select Committee of the House of Lords on the State of Ireland, evidence of Bourke, pp. 180–2; *PP 1830*, vii (665), evidence of Bourke, pp. 501, 503, 513–14; Bourke to the Irish Distress Committee, 8 August 1822.

[20] Ridden, 'Making good citizens', pp. 7–8, 59.

[21] *PP 1830*, vii (665), evidence of Bourke, pp. 511, 516.

paternalistic vision, the populace was prepared for it. While almost all individuals had the capacity to improve themselves to some extent, not all would reach the level necessary to become citizens rather than subjects. Nevertheless, the Irish Liberals believed that the possibility of engagement with the state should be held out to all. This is demonstrated by Bourke's determination to incorporate previously marginalised groups into the colonial polity, whether emancipated convicts and their descendants in Australia; Dutch speakers in South Africa; or the Catholics of both colonies.[22]

The imperative for individual and national progress encouraged the Irish Liberals to consider how such progress could best be supported. In Bourke's view, the answer was education, although its form would vary depending on the nature of the group involved (Ridden, for example, demonstrates that Bourke did not regard Irish girls as requiring the advanced education suitable for Irish boys).[23] Education had 'a direct tendency to improve the habits of the people, both morally and prudentially', and, as it encouraged individuals to become 'good citizens', was 'the business of the state'.[24] In this, and more generally, Bourke appears as a man setting himself apart from, and above, the people he governed. This sense that he was part of a responsible élite was fundamental to Bourke's politics. He sought the improvement of colonial and metropolitan societies, and believed that it was within his power – indeed, that it was his duty – to implement improvement.[25]

Richard Bourke's perception of the British empire, and the place of Ireland – and himself – within it, is also important for this study. Bourke's own feelings about Ireland were complicated: although he returned to Limerick after the Napoleonic Wars, and remained there until 1826, almost all his early life had been spent in London, followed by his military service in South America, Europe and England. Before 1814, Bourke viewed his home society with something of the melancholy and sentimentality of an expatriate: he wrote in 1810, aged thirty-three, that it was 'a misfortune to have been brought up ... so much estranged from Ireland'.[26] In later years, Bourke was determined to make up for this

---

[22] On New South Wales, see pp. 134–5 below. On the Dutch in the Cape Colony, see Bourke to Hay, private, 27 August 1826, unpaginated, CO 323/144, Public Record Office, The National Archives [hereafter PRO].

[23] Ridden, 'Making good citizens', pp. 109–10, and (on the Irish Liberals and education generally) ch. 3.

[24] PP 1830, vii (665), evidence of Bourke, p. 503; Richard to Dick Bourke, 7 November 1835, p. 100, A1733, ML.

[25] PP 1825, ix (181), evidence of Bourke, pp. 183–4.

[26] Bourke to John Le Marchant, 7 November 1810, quoted in King, Bourke, p. 48.

estrangement, despite his continued absence, aside from a brief spell between postings, between 1826 and 1838. For example, Bourke refused the Jamaican government in 1839, despite the opportunity to do some good for 'two or three hundred thousand Blacks', because he might instead do good for 'a much smaller number' of his 'countrymen' in Ireland.[27] Bourke seems to have understood Ireland as similar, but different, to both England and the more distant colonies. Ireland was part of Great Britain; unlike the colonies, it was not subordinate to England.[28] This distinction did not mean that Bourke, or indeed the Irish Liberals generally, could not draw lessons from one society for another. Through its maintenance of roads and its arrangements for paupers, England, for example, served Bourke as both a positive model and a warning for Ireland.[29] Equally, Bourke hoped to encourage harmony in the Cape Colony by providing opportunities for Dutch settlers, just as opportunities should have been provided for Irish Catholics; while his plans for Australian education in the 1830s drew directly on his Irish experience.

Ridden argues that the Irish Liberals developed a flexible 'British' identity in an attempt to justify their position as an élite within Irish society to both the Irish and the English.[30] In an 1834 article decrying the application of the Poor Laws to Ireland, Spring Rice extolled the qualities of 'Britain' as 'the control of religious principle, an obedience to moral duty, the enjoyment of constitutional freedom, the operations of commercial industry, the firm administration of impartial laws'.[31] This malleable identity could be transported to the British empire at large. 'Britishness' was a discourse that Bourke adopted, where necessary, to support the policies that he believed would promote cohesive, progressive and moral societies. In New South Wales, for example, Bourke supported his case for public education by emphasising the colony's British status, and the 'just claim' to 'British institutions' of its inhabitants.[32] The great advantage of 'Britishness' for Bourke, apart from the concept's inherent flexibility, was that it suggested that colonies within the British empire could move towards political maturity without necessarily mimicking English institutions and arrangements. Within the British model regional

---

[27] Bourke to Spring Rice, 29 April 1839, p. 365, A1736, ML.
[28] Ridden, 'Making good citizens', pp. 216–17.
[29] *PP 1825*, ix (181), evidence of Bourke, p. 177; *PP 1830*, vii (665), pp. 508–9. See also Thomas Spring Rice, 'Introduction of Poor Laws into Ireland', *Edinburgh Review* **59** (1834), p. 230.
[30] Ridden, 'Making good citizens', pp. 16–17, 21, 171–2.
[31] Spring Rice, 'Introduction of Poor Laws', p. 261.
[32] E.g. Bourke's speech at the opening of the legislative session, 2 June 1836, encl. in Bourke to Glenelg, 10 June 1836, fo. 218, CO 201/253, PRO.

variations, of religion, polity and society, were acceptable; 'Britishness' conveyed a notion of the tone and values of the society to be created, rather than implying that the society would replicate England.

Bourke's attitudes to colonial governance and the British empire were not, of course, shaped simply by his Irishness, but also by his experiences in the empire itself. In the mid-1820s, he sought a government appointment overseas, largely because he hoped that his wife's ill health would be improved by a change of climate.[33] Elizabeth Bourke had ailed already, on and off, for twenty years, although she did not die until May 1832.[34] Bourke's correspondence reveals that he believed there to be few inducements to colonial life beyond the possibility of an improved climate. In June 1825 he accepted the position of major general on the staff at Malta, but, shortly before his departure the Colonial Office learned that the governor of the Cape Colony intended to return home to answer allegations that had been made against his administration. Bourke was persuaded to go to the Cape instead of Malta: apparently to take up the newly established position of lieutenant governor of the colony's eastern districts, but actually to become acting governor during the governor's absence.[35]

Bourke's two years at the Cape were characterised by considerable uncertainty. He felt that his tenure was always unclear. The governor, Lord Charles Somerset, had taken leave of absence; when he decided not to return in 1827, Bourke was not confirmed as the colony's governor, even though the position to which he had been appointed – lieutenant governor of the Eastern Cape – had been abolished. Bourke's insecurity was exacerbated by the Cape's experienced and opinionated civil servants, especially the colonial secretary, Sir Richard Plasket.[36] Additionally, the commissioners of Eastern Inquiry, who had been in the Cape Colony since July 1823, and were charged broadly with reviewing the establishments of the Cape, Mauritius and Ceylon, continued their work in the colony during much of the first year of Bourke's governorship. Bourke spent his time waiting – in some cases, fruitlessly – for the commissioners' reports on various subjects; dealing with considerable settler anxiety and

---

[33] King, *Bourke*, pp. 55–6.
[34] Bourke had returned from Spain in 1809, declining the opportunity to work as Wellington's private secretary because of her illness: King, *Bourke*, pp. 45–6.
[35] Bourke to Spring Rice, 19 September 1827; Bourke to Spring Rice, confidential, 4 November 1827; Bourke to Sir George Murray, 17 June 1828; Bourke to Goderich, draft, 10 December 1830; fos. 43, 51, 163, 174, Mss. Afr t 7/3, RHL. King, *Bourke*, pp. 56–8.
[36] Zoë Laidlaw, *Colonial connections: 1815–1845: Patronage, the information revolution and colonial government* (Manchester: Manchester University Press, 2005), p. 119.

hostility engendered by the enquiry; and feeling acutely the insecurity of his position.[37] These frustrating experiences in the Cape Colony shaped Bourke's attitudes to both governance and empire. His experiences in southern Africa would also affect Bourke's attitudes to the indigenous peoples he would encounter in New South Wales. The remainder of this chapter will examine how Bourke's colonial policies were influenced by his views of empire, nation and society, as well as his colonial experiences.

BOURKE AND INDIGENOUS PEOPLE

While acting governor of the Cape Colony, Richard Bourke's reputation as a humanitarian defender of indigenous peoples was both developed and undermined. This paradoxical outcome resulted more from British humanitarian campaigns after Bourke left the colony, than from inconsistencies in Bourke's attitude to indigenous peoples. As suggested earlier, Bourke fits within the paternalistic and humanitarian tradition represented by James Stephen in the Colonial Office and other moderate evangelicals. Bourke did not think about indigenous peoples primarily in terms of 'race', but instead by their degree of difference – like the poor of Ireland, or the convicts transported to New South Wales – from himself. Bourke, like many of his contemporaries, understood 'race' in cultural rather than biological terms and possessed an essentially optimistic view of indigenous peoples: they, like others below him on the scale of class or nation, were amenable to improvement, and could be 'civilised' (which would eventually entail conversion to Christianity). Tasmania's Aborigines, for example, were 'savages' in Bourke's eyes, but, through the work of 'diligent and able' missionaries, they could be brought 'towards civilization'.[38] Nationality, if not race, did play a role in this hierarchy of civilisation, as Bourke's decision to remain in Ireland in 1839, instead of helping 'two or three hundred thousand' blacks by becoming governor of Jamaica, suggested.[39]

Like the anti-slavery campaigner, Thomas Fowell Buxton, Bourke's concern for indigenous peoples, and his distress at the negative impact of their contact with European settlers, did not lead him to advocate a complete separation of settlers and indigenes, or an end to British colonisation. *Humane policy*, which dealt with several of Bourke's policies

---

[37] The Commissioners' final reports on the Cape of Good Hope were not completed until 1831.
[38] Bourke to Arthur, 19 March 1832, A2168, ML.
[39] Bourke to Spring Rice, 29 April 1839, p. 365, A1736, ML.

at the Cape, was written by the humanitarian campaigner Saxe Bannister. This extract from the preface encapsulates Bourke's views as well as Bannister's:

> If we, the civilised, could not, physically, exist in the same land with the bar-barian and the savage without destroying them, it would be a paramount duty to discourage the extension of colonies; but history, early and recent, where the civilised have been just, shows all men to be capable of improvement; ... doing justice is the grand means to ensure the amelioration and the mutual safety of the most dissimilar races.[40]

Thus, throughout his governorships at the Cape and in New South Wales, Bourke stressed the need to develop relations with indigenous peoples that – via the civilising influence of missionaries and government functionaries – would benefit them but also protect the settler community.

Bourke's Cape Colony government was responsible for the passage of Ordinance 50 in July 1828, which went some way to asserting – on paper at least – the legal equality of the indigenous Khoi people to European settlers.[41] Instructed by the Colonial Office and guided by the commissioners of Eastern Inquiry, Bourke had asked the commissioner general for the eastern districts, Andries Stockenström, to draft an ordinance which liberalised labour relations for the Khoi people 'and other free blacks', and decriminalised vagrancy. Bourke later claimed to have contemplated introducing Ordinance 50, and the accompanying Ordinance 49, soon after his arrival in 1826.[42] Although this cannot be verified further, the concern to 'remove the potential for class antagonism implicit in relations between Khoi and colonists', reverberated with Bourke's experience of sectarian antagonism in Ireland, whilst mirroring contemporary measures in Britain to foster freer relations between employers and employees.[43]

While Ordinance 50 liberalised relations between the colonisers and the Khoi, Ordinance 49 imposed stricter pass laws on Xhosa and other Africans who entered the colony in search of work. Bourke did not see the two as contradictory: both ordinances attempted to protect indigenous

---

[40] Saxe Bannister, *Humane policy* (London: T. & G. Underwood, 1830), p. vi.
[41] Keegan, *Colonial South Africa*, pp. 102–4; A. Lester, *Imperial networks: creating identities in nineteenth-century South Africa and Britain* (London: Routledge, 2001), pp. 34–5; E. Elbourne, *Blood ground: colonialism, missions, and the contest for Christianity in the Cape colony and Britain, 1799–1853* (Montreal: McGill-Queen's University Press, 2002), pp. 255–7; King, *Bourke*, pp. 119–22.
[42] Richard Bourke to Rev. A. Miles, 31 October 1828, fos. 142, 144, Mss. Afr. t. 7/3, RHL.
[43] Lester, *Imperial networks*, p. 35.

peoples from more powerful settlers.[44] The majority of the Xhosa lived beyond the colony's putative frontier, but, as first Dutch and then British settlers had pressed outwards, conflicts to the north and east pushed more Xhosa towards the colony. Ordinance 49 decreed that interactions between colonisers and Xhosa would be overseen by government, while the Xhosa would be 'civilised' by regulated contact with Europeans.[45] Bourke hoped that both processes would diminish violence between settlers and Xhosa (see chapter 3).

Bourke's predecessor, Lord Charles Somerset, had reintroduced the 'Spoor Law', which permitted settlers who were able to track stolen cattle to retrieve them from Xhosa settlements beyond the colony. The commandos used for the purpose were criticised by both the commissioners of Eastern Inquiry and humanitarian observers for using the (sometimes non-existent) theft of settlers' cattle as a pretext for disrupting the Xhosa's kraals and stealing their cattle.[46] Bourke issued instructions to his frontier commanders in April and August 1826 that this practice was to stop, but his demand that his instructions remain 'quite confidential' (presumably to prevent those Xhosa who were engaged in cattle theft from taking advantage of the altered situation) meant that settler depredations continued.[47]

As Timothy Keegan and others have argued, the practical impact of Ordinance 50, like other efforts of the colonial government to regulate economic and social relations of colonial society, was limited. However, the simultaneous efforts of the London Missionary Society's Dr John Philip to publicise discrimination against the Khoi in Britain, and to encourage the imperial government to give Ordinance 50 the status of an Order in Council (preventing any alteration to its effect without sanction from London) meant that Bourke's measure received metropolitan attention.[48] In the early 1830s, when Governor Cole attempted to reintroduce vagrancy laws, the Khoi people and their humanitarian supporters retrospectively interpreted Ordinance 50 as a far more significant piece of legislation than it actually was.[49] By this time, however, British

---

[44] Keegan, *Colonial South Africa*, p. 105; Peires, 'Matiwane's road', pp. 228–30; Elbourne, *Blood ground*, p. 255.

[45] Bourke to Bathurst, 30 June 1827, cited in Lester, *Imperial networks*, pp. 40–1.

[46] Lester, *Imperial networks*, p. 42.

[47] M. Ryan (Bourke's Military Secretary) to Henry Somerset, 11 April 1826; Bourke to Henry Somerset, 4 August 1826, fos. 1–3, 4, Mss. Afr t 7/12, RHL.

[48] Keegan, *Colonial South Africa*, pp. 103–4, 116–17; Elbourne, *Blood ground*, p. 256; Andrew Ross, *John Philip (1775–1851): Missions, race and politics in South Africa* (Aberdeen: Aberdeen University Press, 1986), pp. 110–11.

[49] Keegan, *Colonial South Africa*, pp. 118–19.

humanitarians were keen to emphasise the role of John Philip, Thomas Fowell Buxton and the London Missionary Society in protecting the Khoi, even if that meant diminishing Bourke's role.

Frontier instability continued throughout 1827 and into 1828. In May, military commanders on the colonial frontier reported that a Zulu invasion of the Xhosa territory which abutted the colony was imminent. Bourke's confidential instructions to his military commanders, William Dundas and Henry Somerset (the son of Lord Charles), were that negotiations with both Zulu and Xhosa leaders were to be preferred over any military action.[50] Only as a last resort were they authorised to lead a raid beyond the colony's boundaries, in order to prevent the Xhosa 'from being driven in *en masse* upon the Colony' and the Zulus from occupying Xhosa country 'immediately on the Border'.[51] Bourke's instructions conveyed indecision, or at least a lack of familiarity with the likely response of his military commanders. Somerset, in particular, had a reputation for provoking clashes, and his military action in this case led to the Battle of Mbholompo. The battle resulted in the massacre of an 'unthreatening' group of African refugees by the colonists' Xhosa supporters; while the colonial militia snatched displaced women and children, presumably for use as labourers in the colony. The episode outraged humanitarians, many of whom dissociated themselves from Bourke's administration.[52]

Divisions between humanitarians and Eastern Cape settlers were widened by the 1834–5 war with the Xhosa. Humanitarians and settlers demonised one another, each side reserving righteousness for themselves. This process also damaged Bourke's reputation: humanitarian narratives emphasised John Philip's stand on behalf of Khoi and Xhosa, rather than Bourke's ordinances; while settler discourse, exemplified by Robert Godlonton's *Irruption of the Kafir hordes*, was critical of Bourke's humanitarianism in the 1820s. During the hearings of the 1835–7 Select Committee on Aborigines, which inquired into the Eastern Cape war and imperial relations with indigenous peoples more generally, Bourke was concerned to protect his reputation for fair dealing with the Khoi and

---

[50] Bourke to Somerset, 25 June 1828, 5 August 1828, 5 September 1828, 11 September 1828, fos. 5–28, Mss. Aft t 7/12, RHL.

[51] Richard Bourke to Henry Somerset, 5 September 1828, fo. 22, Mss. Aft t 7/3, RHL.

[52] Lester, *Imperial networks*, pp. 41–2. William Shrewsbury, the subject of chapter 3, who was stationed at the Xhosa Paramount Hintsa's kraal at the time, was one of the very few white witnesses of the immediate aftermath of the raid. See W. J. Shrewsbury, *The journal and selected letters of Rev. William J. Shrewsbury, 1826–35*, ed. H. Fast (Johannesburg: Witwatersrand University Press, 1994), pp. 86–7, 90–1.

Xhosa. This meant encouraging a renewed emphasis on Bourke's role in Ordinance 50, while arguing that Henry Somerset, not Bourke, was to blame for the 1828 massacre. Although Bourke was by this time governor of New South Wales, his London-based son, Dick, kept him informed of the select committee's proceedings and made sure his father's case was put to the metropolitan authorities.[53] In 1836 Bourke wrote a memorandum, responding both specifically to Robert Godlonton and generally to evidence put forward in the select committee hearings. This memorandum outlined (retrospectively) the principles Bourke had used to reduce frontier violence during his governorship of the Cape Colony and emphasised his attempts to stabilise relations between Africans and Europeans by forbidding colonial excursions beyond the frontier in pursuit of 'stolen' cattle; regulating labour contracts; increasing the number of frontier trading fairs; and supporting the work of mission stations. 'It can not be denied', wrote Bourke, 'that in teaching the savages the arts of life they softened their dispositions.' His policies prepared the Xhosa 'for the reception of [Christianity] and the blessings that follow in its train'.[54]

During his time at the Cape, Bourke did try to reduce the gap between indigenous peoples and European settlers, just as in Ireland he hoped to diminish the differences between the poor and the wealthy. In his next colonial posting, Bourke would attempt to employ a similar approach to both emancipated convicts and the Aboriginal population of New South Wales. Historians have paid less attention to Bourke's attitudes to and relationship with the Aborigines of New South Wales than the Xhosa and Khoi peoples of the Cape Colony. Although participating in the discourse of British humanitarianism, Bourke's interest in the welfare of Aborigines in New South Wales does seem more rhetorical than practical. He arrived in the colony, according to his own account, with a desire to establish model villages like those recently established in the Cape Colony. Although the much-fêted Kat River settlement had begun after his departure from the Cape, Bourke was aware of its glowing reputation among both missionaries and British humanitarians.[55] Kat

[53] Burton to Bourke, 5 November 1835, fo. 71, Mss. Afr t 7/8, RHL; Burton to Dick Bourke, 29 January 1836, fo. 76, *ibid.*; Richard Bourke to Dick Bourke, 31 January 1836, fos. 183–4, Mss. Afr t 7/3, RHL; Dick Bourke to Richard Bourke, 4 July 1836, pp. 149–51, A1739, ML; Richard Bourke to Dick Bourke, 30 December 1836, p. 211, A1733, ML.

[54] Memorandum on frontier policy [1836], fos. 24–7, Mss. Afr t 7/9, RHL; Burton to Bourke, 9 March 1836, 13 June 1836, pp. 468–70, 488, A1738, ML.

[55] By 1834, for example, much was made of the 700 pupils being educated at the settlement's seventeen schools. Keegan, *Colonial South Africa*, p. 118; Lester, *Imperial networks*, p. 37.

River, the humanitarians argued, provided the necessary evidence that
even the most barbarous savages were (just like Bourke's Irish tenants)
amenable to civilising forces.

Bourke corresponded with the governor of Van Diemen's Land,
George Arthur, about establishing a settlement similar to Kat River for
the Tasmanian Aborigines removed to Flinders Island.[56] Four years later,
he encouraged the missionary George Langhorne to establish, if possible,
villages in the newly colonised Port Phillip district along the lines of those
begun by Robert Owen at New Lanark. The 'great object', thought
Bourke, would be 'to wean the Blacks from their wandering habits by
proving to them experimentally the superior gratifications to be obtained
in civilized life'.[57] Like his contemporaries, both paternalistic and
humanitarian, Bourke regarded the settlement of nomadic peoples as the
first step in their conversion and civilisation. Permanent settlements
would lead to agriculture (rather ironically, as Bourke was just discovering
that, for its European inhabitants at least, New South Wales was more
suited to pastoral, than to agricultural, activity); excess produce would
lead to commercial exchange; and commercial exchange would lead to
'civilisation'.[58] Permanent settlements would also enable Aborigines to
receive both practical and religious education. Governor Arthur was
particularly concerned to educate Aboriginal children, arguing that
assimilating the younger generation would lead to the rapid incorporation
of Aborigines into European society.[59]

Bourke's letters from New South Wales indicate that he regarded
Aborigines as 'savages'; although capable, at least theoretically, of conversion and civilisation.[60] In humanitarian circles Australian Aborigines
were perceived as 'probably farther removed from civilization than any
other people on earth'. This, of course, did not absolve the British of
responsibility in their civilisation, but entailed that they 'be led with
greater care from their uncivilized state, and to be the more shielded from

---

[56] Bourke to Arthur, private, 19 March 1832, A2168, ML.
[57] Memorandum for Mr Langhorne, 9 December 1836, Police Magistrate, Box 1, State Library of
Victoria, cited in King, *Bourke*, p. 283, n. 13; King, *Bourke*, pp. 191–5.
[58] On the development of notions of stadial history see: Peter Stein, *Legal evolution: the story of an
idea* (Cambridge: Cambridge University Press, 1980), pp. 24–9, 33–6. On its impact on British
colonialism, see P. J. Marshall and G. Williams, *The Great Map of Mankind: British perceptions of
the world in the age of enlightenment* (London: Dent, 1982), pp. 213–15.
[59] C. Twomey, 'Vagrancy, indolence and ignorance: race, class and the idea of civilization in the era
of aboriginal "protection"', in T. Banivanua Mar and J. Evans (eds.), *Writing colonial histories:
comparative perspectives* (Melbourne: RMIT publishing, 2002), pp. 93–113.
[60] Bourke to Arthur, 19 March 1832, A2168, ML; Bourke to Glenelg, 15 November 1836, fo. 210, CO
201/255, PRO.

our ordinary injustice than any other barbarous people'.[61] The expansion of European settlement to Twofold Bay and Port Phillip would clearly affect the Aboriginal inhabitants of these areas. Although Bourke hoped to regulate relations between settlers and Aborigines, the protection of indigenous peoples ranked below his determination to exert the Crown's right over land, as, for example, when dealing with John Batman's claim to Port Phillip.[62] Bourke believed that the expansion of settled areas was both inevitable and necessary for the growth of New South Wales' economy. Like his superiors in the Colonial Office, Bourke did not contemplate preventing colonial expansion in order to protect indigenous rights.[63] His concern for the Aborigines extended to attempting to regulate relations with them, protecting them from egregious abuse, and encouraging missionary activity, but little further. Bourke's hopes for 'civilisation' were pragmatic: civilised Aborigines, like Khoi protected by Ordinance 50, or Xhosa ensnared in colonial trade, would cease to pose a threat to settler society. As Christina Twomey has observed, finance for the Port Phillip protectorate of Aborigines would come from the government's sale of Aboriginal land. Protection of Aborigines, then, was conditional on European expansion, even though it was that expansion which threatened them.[64]

Bourke's limited concern for indigenous peoples is underlined by his response to an incident which occurred in 1836, during the third expedition of the explorer and surveyor-general, Thomas Mitchell. Mitchell's party mounted a deliberate attack on a group of Aborigines leading to 'a considerable number' being killed.[65] In his expedition report, Mitchell described how his party had surprised the 'treacherous savages', 'pursuing and shooting as many as they could'; he exulted in the killings.[66] Bourke censored the report, omitting the section describing the Aboriginal deaths because he thought it 'so abrupt, and at the same time so alarming'. Public interest was nevertheless aroused, and Bourke was forced to make public the results of an executive council enquiry in

---

[61] Bannister, *Humane policy*, p. ccxxxix.
[62] Bourke to Arthur, 17 August 1835, 21 January 1836, A2168, ML.
[63] Bourke to Glenelg, 10 October 1835, fos. 381–9, CO 201/247, PRO; and CO minute on same, 13 April 1836, fos. 391–8; Glenelg to Bourke, 13 April 1836, in F. Watson (ed.), *Historical records of Australia. Series I, Governors' despatches to and from England*, 26 volumes (Sydney: Library Committee of the Commonwealth Parliament, 1914–1925) (hereafter, *HRA*), Vol. XVIII, pp. 379–81.
[64] Twomey, 'Vagrancy, indolence and ignorance', p. 94.
[65] Bourke to Glenelg, 15 November 1836, fos. 209–10, CO 201/255, PRO.
[66] Extracts from Mitchell's report in the Executive Council minute no. 29, encl. Bourke to Glenelg, 25 January 1837, fos. 88–9, CO 201/260, PRO.

December 1836.[67] The enquiry found that Mitchell's attack had been executed badly, while the number of Aboriginal deaths was exaggerated. Nevertheless, Mitchell was condemned for asserting that 'the slaughter of the Natives' was 'meritorious', rather than justifiable only as a last and desperate resort. The council articulated an 'important public principle' enshrined in Bourke's instructions to the expedition: 'In dealing with ignorant natives ... it is the duty of the civilised intruder to resort to every means consistent with personal safety to disarm hostility by con-ciliation before using force even in self-defence.' Bourke himself was shocked by Mitchell's account of the 'slaughter',[68] but described it offi-cially to Lord Glenelg as 'a very unfortunate conflict with the Aboriginal natives in which I fear a considerable number of these unhappy savages were slaughtered'.[69] Bourke's decision not to hold a public enquiry was criticised mildly by the Colonial Office who thought an opportunity to give an 'impressive lesson ... of the importance attached by the Government to the life of a Native' had been lost.[70] Nevertheless, the conclusion reached by Bourke, the council, and the Colonial Office, was that however indiscreet Mitchell had been in his language, his actions were justifiable.[71]

Richard Bourke's view of indigenous peoples did not change sig-nificantly between 1826 and 1838, although his optimism about their capacity to be 'civilised' diminished. Consistently, his concern was to minimise the threat of disharmony, while creating the conditions in which settlers could thrive and indigenous peoples – whether Khoi, Xhosa, or Australian Aborigines – could be protected and improved by contact with Christian missionaries and fair-minded government officials. Lester's discussion of an 'imported metropolitan model of paternalism', which was a 'combination of a closely monitored bourgeois morality and a more commercial orientation', does seem to fit Bourke's approach and policies.[72] In Bourke's case this paternalism also encompassed his Irish tenants, and his concern to improve Australian convict and emancipist society. Bourke was concerned with creating social harmony, because he

---

[67] Bourke to Glenelg, 15 November 1836, fos. 209–10, CO 201/255, PRO; Bourke to Glenelg, 25 January 1837, fo. 75, CO 201/260, PRO.
[68] Executive Council minute no. 29, encl. in Bourke to Glenelg, 25 January 1837, fo. 90, CO 201/260, PRO.
[69] Bourke to Glenelg, 15 November 1836, fo. 210, CO 201/255, PRO.
[70] Glenelg to Bourke, 26 July 1837, NSW 4/1303, New South Wales Archives.
[71] Executive Council's minute no. 29, encl. in Bourke to Glenelg, 25 January 1837, fos. 87–99, CO 201/260, PRO; Glenelg to Bourke, 26 July 1837, NSW 4/1303, New South Wales Archives.
[72] Lester, *Imperial networks*, p. 60.

believed that it was only within such a context that material and moral progress could be made. Thus he saw placating the disadvantaged in each society in which he worked as fundamental to success; while those who threatened that society from outside should be contained. However, when his schemes to incorporate the disadvantaged or the outsiders failed, Bourke retreated into pragmatic reaction. In the next section, Bourke's vision of society is examined more closely, in a context where he thought he had more chance of success: his policies on education and the constitution.

JURIES AND REPRESENTATIVE GOVERNMENT

When Bourke arrived in New South Wales in 1831, he had a number of improvements for the colony – particularly relating to civilian juries – already in mind. New South Wales was no longer merely a penal settlement; less than half the population of 46,000 in 1830 were convicts, and, despite the arrival of 34,000 transported criminals during the 1830s, they made up only 30 per cent of the 1840 population. The convict roots of the majority of the European population, however, generated the most significant political divide in Australian society during Bourke's governorship. Convicts, emancipists and their children together comprised over 80 per cent of the colonial population in 1830, and still constituted 63 per cent of the 1841 population.[73] As the emancipist population grew, the demands of emancipists and their sympathisers (together designated 'Emancipists') for greater political, legal and economic rights created a direct conflict with the free emigrant or 'Exclusive' section of colonial society. Possessing much of the best land, and all of the (meagre) political and legal power conceded to the settlers, the Exclusives were determined to protect their position and status. The colony was also divided religiously, with sectarian disagreements between the (generally) Anglican élites, Presbyterian emigrants and emancipist Catholics, carried on publicly via the colony's pulpits and newspapers.

Bourke's uncertain experience in Cape Town affected his approach to government in New South Wales. He was determined, for example, to replace the established government officials in Sydney – Tories, through and through – with a more supportive cadre. Bourke thought the existing officials were not only averse to 'all liberal measures of policy' but also

---

[73] D. Neal, *The rule of law in a penal colony: law and power in early New South Wales* (Cambridge: Cambridge University Press, 1991), p. 15.

prejudiced against the emancipists. Bourke claimed that his only support came from 'the body of the People', although he also feared the democratic tendencies of the mob, and gestured darkly towards the population's republican ideas.[74] Bourke's attempts to surround himself with like-minded officials were implemented only gradually and partially; they also engendered the most vicious battles of his Australian career. Bourke's enemies (rightly) decried his manoeuvring as nepotistic, particularly the replacement of the colonial secretary, Alexander McLeay, by Bourke's son-in-law, Edward Deas Thomson. The governor's attempts to remove the colonial treasurer, Campbell Riddell, caused a political crisis which ultimately led to Bourke's resignation.[75]

Bourke had learnt from his Cape Colony experiences in other ways as well: he became more skilled at simultaneously exploiting and diminishing the temporal distance at which he found himself from Whitehall. Bourke managed the distance between Sydney and London, for example, by deliberately overemphasising Alexander McLeay's threats to resign in his despatches to London, because metropolitan endorsement of Bourke's candidate as a successor would be difficult to reverse. In 1836 he chose to misinterpret Colonial Office instructions by refusing the colony's most senior Anglican clergyman, William Broughton, a place on the executive council after he was made a bishop: the constitution identified the 'Archdeacon' as a council member, but not the 'Bishop of Australia'. Knowing that a response from London would take close to a year, and that a metropolitan rebuke would be very carefully weighed, Bourke limited Broughton's power by exploiting the space between London and Sydney.[76] But Bourke also worked to reduce the effect of distance when it suited him. In 1834, he sent his adult son, Dick, to London, to act as an unofficial gubernatorial envoy to the metropolitan government. The relationship between father and son was close, and Dick had spent the previous three years as his father's private secretary. In London, he became skilled at anticipating his father's responses, and worked diligently to keep his father abreast of metropolitan developments; the Colonial Office staff (unofficially) recognised Dick's status, seeking

[74] Bourke to Spring Rice, confidential, 12 March 1834, pp. 214–16, A1736, ML.
[75] S. G. Foster, 'A piece of sharp practice? Governor Bourke and the office of Colonial Secretary in New South Wales', *Historical Studies (Australia)* **16** (1975), pp. 402–24; King, *Bourke*, pp. 232–40; Shaw, *Heroes and villains*, pp. 27–30.
[76] Foster, 'Sharp practice', pp. 417–18. On Broughton see: Bourke to Glenelg, 11 June 1836, 18 June 1836, 25 July 1836, fos. 252–60, pp. 350, 467–8, CO 201/253, PRO; Glenelg to Bourke, 21 December 1835 in *HRA*, Vol. XVIII, p. 223; G. P. Shaw, *Patriarch and patriot: William Grant Broughton 1788–1853: colonial statesman and ecclesiastic* (Melbourne: Melbourne University Press, 1978), p. 103.

clarification from him about his father's despatches and likely response to metropolitan policies.[77] Senior officials, especially the colony's judges, who went to London on leave of absence were also primed to argue Bourke's case with politicians and lobbyists.[78]

In fact, Bourke's determination to secure robust metropolitan support for his New South Wales administration began with a meeting with viscounts Goderich (the Secretary of State for the Colonies) and Howick (the parliamentary under-secretary) shortly before his departure from London in 1831. Bourke placed considerable emphasis on this meeting, believing that he had secured Goderich's and Howick's support for his plans to extend civilian jury trials. The new governor left for New South Wales convinced that his decisions as the 'man on the spot' would be respected. A private letter from Howick in August 1831 reinforced this: although forwarding for Bourke's consideration a memorial, which differed from the governor's stated policies, Howick both referred to the earlier Colonial Office meeting and deferred to Bourke's local knowledge.[79] Of course, British governments changed with considerable rapidity during the 1830s, making the establishment of a connection with any regime difficult: during Bourke's first five years in New South Wales there were six different secretaries of state for the colonies.[80] Bourke at least felt political sympathy with the four Whigs; he had become acquainted with Goderich before he left London, while Spring Rice was one of his closest friends, and Dick worked to cement a strong relationship with Glenelg from 1835 onwards. In addition, Bourke's connections within humanitarian and Whig circles allowed both Dick and him to rely on under-secretaries Howick, Grey and Stephen. The array of personal, semi-official and official forms of correspondence which Bourke used, combined with the Whigs' sympathy for many of Bourke's plans, all helped the governor to secure significant support from the Colonial Office.[81]

Two of the first issues which Bourke confronted in New South Wales were the task of dismantling the Church Corporation and the introduction of civilian juries to try criminal cases. For both, Bourke's policies were influenced by his experience as an Irish landlord and political liberal. His experience at the Cape, by contrast, only rarely influenced the

[77] Zoë Laidlaw, 'Closing the gap: colonial governors and their metropolitan agents', in S. J. Potter, ed., *Imperial communications: Australia and Britain* (London: Menzies Centre, 2005), pp. 60–90.
[78] Laidlaw, *Colonial connections*, p. 74.
[79] Howick to Bourke, 24 August 1831, pp. 88–90, A1738, ML.
[80] Viscount Goderich, Edward Stanley, Thomas Spring Rice, the Duke of Wellington, Lord Aberdeen and Lord Glenelg.
[81] Laidlaw, 'Closing the gap'.

content of Bourke's policies (for example, he thought the New South
Wales' Supreme Court circuit should be organised on the same lines as
the Cape's circuit),[82] but, as seen above, did play a major role in determining his management of the government and his approach to colonial
and imperial politics.

Bourke, Howick and Goderich had agreed to the introduction of a bill
before the legislative council for petit juries in all civil cases at their 1831
meeting.[83] The wider introduction of civilian juries was particularly
contentious because of juries' political significance in a colony without
representative government: as David Neal has argued, 'the right to serve
on juries symbolised citizenship'.[84] Although Bourke's plans to introduce
civilian juries were waylaid, first by the intransigence of the Exclusive
members of the government, and then by changing regimes and vacillation
in the Colonial Office, his original intentions changed little. His lobbying
on jury trials between 1831 and 1837 reveals the types of arguments on which
Bourke drew, and the central place that the involvement of 'the people' in
the governance of their society had in his vision of a morally responsible
and stable community. It is also apparent that Bourke, despite his
opposition to democracy, frequently drew on the (unmeasured) support
given to him by the majority of the colonial population.

Bourke encouraged some of the aspirations of the disenfranchised
Emancipists in New South Wales, advocating a range of rights for
emancipated convicts, and the involvement of a wider cross-section of
colonial society in councils of government. This encouragement was
tempered slightly by Bourke's view that the continuation of transportation contaminated colonial society. Nevertheless, Bourke's disapprobation of the Exclusives, who held sway on the nominated legislative council,
was, if anything, more pronounced than his concern about Emancipists'
morals. In Bourke's view, the Exclusives had been corrupted by easy
access to land, convict labour and power, and did not provide the benefits
of a genuine paternalistic ruling class. Their strength stemmed from their
large land holdings, rather than from 'reputation, talents or numbers'.[85]
Such a view echoed metropolitan sentiment (and contemporary attitudes

---

[82] Bourke to Goderich, 6 February 1832, in *HRA*, Vol. XVI, p. 516.
[83] Bourke to Howick, private, 28 February 1832, in *HRA*, Vol. XVI, p. 542; Howick to Bourke, 24
August 1831, pp. 88–90, A1738, ML; Bourke to Stanley, 12 September 1833, in *HRA*, Vol. XVII.
[84] Neal, *Rule of law*, pp. 168–72; B. Kercher, *An unruly child: a history of law in Australia*
(St Leonards, New South Wales: Allen and Unwin, 1995).
[85] Bourke to Howick, private, 28 February 1832, in *HRA*, Vol. XVI, p. 544; Bourke to Spring Rice, 12
March 1834, pp. 214–15, A1736, ML; Bourke to Stanley, 15 January 1834, in *HRA*, Vol. XVII,
pp. 313–14.

to West Indian slaveowners), which itself reflected a paternalistic metropolitan view of colonial settlers.[86] Furthermore, 'envy and ill will' blinded the Exclusives to the Emancipists' willingness to work for a stable and prosperous society. After all, 'wealthy Emancipists' were just as concerned as their Exclusive counterparts to put down 'robbery and violence' and promote 'the due administration of criminal justice'.[87]

Bourke observed that opportunity in the colony – access to office, to representation, and to land – was 'closed except to a select few'.[88] Even when most colonists supported change in principle, as, Bourke claimed, with the introduction of an elected legislative assembly, the Exclusives would block any innovation which could threaten their privileged position. As a frustrated Bourke wrote to his son in late 1835: 'Nothing but absolute disenfranchisement' for emancipists with 'poverty and [convict] stripes' would satisfy the Exclusives.[89] This inequity, Bourke believed, would limit the colony's capacity to develop as a moral and useful society; just as the exclusion of the Dutch had damaged colonial society at the Cape, and Ireland had been damaged by discrimination against Catholics.[90]

Although Bourke introduced civilian juries on an interim basis and was determined to make them permanent through colonial or imperial legislation, he was thwarted by the legislative and executive councils. In this case, the distance between London and Sydney worked against him. The metropolitan government, wary of provoking the colonial councils, decided that the existing interim arrangements should continue until after the broader question of the New South Wales Act was resolved. The act, which provided the colony's constitution, was to expire at the end of 1836. Bourke argued in his despatches throughout the preceding year that substantially different constitutional arrangements were needed. In particular, he wanted the imperial government to introduce representative government to the colony. Such an arrangement would enfranchise more of the colony's population, while diluting the influence of Bourke's Exclusive opponents.

Bourke's determination to introduce representative government to New South Wales fitted with his Irish Liberal outlook. In order to

[86] See, for example, Richard Whately, *Thoughts on secondary punishments, in a letter to Earl Grey* (London, 1832) and *Remarks on transportation* (London, 1834).
[87] Bourke to Howick, private, 28 February 1832, in *HRA*, Vol. XVI, pp. 543–4.
[88] Bourke to Spring Rice, private, 23 March 1832, pp. 168–9, A1736, ML.
[89] Bourke to Dick Bourke, 26 December 1835, p. 123, A1733, ML.
[90] Bourke to Robert Hay, private, 27 August 1826, [unpaginated], CO 323/144, PRO.

persuade the imperial government that colonial society was ready for greater political responsibility, Bourke had to emphasise the deleterious effects of existing arrangements, underline the readiness of the colonists for greater responsibilities, and demonstrate that his reforms would improve New South Wales. Throughout his tenure, for example, Bourke argued that he and the colonial judiciary thought that the introduction of civil juries and more representative government could be managed with both safety and propriety.[91] Despite the difficulties he encountered, Bourke was optimistic about both the prospects for New South Wales and his own ability to improve the society, as a private letter to Spring Rice in early 1832 suggested. 'I have resuscitated a farming society and hope to make a first attempt at a public library', he wrote. The colony contained:

really some very intelligent persons in the middle classes, but ... they have had no encouragement to show themselves ... I really flatter myself that in three months I have done much towards healing dissensions and bringing people to draw together, and this chiefly by getting rid of absurd mystifications. If I can get Jury trials by civilians substituted for the present military commissions, and open the Council Chambers to the inspection of the Public, I think we shall have peace in Israel.[92]

Bourke's efforts to convince his metropolitan masters that colonial society had progressed sufficiently to cope with the reforms he hoped to institute – reforms which would in turn secure the colony's continuing advancement – meant the governor's despatches had to balance frustrations with government officials and councils, and concern about the immorality engendered by transportation, with optimism about New South Wales' future.

One of Bourke's recurring arguments was based on the rapid growth of New South Wales' non-convict population: the colony contained 'at least 50,000 free inhabitants' in February 1836, with 'a press totally unrestricted, a prevailing intelligence, encreasing [sic] wealth and a quick temperament'. It was no longer possible to govern with a nominated council, there needed to be 'something broader and surer' upon which to draw; a 'wider and firmer basis ... to secure a point of contact with the Colonists from which it might derive wholesome counsel and public support'. The lack of popular support for the council had worried Bourke since at least December 1833.[93] Two years later, colonists from all

---

[91] Bourke to Goderich, 6 February 1832, in *HRA*, Vol. XVI, p. 525; Bourke to Howick, private, 28 February 1832, in *ibid.*, pp. 542–4; Bourke to Stanley, 12 September 1833, *HRA*, Vol. XVII, pp. 213–14.

[92] Bourke to Spring Rice, private, 23 March 1832, pp. 168–9, A1736, ML.

[93] Bourke to Hay, 1 February 1836, fos. 166–7, CO 201/252, PRO; Bourke to Stanley, separate, 25 December 1833, fos. 461–5, CO 201/233, PRO.

parties had agreed that 'an assembly representing the intelligence and wealth of the colony' was required for the 'due administration of its affairs'.[94]

If positive exhortations failed, Bourke had other persuasive arguments. Could power, he asked his metropolitan masters, be exercised with 'advantage or safety' by nominated legislators 'attended with such little responsibility'? The existing constitution of the council not only failed to gather public support but 'frequently produced' the opposite effect. If the imperial government failed to take into account public sentiment, the voice of the colonists would soon 'be forced upon HM's Government', making it 'an important question of present expediency whether it may not be better to effect a change in the gradual manner I have suggested than to delay it until a much greater alteration in the Institutions of the Colony will become inevitable'.[95]

Bourke's arguments also emphasised social advancement and introduced notions of 'British' rights. A private note to Robert Hay, as permanent undersecretary, the Colonial Office's senior civil servant, emphasised the civility of the January 1836 celebrations of the forty-eighth anniversary of the colony's founding. A 'large stone bridge' had been opened with a fête and 'a gallant shew of well dressed Dames and Gentlemen, of Equipages and Horses'. Material gains were accompanied by the improvement of colonial society; even the 'most prudent' colonial inhabitants now recognised that 'whilst the Colony exports the finest wool in large quantities and can produce the wine, oil, fruits and grains which were exhibited, it may import the luxuries of Europe without the guilt of Extravagance'.[96] Bourke also employed the contemporary discourse of Britishness and 'British rights' which had considerable (and flexible) resonance in the colony.[97] His speech to the opening of the colonial legislature in June 1836, formally emphasised the need for the colony's political institutions to match its stature:

Though the period is short since Australia emerged from the wilderness, she is already ranked amongst the most flourishing of British Possessions, and her children justly claim to participate in British Institutions.[98]

---

[94] Bourke to Glenelg, 26 December 1835, in *HRA*, Vol. XVIII, p. 247.

[95] Bourke to Stanley, 25 December 1833, fos. 462–5, CO 201/233, PRO; Bourke to Hay, 1 February 1836, fos. 166–7, CO 201/252, PRO.

[96] Bourke to Hay, 1 February 1836, fos. 166–7, CO 201/252, PRO.

[97] Ridden, 'Making good citizens', pp. 272–95.

[98] Governor's speech at opening of legislative session, 2 June 1836, enclosed in Bourke to Glenelg, 10 June 1836, fo. 218, CO 201/253, PRO.

On almost every occasion when Bourke disagreed with the legislative or executive council, he would emphasise the weight of majority opinion in the colony against the narrow minority represented by the nominated councillors and his senior civil servants. For example, he claimed that the 'great majority of free People' wanted civil juries, rather than military, in early 1832; while in September 1833, Bourke again urged that this was the wish of the 'great majority of the Inhabitants'.[99] The figures were indeed with Bourke. Four thousand colonists signed the petition calling for trial by jury which Bourke referred to in an October 1833 despatch, including 'persons of the largest property and highest respectability in the colony, who must be presumed as deeply interested in the morals of the rising generation and of the due administration of Justice' as any of the council members.[100] By July 1836, Bourke could refer to an emancipist petition signed by six thousand, against the four hundred signatures collected by the Exclusives. 'It cannot be denied', he argued, 'that a vast majority of the Colonists, capable of forming sound opinions, desire the Establishment of Trial by Jury and a Legislature either wholly or in part representative.'[101]

Although it would be some years after Bourke's departure that the first elections for a legislative body would be held in New South Wales, Bourke did help prepare the ground for change. His vision for New South Wales – of a society where all (European) individuals had the opportunity to exercise their rights as British citizens – was significantly shaped by the principles he had adopted in Ireland; while its attempted implementation was affected by his earlier experience as governor of the Cape. However, it was on the next subject, the question of Church and Schools, that Bourke's Irish background, and his skills in colonial governance, really came to the fore.

RELIGIOUS POLICY IN NEW SOUTH WALES

Although a devout Anglican, married to an evangelical, Richard Bourke had supported Catholic emancipation in 1829; and he advocated toleration of all Christian denominations. This avowal was backed up by personal action: in Ireland, the Cape Colony and New South Wales, Bourke had a reputation for advancing not just Catholics, but also dissenters and

---

[99] Bourke to Goderich, 6 February 1832, in *HRA*, Vol. XVI, p. 515; Bourke to Stanley, 12 September 1833, in *HRA*, Vol. XVII, p. 214.
[100] Bourke to Stanley, 2 October 1833, in *HRA*, Vol. XVII, p. 236.
[101] Bourke to Glenelg, 25 July 1836, fo. 420, CO 201/253, PRO.

Quakers. Some of the most notable recipients of his largesse included the Catholic schoolteacher he employed on his Limerick estate; the Quaker botanist, William Harvey, who became treasurer for the Cape Colony government; and the Catholic lawyers, Roger Therry and John Plunkett, who became New South Wales' solicitor general and attorney general respectively. In New South Wales, as in the Cape and Ireland, Bourke would attempt to extend this tolerance to society at large. Bourke's Liberal Anglicanism put him at odds with high church Anglicans in New South Wales, just as it had in Limerick. The most prominent of these colonial Anglicans was New South Wales' archdeacon (and subsequently first bishop of Australia), William Broughton.

When Bourke arrived in New South Wales, he was charged with dismantling the Church Corporation – the system whereby the revenue from one-seventh of the colony's lands was reserved to support the Church of England.[102] After the dissolution, the Anglicans, like other Christian denominations, would receive their funding directly from the government. The change threatened Anglican autonomy and undermined the disproportionate power of the Church of England in the colony.[103] Archdeacon Broughton wanted an established church in New South Wales, but Bourke argued strongly against this: the establishment of an endowed church, was contrary to 'the Spirit of the Age', and would in fact prejudice the population against religion. Bourke instead proposed that government support should be given proportionately, according to congregation size, to the three major religious communities: Anglican, Roman Catholic, and Scottish Presbyterian. Bourke's proposals also entailed the devolution of power to congregations: they would be responsible for maintaining their buildings and finances; and for supporting Sunday Schools. The governor saw the dissolution as affording 'an opportunity for placing upon an equitable footing the support, which the principal Christian Churches in the Colony may for the present claim, from the public purse'.[104]

The dissolution of the Church Corporation also raised questions about how education should be organised in the colony: should the churches receive state funding for educational purposes; or should the state take direct responsibility for education? As it stood, educational opportunities,

---

[102] For the ill-fated history of the Church Corporation, see J. J. Eddy, *Britain and the Australian colonies, 1818–1831* (Oxford: Clarendon Press, 1969), pp. 264–70, and *passim*.

[103] Goderich to Bourke, 25 December 1832, in *HRA*, Vol. XVI, pp. 829–33; Broughton to Bishop of London, 30 September 1832, fos. 434–6, CO 201/235, PRO.

[104] Bourke to Stanley, 30 September 1833, in *HRA*, Vol. XVII, pp. 224–32.

especially for non-Anglicans, were very limited. Bourke was frustrated that Anglican selfishness should hold back the entire society. 'I am sorry to find that the prejudices of one Religion should be allowed to stand in the way of the general education of the people, which in my opinion should not be exclusively placed in the hands of the Clergy', he wrote to his son in London. 'Education is the business of the state.'[105] Bourke's clear view emerged from the Irish Liberal belief that education prepared individuals to act as responsible citizens, as demonstrated by his close involvement with plans for the non-denominational Irish national schools system.[106] He suggested the Irish national schools as a model for New South Wales; hoping 'with some degree of confidence', that providing non-sectarian education on the Irish model would unite 'together in one bond of peace', the people of New South Wales. Colonists would be 'taught' to look up to the Government as their common protector and friend': thus there would be 'secured to the State good subjects and to Society good men'.[107] Bourke was especially committed to non-denominational schools: education would be 'checked and starved by separation' between denominations.[108] Education, Bourke stressed, was particularly important in New South Wales, where the peculiar disadvantages and opportunities of convict society meant it was critical for all classes: 'in no part of the world' was 'the general education of the People a more sacred and necessary duty'.[109] The metropolitan governments of the 1830s echoed Bourke's sentiments, as in Glenelg's reference to the 'sacred and necessary duty' of the colonial government in 1835, and its impact not only on 'higher interests', but also the 'good order and social improvement of the colony'.[110]

Bourke's policies brought him into serious conflict with William Broughton. The colonial government already supported a number of orphan schools and was committed to providing funds to build the King's School, an Anglican boarding school in Parramatta. Bourke objected to educating the sons of 'wealthy Colonists and civil servants' in such style, while the children of the poor were taught 'in mere Hovels under convict school masters'.[111] Although the New South Wales population was far

[105] Richard Bourke to Dick Bourke, 7 November 1835, p. 100, A1733, ML.
[106] *PP 1825*, ix (181), evidence of Bourke, pp. 183–4; *PP 1830*, vii (665), evidence of Bourke, pp. 503–4, 513–14; Ridden, 'Making good citizens', pp. 55–9, 95–100.
[107] Bourke to Stanley, 30 September 1833, in *HRA*, Vol. XVII, pp. 229–31.
[108] Richard to Dick Bourke, 7 November 1835, p. 100, A1733, ML.
[109] Bourke to Stanley, 30 September 1833, 15 January 1834, in *HRA*, Vol. XVII, pp. 232, 313–14.
[110] Glenelg to Bourke, 30 November 1835, in *HRA*, Vol. XVIII, p. 202.
[111] Bourke to Stanley, 10 March 1834, in *HRA*, Vol. XVII, p. 393.

more religiously mixed than the Irish population, Bourke drew on his Irish experience to outline a system where government schools were built as population growth demanded them. These schools would be attended by children of all religious denominations, although their religious instruction would take place separately.[112]

Bourke did not merely rely on his Irish Liberal principles and experience in the debate on Australian education; changing imperial policy on education required both careful management and the utilisation of Bourke's imperial connections. The arguments that Bourke put to the Colonial Office on religion drew, like his plans for the New South Wales constitution and the introduction of jury trials, not only on assertions of their practical and moral importance, but on his avowals of the support of the vast majority of the inhabitants of the colony. Bourke claimed that his arrangements were approved by 'the great majority of the colonists' and thus promoted 'with the best assurance of success the religious instruction and general education of this People'. A favourable petition got up at a public meeting, which was 'numerously signed', had recently been presented to the governor and legislative council. Bourke supported his arguments with statistics giving the proportion of the population adhering to each of the main religions: although there had been no census, he calculated, for example, that about one-fifth of the population were Catholics, while the Presbyterians formed a smaller proportion, but were 'amongst the most respectable' of the colony's inhabitants. His figures were more convincing when it came to government expenditure. While £11,542 was spent annually on the Anglican Church; the Catholic establishment received only £1,500; and the Scottish Presbyterians, £600.[113]

Broughton's opposition to Bourke on the question of the colonial church and education did have theological and philosophical roots, but the archdeacon was also concerned that the Anglicans lost as little power as possible in the colony.[114] Broughton campaigned ferociously on both questions. Recognising his implacable differences from Bourke, he applied for leave of absence in 1834, in order to lobby ecclesiastical and political figures in London, including his patron, the Duke of Wellington.[115] Bourke was well aware of the damage Broughton might do

[112] Bourke to Stanley, 30 September 1833, in *HRA*, Vol. XVII, pp. 230–2. [113] *Ibid.*, pp. 224–6.
[114] On Broughton, see Shaw, *Patriarch and patriot*.
[115] Bishop of London to Stanley, 3 May 1833, fo. 433, CO 201/235, PRO; Broughton to Bishop of London, 30 September 1832, fos. 434–9, CO 201/235, PRO; Broughton to Spring Rice, 29 August 1834, 1 September 1834, 3 September 1834, fos. 74, 76–80, 84, CO 201/244, PRO; Broughton to Grey, 10 September 1834, fos. 86–7, CO 201/244, PRO; Laidlaw, 'Closing the gap'.

to his plans in England, and the archdeacon's departure spurred the despatch of Dick Bourke as his father's metropolitan envoy. Until then, Bourke had relied on unofficial and official communications to the Colonial Office and to his friend Spring Rice. The prospect of Broughton making his case in person encouraged the governor to place his own informed and reliable representative in the metropole. With Spring Rice's assistance, Dick would 'give much useful information' to the Colonial Office and remove 'any unfavourable impressions' created by Archdeacon Broughton.[116]

The metropolitan government wanted to avoid potential sectarian antagonism in New South Wales,[117] but Broughton's strident protests did capture ministers' attention. The archdeacon was unfortunate that his arrival in London coincided with two quick changes of government in late 1834 and early 1835, which threw the Colonial Office into some disarray. Several possible schemes for New South Wales education seem to have been mooted at the time: Dick Bourke wrote that the system recently approved for the West Indies – of separate schools for separate denominations, funded according to proportion of the population – was being considered as a compromise. In fact this was never taken up; the metropolitan government, like Bourke, decided it was impractical and expensive.[118] Informed and cajoled by a persistent Dick Bourke, the Colonial Office officials were persuaded of his father's case.[119] In 'those communities, formed and rapidly multiplying under most peculiar circumstances', with large Catholic and Presbyterian communities, the imperial government agreed that 'the attempt to select any one Church as the exclusive object of public endowment ... would not be tolerated'. Thus, by November 1835, the Colonial Office had adopted Bourke's solution as if it were their own. Glenelg forwarded Bourke documents relating to the Irish national schools, with his endorsement and encouragement to bring every denomination into the scheme.[120]

---

[116] Bourke to Spring Rice, confidential, 12 March 1834, pp. 209–13, A1736, ML.

[117] Glenelg to Bourke, 30 November 1835, 27 February 1837, in *HRA*, Vol. XVIII, pp. 202–6, 695–7.

[118] Dick Bourke to Richard Bourke, 24 June 1835, p. 70, A1739, ML; Richard Bourke to Dick Bourke, 7 November 1835, pp. 99–100, A1733, ML.

[119] The correspondence between Dick and Richard Bourke provides extensive evidence of Dick's frequent appearances at the Colonial Office, and the regard in which he was held by senior political and permanent staff there. See particularly, Dick to Richard Bourke, 1 September 1834, 20 September 1834, 15 April 1835, 24 June 1835, 29 March 1836, 29 December 1836, pp. 16–18, 22–3, 51–4, 68–71, 128–9, 173, A1739, ML.

[120] Glenelg to Bourke, 30 November 1835, in *HRA*, Vol. XVIII, pp. 203–6; Grey to Bourke, 31 December 1835, in *ibid.*, p. 253.

Broughton was entreated to return to the colony as the first bishop of the new diocese of Australia.

Unsuccessful in the metropolis, and convinced that Bourke was utterly wrong, Broughton nevertheless returned to the colony as bishop of Australia. Bourke's fears that Broughton intended to undermine the new education policies in the executive council were probably well grounded, and certainly genuine. The governor maintained that this potential insubordination justified the bishop's exclusion from the council, despite specific instructions from London.[121] As mentioned earlier, Bourke thus exploited the distance between metropole and colony, a gap that he had earlier sought to diminish by the despatch of Dick as his envoy. Broughton responded to his exclusion by chairing a public meeting, and whipping up a colonial storm on an issue that had earlier received relatively little attention from those beyond the clergy and supporters of the King's School.[122] The antagonism generated was so disruptive that Bourke's plans for national schools were placed on hold by the imperial government, 'a great personal disappointment' to him.[123]

Plans for the non-denominational education of New South Wales' children provide perhaps the clearest case of Bourke transferring his experience of Ireland directly to a different colonial setting. It should be remembered, however, that Bourke had not seen the Irish national schools system implemented, and that his conviction about the right form of education, and his enthusiasm for the project stemmed more directly from his Irish Liberal worldview, than from his practical experience.

RICHARD BOURKE AND BRITISHNESS

Richard Bourke's understandings of nation, race, empire and society were shaped in Ireland and England, but challenged in the Cape Colony and New South Wales. These colonial challenges forced Bourke to articulate and defend his ideas, allowing historians to assess their importance to him. Bourke placed himself in a paternalistic relationship to the societies in which he lived and worked, whether Irish or colonial. It was, he believed, his responsibility to work for more harmonious, prosperous and moral societies. Yet despite positioning himself above society, Bourke was

---

[121] Bourke to Glenelg, 11 June 1836, 18 June 1836, 25 July 1836, fos. 252–4, 350, 467, CO 201/253, PRO.
[122] Bourke to Glenelg, 8 August 1836; Bourke to Glenelg, separate and confidential, 8 August 1836, fos. 52–9, 114–21, CO 201/254, PRO; Bourke to Glenelg, 7 October 1836, in *HRA*, Vol. XVIII, pp. 565–70.
[123] King, *Bourke*, pp. 230–2; Glenelg to Bourke, 27 February 1837, in *HRA*, Vol. XVIII, pp. 695–701.

concerned by that which connected him to other people; it was when he could find no connection, as with the aboriginal peoples of New South Wales, that his vision of a tolerant, liberal, and 'British' society faltered. In other respects, Bourke's Irish Liberal convictions helped him to introduce reforms such as Ordinance 50 to the Cape Colony and to open up important debates about the nature of the New South Wales polity.

But Bourke's liberal ideals might well have come to nothing, if not combined with two other attributes: his excellent metropolitan connections; and his understanding of the nature of colonial governance. Through his Westminster and Oxford education, his seventeen years' active military service during the Napoleonic wars, his Irish connections to Westminster, and his daughters' fortuitous marriages, Richard Bourke possessed a formidable set of British imperial networks. These connections helped him acquire office, gave him confidence, and provided him with avenues of communication to the most influential of metropolitan figures. While they could not secure the extension of his tenure at the Cape, Bourke's growing experience as a colonial administrator enabled him to use his connections more effectively while governor of New South Wales. Although Bourke by no means accomplished all he had hoped, he did learn to manage the distance between London and Sydney effectively. This was achieved not only through the placement of personal envoys in Britain or the provision of carefully considered (and sometimes misleading) responses to Colonial Office despatches, but also through the establishment of a coterie of supporters among his official subordinates and clever allusions in his despatches to the threat and the benefits of popular support. Thus studying Richard Bourke in his full imperial context – his full British context – allows historians to better appreciate not only the web of personal and institutional connections that linked and shaped all parts of the early nineteenth-century empire, but also the way in which ideas – of subjecthood, citizenship, and 'Britishness' – were moulded by context and location as well as individual concerns.

CHAPTER 5

George Grey in Ireland: narrative and network

Leigh Dale

> Noticeably ... the outwardly successful career is often the well-architected career, for in all life the careerist exists and thrives, liking his mission
>
> James Milne, *Memoirs of a bookman*, p. 301.

Sir George Grey (1812–98: see Fig. 5.1) is said to have numbered many of the luminaries of the Victorian age among his correspondents and patrons – Thomas Carlyle, William Gladstone, the queen herself. His associates spanned not merely the usual family members and professional contacts, but those with a scholarly interest in ethnography, linguistics, geology, geography, anthropology and ornithology, and an equally active network of people in public life, including indigenous leaders in southern Africa and New Zealand. In this essay I want to consider the ways in which that material nineteenth-century network has been represented in, and perhaps even superseded by, a *textual* network through which Grey's reputation has been made and unmade. In doing so, I want to contest a key claim in the existing biographical record: the belief that George Grey developed the liberal views for which he was famed during the time he was an unwilling member of the occupying army in Ireland. I want to suggest, instead, that during this period he learned the political philosophies, and the rhetorical and material strategies of domination, that would inform his viceregal rule.

In concentrating on textual networks in this essay, I do not wish to imply that personal networks of patronage did not play a central role in Grey's own lifetime. A brief example will serve to emphasise the importance of his connections: when he went exploring, while in his mid-twenties, Grey travelled on the same ship on which Charles Darwin accompanied Captain Robert FitzRoy, the *Beagle*. Grey was an acquaintance of Darwin's, and

Acknowledgements: I thank the editors, along with Sarah Ferber and, particularly, Marion Diamond, for their comments, and the Arts Faculty, University of Queensland for funding this research.

Fig. 5.1 Sir George Grey, c. 1855, B5969, by permission of the
State Library of South Australia.

claimed to have become a 'frequent caller' during his relatively brief periods
of residence in London.[1] Darwin's *The voyage of the Beagle* was dedicated to
geologist Sir Charles Lyell, with whom Grey became a correspondent and,
by his own claim, friend.[2] In the meantime former sailor Robert FitzRoy
became governor of New Zealand; when FitzRoy was dismissed from
his position in 1845, it was Grey who took his place. Equally, the span of
his reputation is broad: I purchased a 1907 biography, written by an
Australian scholar, in a bookshop in Cape Town. That particular volume
had English and American publishers, and was a cast-off (I hope!) from the

[1] J. Milne, *The romance of a pro-consul: being the personal life and memoirs of the Right Hon. Sir George Grey, KCB* (London: Chatto and Windus, 1899), p. 40.
[2] *Ibid.*, p. 47; see also J. Rutherford, *Sir George Grey KCB, 1812–1898: a study in colonial government* (London: Cassell, 1961), p. 584.

Massachusetts Public Library. Grey's reputation – and debates about it – span the English-speaking world.

THE IMPERIAL CAREER

By any measure Grey had a stellar career in imperial service (see Map 5.1 for his career path), notwithstanding the controversies that also saw him twice recalled from his position. Named governor of South Australia before he was thirty, after the publication of a two-volume account of his journeys of exploration in northern Western Australia made in his mid-twenties, he was knighted on completion of this appointment in 1845.[3] As governor of New Zealand (1845–54 and 1861–7) he managed to please and antagonise almost every sector of the population from missionaries to the New Zealand Company: 'In the eight years of his first New Zealand governorship, Grey bought nearly 30 million acres of Maori land in the South Island and about 3 million acres in the North Island.'[4] Grey remains a major figure in New Zealand historiography and scholars from that country have taken the leading parts in debates over Grey's role and reputation: no less than five biographies are by authors based in New Zealand.[5] Much modern debate is concerned with challenging the mythology of Grey as a governor who 'knew the Maori', a reputation based on Grey's studies of the language, and his patronage of widely circulated publications of Maori literatures. Extracts from these books were studied in New Zealand schools for much of the twentieth century, fortifying his reputation in the public imagination.[6] When Grey completed his second term in New Zealand he was refused any further appointment in the colonial service, but later became prime minister and

---

[3] G. Grey, *Journals of two expeditions of discovery in North-west and Western Australia during the years 1837, 38 and 39 ... with observations on the moral and physical condition of the aboriginal inhabitants*, 2 vols. (Adelaide: Libraries Board of South Australia, 1964 (1841)). John Lort Stokes criticised Grey for overstating the quality and value of the lands: see A Naval Officer [Stokes], 'Voyage of the HMS Beagle on a survey of the coast of Australia', *Nautical Journal* 10 (1840), pp. 579, 702–14, 784–8. For a defence of Grey see 'The new country to the northward', *Western Australian Inquirer* (26 September, 3 October and 10 October 1849), G.13.1.17 and G.39.d.28 respectively, South African Public Library (SAPL), Cape Town.

[4] See Rutherford, *Sir George Grey KCB*, p. 163.

[5] See also Harry Bioletti, *Whatever happened to Lady Grey? or, The many shades of Grey: being a look into the private lives of Lady Eliza Lucy Grey and her husband Sir George Grey* (Auckland: H. Bioletti, 2001).

[6] Like Grey's researches in Aboriginal linguistics in Australia in his *A vocabulary of the dialects of south western Australia*, 2nd edn. (London: T. & W. Boone, 1840), and his patronage of the collection of publications about southern African languages (preserved in the SAPL), this material provides a rich if ambiguous legacy.

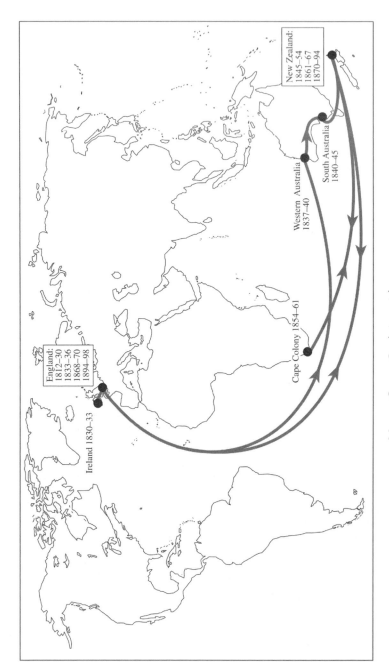

Map 5.1 George Grey's imperial career.

served as a member of parliament there. Indeed, such was his political longevity that he was one of the New Zealand delegates to the Australian federation convention, held in 1891.

Perhaps Grey's greatest challenges came when he was governor of the Cape Colony (1854–9; 1860–1), where again his reputation was made and unmade. It is felt by many historians (and the Grey biographers) that a more complex political and cultural landscape in the Cape and beyond was much less yielding to Grey's undoubted administrative talents. He reduced the expenditure that the colony had absorbed in previous decades through a series of devastating wars, and significantly improved the colony's civic and industrial infrastructure, but was derided by liberal and hardline colonists alike for what was seen either as uncompromising brutality towards or excessive accommodation of indigenous peoples. The key event in his administration was the cattle-killing movement. He was controversially recalled in 1859 for disobedience in prematurely (albeit prophetically) advocating the union of the English and the Boer republics, but subsequently reappointed (and subsequently hosted the young Prince Alfred), before successfully pleading to return to New Zealand in 1861. These comments from a contemporary give a good sense of the prevailing views of colonial observers, incorporating as they do both mythology and skepticism:

Sir George Grey was one of our Governors who declined to act upon any Imperial policy which he thought detrimental to the best interests of the people of the country. . . . Difficulties to Sir George were opportunities for bringing his genius into play. Who else could have turned the wholesale Kafir cattle-killing to such good account as he did? . . . The Kafirs were the uncompromising and bloodthirsty enemies of the country, and he fed them. Never did a Governor's policy, founded upon gospel principles, bring a richer reward. It was during Sir George's time that the Cape commenced to make its advance in material progress. . . . He turned the sod of the first railway and laid the foundations upon which British Kaffraria was built – laid them solid and sure, turning territory which had heretofore been a battle ground on which the lives of thousands of Her Majesty's subjects had been sacrificed into a land of peace and plenty . . . There is hardly a district in the Cape Colony in which Sir George did not lay the foundation of some public undertaking, either institution, bridge, library, or other kind of work. . . . Sir George had won a good deal of his popularity by a large public expenditure in the country . . . leaving it to whoever might succeed him to let the Parliament know that the Colony was on the very verge of bankruptcy and to take upon himself the task of retrieving the Colony from that position.[7]

[7] R. W. Murray Sen. *South African reminiscences: a series of sketches of prominent public events which have occurred in South Africa within the memory of the author during the forty years since 1854, and of*

As these comments demonstrate, many colonists admired George Grey for his apparent preparedness to speak in their interests in his communications with England, while close observers were also aware that he was adroit in cultivating popularity and scrupulous (perphaps obsessive) in documenting public approval. When dismissed from his post in South Africa several dozen petitions, signed by many hundreds of people, endorsed his rule; dutifully he forwarded each of them to the Colonial Office for presentation to Queen Victoria. They were among literally scores of testimonials he sought and received from indigenous peoples and from colonists as to the probity and wisdom of his administration.[8]

Political opponents condemned Grey for what they saw as his self-serving representations in his formal dispatches to the Colonial Office. This sceptical view has become the modern orthodoxy, famously summed up by eminent historian Ian Wards who remarked that Grey 'lied about virtually everything'.[9] At this point it is important to acknowledge that there are subtle but significant differences between the views in the various southern colonies with which Grey was associated: in Australia, Grey's popular reputation is that of the explorer (of Western Australia) and the brilliant young statesman on the rise (in South Australia), although there has certainly been criticism. In New Zealand it seems that regard for and interest in Grey, strong until the more general revisionist mood of the 1960s and 1970s which affected school curricula and popular forms of representation, coincides with the general scholarly scepticism already remarked on. In southern Africa the scholarly challenge has come much later, if even more forcefully, but much of the apparatus through which Grey has been revered seems to remain intact.[10]

There is no easy or consistent cleavage by which one can characterise Grey's supporters or critics. Some colonists regarded him as dangerously radical in his views, proposing education and the provision of healthcare for indigenous peoples; some of his closest colleagues expressed their revulsion for his maltreatment of those same people, particularly in relation to the seizure of land. A contemporary who worked as his private

the public men, official and unofficial, who have taken part in them (Cape Town, Port Elizabeth and Johannesburg: J. C. Juta, 1894), p. 35; pp. 44–5.

[8] MSB 222 1(1), in the SAPL is a bound volume consisting of votes of thanks to Grey. There are nearly 20 petitions, which taken together have many hundreds of signatures.

[9] Quoted in G. Parsonson, 'The colourful life and times of an upper-class hero', Review of Edmund Bohan, *To be a hero: Sir George Grey, 1812–1898, Evening Post* [New Zealand], 30 October 1998, p. 5.

[10] Indicative of the frustration this prompts is Gail Weldon's textbook *George Grey and the Xhosa: fact and opinion* (Pietermaritzburg: Heinemann-Centaur, 1993).

secretary in New Zealand explained his resignation from his position in these terms:

It was not the mere peril and care and worry of the life which made me give it up, but the change was hastened on because I was vexed by some things which the Governor had lately done in the South, and I thought they were not as straight-forward in our dealings with the Māori as we should have been. I was very unwilling to be an agent in a policy against which my private conscience revolted.[11]

'Grey sceptics' – among whom could be numbered almost every single modern commentator, with the notable exception of his most recent biographer Edmund Bohan – point in particular to the contradiction between Grey's reputation for benevolence, and his record of initiating, compounding, and exploiting the dispossession and maltreatment of indigenous peoples. But no clear line can be drawn between scholarly studies and popular texts in terms of their attitude to Grey, although it *is* possible to say that the latter material is generally more reverential. Put another way, the public criticisms of Grey that were made in his own lifetime have more often filtered into the scholarly than the popular record. There is a crucial qualification to this claim: in 1977 Keith Aberdein's novel *The governor* was made into a television series by TV NZ.[12] The source for Aberdein's luridly imagined account of Grey's life is the off-hand remark, made by Edward Clarke in a letter to his aunt George Eliot, that Grey kept 'a Maori harem'.[13] It is not clear to what extent the novel and the television series have challenged or changed public perceptions of Grey in New Zealand, perhaps because academics are reluctant to admit having encountered them.

More substantively, it is Grey's reputation as a statesman who was instrumental in 'spreading civilisation' that is the staple of most of the popular material that considers his life, although it is also in evidence in a significant proportion of scholarly commentary. The précis of the first chapter of G. C. Henderson's 1907 biography offers a neat summary of the imperial version of Grey and his work:

Influence of the French revolutionary teaching on England and on Sir George Grey – His love of nature and his enthusiasm for humanity – Continuity of his work shown by reference to his public policy – His views on the Land Question,

---

[11] G. Clarke, *Notes on early life in New Zealand* (Hobart: J. Walch, 1903), p. 97.
[12] K. Aberdein, *The governor* (Wellington: Hamlet Books, 1977).
[13] G. Haight, ed., *The George Eliot letters*, Vol. VIII (New Haven and London: Yale University Press and Oxford University Press, 1954–78), pp. 421–4. See G. J. Tee, 'Edward Clarke, author of the Thames Miner's Guide (1868)', *Turnbull Library Record* **14** (May 1981), pp. 5–12. Rutherford is dismissive of speculation: *Sir George Grey KCB*, p. vii.

Extension of the Franchise, and Education of the Masses – His enthusiasm for Empire, and his attachment to the principle of self-government – His arguments reviewed in relation to the problem of Imperial Unity – Merits and defects of Sir George Grey's native policy – His extraordinary personal influence over primitive and aboriginal races – General observations on the work which he accomplished in South Africa and Australasia – His place among the builders of Empire in the Southern Hemisphere.[14]

Within these narratives of George Grey's 'exemplary life' there is emphasis given to the claim that his experiences as a young soldier in Ireland had a formative and enduring impact on him. And almost without exception, commentators (including Henderson) remark frequently and at length on the contradictions within Grey's character, and contradictions between his character and his public policy. Hence modern commentary: typical is the writer who says that 'The ambiguous legacy of Grey's governorships in New Zealand ... and in South Africa ... is compounded by a personality prone to authoritarianism and deceit. As the historian Keith Sinclair put it, Grey's "conduct is a never-failing source of astonishment. Such a mixture of greatness and pettiness, breadth of intellect and dishonesty, is rarely met with".'[15] The argument is underpinned – again, the example is symptomatic – with a recitation of Grey's growth to intellectual maturity via three main sources: a 'pietistic mother'; the cleric, archbishop of Dublin Richard Whately, 'who inspired the young Grey with liberal views' on a range of issues; and six years in Ireland, which 'exposed young Grey to an unimaginable poverty, which profoundly affected him. As a result he decided to forego a military career for a profession dedicated to administration and reform.'[16]

The primacy given to this relatively limited set of causes of Grey's 'personal growth' is the basis for considering Grey's militantly benevolent imperialism, and specifically the paradox of his liberal views and his authoritarian policies. In such circumstances I am motivated to ask two questions.

- Why have the stories of 'George Grey and Ireland', the foundation of so much modern critique as well as of the earlier biographies of Grey, received little or no critical attention?

---

[14] Geo. C. Henderson, *Sir George Grey: pioneer of empire in southern lands* (London and New York: J. M. Dent & Co. and E. P. Dutton & Co., 1907), p. xiii.
[15] J. Gump, 'The imperialism of cultural assimilation: Sir George Grey's encounter with the Maori and the Xhosa, 1845–1868', *Journal of World History* **9** (Spring 1998), p. 90; quoting K. Sinclair, *The origins of the Maori Wars* (Wellington: New Zealand University Press, 1957), p. 33.
[16] Gump, 'The imperialism of cultural assimilation', pp. 91–2.

- Why have the contradictions that riddled his administration and his policy been attributed to his personality, rather than to the contradiction inherent in the claims to benevolence that aimed to legitimate British imperial practices?

We need to begin by considering the biographical edifice surrounding Grey.

The sources on Grey's life are numerous, indeed almost overwhelming. There are two major scholarly works: James Rutherford's *Sir George Grey KCB, 1812–1898: a study in colonial government* (1961) which had been preceded by a preliminary study, and George Cockburn Henderson's *Sir George Grey: pioneer of empire in southern lands* (1907). Each author spent many years researching his subject across the southern colonies: Rutherford ruefully admits to ten, 'instead of the three or four I once hopefully contemplated'.[17] Although this essay is critical of Rutherford, I should state that I am completely in awe of the scope and detail of his research. Apart from Aberdein's novel, already noted, there are five popular works (one unsighted), two of which appeared in the 1890s: James Milne's *Sir George Grey: the romance of a proconsul* (1899), and William Rees and Lily Rees' *The life and times of George Grey* (1892).[18] James Collier's *Sir George Grey* (1909) aims to challenge the very positive portrait offered by Rees and Rees;[19] contrastingly, Edmund Bohan's fairly recent study *To be a hero* sets out to counter modern scholarly criticisms, in a work that, while sometimes quite critical of its subject, clearly aims to restore the authority of the populist version of Grey.[20]

The main source for condemnation of Grey is his mid twentieth-century biographer, James Rutherford. Rutherford, in detailed analyses of Grey's actions as governor and of his participation in New Zealand politics in particular, has written what is by far the best known and probably the most authoritative of the six biographies. He comes to the conclusion that 'What made Grey such a "terrible and fatal man", in Tancred's trenchant phrase' were the particularly lethal effects of combining 'romantic idealism' with 'a fierce determination to carry his ideas into practice'.[21] Curiously, Rutherford cites as evidence for these characteristics not Grey's imperial policies or practices, but his running away

---

[17] Rutherford, *Sir George Grey KCB*, p. viii.
[18] W. L. Rees and L. Rees, *The life and times of George Grey, KCB* (Auckland: Brett, 1892).
[19] J. Collier, *Sir George Grey, governor, high commissioner, and premier: an historical biography* (Christchurch: Whitcombe and Tombs, 1909).
[20] E. Bohan, *To be a hero: Sir George Grey, 1812–1898* (Auckland: HarperCollins, 1998).
[21] Rutherford, *Sir George Grey KCB*, p. 655.

from school before he was ten; his suggestion that a fellow soldier not be
flogged; and his abandonment of his military career 'to go in search of
new lands on which to settle the Irish people'.[22] What makes these pieces
of evidence curious is that they come not from the meticulous research
that underpins much of Rutherford's 700-page study, but from Grey's
own account of his childhood and early adulthood – that is to say, they
are part of the Grey mythology, founded on the works by Milne and by
Rees and Rees, that Rutherford's volume sets out to disassemble.

Few scholars of the past decades refer to any other work than
Rutherford's – the Henderson is perhaps unjustly neglected, for although
frankly and untiringly boosterish in relation to empire it is also scholarly,
and more sceptical of its subject than either its title or general ideology
might suggest.[23] James Milne's book is much derided by later writers for
its sycophancy. Its author claimed to have had extended interviews with
Grey in London in his late old age and to have transcribed that material,
supplemented where appropriate by research. Equally uncertain in its
provenance is the book by the Reeses, father and daughter: William Lee
Rees was an ally of Grey in New Zealand politics. But precisely *because*
they so transparently aim to speak for their subject, these books are crucial
sources for understanding the ways in which Grey wanted historians, and
the reading public, to see him as having acted. And they are important in a
second way: both books, although disparaged, have nonetheless been
essential sources for later scholars, who have tended to turn to them –
especially Milne's – for their most telling personal anecdotes of Grey and
his life, anecdotes which have in turn been recycled through popular and
general sources as scholarly truth. Thus, although these two books have
been discarded in the historical record, I regard them as crucial sources for
tracing the source of scholarly legend.

Apart from the Rutherford volume and subsequent general studies in
New Zealand, some of the most useful correctives to the Grey mythology
have come from careful investigation of specific events in which Grey
participated, a point demonstrated by the work of J. M. R. Cameron (in
relation to Australia) and Jeff Peires (in southern Africa). Cameron's essay
on Grey's preparations for his journeys of exploration, which makes
extensive use of the records of the Royal Geographical Society (RGS),

---

[22] *Ibid.*, p. 655.
[23] Henderson declares that 'it is high time that the reputations of sincere and honest men at the
Colonial Office were vindicated against the unjustifiable censures passed on them by an author
who has assumed the *rôle* of an advocate' (*Sir George Grey*, p. 298), a *double-entendre* surely directed
at Rees, a former lawyer.

reveals Grey's ruthlessness, his authoritarianism, and his willingness to seek and to deploy patronage in furthering his own career and interests. Cameron recounts that Grey, caught up in RGS politics and subordinated to the ambitions of its president Sir John Barrow, complained forcibly to James Stephen, undersecretary for the colonies,

of the steps the Society had taken to progressively debase his original conception and diminish his role to the point where he was now a mere agent of the society, 'in an expedition which I never contemplated undertaking *and does not hold out to me any prospect of such results, as those the hope of obtaining which has been my sole motive from the beginning of the affair.*'[24]

Apart from the single-minded ambition on display here, the forcefulness of Grey's complaint is surely evidence of his high social standing and extraordinary self-confidence. Jeff Peires, in *The dead will arise*, carefully and far more devastatingly demonstrates the ways in which Grey actively impeded the work of a famine-relief committee in the eastern Cape region, thereby exacerbating widespread starvation that had been caused by the proliferation of a prophecy movement among the Xhosa in 1856–7. This movement, which saw the proliferation of demands that the Xhosa people kill their cattle and destroy their crops, ultimately caused tens of thousands of deaths, the displacement of further thousands, and the effective destruction of Xhosa society.[25]

LEGENDS OF IRELAND

In almost every discussion of Grey's life and work, the experience of Ireland is represented as being central to the formation of his character, specifically to the development of liberal social views. It is, commensurately, central to the ways in which biographers (and thence historians and cultural critics) understand Grey as a man of deeply contradictory character traits.[26] The first published biography asserted that 'The scenes of wretchedness which the young officer witnessed were never forgotten by him'.[27] Setting a pattern that most modern commentators follow, Rutherford concludes that

---

[24] J. M. R. Cameron, 'George Grey goes exploring: the interplay of personalities, politics and place', *Journal of the Royal Australian Historical Society* **78** (June 1992), p. 63. Emphasis added.

[25] J. Peires, *The dead will arise: Nongqawuse and the great Xhosa cattle-killing of 1856–7*, 2nd edition (Johannesburg and Cape Town: Jonathan Ball, 2003).

[26] The exception is Cameron, who for obvious reasons emphasises the significance to Grey's career of his journeys of exploration: Cameron, 'George Grey goes exploring'.

[27] Rees and Rees, *The life and times of George Grey*, p. 13.

Ireland changed [Grey's] outlook. Here he encountered an accumulation of human misery which both oppressed and inspired him, and under the impact of this experience his radical convictions overcame the aristocratical instinct which had inspired his notions of an army career. Henceforth his life's ambition was to serve the common people in the capacity of a civil administrator and reformer.[28]

How do such accounts of the effect of Ireland on Grey mutate into popular sources? By refining a story of transformation into unadulterated cliché, like this:

> In England an aristocratic, quick-tempered and proud young army officer, Captain George Grey, had decided that, at 24, he was weary of keeping order amongst the unruly Irish.[29]

Grey had entered the Junior Department of the Royal Military College (RMC) at Sandhurst in Surrey, at a young age – Henderson claims that the year of his enrolment was 1826, making him thirteen or fourteen.[30] The College's own website notes that during this period, 'the RMC gained a reputation for disorderly behaviour, rioting, and bullying comparable with unreformed public schools of the period, with the average age of the cadets being about fifteen'.[31] On graduation from Sandhurst after three years, Grey became an ensign in the 83rd Foot Regiment. When Grey joined on 14 January 1830, members of the first battalion of the 83rd were serving in Glasgow. But in August that year they were ordered to Belfast.

It is difficult to flesh out the details of this period of Grey's life, let alone to imagine what it might have meant to be a teenage member of an occupying force, coming to terms with life on active service. In some significant ways the hardships of army life were diminished by having an officer's commission – one was exempted from the punishment of flogging, for example. The officers were an élite, expected to defray the expense of service with a private income. Gwyn Harries-Jenkins notes that for a line regiment like the 83rd a minimum of £100 pounds a year was specified, but double that was recommended.[32] Apart from the expense (including the purchase of commission and promotions), 'Within the closed world of the officers' mess a way of life was maintained

---

[28] Rutherford, *Sir George Grey KCB*, p. 5.
[29] M. McEwan, *The westerners*. Diana Chiccio (ed.), Australian explorers 9 (Sydney: Bay Books, 1979), p. 5.
[30] Henderson, *Sir George Grey*, p. 20.
[31] http://www.atra.mod.uk/atra/rmas/history/history5.htm, accessed 4 December 2004.
[32] G. Harries-Jenkins, *The army in Victorian society* (London: Routledge and Kegan Paul, 1977), p. 98.

which reflected very closely the leisured life of the landed interest': officers expected days off for hunting, and extended periods of leave for 'the season'.[33] Harries-Jenkins claims that the standard of education was 'appallingly low'; the emphasis was on manners, values, attitudes, and squirely accomplishments, on 'character rather than intellect'.[34]

Apart from the collision between this kind of regimental culture, and the values and politics of the majority of the Irish population, there were more complicating factors for Grey himself. These include the fact that his regiment, the 83rd, was the 'Royal Irish Rifles'. Being an Irish regiment is likely to have meant a somewhat higher proportion of Irish recruits (particularly among enlisted men and NCOs) than usual, lending further complication to the relationship between the occupying force and the local population. And Grey was a very junior officer whose father had been a lieutenant colonel in the 30th Foot, and who had died in the Peninsular Wars while leading his regiment in a charge at the Battle of Badajoz. In addition to the reputation gained through this kind of death, it may have further affected Grey that his father had (judging by regimental records) been known to at least some of his son's commanding officers. More complicatedly still, his mother, born Elizabeth Anne Vignoles, was the daughter of the Reverend John Vignoles, of Cornahir [Coruaher] in County Westmeath in the centre of Ireland, not far from where Grey was serving from April 1833 to early 1834.[35]

As George Henderson points out, the early 1830s was a period of tumult in Europe, with uprisings in France, Poland, Italy, Germany, Belgium and the Netherlands.[36] In Ireland there had been some very limited political reform in 1829, following unrest created by the abolition of the Irish parliament and union with England in 1800.[37] An acquaintance of Richard Whately recalled the mood at the time, when 'An organized determination to pay no more tithes animated the length and breadth of Ireland':

two parsons were murdered, and great atrocities were committed on both sides ... [When an Anglican priest at Skibbereen, in Cork, was refused admission to seize potatoes from a barn] he ordered the yeomanry to fire, and

---

[33] *Ibid.*, p. 100, p. 98.   [34] *Ibid.*, p. 103.

[35] Rutherford, *Sir George Grey KCB*, p. 3, fn. 1; Henderson, *Sir George Grey*, p. 19 (who offers the alternative spelling); Collier, *Sir George Grey*, p. 4.

[36] Henderson, *Sir George Grey*, p. 21.

[37] R. V. Comerford, 'O'Connell, Daniel (1775–1847)', *Oxford dictionary of national biography* (Oxford University Press, 2004 at http://www.oxforddnb.com/view/article/20501), accessed 28 Nov. 2004.

twenty-nine persons fell dead. Blood was also shed at Carrickshock, Rathcormac, Castlepollard, Gortave, Dunmanway, and Newtownbarry. At the latter place stones appear to have been thrown in resistance to the Rev. Mr M'Clintock's claims, and the military fired, killing fourteen and wounding twenty-six persons.[38]

Analysis of the 83rd regiment's muster books and pay lists for the period 1830 to 1839 suggests that from 1831 to 1833 Grey had periods of service in Belfast, Omagh and Enniskillen in the north, Foxford and Castlebar in County Mayo on the west coast, and Wexford and Tipperary in the south of Ireland, giving him a relatively wide experience of the country in a time of considerable political turbulence.[39] Grey claims that the duties of the regiment included being on guard during nationalist political meetings, like those addressed by influential leader Daniel O'Connell. Milne records that Grey's sympathy for O'Connell's cause was prompted by hearing him speak, which Henderson in turn asserts was a key element in Grey's decision to turn to the imperial civil service. Grey's claims to have been present at a meeting in Limerick that was addressed by O'Connell are not contradicted by the historical record – indeed O'Connell's own letters from late 1832 record that he 'made a great speech yesterday, and another today'.[40]

The tangled web of personal and political circumstances hints that a more complex story of Grey's time in Ireland might be told than the historical record permits, and it certainly suggests that a simple narrative of growth to radicalism is inadequate. And as well as dealing with violence, there is evidence that the time was unpleasant for Grey in a different way: he was listed as being sick in two musters in 1832, and that year the entire regiment was ordered into barracks during an outbreak of cholera, in which twelve soldiers died.[41] It is perhaps not surprising that in February 1834, when the regiment was ordered to Cork for embarkation to Canada, Grey was not with them. He returned to the Senior

---

[38] W. J. Fitzpatrick, *Memoirs of Richard Whately, archbishop of Dublin, with a glance at his contemporaries* (London: Richard Bentley, 1864), p. 77, p. 80, pp. 80–1.

[39] The information on Grey is compiled from Regimental muster books and pay lists, 83rd Foot, 1st Battalion, War Office (WO) 12 8691, 8692 and 8693, PRO, Kew.

[40] Milne, *Romance of a pro-consul*, p. 33; Daniel O'Connell, Letter 18 December 1832, Letter 1943, *The correspondence of Daniel O'Connell Vol. IV: 1829–1832* (Dublin: Stationery Office, for the Irish Manuscripts Commission, 1977), p. 475.

[41] In late June 1832 all those at HQ were confined to camp at Ballinew until early September after the cholera outbreak; ten men died at Castlebar, and two officers at Ballinew. Information collected from *Memoirs and services of the eighty-third regiment, (County of Dublin), from 1793 to 1863: including the campaigns of the regiment in the West Indies, Africa, the Peninsula, Ceylon, Canada and India* (London: Smith, Elder, 1863).

Military Academy at Sandhurst for further study.[42] Rutherford was aware of this further period of study but not of its length, stating that Grey was six years in Ireland.[43] His error, repeated in almost every modern source, has two effects: first, it nearly doubles Grey's period of active service (which could have been four years, or perhaps three and a half); second, it encourages the belief that Grey's response to his time in Ireland was to leave the Army. On the contrary: his response was to further his military training for at least two and possibly for three more years. But Grey's own versions of his youthful experiences say nothing of this, highlighting instead the transformation in his political values effected by his observation of poverty and injustice.

In the reminiscences taken down by Milne, Grey records that, after escorting church officials to collect tithes, he submitted a report to his superiors stating the truth of the methods of collection and an account of the feelings of the Irish people about the practices. The commanding officer requested that Grey rewrite the report so that it expressed more orthodox opinions [at least in military terms], but Grey refused: ' "Sir ... I have stated just what happened and should wish, with your permission, to abide by my report." He awaited results with a mixed interest, but the farthest history of that temerarious despatch he never learned.'[44] Speaking in the 1890s to Milne, Grey is retrospectively establishing a precedent for one of the defining aspects of his career: his preparedness to challenge the imperial and military authorities. In this account of his actions (while still a teenager), Grey produces a template which readers can use to interpret negative accounts of his later behaviour as a senior member of the imperial civil service.

This is a crucial story. It is Grey's first 'dissident' despatch, by a man for whom despatch writing came to be one of the principal arts of his career, central to the making of his public reputation. The story is told by Grey to Milne, more than seventy years after an actual (?) event. Rutherford's use of an extensive quotation from Milne, while it seems to verify the story, permits the reader to forget that the account is second hand and has the effect of amplifying Grey's voice. In Rutherford we read as *Grey*'s words Milne's ghosted narration: 'my heart was wrung at what I witnessed ... it seemed to me nothing less than blasphemy, a mockery of

---

[42] Henderson, *Sir George Grey*, p. 24. Henderson says Grey returned to Sandhurst soon after his promotion to Lieutenant [on 29 March 1833: see WO 25 495, PRO for this and the following], but in WO records Grey is listed as being with his regiment until the same period the following year, although the same records do not list Grey for 1834.

[43] Rutherford, *Sir George Grey, KCB*, p. 5.   [44] Milne, *The romance of a pro-consul*, p. 30.

all true religion, and I thought it terrible to have to bear a part in the business'.[45] The incident is solidified in the historical record by Rutherford's apparently judicious summary – taken from Milne – of the aftermath: 'He salved his conscience by submitting a report, against the wishes of his commanding officer, which set forth the feelings of the peasantry and suggested amelioration, but no notice was taken of it.'[46] Thus can Rutherford conclude, 'Ireland changed his outlook.' This is a more spectacular way of representing a change of career than to say something like, having been appalled by his experiences in Ireland, but nonetheless feeling the pressure of expectation created by his father's exploits, Grey decided that it would be possible to combine the search for glory and the need to escape by embarking on a series of journeys of exploration. And something of this account might help to explain the ruthlessness, documented by Cameron, with which Grey pursued the latter ambition.

SEEING THE LIGHT

Let us consider in a little more depth the ways in which the experience of Ireland has accumulated in Grey historiography, specifically, as the cause of and the evidence for his radical views. As noted, James Milne's *The romance of a pro-consul* is the ur-text for much Grey mythology. In the chapter that deals with his time in Ireland Grey is quoted as expressing his sympathy for an Irishman who, in the memoirs of his long period in prison, describes the torture of the irregular flashes of the watchman's lantern in his cell. Grey's feelings are so intense that the story haunts him: 'It gnawed. His heart was full, and perhaps also his mind with the idea, "Is it ours to impale the soul as well as the body of a fellow-creature? Surely that is reserved for a higher tribunal!"'[47] Similar sentiments are shown in a second anecdote, in which Grey recalls his revulsion at being present at a toast lauding 'The Protestant King and confusion to Roman Catholicism'.[48] As with the story of the tithe collecting, the account serves as proof of a generalised Christian feeling, rather than of affiliation to a particular theology or church. And the stories also draw attention, in quite obvious ways, to the recognition of the power of intensely felt sentiment, quite at odds with what we might expect in a portrait of an

[45] *Ibid.*, p. 29; Rutherford, *Sir George Grey KCB*, p. 6.   [46] Rutherford, *Sir George Grey KCB*, p. 6.
[47] Milne, *The romance of a pro-consul*, p. 28.   [48] *Ibid.*, p. 29.

imperial statesman: Milne describes Grey in Ireland as 'young, sensitive, sympathetic, and the environment moulded him'.[49]

I want to suggest that there is a recognisable and easily available template for this mode of storytelling: the many thousands of works of evangelical Christianity which proliferated in the early part of the nineteenth century, and which continued to inform the work of some of England's greatest writers throughout the Victorian period.[50] By this I do not mean to contend that Grey himself could be categorised as an evangelical Christian – indeed, aspects of his self-presentation showed a singular flexibility. He could appeal (in the late 1830s and 1840s) to influential evangelical patrons at the Colonial Office; demonstrate awareness of the strongly anti-missionary views of most colonists (particularly from the mid-1840s to the mid-1860s); and simultaneously maintain working relationships with senior Anglican clerics in the colonies for much of his time as governor – a balancing act of near genius. So while rejecting specific elements of evangelical belief, Grey was very much alert to key elements of evangelical thought – necessarily so, when he sought the patronage of known evangelicals such as James Stephen and Lord John Russell at the Colonial Office at the beginning of his career, and experienced immediately the good effect to which such self-presentation could be put. The argument here, following Elizabeth Jay, is that the key tropes and modes of self-presentation from evangelical literature persisted long after the high tide of evangelical influence had receded, and the suggestion is that they could be brought back into circulation by Grey and his biographers late in the nineteenth century to make sense of the trajectory of his own life, using what were, by now, highly conventional if markedly quaint literary forms and terms.

The most obvious marker of the evangelical mode in Grey's self-presentation is his oft-repeated expression, particularly in the decades of his life after his imperial civil service had been completed, of an intense personal piety. But in Grey's voice and mind, what one writer would describe as the distinctive traits of the evangelical character and experience, 'a perpetual call to seriousness – to a sense of personal responsibility'[51] was

---

[49] Milne, *The romance of a pro-consul*, p. 29.
[50] See E. Jay, *The religion of the heart: Anglican evangelicalism and the nineteenth-century novel* (Oxford: Clarendon Press, 1979), p. 8, p. 9. The Religious Tract Society alone had circulated 'over 500 million copies of 5,000 separate titles and [by 1849] was issuing tracts from its central repository at the rate of 20 million a year'. I. Bradley, *The call to seriousness: the evangelical impact on the Victorians* (London: Jonathan Cape, 1976), p. 42.
[51] Bradley, *The call to seriousness*, p. 18.

transformed into a powerful sense of divine approval for the imperial mission and the infallibility of his own judgement:

'It was a comfort to me, in trying hours, to feel that I was working according to the way of my Maker, so far as I could comprehend it. Perhaps I most experienced this nearness of an all-wise Providence while I was amid the heathen acres of the far south. You seemed to be communing with the Great Spirit more intimately in those lonely haunts than elsewhere. I have always been supported by the belief in God's goodness, as manifested to me. My judgement is that man cannot prosper if he falls from faith, by which I mean trust in a Supreme Being.'[52]

Ironically it is the very godlessness of the people of the southern lands that allows closer communication with the Christian deity. More usefully for Grey, a person of aristocratic background like himself could overwrite his family legacy of advantage by deploying a narrative instantly recognisable in the late Victorian period, which welcomed the rise of the middle classes: the exemplary life in which effort replaced inheritance; agonised deliberation replaced aristocratic command; and revelation was experienced as a series of revelatory moments in which the distant truth and the rocky path towards it were brilliantly illuminated. It is the kind of life infused, in Matthew Arnold's words, by what was experienced

'as an energy driving at practice, a paramount sense of the obligation to duty, self-control, and work, and an earnestness in going manfully with the best light we have'. Nowhere were those particular attributes more clearly displayed than in the lives and attitudes of those children of Evangelical families who went on to achieve public and intellectual distinction in the nineteenth century.[53]

By telling this kind of story, Grey could literally overwrite his own class background and insert himself into the middle class, monumentalising a 'moment of conversion' to the cause of imperialism and the 'spread of civilisation'.

James Stephen was of the view that

only direct rule by Britain could secure the natives of Africa against slavery and exploitation ... The role of trustee and tutor to native peoples to which the Evangelicals called their countrymen was their most significant contribution to the development of the Victorian imperial idea.[54]

Thus Ian Bradley contends that it was in the arena of imperial policy-making that the evangelical movement had its most distinctive and its

---

[52] Milne, *The romance of a pro-consul*, p. 211. The quotation is in inverted commas, following Milne.
[53] M. Arnold, 'My countrymen' [Preface to *Culture and anarchy*], quoted in Bradley, *The call to seriousness*, p. 195.
[54] *Ibid.*, p. 89.

most powerful effects; indeed it might even be that the 'heathen acres of the far south' offered more fertile fields for the proliferation and enhancement of these narratives than England itself. The flexibility of the imperial vision of spreading civilisation, in terms of its holders' ability to co-opt the language of divine mission, is shown in George Grey's account (as it is presented in Milne), of his decision to set aside the constitution for New Zealand sent by the Colonial Office in 1846, and to draft by himself the charter that would bring the nation into being:

'In the end, when my thoughts had bent to a shape, I went up into the mountains between Auckland and Wellington, camped on Ruapehu, in a little gypsy tent, and set to the task. A few Maoris accompanied me to carry the baggage; nobody else, for I could not have drawn the constitution with a cloud of advisors about me.

'Where did I get my inspiration? Oh, by talking to the hills and trees, from long walks, and many hints from the United States constitution ... '

Sir George held man's highest education to be that, which taught him the rights and duties of citizenship ... Therefore, he conceived the best system of government, to be one wherein the opportunities for the exercise of citizenship were the fullest. What could be more pathetic than the cramping of aspirations, such as had been seen in the case of Ireland?[55]

Rutherford derides this account as 'an old man's humour running to romance', attributing Grey's rejection of the Colonial Office draft – a bold step – to his desire to protect Maori interests.[56] Rutherford is probably right to dismiss such stories as fanciful, but if we stop there, we lose the opportunity to explore the question of why they have so long had such purchase in popular imagination, and from what kind of other narratives they derive. To take the second question first, we can note the parallels between Milne's 1899 account of the circumstances in which the constitution of New Zealand was drafted and J. A. La Nauze's description of the drafting of the Australian constitution in late March 1891, following the convention in Sydney earlier at that month at which Grey had been one of three New Zealand representatives. The drafting committee retreated aboard the steamer *Lucinda*, cruising the waters of Broken Bay and later lying 'at peace in the beautiful waters of the estuary of the

---

[55] Milne, *The romance of a pro-consul*, pp. 117–18.
[56] Rutherford, *Sir George Grey KCB*, p. 143. More skeptical is Henderson, who says that 'Reading between the lines of the dispatches which he wrote before 1850 it would appear that the suspension of the Charter of 1846 was due mainly to his anxiety of the welfare of his native schemes, and for the maintenance of that personal ascendancy which he was rapidly acquiring over the natives themselves', *Sir George Grey*, p. 124.

Hawkesbury River'.[57] Grey's story, more consciously poetical, also recalls
the journeys of Moses to Mount Sinai in the book of Exodus.

More broadly, within the terms of evangelical convention, the trope of
a traumatic and intense experience producing an equally deeply felt
change of heart was easily recognisable: Milne's book is structured around
the 'vivid and compelling personal experiences' which Bradley claims
were markers of the evangelical 'way of life' – moments like Ireland, or
the experience of the New Zealand wilderness.[58] Put another way, Grey
and his hagiographers seem comfortable in making sense of his life in
terms of moments of quasi-spiritual enlightenment in rhetorical terms
that resonated with popular genres.[59] What is perhaps more surprising is
that there is seepage of this narrative mode into the later sources, deepening the grooves carved by evangelical habits of expression. Analysing
Grey's participation in New Zealand politics in the 1870s, Henderson
reminds his reader that 'Before setting out on his expedition to Western
Australia, Grey had served as a military officer in Ireland, and the condition of the peasants had made an indelible impression on his mind.'[60]
And echoing Milne, Rutherford writes (more than half a century later)
that being

Young, sympathetic and highly sensitive, he was deeply touched by the sufferings
of the Irish poor, whom he found half-starved, ill-clad, crowded like animals in
wretched, unfurnished hovels, eking out a meagre subsistence on patches of land
which they occupied on the most precarious of tenure.[61]

Rutherford here replicates – and perhaps magnifies – Grey's distaste for
the poverty of the people over whom he exercises military jurisdiction,
and continues the well-worn story of the horrors that Ireland presents to
the sensitive mind. In doing so, he provides a superb summary of the
classic evangelical response to such scenes, which unhesitatingly coupled
middle-class capitalist aspiration with intensely felt piety in terms that
become almost epic:

The tragic poverty of the Irish peasantry moved Grey to propound the twofold
remedy of colonial emigration and political liberation ... He wished to call in a
new world to redress the social balance of the old. His new-found idealism

---

[57] J. A. La Nauze, *The making of the Australian Constitution* (Melbourne: Melbourne University
Press, 1971), p. 65. La Nauze notes Grey's presence at the convention in Sydney earlier that month,
p. 30. I thank Marion Diamond for noting this similarity in the two stories.
[58] Bradley, *The call to seriousness*, p. 22.
[59] William Rees was a one-time member of the clergy. See T. Brooking, 'Rees, William Lee 1836–
1912' (*Dictionary of New Zealand biography*, at http://www.dnzb.govt.nz/), accessed 7 Dec. 2004.
[60] Henderson, *Sir George Grey*, p. 245.   [61] Rutherford, *Sir George Grey KCB*, p. 6.

revolted against the artificialities and injustices of the older feudalised society, against the tyranny of large landed estates, great capitalist fortunes, wealthy monopolistic institutions in church or state ... New nations should be founded, which should be lands of opportunity where the poorer classes could develop a simpler, happier and more natural life.[62]

EASY LESSONS ON MONEY MATTERS

In explaining the development of views such as these, Grey himself named his three most significant intellectual mentors as Thomas Carlyle, James Stephen and Richard Whately (1787–1863), all of whom he numbered as acquaintances. Carlyle and Stephen I will not consider here; my focus is on Whately, the least historically conspicuous of these figures. Whately was associated with humanitarian advocates of social and political change, although he was by no means an undiluted radical, or even liberal. (In terms of imperial networks, it is worth bearing in mind that the Whately family maintained a lifelong friendship with the family of Thomas Arnold.) And Whately, like Grey, may have felt that he was undertaking a civilising mission when he became archbishop in Dublin – certainly his daughter claimed that it was his sense of 'duty' that impelled him to accept the position.[63] As archbishop he played a central role in various political deliberations and reforms, notably as chair of the Poverty Inquiry Commission of the 1830s, and through his active participation on the Board of Education, which oversaw significant reforms in the administration of education and the development of school curricula.[64]

Whately forms an important part of Grey's network of patronage, in part because of his identification as a moderate and judicious administrator, and in part because of his diverse credentials: professor of political economy at Oxford, archbishop of Dublin, and the author of widely used textbooks. While Whately is spoken of in the various Grey biographies as a magnetic mentor who had a decisive influence on Grey, he seems to have struck many of his contemporaries as abrasive and impatient – his biographer, a colleague and (apparently) a friend, remarks in passing that

---

[62] *Ibid.*, p. 7.
[63] E. J. Whately, *Life and correspondence of Richard Whately, DD, late archbishop of Dublin*, new edition, in one volume (London: Longmans, Green and Co., 1868), p. 59.
[64] See D. H. Akenson, *A Protestant in purgatory: Richard Whately, archbishop of Dublin*, Conference on British Studies Biography Series, Vol. II, New Series (Hamden, CT: Archon Books, for the Conference on British Studies and Indiana University at South Bend, 1981).

'he had not a winning way'.[65] The exact extent of Grey's acquaintance with Whately is unclear: there is no mention in books on Whately of encounters with Grey in Grey's childhood or after, although perhaps that is not surprising given the age difference. Milne refers to a holiday spent together after Grey had fled school, whereas Rees and Rees contend that the two had 'constant intercourse' when they were in Ireland.[66] When Whately arrived in Dublin, around October 1831, the young man whom he had known as a child had been in the country for at least a year. Rees and Rees assert that 'the young soldier was a great favourite with the archbishop, and had every opportunity of profiting by the wise counsels of his illustrious friend', but no other source supports this claim and no evidence is cited.[67] The suggestion that there was some contact in this period is given limited credence by the fact that when Grey returned from his journeys in Australia to oversee the publication of his journal in 1840, Whately wrote to Lord John Russell, then secretary of state for the colonies, to recommend his young relative for a position.[68] Nevertheless, the legend of Whately's influence on the young man, whether as a child of eight, or as a young man in his early twenties, is central to the (re)construction of Grey as a person profoundly influenced by liberal thought, which informed his 'enlightened' view of indigenous peoples of the empire.

The first significant expression of these views comes in George Grey's various publications arising from his time in Western Australia. On completing his journeys of exploration he had received a minor appointment as resident magistrate in Albany, on the southern coast of that colony, after which he returned to England. From his time in Western Australia come the two-volume *Journals*; a *Vocabulary* of Aboriginal languages, initially printed in Perth – dedicated to the Royal Geographical Society, who had sponsored his journeys – with

---

[65] Fitzpatrick, *Memoirs of Richard Whately*, p. 57. For an unashamedly derogatory portrait of Whately as perennially discontented, alienated from his colleagues at Oxford and fearful of assassination in Ireland, see T. Mozley, *Reminiscences chiefly of Oriel College and the Oxford Movement*, 2 vols. (London: Longmans, Green, and Co., 1882), Vol. I, pp. 266–71.

[66] Rees and Rees, *The life and times of George Grey*, p. 10. Milne, *The romance of a pro-consul*, p. 24. Whately is said to have known Grey as a child when both were in Cheltenham, and Whately was courting Elizabeth Pope (Rutherford, *Sir George Grey KCB*, p. 4).

[67] Rees and Rees, *The life and times of George Grey*, p. 12.

[68] Writing to Nassau Senior two years earlier, Whately had speculated that James Stephen had heard of the plans for the systematic colonisation of New Zealand from 'Lieutenant Gray' [*sic*] – the misspelling hints at a more slight acquaintance than Rees and Rees would entertain, although the letter might have been transcribed by one of Whately's staff. See Letter 8 November 1837, in Whately, *Life and correspondence*, p. 134.

a revised and expanded edition subsequently published in London;[69] and a pamphlet, *Report on the best means of promoting the civilization of the aboriginal inhabitants of Australia*, a revised edition of which was published as an appendix to the *Journals*. There is a considerable intellectual energy at work in these publications, and the journals received high-profile and positive reviews. Particular attention was paid to Grey's compassionate views of Aborigines.[70] In a very short time Grey had brought himself to the attention of scholarly readers in the fields of colonialism, geography, anthropology, linguistics and philanthropy – no doubt the 'results, as those the hope of obtaining which has been my sole motive from the beginning of the affair'.

Grey's scheme for 'Promoting the civilization of the aboriginal inhabitants of Australia' made it clear that he was 'laying aside all thought of their amalgamation with Europeans'.[71] But the revolutionary and – to a British audience – radical aspects of his argument were his advocacy of the integration of colonised peoples into the colonialist economy, and of the extension of not simply the responsibilities but the *rights* of life under British law – in short, to make Aborigines British subjects. Certainly Grey showed himself capable of empathy: in recounting the (mis)fortunes of a man who, taken up and then abandoned by white patrons, decided to return to his culture of origin, he says simply and forcefully, 'and I think that I should have done the same'.[72] Crucially, in terms of bolstering the appeal to the evangelical patrons who held sway in the Colonial Office, it was on the basis of this empathy that Grey disputed the practices which assumed the absolute and enduring separation of coloniser and colonised. Perhaps readers like Stephen and Russell chose not to notice that Grey spoke from the position of the anti-evangelical colonist, invoking the authority of the 'man on the spot' who, *contra* metropolitan theory, is able to properly discern what it really is that indigenous peoples need. Grey disputed the views of those who advocate separatism, views which 'originated in philanthropic motives, *and a total ignorance of the peculiar traditional laws of these people*'.[73] He made the classic, colonialist recourse to a 'true humanity' to justify his vision of colonisation, a vision that was given political traction by its moral certainty.[74]

---

[69] G. Grey, Esq, Lieut. 83rd Regiment, *Vocabulary of the dialects spoken by the aboriginal races of SW Australia*. To the President and Members of the Royal Geographical Society (Perth: Printed by C. Macfaull, 1839); G. Grey, *A vocabulary of the dialects of south western Australia*, 2nd edn (London: T. & W. Boone, 1840).
[70] A small collection of reviews, several unsourced, is in the SAPL at G.13.1.17.
[71] Grey, *Journals*, Vol. II, p. 367.   [72] *Ibid.*, p. 371.   [73] *Ibid.*, p. 374. Emphasis added.
[74] *Ibid.*, p. 376.

Grey's 'modest proposal' urged the implementation of a system of indenture which would disperse the task of 'civilising' Aborigines across the colony, delegating it to colonists who would employ and 'train' individuals. Where there are towns, Aborigines should be gathered together and employed in building or repairing roads; institutions for education and medical care should also be accessible.[75] The complete ignorance of, or disregard for, Aboriginal cultural values, in which relationships to kin and place are primary, is staggering. But Grey argues that the dearth of labour in the Australian colonies provides the British imperial authorities with an almost unsurpassed opportunity 'for the development of the better qualities of the Aborigines, and ... so fair a chance of their ultimate civilization'.[76] His key point is that Aboriginal economies are not organised in such a way as to motivate individuals to produce a surplus, and condemns the 'evil consequence' of 'a native finding he can gain as much by the combined methods of hunting and begging, as he can by working', finding the former a 'much more attractive mode of procuring subsistence'.[77] By way of contrast, if Aborigines can be employed in labour on public works and paid fairly and promptly – a programme which he claimed to have begun in a modest way in Albany – they would quickly learn the value of money and the benefits of participating in a capitalist economy.

The influence of Grey's plan for indigenous peoples has been debated, but it certainly added lustre and complication to his reputation, its political economy read as philanthropy. The biographies claim that, from the sending of that document came a personal meeting with Russell, and (with the support of James Stephen), Grey's appointment as governor of South Australia.[78] Stephen's support seems to have been fortified by having met Grey in late 1836, when he was arranging his journeys of exploration. In Cameron's words, Stephen 'later confessed to being captivated by Grey's enthusiasm, enterprise and intellect'.[79] It was surely his seemingly *practical* approach to the problem of implementing an evangelical agenda in hitherto 'recalcitrant' colonial and indigenous populations that was so eye-catching to a Colonial Office which, in the 1830s and 40s, struggled to find policies informed by evangelical sympathies, let alone the people to implement them effectively. But I want to try and reconnect the arguments of this 'founding document' of Grey's

---

[75] *Ibid.*, p. 386.   [76] *Ibid.*, p. 365.   [77] *Ibid.*, p. 368.
[78] Henderson, *Sir George Grey*, pp. 38–40; Rutherford, *Sir George Grey KCB*, pp. 19–20.
[79] J. M. R. Cameron, citing Colonial Office records, in his 'George Grey goes exploring', p. 51.

views on race with his claim to have been influenced by archbishop Richard Whately, and in doing so to examine more closely the terms of Grey's reputed humanitarianism.

One of Whately's best-known publications was a small primer on money management. *Easy lessons on money matters, for the use of young people* appeared in 1837, the year Grey first came to Australia.[80] That Grey was an aficionado of Whately's voluminous other writing is difficult to substantiate: the Auckland city library and the South African public library in Cape Town have relatively few of Whately's later publications. But what each library *does* have is a copy of *He pukapuka ako tenei i nga ritenga pai e-maha, o roto o te taonga nei o te moni, i nga tikanga pai hoki, o te hokohoko, o te aha, o te aha* – Whately's primer on *Money matters*, 'Translated into the New Zealand language, under the direction of the government' by H. T. Kemp, at the instruction of George Grey, and 'published under the direction of the Committee of General Literature and Education, appointed by the Society for Promoting Christian Knowledge'.[81]

What effect might the circulation of such a document have had in New Zealand? By the mid-1850s, Maori traders were responsible for some fifty per cent of New Zealand's exports, and had a major role in shipping and flour milling.[82] They were, in other words, playing a central role in the colonial economy. Two explanations are possible: that Whately's words had been used to extraordinarily good effect, or, that the Maori traders had no particular need of Whately's 'easy lessons'. Certainly Whately himself was of the former view, proudly writing to Mrs Thomas Arnold that 'I forgot whether I told you that Governor Grey has sent me some copies of a translation into Maori of the "Lessons on Money Matters," which he says has proved highly acceptable to the natives'.[83] Thus Whately, and Grey, could claim – not least in their own minds – to have been instrumental in the spread of a form of political philosophy and practical financial advice from Oxford, via Dublin, to the very ends of the earth, and in the commensurate transformation of 'a race of men' from

---

[80] COPAC (Britain) lists an enlarged edition (1835), a third (1836), sixth (1842), twelfth (1850), fourteenth (1855), fifteenth (1858) and sixteenth (1862).

[81] Kemp also translated *Pilgrim's progress* and *Robinson Crusoe* at Grey's request. The information on the translation of Whately's book comes from the ACL catalogue entry. Information on translations comes from Rutherford, *Sir George Grey KCB*, p. 277, and is confirmed by the ACL catalogue.

[82] S. Webster, 'Maori *Hapu* as a whole way of struggle: 1840s–50s before the Land Wars', *Oceania* **69**, 4 (1998), pp. 23–4, p. 21.

[83] Whately, *Life and correspondence*, p. 297. See also Akenson, *A Protestant in purgatory*, p. 179.

'savagery to civilization'.[84] The very act of having the pamphlet translated is indicative of Grey's view that it was possible, and highly desirable, to integrate colonised people into the lower rungs of a capitalist economy. It was the 'radical' alternative to extermination.

Whately's modern biographer Donald Akenson argues that Whately's primer of political economy – which endorsed frugality, self-discipline and the intrinsic moral value of labour, and which emphasised the devolution of economic responsibility onto the individual – allows us to understand what otherwise seems like the striking contradiction between private generosity and public stringency which marked Richard Whately (and George Grey). Whately is estimated to have given many thousands of pounds to individuals, while Grey's immense personal generosity was demonstrated in his use of his own income to alleviate distress in several colonies and in his massive donations of books to found libraries in Auckland and Cape Town. But each was also determined never to allow this private generosity to inform public policy, and indeed, this apparent contradiction was a matter of considerable personal pride to both. Their 'liberal' views were manifested (only) in their belief that policy could and indeed must be used to increase employment in times of hardship. Hence both were strong advocates of extensive programmes of public works[85] – indeed such a programme was at the heart of Grey's 'new' policy for indigenous peoples.

Such welfare-driven policy could coexist with faith in the value of the free market – of goods and of labour. Such views, indeed, are a commonplace of modern economics. And they are perhaps not the only lesson that Grey took from Whately and his time in Ireland. Whately's 'Poverty Inquiry' had recommended a set of measures which were to find parallels in Grey's actions in New Zealand and, particularly, in the Cape colony and the region known as 'British Kaffraria'. R. B. McDowell reports that the commissioners' plans, outlined in the report of 1836 (which was largely drafted by Whately), were 'bold' ones, establishing a board to 'plan and supervise wide schemes of national improvement': 'The board was to partition and improve waste lands by drainage, road building and fencing on a large scale', while also overseeing local institutions which would provide care for 'the infirm, sick, aged and lunatic

---

[84] Akenson points out the mind-boggling scale of the distribution of Whately's writings; he estimates that Whately's theories of political economy were disseminated to millions of schoolchildren in Britain and beyond during the nineteenth century. See *A Protestant in purgatory*, p. 179.

[85] *Ibid.*, p. 128.

poor'.[86] Whately himself made clear the connection that he saw between integration into the economy and the extension of political control, when he explained what happened when colonising powers *neglected* their obligation to impose civilisation:

I have remarked in the Lectures on Political Economy (Lect. 5), that the descriptions some writers give of the Civilization of Mankind, by the spontaneous origin, among tribes of Savages, of the various arts of life, one by one, are to be regarded as wholly imaginary, and not agreeing with anything that ever did, or can, actually take place. Numerous are the accounts we have, of Savages who have *not* received such aid, we do not hear, in any one instance, of their having ceased to be Savages.[87]

George Grey's statement of his intentions in relation to the various indigenous peoples of the Cape Colony and 'British Kaffraria' to the secretary for the colonies shows various similarities with Whately's programme for Ireland. He plans

to attempt to gain an influence over all the Tribes included between the present North Eastern boundary of this Colony and Natal, by employing them upon public works which will tend to open up their country, by establishing Institutions for the education of their children, and the relief of their sick, by introducing among them institutions of a civil character suited to their present condition, and by these and other like means to attempt gradually to win them to civilisation and Christianity, and thus to change by degrees our at present unconquered and apparently unreclaimable foes, into friends who may have common interests with ourselves.[88]

Both Whately and Grey envisioned the creation of a literate labouring class whose very education and labour would ensure moral improvement and commitment to imperial ideology – what Antonio Gramsci would later call hegemony. Translated to the colonial context, such policies aim at the deliberate creation, on the basis of race, of a perpetual servant class.

There is a coda to this argument about Whately's influence on Grey. As well as being the author of works on political economy, Whately also wrote two textbooks, on rhetoric and on logic. The remark in Whately's preface to his *Elements of rhetoric* that 'A brief outline of the principal part of the following Work was sketched out several years ago for the private

[86] R. B. McDowell, *Public opinion and government policy in Ireland* (London: Faber and Faber, 1952), p. 192.

[87] R. Whately, *Elements of rhetoric: comprising an analysis of the laws of moral evidence and of persuasion, with rules for argumentative composition and elocution*, D. Ehringer (ed.), 7th edition (Carbondale: Southern Illinois University Press, 1963), p. 71.

[88] George Grey, Dispatch, 22 December 1854, Colonial Office 48/361, quoted in Rutherford, *Sir George Grey KCB*, p. 313.

use of some young friends', and the frequent occurrence of a set of highly stylised rhetorical flourishes in Grey's dispatch writing, offers the intriguing possibility that Grey was a dedicated student of Whately's lessons on rhetoric.[89] Whately's firm prescription was that any writer must bear in mind that

The process of *investigation* must be supposed completed, and certain conclusions arrived at by that process, *before* [the writer] begins to impart his ideas to others in a treatise or lecture; the object of which must of course be to *prove* the justness of those conclusions.[90]

This seems remarkably similar to Grey's claim, in Milne, that a 'man's responsibility, in the largest sense, is, after adequate deliberation, to proceed as he determines to be just and wise'.[91] And the many trenchant critics of Grey's dissembling in dispatches might ponder Whately's view that a writer or speaker

will not always find it expedient to adhere to the same course of reasoning by which his own discoveries were originally made; other arguments may occur to him afterwards, more clear, or more concise, *or better adapted to the understanding of those he addresses.*[92]

ARE WE THERE YET?

Only by excavating the tropes of nineteenth-century language can we start reconstructing the immigrant's psychic and mental maps and relating them to the new landscape.[93]

This evocative and provocative comment comes from Erik Olssen's essay 'Where to from here'. When considering the ways in which Grey translated his policies from colony to colony and drew on his experience of 'other' places, it is worth bearing in mind that ideas can be taken up in ways quite unexpected by those who initially espouse them, and that Grey's 'psychic and mental map' was related not so much to new landscapes as to indigenous societies which, fatally, he 'recognised' as 'Irish'. Translating these events into narrative, late in his life, George Grey made flexible and powerful use of conventions for the expression of humanitarian feeling, as he spoke and wrote with a keen eye to what history would make of his actions.

---

[89] R. Whately, *Elements of rhetoric*, p. xxxiii.   [90] *Ibid.*, p. 5.
[91] Milne, *The romance of a pro-consul*, p. 115.   [92] Whately, *Elements of rhetoric*, p. 5.
[93] E. Olssen, 'Where to from here: reflections on the twentieth-century historiography of nineteenth-century New Zealand', *New Zealand Journal of History* **26**, 1 (1992), pp. 54–77, p. 73.

I have suggested that we must renew our skepticism of the scholarly record, paradoxically by bringing back into focus the apocryphal sources on Grey and his life, and asking what purposes they served and to which readerships they spoke. This will allow us to identify connections between place and policy that we might otherwise find merely ironic:

> One of [Grey's] first actions on reaching the frontier [in the eastern Cape] in 1857 was to cause Maclean to issue a Government Notice ... ordering four ... thieves caught on the Crown Reserve to be transported, announcing that persons convicted of armed robbery would be punished by death, and warning the chiefs that marauders would be fired upon. Thus was British law to supersede Kafir custom. It came in the form of martial law and read like an Irish coercion act.[94]

As his tone indicates, Rutherford here sees Grey's actions as further indication of his hypocrisy; but perhaps Ireland, that place of magical transformation, was at the heart not only of Grey's personal development, but the development of his notions of policy. For in fact, *contra* the constant assertions as to the centrality of Ireland in his personal development, I can find no evidence, in his own writing, that his 'radical' views impinged on Grey's own political consciousness before his return to England in 1868, at the end of his career as a colonial governor – although perhaps only a complete fool would ever have committed such views to paper, and Grey was far from that.

In the two years in which he remained resident in England in the late 1860s, there is ample evidence that Grey became concerned about the issues raised by self-government and Ireland. But these issues had been commonplace ones in each of the colonies in which he had served. Paradoxically, the suppleness of Grey's political values enabled him to apply, subsequently, to Ireland the ideas from campaigns for colonial self-government that he had so determinedly and effectively resisted in his time as governor, particularly in South Africa and New Zealand: we can contend that by now, the colonies influenced his political views on Ireland. The traffic in public policy flowed both ways. And we do not always need the sometimes speculative apparatus that I've developed in this essay to call the biographical fact of Grey's 'Irish experience' into question. We need only to consider George Henderson's remark that 'At the age of twenty-four there was every indication that the young lieutenant would make his way in the service, and attain distinctions that would do credit to the memory of his gallant father'.[95] Henderson, perhaps the most

---

[94] Rutherford, *Sir George Grey KCB*, p. 365. [95] Henderson, *Sir George Grey*, pp. 24–5.

committed imperialist of all the biographers, saw logic and continuity in Grey's move from active service to Sandhurst, in furthering his military career.

Why Ireland? Ireland stands in complex relationship to the more widely recognised parts of the British empire, its colonisation so long sustained, and so tightly woven into the political and cultural fabric that it can be difficult to recognise the ways in which it might be part of the imperial network. Ireland offered a young George Grey not only a model of political intervention, but a model of racial prejudice, of political domination, of land seizure and cultural genocide. It is probably unnecessarily unkind to suggest that in Grey's memoirs, as transcribed by Milne, occasional correspondents became chums and long-time intellectual companions; luminaries of the age became patrons and mentors; great events of history became the backdrop to his own personal development: such claims are difficult to substantiate because of the relative lack of personal correspondence preserved in the otherwise voluminous Grey records. Certainly Grey's web of correspondents and confidantes seems to have sustained him early in his career materially, and later through the ways in which he memorialised those connections. In the terms of enquiry established by this volume, we can see that Grey did not so much adapt in response to particular situations – take with him lessons from one place to another – as he claimed to have done, but rather that he laid over each colonial place the ideas about 'native peoples' that were part of his general philosophy of the relationship between society and the individual, views which gave primacy to instilling a rudimentary version of middle-class notions of self-help. It is the same paradigm that is underpinning current federal government policy towards indigenous peoples in Australia. And (one might argue, like John Howard's current Australian government), Grey's views can be seen to harden into calculated self-interest and naked ambition not in response to changing ideologies of race, but in response to opportunities provided by defeats, or weakenings in the resistance, of colonised peoples, and changing tides of public opinion which he himself helped to direct. It is crucial to our understanding of the atrocity that is imperialism that we do not attribute these actions to an aberration of personality, that we do not see an authoritarian or duplicitous personality as a *disruption* to the processes of conquest and domination. Chillingly, what we can most properly take at face value is Grey's oft-repeated contention that he acted only after careful deliberation as to the best line of policy. Grey's commitment to the authority of his own judgement found echo in the methods of

Whately's rhetoric and of his logic, and in the evangelical philosophies that infused the world in which he grew up, and which find renewed vigour in our own time. Perhaps it is not so much George Grey who should be the target of our skepticism as the more general will to good will, the desire for the *appearance* of kindness.

The historiography of George Grey too often turns to personality to explain invasion, duplicity, annihilation and assimilation, as though these practices were somehow aberrant in, rather than intrinsic to, imperialism. Such tricks of mind leave intact in our imaginations (and in the world at large) the same edifices of belief – in civilisation, in capitalism, in the individual and the power of their conscience – that enable and condone conquest through physical and cultural violence. In this essay I have tried to restore some historical context to the writing of the histories of George Grey: the importance of Ireland as a trope of specifically colonial origins; the tropes and conventions of evangelical writing; popularised notions of political economy which to this day inform common-sense under-standings of the relationship between the individual and society, and of model citizenship and proper forms of aspiration; and the centralising of personality in imperialist biography, for each of these ways of thinking about George Grey has seeped into the foundations of accounts of his-torical events. And I have tried to suggest that networks need to be understood as working not only in a material sense, nor in terms of ecologies of values, but in terms of narratives and their conventions, shaping our readings of history through invisible because habitual practices of reading and interpretation. For at times it seems that the intertwining stories of George Grey have become so dense that even the most hostile critics of his life and work are yet trapped within the textual webs that he himself spun, late in his life, to defend and to define his reputation as the greatest imperial administrator of the Victorian age.

CHAPTER 6

Wonderful adventures of Mrs Seacole in many lands (1857): colonial identity and the geographical imagination

Anita Rupprecht

INTRODUCTION

Mary Seacole (Fig. 6.1), a Jamaican creole 'doctress' of mixed race, arrived in London in October 1854.[1] It was at the height of a public outcry over the condition of the British army in the Crimea. The first detachments of troops had departed in February. By early autumn, the public learned that the soldiers stationed on the Bulgarian coast were suffering from malaria and cholera. Already in poor health, they experienced heavy losses in the first military campaigns. Subsequently, they became entrenched for the winter in Balaclava without adequate protection from the severe weather or a reliable supply system. The public outcry produced a governmental crisis, and, in January 1855, a motion to enquire into the condition of the army and the supply services had the support of a large majority in parliament. Aberdeen resigned, and Palmerston became prime minister.[2] The enquiry went ahead, and the British army received

---

[1] Seacole represents herself as a 'Creole' in her autobiography. The shifting meanings of the word 'creole' reflect the complex historical and cultural transformations of the Caribbean as migrants, forced and free, came to claim the region as their own, and to see themselves as belonging to it. Originally a term differentiating white settlers born in the Caribbean from their European-born counterparts, it was rearticulated in the eighteenth century by Caribbean-born slaves and free people of colour as a way of distinguishing themselves from newly arrived Africans. See, Edward Kamau Brathwaite's *The development of creole society in Jamaica, 1770–1820* (Oxford: Oxford University Press, 1971) that has established the centrality of the term to Caribbean intellectual life. For the development of the term in relation to the complexity of Caribbean slave societies see amongst others, David Lambert, *White creole culture, politics and identity during the Age of Abolition* (Cambridge: Cambridge University Press, 2005); Gad J. Heuman, *Between black and white: race, politics and free coloureds of Jamaica, 1792–1865* (Westport, CT: Greenwood, 1981); Hilary Beckles, 'On the back of blacks: the Barbados free coloureds': pursuit of civil rights and the 1816 slave rebellion', *Immigrants and Minorities* 3, 2 (1984), pp. 167–88; and Arnold A. Sio, 'Marginality and free coloured identity in Caribbean slave society', in G. Heuman and J. Walvin (eds.), *The slavery reader* (London: Routledge, 2003), pp. 668–81.

[2] The *Times* ended its support for the war in early 1855. It reported: 'If government ... choose[s] to sell themselves to the aristocracy, and through the aristocracy to their enemies, it is their own affair; we wipe our hands of the national suicide.' Matthew Paul Lalumia, *Realism and politics in Victorian art of the Crimean War* (Ann Arbor: UMI Research Press, 1984), p. 52.

Fig. 6.1 Mary Seacole painted in 1869 by London artist Albert Charles Challen. This is the only known portrait of Mary Seacole. She is pictured wearing a red creole scarf and the three medals awarded for her services to the military in the Crimea. Courtesy of Helen Rappaport/National Portrait Gallery, London.

renewed support.[3] The *Times* had set up a fund for public contributions, and the government acceded to demands for more female nurses, an initiative to match the French Sisters of Charity. The Catholic Church had already responded by sending their Sisters of Mercy, and the officially organised party headed by Florence Nightingale was now to be extended. Seacole's plan was to volunteer her services to this nursing delegation.

---

[3] For a useful overview of the Crimean campaign, public opinion and the ensuing reform of the British army and navy, see E. L. Woodward, *The Age of Reform: 1815–1870* (Oxford: Clarendon Press, 1938), pp. 242–84. For historical background on the Crimean War, see amongst others David M. Goldfrank, *The origins of the Crimean War* (London: Longman, 1994); Trevor Royle, *Crimea: the great Crimean War 1854–1856* (London: Little, Brown and Co., 1996).

Seacole approached the War Office, the quartermaster general, the medical department where Elizabeth Herbert was recruiting for Nightingale, and finally the Crimean Fund in the hope of a free passage. All official parties rejected her applications. She recorded her disappointment in an autobiography, *The wonderful adventures of Mrs Seacole in many lands*, published in London in 1857. 'Was it possible that American prejudices against colour had some root here? Did these ladies shrink from accepting my aid because my blood flowed beneath a somewhat duskier skin than theirs?'[4] It was almost certainly not Seacole's colour that caused her to be turned down, or more specifically, not only her colour. The selection process was carried out by the wives of government ministers, and based on metropolitan class hierarchy.[5] Herbert was recruiting middle-class 'lady volunteers' to bring order and discipline to the overcrowded Crimean hospitals. It was understood that feminine moral and spiritual authority could only be exported if nursing was kept free from the corrupting influence of paid-wage labour. Given this remit, it was virtually impossible for previous experience to be a criterion for acceptance as a 'volunteer'. Herbert was also struggling to recruit working-class nurses, and the issue of wages served as one way of marking the ranks.[6] Seacole, a middle-aged Jamaican woman who had just spent three years carving an independent living as a private medical practitioner and hotelier in the central American jungle, simply could not qualify as a 'lady volunteer'.

Seacole was carrying several letters of reference. One was from the 'Late Medical Officer' of the West Granada Gold-mining Company, though it is unclear if anyone read it. The document is included in *Wonderful adventures*. It testifies to the fact that Seacole had official connections: the writer claims to have been introduced to her through the consul at Colon on the isthmus. He confirms 'her professional zeal and ability in the treatment of aggravated forms of tropical diseases', stressing the point by noting that she was more able than other local practitioners who had 'qualified in the North' (pp. 123–4).

---

[4] Mary Seacole, *Wonderful adventures of Mrs Seacole in many lands*, [1857], Ziggi Alexander and Audrey Dewjee (eds.) (Bristol: Falling Wall Press, 1984), p. 126. All subsequent references to this edition are cited in the text.

[5] For an analysis of the way class was the principal determining factor in the selection of paid nurses and 'lady volunteers', see Anne Summers, 'Pride and prejudice: ladies and nurses in the Crimean War', *History Workshop Journal* 16 (1983), pp. 32–54. See also Summers' later study, *Angels and citizens: British women as military nurses 1854–1914* (London and New York: Routledge & Kegan Paul, 1988), pp. 26–66.

[6] See Ziggi Alexander and Audrey Dewjee's 'Introduction' to *Wonderful adventures*, pp. 17–29.

The stark contradiction between the letter of reference and Seacole's failure to be recruited by the British state institutions can be understood in relation to what Ann Laura Stoler and Frederick Cooper have broadly termed 'colonial culture in a bourgeois world'. That is to say, the event and the document occupy a 'shared but differentiated space of empire' where new 'hierarchies of production, power, and knowledge . . . emerged in tension with the extension of the domain of universal reason, of market economics, and of citizenship'.[7] Seacole's autobiography tells a British reading public the story of how she negotiated the terms of this tension in order to fulfil her ambition. She did eventually travel to the Crimea but it was the market, rather than state sponsorship, that mediated her journey. Once in the Crimea, she combined commercial enterprise with imperial duty, and became a popular heroine after the war. The fact that she had performed a socially useful act that was nonetheless supported by a commercial network ensured her fame. It also spoke to the shifting values of the mid-nineteenth century.

Seacole's popular celebrity coincided with her financial ruin, and she published *Wonderful adventures* for money. William H. Russell, the celebrated *Times* war correspondent wrote her 'Preface'. He remarked:

If singleness of heart, true charity, and Christian works; if trials and sufferings, dangers and perils, encountered boldly by a helpless woman on her errand of mercy in the camp and in the battle-field, can excite sympathy or move curiosity, Mary Seacole will have many friends and many readers [p. 49].

The rhetoric is unsurprisingly sentimental. The claim, however, that Seacole will either 'excite sympathy' or 'move curiosity' highlights the complex position Seacole occupied in relation to her reading audience. Russell's phrasing identifies her femininity as the locus for admiration but it also refers to the codification of colonial intimacy via shifting conceptualisations of identity and difference. In fact, Seacole's autobiographical representation of her extraordinary career consistently complicates that crude conceptual binary in ways that offer a powerful critique of any transcendent colonial determination of her 'character'.[8] Instead, her implication within, and dependence upon, the commercial and military networks that mapped the unlikely route from the

---

[7] Ann Laura Stoler and Frederick Cooper (eds.), *Tensions of empire: colonial categories in a bourgeois world* (Berkeley: University of California Press, 1997), p. 3.

[8] Rhonda Frederick, 'Creole performance in *Wonderful adventures of Mrs Seacole in many lands*', *Gender and History*, **15**, 3 (2003), pp. 487–506, also argues that Seacole's autobiography complicates the reductive binaries that structure cultural categories. She focuses on the way that Seacole negotiates them with particular reference to the black/white binary associated with racial difference.

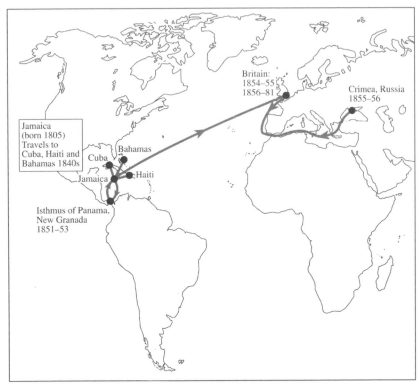

Map 6.1 Mary Seacole's imperial career and major sites of dwelling.

Caribbean to the Crimea mean that her diasporic identity is produced via a set of complex relational dynamics associated with her cross-continental mobility (see Map 6.1).

Wonderful adventures includes a brief account of Seacole's early life in Jamaica, a period spent in central America and finally, via London, her experiences in the Crimea. The text dramatises her journey, therefore, through some of the most contested sites of distant European empire building, revealing the ways in which the three destinations were connected by the globalising forces of nineteenth-century, geopolitically oriented, imperial power relations. In many ways, Seacole's itinerary was enabled by the fact that Jamaica, central America, and the Crimea were characterised by historically contingent concentrations of highly differentiated constituencies brought together in specific circumstances. Each place offered a temporary context where the mobility of colonial culture provided unique opportunities for self-making. Nevertheless, while the sugar colony, the ex-colonial frontier, and the European war zone were linked within global, militarised networks, they were also characterised by radically variant power relations. In these terms, reading Seacole's autobiography contextually, historically and spatially reveals the geographically and temporally discontinuous sets of criteria that were used to define access to privilege in various commercial and imperial ventures. After all, it seemed that Seacole had to prove herself abroad, in the service of the empire to which she belonged, before she could be recognised at 'home'.

In the early nineteenth century, De Pradt, an archbishop and *philosophe* of Napoleon's empire observed that 'as England has adopted the most ingenious mechanical improvements, almost all of the world' has been 'changed into an empire the more powerful too, the more it is voluntary'.[9] Colonial ideologies of voluntary subjecthood were differently constituted given the diversity of colonial projects prosecuted by the British during the nineteenth century. Seacole's own imperial affiliation can be understood in relation to the consolidation of a distinctive creole identity among free coloured people in the Caribbean during the period of slavery.

CREOLE JAMAICA

As one of England's oldest and richest colonies, Jamaica was pivotal within the global commercial and maritime networks that sustained English economic superiority. Catherine Hall's description of the island as 'that sugar-laden extension of the metropolis' highlights the intimacy of the exchanges between the imperial centre and the colony, while the differentiations of race, class, origin, language, religion and politics which characterised island society were the result of multiple convergences of identities from across the world.[10] Social relations were marshalled by a colonial assembly often at odds with London and by the everyday violence of slavery, and were underscored by the antagonisms, affiliations and dependencies associated with licit and illicit commercial opportunism.

Like Britain, colonial Jamaica was a world of exceptional social complexity. Metropolitan Victorians were obsessed with the terms of social status as changes in social identity brought about by the Industrial Revolution collided with an elaborate and pre-existing hierarchy of ranks

---

[9] Dominique Dufour de Pradt, *The colonies, and the present American Revolutions* (London: 1817), p. 121.

[10] Catherine Hall, *Civilising subjects: metropole and colony in the English imagination 1830–1867* (Cambridge: Polity, 2002), p. 70.

and orders. In this highly mobile social context, the contingent relations between how an individual appeared, what they did, and who they were, were endlessly debated. Similar anxieties and obsessions dominated the critical space of the colony; the meanings and mutable significances of social station, licence and legitimacy were, however, further magnified by the fact of minority white rule. 'Race' could be interpreted through a variety of categories such as country of origin, language, religion, property ownership, and political rights as well as by the immediate visibility of skin colour. The historical legacy of custom, tradition and interaction meant that skin colour or 'appearance' alone did not always act as a reliable or sufficient marker of identity. As in Britain, normative identities were stabilised via the demand that outer appearance marked an internal difference of 'character'. In this way differences could be secured between black and white, English and Scot, missionary and merchant.

And yet the cultural hybridities born, at least, from the conjunction and cross-fertilisation of African, European and indigenous social practices opened up possibilities for the everyday subversion of racialised social categories. The temporal and spatial dimensions of identity formation were contested, or reconfigured as unequally positioned individuals engaged with each other in activities such as exploiting cultural capital, currying favour, 'going native', maintaining customer relations, getting married, plotting insurrection, or simply scraping a living. In this fragile and often violent colonial context, familial networks, customer bases, established reputation, and community contacts were important sources of security, identification and imagined possibility.

Jamaica had the largest population of free people of colour in the British colonies.[11] As a group they were denied basic civil and political rights. While some had managed to secure financial status either through inheritance from white planters or successful entrepreneurship, most operated at the edges of the colonial economy. Gravitating towards the economic opportunities offered by the urban centres, they formed a significant segment of the artisan, small trading and crafts communities.

Despite their marginality, creoles established, over time, a sense of their own origin, and a settled history. As Arnold Sio notes, although they were caught in ambiguous social positions that directly complicated colonial determination, the idea that creoles were 'genuinely indigenous to the

[11] See Edward Kamau Brathwaite, *Contradictory omens: cultural diversity and integration in the Caribbean* (Mona, Jamaica: Savacou Publications, 1974); Barry Higman, *Slave population and economy of Jamaica, 1807–1834* (Cambridge: Cambridge University Press, 1976); and Gad J. Heuman, *Between black and white*, pp. 3–20.

area' stabilised a sense of collective identity.[12] In this way they were able to distance themselves from the dispossessed slaves, while whites could be regarded as 'alien' or 'transient' or as foreign interlopers not only to individual islands but also to the Caribbean as a whole.[13]

Territorial affiliation alone, however, did not counter the social and political exclusions of a racially stratified society bolstered by law. Between 1813 and 1830, those creoles who could do so campaigned for the civil and political rights of citizenship withheld by the Jamaican assembly but championed in the 'mother country'.[14] The rights of creoles also became a focus for metropolitan reformists whose opposition to the colour prejudices of slave society formed part of the 'gradualist' lobby.[15] During the deepening crisis over abolition, the assembly attempted to embrace the creole population by granting the 'same rights, privileges, immunities, and advantages' to 'all free blacks and browns' as those attached to white men.[16] The imperial/colonial fracture remained, however, and creoles continued to express their imperial loyalty by supporting full emancipation.

The metropolitan allegiance achieved within the context of the abolition campaign and the subsequent emancipation period, was uneven and gendered. Only élite creole males who were educated and propertied would have been able to petition for political rights. Women largely remained in economically dependent positions, and were vulnerable to sexual exploitation. Nevertheless, Seacole grew up in a context that saw the consolidation of a specifically creole identity that encapsulated a strong sense of homeland, cultural confidence, *and* a sense of imperial affiliation.

Seacole's more personal identifications extend from her confident possession of a sense of place as an hotelier and 'doctress'. Jamaican lodging houses, inns and taverns provided localised contexts for the magnification of colonial intimacies and boundary crossings. Traditionally run by creole and black women, they catered for a cosmopolitan array

---

[12] Arnold A. Sio, 'Marginality and free coloured identity in Caribbean slave society', p. 673.

[13] David Lambert, *White creole culture*.

[14] Mavis C. Campbell, *The dynamics of change in a slave society: a sociopolitical history of the free coloureds of Jamaica, 1800–1865* (London: Associated University Presses, 1976); and Gad J. Heuman, *Between black and white*.

[15] Edith Hurwitz, *Politics and the public conscience: slave emancipation and the Abolitionist Movement in Britain* (London: Allen and Unwin, 1973); Robin Blackburn, *The overthrow of colonial slavery 1776–1848* (London: Verso, 1988), pp. 419–72; Thomas C. Holt, *The problem of freedom: race, labour and politics in Jamaica and Britain, 1832–1838* (Baltimore: Johns Hopkins University Press, 1992).

[16] Mavis C. Campbell, *Dynamics of change*, p. 140.

of merchants, civil servants, travellers and military personnel on an everyday basis.[17] The women who ran these houses inhabited complex social situations. Selling domestic comforts, and often administering medical care, to a transient, largely white male crowd, they would have found that the boundaries between business, entertainment and dependency were easily blurred. As Paulette Kerr notes, evidence that might provide an insight into the everyday relations between creole women lodging-house keepers and their clients is limited.[18] In this sense, Seacole's autobiographical accounts of her familial inheritance and her early socialisation within creole boarding-house culture are significant despite, or perhaps because of, their brevity.

The context within which Seacole eventually wrote the autobiography may have been partially responsible for her silences. Popular metropolitan imaginings of the Caribbean shifted in the wake of emancipation. The sharp decline of the sugar economy contributed, in part, to the perception that ex-slaves had not been successfully transformed into willing colonial subjects. Debates were reactivated concerning the connections between labour discipline, social improvability and the question of racial inheritance.[19] For example, Carlyle's infamous 'Essay on the nigger question', published in 1849, lambasted the liberal 'Exeter Hall' lobby for their hypocritical philanthropic optimism.[20] The article was an extreme piece of vitriol aimed at those political economists who supported the universal tenets of free wage labour. But the specific direction of Carlyle's argument to the Caribbean situation powerfully reinforced stereotypical assumptions about 'lazy blacks' whether they had been enslaved or not.[21] New scientific theorisations of inherent racial difference were also bleeding into the popular imagination through the dramatic expansion of the print

---

[17] Aleric Josephs, 'Mary Seacole: Jamaica nurse and doctress, 1805/10–1881', *Jamaican Historical Review* **17** (1991), pp. 48–65; Paulette A. Kerr, 'Victims or strategists? Female lodging-house keepers in Jamaica', in V. Shepherd, B. Brereton and B. Bailey (eds.), *Engendering history: Caribbean women in historical perspective* (New York: St Martin's Press, 1995), pp. 197–212.

[18] Paulette A. Kerr, p. 198.

[19] Thomas C. Holt, 'The essence of contract: the articulation of race, gender, and political economy in British emancipation policy, 1838–1866', in F. Cooper, T. C. Holt and R. J. Scott (eds.), *Beyond slavery: explorations of race, labour and citizenship in postemancipation societies* (Chapel Hill: University of North Carolina Press, 2000), pp. 33–60.

[20] Thomas Carlyle, 'Occasional discourse on the nigger question', in *Critical and miscellaneous essays* Vol. VI (London: Chapman and Hall, 1869), pp. 183–240. First published in *Fraser's Magazine*, December, 1849 and reprinted as a separate pamphlet in London in 1853.

[21] For discussions of Carlyle's essay, see Simon Gikandi, *Maps of Englishness: writing identity in the culture of colonialism* (New York: Columbia University Press, 1996), pp. 57–68; Catherine Hall, *Civilising subjects*, pp. 349–54, 378–9; and David Theo Goldberg, *The racial state* (Oxford: Blackwell, 2002), pp. 57–73.

media. There were also renewed anxieties about the consequences of racial miscegenation. Not only did it bespeak sexual impropriety in the colonies but fears were also expressed concerning the dissipation of English national vitality both in terms of blood and property.[22]

It is impossible to say just how far these circulating debates influenced Seacole's narrative self-representation. The opening paragraphs of *Wonderful adventures*, however, lay claim to a West Indian creole heritage at the same time as offering a complex corrective to any easy assumptions that a British readership may have made about the racial provenance of Seacole's 'character'. She declares that she is a creole *and* that she has 'good Scotch blood' coursing through her veins. Countering any theory of racial degeneracy, Seacole also refers her readers to the complexity behind any straightforward link between whiteness and metropolitan imperial identity. The Scots remained at one remove from the idealised norm at the same time as they were accommodated within the image of Anglo-Saxon imperialism, particularly when figured as successful settlers or as a loyal colonial military. Although her father was 'a soldier of an old Scotch family', she makes no allusion to the circumstances of the private relationship between her mother and her father (p. 55). She notes that her early years were spent in the care of an 'old lady' but discreetly offers no explanation for why this might have been the case.

Setting the scene for her Crimean heroism, Seacole states that she owes to her father her enduring 'affection for a camp-life' and 'sympathy' for what she has 'heard her friends call the pomp, pride, and circumstance of glorious war'. As this statement illustrates, the socially produced dimensions of her self-image complicate the notion of biological imprint as she alludes to observations that others have made of her. Distancing herself from the white myth of native 'laziness', she continues:

Many people have also traced to my Scotch blood that energy and activity which are not always found in the Creole race … and perhaps they are right. I have often heard the term 'lazy Creole' applied to my country people; but I am sure I do not know what it is to be indolent. All my life long I have followed the impulse which led me to be up and doing [p. 55].

If the narrative is to be an account of Seacole's success, her opening paragraph establishes the complex lineaments of her narrative persona. A sense of cultural rootedness, authorised by the assertion of a strident individualism, and then modulated by an overdetermined deference to

---

[22] For an extended analysis of the nineteenth century metropolitan interest in miscegenation see Robert Young, *Colonial desire: hybridity in theory, culture and race* (London: Routledge, 1995).

the observations and prejudices of others, reveals just how much is at stake in the process of autobiographical writing.

Early in the narrative, Seacole notes that she had travelled to London in her youth. She writes:

Strangely enough, some of my most vivid recollections are the efforts of the London street-boys to poke fun at me and my companion's complexion. I am only a little brown – a few shades duskier than the brunettes whom you all admire so much; but my companion was very dark, and a fair (if I can apply the term to her) subject for their rude wit ... there were no policemen to awe the boys and turn our servants' heads in those days [p. 58].

The memory reconfirms for Seacole's readers that she is not 'wholly black' and that she is acutely aware that the meaning of her light skin is contingent upon her social and cultural context. If her colour and occupation ensure a degree of social standing in Jamaica, she tacitly demands the same respect in England. By articulating this memory in 1857, Seacole further repudiates Carlylean mythology. She appeals to a progressive conscience by noting that things have since improved by force of the metropolitan law. This type of overt racism is now the result of class ignorance.[23]

The importance of Seacole's creole identity is affirmed when she claims that it was 'natural enough' for her to 'inherit her mother's tastes' (p. 56). In fact Seacole never mentions her father again. Instead, albeit briefly, she stresses the centrality of her formative years to her subsequent adventures. Seacole focuses attention on her mother's medical reputation with the military personnel and their families stationed at the nearby Up-Park and Newcastle camps. Her desire to become a doctress is attributed to the assistance she gives her mother as she regularly nursed the invalid officers and their wives. Far from refuting her West Indian identity, this carefully rendered explanation makes it clear that it is a maternally inherited set of culturally specific skills that have enabled her to stake her claim both within the unstable racial hierarchies of Jamaica, and within the broader imperial polity.[24]

Creole healing was essentially folk medicine rooted in African medicinal practices that had been adapted and indigenised throughout the

[23] Presumably Seacole visited London before Robert Peel had established the metropolitan police force in 1829.

[24] Amy Johnson, 'Authority and the public display of identity: Wonderful adventures of Mrs. Seacole in many lands', *Feminist Studies* **20** (1994), pp. 537–57 argues that Seacole 'repudiates the West Indies as the authorising context of her identity' in favour of a colonial British subjectivity, p. 538.

period of slavery.[25] That Seacole is concerned to establish for the reader her own reputation amongst the military testifies to the fact that it also had become indispensable to white survival in the West Indian colonies. While European doctors struggled to treat malaria, typhoid, cholera and the other tropical fevers which produced an inordinately high mortality rate amongst colonial personnel, private officers had long relied on local medical care administered by creole doctresses.[26] Nevertheless, Seacole carefully legit-imates these skills by noting that she also learned from the colonial doctors. Thus, she makes it clear that she spent her early life negotiating with the military by supplying the private and domestic services that were necessary to support their authority. The specification of this context enables her to stress her 'native' identity, establish the British as 'foreigners', and suc-cessfully avoid commenting on the violence of post-emancipation Jamaica. Given her, and perhaps her editor's, sensitivity to the perceived crisis in the British West Indies, Seacole avoids commenting on the civil unrest that swept the island in the 1840s, noting only that the great fire of 1843 destroyed her Kingston home. The event is registered only in terms of her own ability to recover from financial disaster. For her, it is the ineluctable inhospitality of Jamaica's climate that seals the fate of so many Europeans rather than the colonial enterprise itself. She declares:

It was a terrible thing to see young people in the youth and bloom of life suddenly stricken down, not in battle with an enemy that threatened their country, but in vain contest with a climate that refused to adopt them. Indeed, the mother country pays a dear price for the possession of her colonies.

I think all who are familiar with the West Indies will acknowledge that Nature has been favourable to strangers in a few respects, and that one of these had been in instilling into the hearts of Creoles an affection for English people and an anxiety for their welfare which shows itself warmest when they are sick and suffering [p. 108].

Readers in the 1850s who had knowledge of the dire economic and social situation in the Caribbean since the abolition of slavery, and par-ticularly after the repeal of the Sugar Duties in 1846, would surely have read these comments with some sense of irony.

---

[25] Richard Sheridan, *Doctors and slaves: a medical and demographic history of slavery in the British West Indies, 1680–1834* (Cambridge: Cambridge University Press, 1985); Todd L. Savitt, *Medicine and slavery: the diseases and health care of blacks in antebellum Virginia* (Urbana: University of Illinois Press, 1978); and Orlando Patterson, *The sociology of slavery: an analysis of the origins, development and structure of negro slave society in Jamaica* (Rutherford: Fairleigh Dickinson University Press, 1969).

[26] See David Patrick Geggus, *Slavery, war and revolution: the British occupation of Saint Domingue, 1793–1798* (Oxford: Clarendon Press, 1982), p. 371.

Seacole's social and military connections would have been improved by her marriage in 1836 to Mr Seacole, a godson of Nelson. The couple opened a store in Black River but he is presented as a 'delicate' man, who soon succumbed to the tropics. Widowed and later orphaned after the deaths of her guardian and her mother, Seacole casts her early life within a colonial version of Smilesean self-help, accepting the vagaries of the market, and other personal difficulties with the stoicism of a utilitarian businesswoman.[27] Seacole notes that she began trading beyond Jamaica, travelling to New Providence, Haiti and Cuba. After the Jamaican cholera epidemic of 1850, she decides to join her brother in exploiting the commercial opportunity that had developed on the isthmus of Panama as a result of the California Gold Rush. She leaves her business in the hands of a cousin, and travels to Chagres loaded with clothes, preserves and other saleable products.

SELF-MAKING IN PANAMA

Even before the United States had acquired California after the Mexican War (1846–8), many heading for the west coast used the isthmus crossing in preference to the arduous journey across the continent or the lengthy maritime route via Cape Horn. The discovery of gold in 1848 generated a huge increase in traffic as migrant opportunists increasingly chose the fastest route possible. Seacole and her brother would have had no trouble getting to Chagres from Jamaica as the Royal Mail Steam Packet Company ran steamers from England to the Caribbean which regularly docked on the Atlantic coast of the isthmus. Kingston and Chagres were also stopping points on a through service that ran from England to the west coast of South America using the Panama link.[28]

By 1850, New York financiers had secured exclusive concessions from Colombia to build a railroad linking the Atlantic and the Pacific. It was completed in 1855 but before then the twenty-one miles of swamp had to be traversed by a combination of foot, mule and boat depending on the season. At the height of the 'Rush' many more migrants arrived than could leave, given the shortage of shipping services on the Pacific coast. Malaria, 'Panama Fever' and cholera were rife while prices for food,

---

[27] Samuel Smiles, *Self-help: illustrations of character and conduct* (London: John Murray, 1859). Tim Travers notes that the phrase was already common parlance before 1850. See his *Samuel Smiles and the Victorian work ethic* (London: Garland, 1985), p. 238.

[28] John Haskell Kemble, 'The Gold Rush by Panama, 1848–1851', *Pacific Historical Review* **18** (1949), pp. 45–56, p. 46.

lodging and transport services were hugely inflated, producing vast profit for those who provided them. Tensions ran high as the isthmus became a kind of frenzied, sometimes blocked, crossroads where impatient gold-seekers and returning 'Yankees' often treated the local population with violent contempt. By the time Seacole published her narrative, British readers may well have been aware of the infamous 1856 race riot that became known as the 'Watermelon War'.[29]

While the route across the isthmus was well worn, and guidebooks had been available since 1846, the region was also regarded as a forgotten frontier.[30] Anthony Trollope, travelling in central America in the 1850s, thought political independence to be disastrous for the region. Imagining Panama in historical flux, as the decaying Spanish colony was overtaken by independence and nationhood, he wrote:

Now the whole country has received the boon of Utopian freedom; and the mind loses itself in contemplating to what lowest pitch of human degradation the people will gradually fall . . . Civilization here is retrograding . . . It is making no progress.[31]

Seacole's episodic account of her time in Panama largely accords with Trollope's assessment although her judgements concerning the various constituencies she encountered tell a more complicated story. Seacole presents a damning portrait of Panama as she observes an anarchic social context where economic rationality has given way to violent and corrupt excess, and where civility has fallen foul of unregulated self-interest. But she also reflects critically on the growing imperial interest that America is taking in the region, and on the institution of slavery.

Seacole certainly echoes Trollope as she regards the prospectors, their female companions, emigrants, touts, convicts, gamblers, drunks, sailors, Spanish Indians, and ex-slaves as the 'refuse of every nation'. Her narrative encodes Panama's inhospitable geography through the rhetoric that Mary Louise Pratt attaches to the 'capitalist vanguard'. Seacole casts travel as a triumph in its own right, and destinations as objects of mastery rather than places.[32] As Seacole describes her journey from Navy Bay by boat up

[29] Mercedes Chen Daley, 'The Watermelon Riot: cultural encounters in Panama City, April 15, 1856', *Hispanic American Historical Review* **70** (1990), pp. 85–108.

[30] John Haskell Kemble, p. 47.

[31] Anthony Trollope, *The West Indies and the Spanish Main* (London: Chapman & Hall, 1860), p. 243. For discussions of Trollope in this context see J. H. Davidson, 'Anthony Trollope and the colonies', *Victorian Studies* **12** (1969), pp. 305–30; Catherine Hall, *Civilising subjects*, pp. 210–22; and Simon Gikandi, *Maps of Englishness*, pp. 92–114.

[32] Mary Louise Pratt, *Imperial eyes: travel writing and transculturation* (London: Routledge, 1992), pp. 146–55.

the River Chagres to Gorgona and then Cruces, she writes: '[I]t seemed as if nature had determined to throw every conceivable obstacle in the way of those who would seek to join the two great oceans of the world' (p. 63). To the eye of a traveller, both landscape and its inhabitants are subject to neglect, in dire need of authoritative rationalisation, and constitute therefore logistical obstacles to her sense of purpose and order. The half-finished railway appears as a sign of stalled civilisation. Her reaction to the pitiful sight reveals, moreover, her understanding of the contradictions that accompany the march of progress.

Every mile of that fatal railway cost the world thousands of lives. I was assured that its site was marked thickly by graves, and that so great was the mortality among the labourers that three times the survivors struck in a body, and their places had to be supplied by fresh victims from America, tempted by unheard of wages. It is a gigantic undertaking, and shows what the energy and enterprise of men can accomplish [p. 65].

The representation of the isthmus as a site of degenerative excess reveals the intricate interdependence of subjectivity and place in Seacole's autobiography. Cast as geographically intransigent and socially unstable, the region becomes a particular kind of anachronistic space that serves as a context for magnifying Seacole's own 'exceptionalism'.[33] In many ways, Panama bore similarities to Jamaica. It was also a place where the fantastical promise of riches had produced an unprecedented concentration of constituencies, and had made for a very specific set of social complexities born out of exploitation and violence. Yet, for Seacole, Panama is beyond colonial authority, and outside the racialised bipolarities of everyday slave society. Here, she is able to comment freely on the contingencies of social identity formation. If her status as a light-skinned creole, her connection to the military, and her identification with empire enabled her to abstract herself from the politically volatile situation in Jamaica, Panama serves as a site of (dis)placement that paradoxically reveals the situated nature of her agency.

When she first arrived in Cruces, Seacole lived with her brother Edward who had opened the 'Independent Hotel'. She quickly opened her own establishment on the opposite side of the street. An outbreak of cholera introduced her to the full diversity of local isthmus life, and established her

---

[33] Amy Robinson, 'Authority and the public display of identity' argues that Seacole's autobiography illustrates the ways in which 'exceptionalism' becomes the 'province of the female colonial voice' in the mid-nineteenth century, p. 537. Her insight informs this discussion although I am also interested to analyse the differently structured processes, and places, within which 'exceptionalism' acquires meaning.

reputation as a reliable doctress. As she notes, there was no other medical expert in Cruces except a 'timid little dentist, who was there by accident' and later a Spanish doctor who was too frightened and inexperienced to be effective. Her medical success ensured that the Americans soon christened her 'the yellow woman from Jamaica with the cholera medicine'. As she points out, her doctressing is not a charitable enterprise, and, while she administers to all, she charges those who can pay. As she wryly notes, 'The best part of my practice lay amongst the American store and hotel-keepers, the worst among the native boatmen and muleteers' (p. 79).

Seacole's narrative modulates between interesting anecdote and personal observation in a way that establishes a sense of herself as belonging to the local community of small traders who battle with violence, theft and corruption while making good money. Pitted, as she is, with this constituency, Seacole's most strident criticism is reserved for the American travellers. While she berates the Spanish Indians for their superstitious Catholicism, the native army for their shoddy uniforms, and the ex-slave magistrate for his creative use of the law, she is most concerned to point up the crude epidemiological racism exhibited by the Americans even if she often cloaks her comments with irony. When writing about Jamaica, Seacole says nothing about her slave descendency. Her location in Panama, however, enables her to establish her moral authority with regard to her post-emancipation British audience.

On first arriving in the isthmus, Seacole describes her attempt to hire a boat of her own as she is making her way to her brother. She is carrying luggage but she is also frightened of sharing with the Americans. She explains this by directly addressing her British readership:

[M]y experience of travel had not failed to teach me that Americans (even from the Northern states) are always uncomfortable in the company of coloured people and very often show this feeling in stronger ways than by sour looks and rude words. I think if I have a little prejudice amongst our cousins across the Atlantic – and I do confess a little – it is not unreasonable. I have a few shades of deeper brown upon my skin which shows me related – and I am proud of the relationship – to those poor mortals whom you once held enslaved, and whose bodies America still owns. And having this bond, and knowing what slavery is; having seen with my own eyes and heard with my own ears proof positive enough of its horrors – let others affect to doubt them if they will – is it surprising that I should be somewhat impatient of the airs of superiority which many Americans have endeavoured to assume over me? [p. 67].

This is a complex digression for several reasons. Rhonda Frederick, arguing for the particularity of Seacole's 'Creole performance' in the autobiography, suggests that Seacole 'undoubtedly wants her readers to know that her skin is *light brown* and that she is *related to*, but *not* one of, Jamaica's black and formerly enslaved population.'[34] This much is true, but Seacole's comment resonates beyond the affirmation of her light skin. It is also a critique of the North American reliance on appearance as *the* definitive marker of difference, and it thus highlights the complex articulation of race, class, culture *and* politics that mark Seacole's particular social perspective. In order to explain her relation to, and distance from, Jamaica's ex-slaves, Seacole adopts abolitionist rhetoric of the type that was also echoed in many slave narratives by calling upon the authority of first-hand witness to authorise her comments.[35] This rhetoric would have carried particular significance for her British readers. During the 1850s, many Britons were energetically engaged in defining the nation against American slavery.[36] British activists had become involved in the North American antislavery campaign, and were hosting African-American abolitionist lecture tours. Seen in this context, the tension between Seacole's personal experience of American prejudice and her elicitation of British sympathy is particularly charged. She appeals to the nation's sense of moral destiny but she also tacitly reminds her British readers of the racist attitudes that remain as a legacy of their own slaving past, her own rejection by British institutions, and the ongoing violence of contemporary imperial ventures.

Seacole's commentary on Panamanian life concentrates on the unpredictable solidarities, sympathies and divisions that are formed as class and racial hierarchies are reworked in the context of free market culture. In particular, her disgust with 'Yankees' of the 'lowest sort' who abuse their 'freedom and independence' contrasts with her praise for the free-black population of the isthmus for whom the same atmosphere of 'freedom and equality' is used to acquire 'positions of eminence' in the new republic (p. 93).

[34] Rhonda Frederick, 'Creole performance', p. 496.
[35] For the circulation of slave narratives in Britain, see Clare Taylor, *British and American Abolitionists: an episode in transatlantic understanding* (Edinburgh: Edinburgh University Press, 1974); William L. Andrews, *To tell a free story: the first century of Afro-American autobiography, 1760–1865* (Chicago: University of Illinois Press, 1988).
[36] For the English interest in American slavery and abolition after 1830, see among others, R. M. J. Blackett, *Building the antislavery wall: black Americans in the Atlantic Abolitionist Movement, 1830–1860* (Ithaca: Cornell University Press, 1983); Marcus Wood, *Blind memory: visual representations of slavery in England and America 1780–1865* (Manchester: Manchester University Press, 2000); and Audrey Fisch, ' "Repetitious accounts so piteous and so harrowing": the ideological work of American slave narratives in England', *Journal of Victorian Culture* 1 (1996), pp. 1–33.

As an independent nation, New Granada had outlawed slavery, and the isthmus had become an economic destination for free blacks and runaway slaves escaping from the southern American states. Others escaped from their North American owners while in transit. California had banned slavery but many migrants took their slaves with them as a means to counter labour competition from Mexican and South American *peones*.[37] Despite Seacole's criticism of Spanish-Indian degeneracy, she identifies with their antipathy towards the Americans. She approves of their involvement in small acts of anti-imperialist resistance, and of their active role in helping to free migrant slaves. It appears that she became actively involved, recounting an instance where she and the settled population of Gorgona freed an abused slave from her American mistress. Together they set up a fund to buy the slave-woman's child which had been left in New Orleans (p. 102).

Seacole eventually engaged in prospecting herself. Gold mining was associated with commercial greed, and historically connected with Spanish and Portuguese imperial futility, so she is careful not to celebrate her endeavours. In fact, she makes a point of telling her readers that, from her point of writing, she has not yet extracted herself from the unfortunate investment. The narrative positioning of the disappointing gold-mining episode, just before she leaves for the Crimea, reinforces the representation of herself as a woman fitted for a life of maternal service and duty rather than for the unfeminine world of prospecting. It also offers a directly material cause for how the possibility of travelling to the Crimea first developed. Seacole had been invited to invest in mining by another itinerant entrepreneur, Mr Day, a distant associate of her late husband, and superintendent for the New Grenada Gold-mining Company at Escribanos. Having moved from mining to shipping, Day met her again in London, and it was his last-minute financial backing that secured the unlikely route from central America to the Crimean battlefield.

DRAMATISING IMPERIAL DUTY: THE CRIMEA

Seacole advertised ahead of her departure from London in January 1855. One of her business cards is inserted in the autobiography as a sign of her

[37] For the issue of slavery in California, see Carey McWilliams, *California: the great exception* (Berkeley: University of California Press, 1999), pp. 39–49; Rudolph M. Rapp, 'The negro in Gold Rush California', *Journal of Negro History* **49** (1964), pp. 81–98, and William E. Franklin, 'The Archy Case', *Pacific Historical Review* **32** (1963), pp. 137–54.

professionalism and patriotism. Unlike her brother who had named his Panamanian establishment the 'Independent Hotel', hers was called the 'British Hotel'. The card 'respectfully announced to her former kind friends, and to the Officers of the Army and Navy generally' that she was headed for Balaclava to 'establish a mess-table and comfortable quarters for sick and convalescent officers' (p. 127).

The second half of *Wonderful adventures* narrates the successful realisation of Seacole's plan, and, as she stresses, it is the part of her life that most merits public attention. Nevertheless, as the inclusion of the carefully worded advertisement signifies, such recognition could not be taken for granted. The ensuing part of the narrative is repeatedly interrupted by a variety of further textual supplements designed to ratify her story.[38]

Letters of commendation begin to pepper the text, and constitute almost all of one chapter entitled, 'My work in the Crimea'. All of the documents testify to Seacole's nursing skills, her kindness, and her expert provision of domestic comforts. Some are dated, and had been sent after the war in support of Seacole's financial distress. Others serve as documentary evidence of her activities in the field. The diversity of the selection generalises Seacole's reputation but the letters also confirm her place outside the institutional fold of the official nursing organisations.

Their narrative organisation also indicates the relationship between the specific geographical location of Seacole's establishment and the network of class relations that linked London and the Crimea. The British Hotel was situated some distance from the officers' camps on the Heights. While Seacole's customers included high-ranking officers, more often she dealt with their servants who travelled down the muddy road with lists of required supplies. The hotel was halfway between Balaclava and Kadikoi along the major military supply route and near the Land Transport Corps hospital. Although the Land Transport and Army Works Corps were not directly involved in armed combat, fear, rumour and an exaggerated reliance on fate meant that they were intensely suspicious of being sent to the military hospitals when they were sick or otherwise injured. Many believed that they would never return alive. As a consequence, many of Seacole's regular patients belonged to these lower ranks, and this is reflected by the extended selection of their letters of recommendation.

---

[38] Sarah Salih, '*The history of Mary Prince*, the black subject, and the black canon', in B. Carey, M. Ellis, and S. Salih (eds.), *Discourses of slavery and abolition: Britain and its colonies, 1760–1838* (Basingstoke: Palgrave Macmillan, 2004), pp. 123–38, argues powerfully that editorial and critical approaches which seek to position early black writing as inaugural or canonical often overlook the intra- and inter-textual nature of these texts.

A referenced extract from William Russell's recently published 'Letters from the seat of war' is included to secure their authority.

The magazine *Punch* had published a popular ballad celebrating Seacole's work in December, 1856.[39] The 'Stir' is reprinted after the letters. It is only after the comprehensive layering of increasingly public documents that Seacole again refers to her initial rejection by the British authorities. 'Reader, now that we have come to the end of this chapter, I can say what I have been in all anxiety to tell you from its beginning. Please look back to Chapter 8, and see how hard the right woman had to struggle to convey herself to the right place' (p. 175).

The abundance of legitimising contextual material has several conflicting effects. The glowing references evidently bolster Seacole's appeal for public recognition. Her anxious deference, however, letting 'other voices speak' for her, also reveals the self-conscious fragility of her claim. Moreover, the inclusion of the mutually substantiating, hard documents confirms that Seacole's willed inclusion in a narrative of patriotic war service is based on the fact that she displayed acts and qualities which were valued and celebrated – expert nursing, evident bravery and imperial loyalty – at a particular historical point of perceived national crisis.

Wonderful adventures entered a print field already flooded with Crimean war memories in the form of newspaper reports, memoirs, published diaries, and literary, dramatic and poetic works, and just as the first news stories about the Indian Mutiny were appearing in the national press.[40] The unprecedented public controversy over the Crimean war, energised by the vastly expanded media industries, facilitated the beginning of a transformation in popular perceptions of the military. As Olive Anderson has argued, the period saw the beginning of a 'decisive shift' from the 'brutal and licentious soldiery' of the Napoleonic wars to the 'unprecedented adulatory attitudes towards Britain's professional soldiers' which subsequently characterised late imperial jingoism.[41] Seacole's documentary deference to the newly envisioned military thus played directly to the cultural imaginaries that helped to shape dominant metropolitan interpretations of the Crimean war. Moreover, *Wonderful adventures* further articulates cross-class, nationalist sentiment by echoing

[39] 'A stir for Seacole', in *Punch*, December 6th, 1856.
[40] For analysis of the Indian Mutiny as the first 'national-popular' colonial war fought by Britain in its Empire, see Graham Dawson, *Soldier heroes: British adventure, empire and the imagining of masculinities* (London: Routledge, 1994), pp. 79–114.
[41] Olive Anderson, 'The growth of Christian militarism in mid-Victorian Britain', *English Historical Review* **84**, 338 (Jan. 1971), p. 49.

popular mythologies of manifest destiny, heroic sacrifice and Christian militarism. One example of this type of rhetoric illustrates the way in which these ideologies enable the elevation of Seacole's personal experience. Here, as elsewhere, her independent, masculinist, commercial venture is translated into the expression of sentimental imperial maternalism:

There was one boy in the Artillery, with blue eyes and light golden hair, whom I nursed through a long and weary sickness, borne with all a man's spirit ... It was a long time before I could banish from my mind the thought of him as I saw him last, the yellow hair, stiff and stained with his life-blood, and his blue eyes closed in the sleep of death [p. 191].

If the sentimentalised rhetoric and the extra-textual documents were designed to confirm Seacole's imperial loyalty, she was also clearly aware of the originality of her own particular perspective on the war. As most published memoirs were written by British soldiers and civilian eye-witnesses, the novelty of *Wonderful adventures* stems from the descriptions of the practical difficulties, social scenes, and unusual events that characterise life at the 'British Hotel' as much as from her own curious trajectory from Jamaica via Panama.[42]

As the route to Constantinople 'was already worn threadbare by book-making tourists', Seacole dramatises her own voyage and arrival via a set of fortuitous, yet half-expected, reunions with a set of old friends and customers from Jamaica (p. 128). She meets two injured soldiers of the 48th in Gibraltar, and several medical officers in Malta, one of whom gives her a letter of introduction to Florence Nightingale. Once at the Scutari hospital, she finds other soldiers who had known her at Up-Park camp.

The sense of social ease that accompanies Seacole's reconnection with her familiar, and familial, role amongst the wounded military men stands in stark contrast to the cold reception of Selina Bracebridge, one of the 'lady volunteers' who 'felt more surprise than she could politely show' upon meeting her (p. 135). The exchange between the two women reveals much about Seacole's determination to carry out her plan. She suffers another rejection by being told, too quickly, that there is no official vacancy at the hospital. In response, she fails to recognise Bracebridge's social superiority by suggesting that she is not interested in staying at

---

[42] For a contextualisation of Seacole's autobiography amongst other Crimean memoirs, especially those of Lady Alicia Blackwood and Mrs Frances Duberly, see Sandra Gunning, 'Travelling with her mother's tastes: the negotiation of gender, race, and location in *Wonderful adventures of Mrs Seacole in many lands*', *Signs: Journal of Women in Culture and Society* **26** (2001), pp. 949–81.

Scutari but is 'bound for the front in a few days'. The letter of reference secures the audience with Nightingale but Seacole does not press her case. She merely requests a bed for the night. The fact that Seacole was offered accommodation in the washerwomen's quarters confirms Anne Summers' observations on the policing of class and gender boundaries in the Crimean hospitals. Female middle-class moral authoritarianism simply 'could not contain working women of a more independent type'.[43] As Summers notes, knowledge of their own agency, given the shortage of labour in the hard-pressed hospitals, threatened to destabilise the attempted replication of British-based domestic hierarchies in a war zone. Though Seacole glosses the indignity, she was, in the end, treated like a servant. Significantly, she relates her easy conversation with the washer-woman as they spend the night swapping stories about themselves. At this point in *Wonderful adventures*, the narrative tenses slide from past to present, and back into the past again, as the memory is freshly recalled during the act of writing it down (p. 136). It is the only moment of intimate female solidarity that Seacole recorded in her entire auto-biography.

While Seacole's social mobility was brought up short by her confrontation with metropolitan feminine middle-class authority at Scutari, the male-dominated front, almost literally, offered another world. Inhabited by Tartars, the Crimean peninsular was occupied between 1854 and 1856 as the allies laid siege to the Russians in Sebastopol. In many ways it was transformed into a temporary mini-state covering clearly defined territory, bounded by the Black Sea with a hostile border to the north. The French and the British were encamped on the higher ground above the southern port of Balaclava, and supply roads and a railway were under laborious construction for most of the war. Like any other battle zone, the Crimea quickly generated a particular economy – a culture of circulation marked by imports, exports, systems of exchange, finance and credit, divisions of labour and specialisations – which both set it apart and connected it to the outside world. The area was rapidly domesticated by the localised naming of the sites of battles, encampments and supply routes. The place where the ill-fated Charge of the Light Brigade took place was called thereafter 'Valley of the Shadow of Death'. The British Hotel was located at 'Spring Hill'.

For Britain, the unlikely alliance with France and Turkey brought a set of exotic and not so exotic 'others' together as soldiers and settlers. The

<hr>

[43] Anne Summers, 'Pride and prejudice', p. 41.

British forces included the Scottish Highlanders, Irish recruits seeking employment after the famine, as well as the English ranked in relation to class background.[44] The French deployed their distinctively attired armies which traditionally served in colonial North Africa: the Zouaves and the Chasseurs d'Afrique. The Turks recruited from a variety of ethnic groupings across the Ottoman Empire. Sardinian Grenadiers also supported the British. The Crimea, moreover, developed its own distinctive social hierarchies, its own particular rules (official and unofficial), and its own, highly complex, everyday culture.[45] Seacole's autobiography underscores the fact that she, and the British Hotel, were integral to the social and cultural geography of the occupied region. Her reputation had preceded her via the military network, and her hotel quickly became a perpetually busy focal point for everything from entertainment and relaxation to saving lives and selling homemade handkerchiefs. For Seacole, if we follow the autobiography, this Crimea (only partially represented here), served as both erasure and as a kind of historical beginning. Arriving only a little belatedly, she joined her heroic 'sons', and positioned herself centrally within a freshly constructed order of things.

In many ways, life in the Crimea enabled Seacole to determine her 'Britishness'. She portrayed herself as an affective conduit between the security of home and the front via her care for the displaced soldiers, while the British Hotel served as a comforting haven from the everyday grind of static warfare. Any singular interpretation of her sense of belonging does not do justice to her account however. There is no doubt that she delights in becoming known as 'Mother Seacole' to her specifically British 'sons' rather than 'the yellow woman from Jamaica with the cholera medicine'. But she also makes much of her interaction with the cosmopolitan (male) crowd, while her maternalist nursing ensured a greater intimacy with the men than if she had been simply a commercial trader. Her particular vantage point enabled her to practise elements of her creole cultural heritage – through her medical work, her West Indian cuisine and, in fact, by employing two 'wholly black' cooks – in ways that resonated with her old Jamaican life. In short, Seacole expresses her sense of belonging through a complex amalgam of memory, invention and

---

[44] Ziggi Alexander and Audrey Dewjee, 'Introduction' to *Wonderful adventures*, note that the 2nd West India Regiment volunteered for posting to the Crimea but were turned down by the British government, p. 12.

[45] I am indebted to Chris Ward, 'Impressions of the Somme: an experiment', *Representing History* **1**, 3 (1997), pp. 275–310, for inspiring me to think about the Crimea in terms of the relations between the representation of experience and the local cultural geography of the war zone.

projection informed by the existence of cross-empire networks. The representation of her agency and aspirations are both idealised *and* entirely contingent on the local conceptualisations of identity constituted within the war zone. In the Crimea, she is British, Jamaican, creole, a member of the allied forces, briefly Crimean, a matriarch, an anti-czarist, an indiscriminate humanitarian nurse, and an independent small trader. To press a point to her British readers, she is only 'black' in the Crimea when confronted by Americans (p. 216).

THE SPECTACLE OF WAR: *WONDERFUL ADVENTURES OF MRS SEACOLE IN MANY LANDS*

From a contemporary postcolonial perspective, Seacole's text raises important issues about the politics of criticism. The ideological demands associated with reading a colonial text that 'writes back' have elicited several critical analyses premised on identifying moments of anti-imperial resistance in *Wonderful adventures*.[46] It has to be stated though that the strident intentionality of Seacole's individualist patriotism ensures that direct criticism of either British imperialism or colonialism is muted at best. Recent postcolonial readings have also been interested to unearth and claim an authentic or emergent West Indian national consciousness for Seacole.[47] This approach is also problematic, not least because the textual incursions made by the multiple authorising documents, references to an editor, and the necessity of a legitimising preface, all signal the dangers of conferring upon Seacole an entirely autonomous authorial voice. Moreover, both critical approaches risk glossing the text's multiple articulations by lifting it too far from its interconnected territorial contexts. Given these interpretative difficulties, one might ask how the text speaks back to our efforts to engage with the global dynamics of extranational colonial and imperial histories.

---

[46] Bernard McKenna, '"Fancies of exclusive possession": validation and dissociation in Mary Seacole's England and the Caribbean', *Philological Quarterly* **76** (1997), pp. 219–39, argues that Seacole's narrative 'subtly undermine[s] the imperium', p. 220. Catherine Judd, *Bedside seductions: nursing and the Victorian imagination, 1830–1880* (Basingstoke: Macmillan, 1998), pp. 101–21, reads the narrative for its 'oblique resistance' through Seacole's 'rewriting of the Homeric epic' and 'the popular hagiography of Florence Nightingale', p. 101.

[47] Sandra Pouchet Paquet cites Seacole's narrative as an early example of a 'West Indian autobiographical consciousness' in 'The enigma of arrival: *The wonderful adventures of Mrs Seacole in many lands*', *African American Review* **26** (1992), pp. 651–63, p. 652. Rhonda Frederick argues that 'Seacole's narrative self is an example of a Creole identity that highlights the inherent complications in master narratives and that exemplifies an emergent Caribbean subjectivity' in 'Creole performance in *Wonderful adventures*', p. 504.

Seacole's autobiography presses up against its contemporary world even though a complicated historical politics surrounds the legitimising conventions that were necessary for it to claim its status as 'truth'. Yet it is also important to acknowledge the fact that Seacole's public recognition and historical importance were secured specifically by her participation in a modern imperial war. The Crimean episode set a number of important precedents in any modern cultural history of globalisation. It was the first war to be 'covered' by the immediate presence of media correspondents, the first to be relayed instantly by telegraph, and the first to be photographed. It was only after this war that media censorship became a state issue.[48] Brought into the realm of technologised spectacle, the war was a tourist destination for the curious, an avenue for displaced outpourings of nationalist sentiment, and, perhaps more than ever before, it was intensely dramatic.

The Crimean topography contributed to the particular dramatisation of this war. As he watched a Russian counter-attack in October 1854 from the plateau overlooking Balaclava, William Russell reported that he could see the disaster unfold 'as the stage and those upon it are seen from the box of a theatre'.[49] Russell, a self-made Irishman, was Seacole's greatest champion, and one cannot escape the sense that the theatrical rhetoric of war journalism is carried through into her autobiography. She, too, is enthralled by the views from Cathcart's Hill, and she repeatedly casts herself as actor, character and spectacle amongst 'scenes of horror and distress'[50] (p. 197).

Paul Fussell discusses the relationship between modern war and the theatre in his classic cultural analysis of British experiences and memories of the Great War. He argues that war was not only observed in theatrical terms but that it was also experienced through them. As he notes, the 'palpable character conventions of the army, with its system of ranks, its externalisation of personality, its impatience with ambiguity or subtlety' inevitably lead to dramatic interpretation.[51]

It is tempting to read Seacole's literary representation of herself in relation to these terms. As Fussell also points out, however, it is the sheer extremity or absurdity of the war context that leads to the performative

---

[48] Peter Young and Peter Jesser, *The media and the military from the Crimea to the Desert Strike* (Basingstoke: Macmillan, 1997), pp. 20–4.

[49] Philip Knightley, *The first casualty: the war correspondent as hero, propagandist, and myth maker from the Crimea to Vietnam* (London: André Deutsch, 1975), p. 11.

[50] Seacole constantly uses dramatic rhetoric throughout the description of her experiences in the Crimea. See, for example, pp. 134, 143, 186, 205–6.

[51] Paul Fussell, *The Great War and modern memory* (Oxford: Oxford University Press, 1975), p. 204.

deflection of events and their meanings. If we follow his argument, Seacole is not simply using theatrical metaphor for dramatic effect. In fact, one might argue that she harnesses the subversive power constituted by the conjunction of theatre and war. She describes a host of occasions in which the processes through which normative social identities become stabilised are deliberately confused. For example, she coaches the company of the 1st Royals to dress and behave like women for a theatrical entertainment, and she notes the soldiers' attempt to make their race course look like Ascot or Epsom: 'some soldiers blackened their faces and came out as Ethiopian Serenaders'[52] (p. 217). Elsewhere, she is mistaken for a Russian spy and arrested by the French as the result of an American sailor fooling about.

As these anecdotes intimate, Seacole continuously draws attention to herself in relation to the defamiliarising processes of the war zone. Riding into Tchernaya, after hostilities have ceased, she writes, 'very much delighted seemed the Russians to see an English woman. I wonder if they thought they all had my complexion' (p. 223). Later, she travelled to Simpheropol where her companions

tried hard to persuade the Russians that I was Queen Victoria, by paying me the most absurd reverence. When this failed they fell back a little, and declared that I was the Queen's first cousin. Anyhow, they attracted crowds about me, and I became quite a lioness in the streets of Simpheropol, until the arrival of some Highlanders in their uniform cut me out [pp. 224–5].

The Highlanders, of course, could be seen as another set of 'cross-dressers' who would have fascinated the Russians. These last two events could easily be read as culminating narrative moments designed to realise Seacole's fantasy of imperial belonging. Read within the wider context of the autobiography, though, they also provide evocative reminders of her struggle with the temporal and spatial discontinuities of identity formation in the context of a route that breached the boundaries of empire. These representational complexities are too often missed by colonial histories traditionally wedded to the internal, or territorially defined, dynamics of the imperial ambit. Moreover, the autobiography, as it charts Seacole's life, speaks back to both metropole and colony by constantly calling attention to the idealised power of naming and its association with imperial channels or networks of violence and war.

---

[52] For the popularity and success of 'minstrelsy' in mid-nineteenth-century Britain, see J. S. Bratton, 'English Ethiopians: British audiences and black-face acts, 1835–1865', *Yearbook of English Studies* **2** (1981), pp. 127–42.

The abrupt end of the Crimean War ruined Seacole financially. The departure of the troops meant that the market collapsed, and she was forced to destroy the remainder of her stocks.[53] If the war made her famous, it also made her homeless. As the military machine rolled onwards, many soldiers were immediately redeployed further east to deal with the Indian crisis. The autobiography records Seacole's affinity with the recruits who were not posted on. She writes of one soldier, 'with him I acknowledged to have more fellow-feeling than with the others, for he, as well as I, clearly had no home to go to' (p. 226). This single quotation complicates the suggestion that a notion of autonomous performativity offers a theory of cultural agency for this text by highlighting the fact that performed identities do not, or cannot, make sense without boundaries or a spatial setting. As Seacole's defining context collapses around her, the pathos of her final image is most apt. She records that she took one last look at the spectacle of the burning Crimea from Cathcart's Hill:

It was with something like regret that we said to one another that the play was fairly over, that peace rung the curtain down, and that we, humble actors in some of its most stirring scenes, must seek engagements elsewhere [p. 230–31].

CONCLUSION

Although there is some indication that Seacole desired to move on to India with the British troops, she returned to London in 1856 and, successfully recovering from bankruptcy, settled there until her death in 1881. It appears that she did not give up her connections with Jamaica. She left in her will a substantial sum of money and property in Kingston and London.[54] The autobiography was an immediate success when it was first published though, despite being decorated by the English, French, and Turkish authorities, she was quickly erased from the public narrative of British imperial heroism. The bronze Crimean War memorial erected in London in 1915 celebrates Sidney Herbert, Secretary for War, and Florence Nightingale but not Mary Seacole. *Wonderful adventures* was finally edited and republished in 1984 but it is only in the last ten years that it has become of significant interest in British and American critical contexts. More recently, in February 2004, Mary Seacole topped a popular poll of 'One hundred great black Britons'. A public campaign has been

[53] Russell notes that the 'abrupt' end of the war was financially ruinous for the sutlers in *The Great War with Russia, the invasion of the Crimea: a personal retrospect* (London: George Routledge & Sons, 1895), pp. 286–7.
[54] See Ziggi Alexander and Audrey Dewjee, 'Introduction' to *Wonderful adventures*, pp. 29–41.

launched to have a statue of her erected in London, and to have a blue
heritage plaque attached to one of her old residences.[55] Thus, Seacole has
become iconic within the current metropolitan revisioning of the cultural
memory of empire. Her life, however, raises important political questions
about how such public revisionings are to be framed. In other words, it is
crucial that Seacole's achievements, won via her determined negotiation
of the structural obstacles imposed by imperial institutions and market
forces, are acknowledged. On the other hand, an uncritical recuperation
of Seacole's personal 'success' risks the nostalgic reinscription of those
same imperial processes that first brought her to the attention of the
Victorian reading public one hundred and fifty years ago.

[55] For the 'One hundred great black Britons' poll, see www.100greatblackbritons.com. For an
extensive summary of the various ways in which Seacole is currently commemorated including the
campaign to erect a statue in London, and the reinstallation of a blue heritage plaque, see
www.maryseacoleappeal.org.uk and www.maryseacole.com/maryseacole/biography/.

CHAPTER 7

Inter-colonial migration and the refashioning of indentured labour: Arthur Gordon in Trinidad, Mauritius and Fiji (1866–1880)

Laurence Brown

On 23 March 1875, Sir Arthur Gordon (Fig. 7.1) began the two-month journey from London to the Pacific to take up his appointment as the first governor of the new British colony of Fiji. Accompanied by his wife, two young children and several hand-picked staff, the Gordon party found themselves in close contact with their fellow passengers bound for the colonies, including Australian settlers, English tea planters, and Dutch emigrants to Java.[1] Reaching Singapore in early May, the Gordons boarded the *SS Brisbane*, along with 550 Chinese labourers travelling to Queensland. With the Chinese crowded across the main deck, Arthur Gordon complained that 'the smells from this live cargo are indescribable and detestable'.[2] Yet, the aromas of Chinese cooking were the only significant encounter between the governor and the mass of migrant labourers, for Gordon also noted that he seldom saw or heard the Chinese below.[3] This social separation between the *Brisbane*'s passengers has been replicated in imperial historiography, as rarely have the different layers of élite and subaltern migration been brought together to analyse their common passages across empire.

The divided historiography of inter-colonial migration has significant implications for our understandings of nineteenth-century colonialism. Imperial biographies and the new colonial history have both emphasised the mobility of colonial governors across the British empire, although the former have tended to depict individuals carrying with them consistent policies of rule, while the latter have emphasised the ways in which administrators were remade and forced to adapt as they circulated

---

[1] Arthur H. Gordon, *Fiji: records of private and of public life, 1875–1880*, Vol. I (Edinburgh: Clark, 1901), pp. 71, 75 and 85.
[2] *Ibid.*, p. 105.   [3] *Ibid.*, p. 109.

Fig. 7.1 Arthur Charles Hamilton-Gordon, 1st Baron Stanmore, after a photograph
by Bassano. Wood engraving, 1896, NPGD6840, by permission
of National Portrait Gallery, London.

through distinctive environments.[4] In contrast, social histories of
indentured Africans, Asians and Pacific islanders have tended to focus on
the linear movements of subaltern immigrants between their societies of
origin and the plantation colonies.[5] As a result, historians of indentured
immigration have tended to portray migration under indenture as

[4] For imperial biographies of Gordon see J. K. Chapman, *The career of Arthur Hamilton Gordon*
(Toronto: University of Toronto Press, 1964); I. M. Cumpston, 'Sir Arthur Gordon and the
introduction of Indians into the Pacific: the West Indian System in Fiji', *Pacific Historical Review*
25 (1956), pp. 369–88. For a survey of recent approaches to colonial biography see the introduction
to this book.
[5] M. Schuler, *'Alas, alas, Kongo': a social history of indentured African immigration into Jamaica,
1841–1865* (Baltimore: Johns Hopkins University Press, 1980); W. Look Lai, *Indentured labor,
Caribbean sugar: Chinese and Indian migrants to the British West Indies, 1838–1918* (Baltimore: Johns
Hopkins University Press, 1993); M. Carter, *Servants, sirdars, and settlers: Indians in Mauritius,
1834–1874* (Delhi: Oxford University Press, 1995); B. V. Lal, *Girmitiyas: the origins of the Fiji Indians*
(Canberra: Journal of Pacific History, 1983); P. Corris, *Passage, port and plantation: a history of
Solomon Islands labour migration, 1870–1914* (Melbourne: Melbourne University Press, 1973).

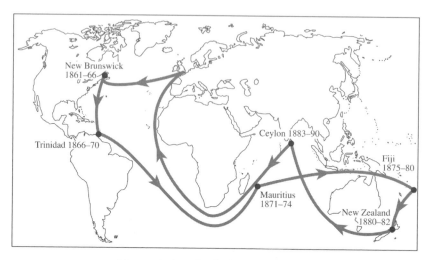

Map 7.1 Arthur Gordon's imperial career.

determined by the local forces of environmental constraints and economic demands (such as famine in India or labour shortage in the Caribbean), rather than driven by the global circulation of people and ideas.

In part to explore the inter-colonial linkages which shaped the expansion of indentured immigration projects across empire, this chapter follows the career migrations of Arthur Hamilton Gordon, who served as the governor of Trinidad, Mauritius and Fiji between 1866 and 1880 (Map 7.1). Whereas global histories of indenture have largely homogenised the conditions of contract, Gordon's movements provide a 'lens' on the significant material differences between indentured schemes across empire.[6] Exploring Gordon's interventions in debates on migrant labour highlights the constraints faced by transient administrators in distinctive colonial environments. His journey from Trinidad to Fiji also casts new light on the circulations across the colonial 'periphery' by other imperial functionaries, planters, missionaries and labourers. These trans-imperial connections reveal the fluid refashioning of indentured immigration by élite and subaltern migrants during the late nineteenth century.

---

[6] C. Hall, 'Histories of difference: new narratives of nation and empire', Allan Martin Memorial Lecture, Australian National University, Canberra, 5 April 2005.

A GRAND SEIGNEUR IN THE COLONIES

Born in 1829, Arthur Gordon was the youngest son of Lord Aberdeen, then serving as Britain's foreign secretary. After studies at Cambridge, Gordon served as private secretary to his father, who was prime minister from 1852 to 1855. With paternal support Arthur Gordon was elected into the House of Commons in 1854 at the age of twenty-four, although he lost his seat in Beverley three years later. Out of parliament, Gordon briefly acted as private secretary to his close friend William Gladstone on the latter's mission to the Ionian Islands. Returning to England in 1859 to nurse his father, whose health had collapsed, Gordon approached the Duke of Newcastle for an appointment in the colonial service.[7]

Alongside the increasing professionalisation of colonial administration, the 1860s were marked by a significant influx of former politicians into governorships across empire.[8] Financially independent and with his close personal connections to Britain's political élite (including Newcastle and Gladstone), Gordon was confident that he might begin his imperial career in a significant colony such as British Guiana or Trinidad. Such self-assurance meant that he expected to rise rapidly through the hierarchy of colonial appointments. Between 1861 and 1890, Gordon was appointed to six colonial governorships (New Brunswick, Trinidad, Mauritius, Fiji, New Zealand and Ceylon) with increasing salaries and status, yet he was constantly lobbying for more prestigious posts and twice resigned his commission.[9] Gordon's initiatives in seeking to shape his career path across empire, reflect his confidence as a political insider who looked to his powerful friends in London, rather than for support from the local communities he ruled.

In describing his father, Gordon wrote that 'he was essentially [a] *grand seigneur* and that his own feeling of his position as such had an influence of a very marked description over all he did'.[10] Such a description was equally applicable to Gordon's own approach to service in empire. He shared the hierarchical obsession of many other aristocratic emigrants to empire who were alienated from Britain's expanding political franchise

[7] Chapman, *The career of Arthur Hamilton Gordon*, pp. 3–15.
[8] A survey of British colonies revealed that in 1865, of 33 governors, 11 were professionals, 12 were from the military and 4 were former politicians. By 1871, of 30 appointments, 10 governors were professionals, 7 were from the military and 9 were former politicians: H. L. Hall, *The Colonial Office: a history* (London: Longmans, 1937), pp. 88–9.
[9] P. Knaplund (ed.), 'Gladstone-Gordon correspondence, 1851–1896', *Transactions of the American Philosophical Society* **51**, 4 (1961), pp. 48, 52, 54, 57.
[10] Gordon to Guizot, 8 August 1867, Add 49235, Stanmore Papers, British Library, London.

and declining rural economy.[11] This awareness of 'his position' as a gentleman was expressed throughout Gordon's voluminous correspondence in the colonies, which he published for a public audience after his retirement.[12]

His élite background meant that Gordon saw himself as fundamentally different from the professional careerists emerging in the Colonial Office in London and overseas. While those who depended on their governor's salaries often bent to the pressure of the colonial élites they ruled, Gordon saw colonial rule as a public duty by an independent paternalist aristocracy.[13] Such attitudes made him an exceptionally autocratic governor, and during his first commission in New Brunswick he was so alienated from settler democracy that for the rest of his career, he sought posts in Crown colonies whose absence of local legislatures allowed him greater powers.[14] After leaving Canada, Gordon described himself as 'evidently a man to whom, as to the majority of men, it is far easier to wield a despotic rule vigorously than to exercise a limited authority with tact and persuasiveness'.[15]

In October 1866, Gordon sailed from New Brunswick to Trinidad to take up his second commission as governor. At the time, the island colony was enjoying considerable economic growth as sugar exports doubled over the 1860s, to reach 60,000 tons by 1871. During the same period, the number of indentured Indians in Trinidad had grown by over 40% to reach 22,800 immigrants.[16] The newly arrived governor saw his role as directly managing the rising local economy. After eight months of visiting across the island, Gordon complained that,

People here are apathetic and unenergetic. They think only of sugar (which they make very badly) and cacao. Now there can be no doubt that cotton, tobacco,

---

[11] D. Cannadine, *Ornamentalism: how the British saw their empire* (London: Penguin, 2001), pp. 28–32.

[12] As governor of Mauritius, Gordon edited his father's correspondence for publication, and he was particularly conscious of writing for posterity in his own official letters: A. H. Gordon, *Mauritius: records of private and of public life, 1871–1874*, Vol. I (Edinburgh: Clark, 1894), p. 48.

[13] For examples of governors whose social and economic status was more fragile than Gordon's, and who were therefore more flexible in responding to colonial demands, see the careers of Edward Eyre and Francis Hincks: C. Hall, *Civilising subjects: metropole and colony in the English imagination 1830–1867* (Cambridge: Polity Press, 2002), pp. 23–65; Laurence Brown, 'Experiments in indenture: Barbados and the segmentation of migrant labour in the Caribbean 1863–1865', *New West Indian Guide* **79**, 1–2 (2005), pp. 31–54.

[14] Chapman, *The career of Arthur Hamilton Gordon*, pp. 18–44.

[15] Gordon to Rate, 8 June 1867, Add 49235, Stanmore Papers; after arriving in Trinidad, Gordon celebrated that 'Here all power of every description is centered in the hands of the Governor alone. The Executive Council never meets except perhaps once a year on some formal occasion and in the Legislative Council nothing is proposed except by the Governor or by his direction': *ibid.*

[16] Look Lai, *Indentured labor, Caribbean sugar*, p. 302.

and coffee would all pay well, especially the two former. We want a few go ahead Yankees or shrewd Englishmen to take up such things. I will give them land cheap (there is plenty of it) and as much immigrant labour as they please.[17]

State intervention through land grants and the allocation of migrant labour were central to colonial development projects across the British empire during the nineteenth century, but these were closely supervised by the Colonial Land and Emigration Commission in London. Gordon's enthusiastic promises of land and labour reveal his sense of independence from the metropole and his desire to leave his own mark on the colony.

Gordon also sought to recruit capital from Canada, guaranteeing government backing and the economic support of Trinidad's leading sugar planters. He wrote,

I am convinced that if this colony is ultimately to succeed in its struggle for prosperity it is essential that it should have another bank and equally essential that it should have central factories in the Martinique plan. That every sugar farmer should grind his own canes and make his own rum is in my eyes as absurd as it would be for every corn farmer to grind his own wheat and brew his own liquour.[18]

Gordon's awareness of the centralisation of sugar production in French Martinique during the mid-1860s (fuelled by earlier banking reforms), shows how quickly he formulated his own vision for colonial development and economic modernisation. However, it was only after his departure from Trinidad that central sugar factories were constructed on the island, and these would be financed by capital from Britain rather than a local bank under government patronage.[19]

Gordon's predecessor as governor of Trinidad was Sir John Manners-Sutton, whom Gordon had met when succeeding Sir John as governor of New Brunswick in 1861.[20] Arriving at the Governor's Cottage in Port of Spain, Gordon took on Manners-Sutton's servants including a mulatto housemaid, black coachman and black cook.[21] He also took over his predecessor's policies on land reform and immigration. Squatting had been seen as a major threat in Trinidad in the wake of emancipation when many former slaves deserted the plantations, but these pressures had weakened by the mid-1860s as plantation production was expanding and

---

[17] Gordon to Rate, 8 June 1867, Add 49235, Stanmore Papers.
[18] *Ibid.*
[19] R. W. Beachey, *The British West Indies sugar industry in the late nineteenth century* (Oxford: Blackwell, 1957), p. 84.
[20] Chapman, *The career of Arthur Hamilton Gordon*, p. 16.
[21] Manuscript on Trinidad, p. 53, Add 49271, Stanmore Papers.

indentured immigration reached record levels. Manners-Sutton had received a petition in 1865 from French and Spanish creoles seeking to legalise the small cocoa farms that had been established on Crown lands, and Gordon subsequently endorsed a scheme to regularise land settlement in the Montserrat Ward of Western Trinidad.[22] However, these land grants to smallholders were eclipsed by the extensive acreages Gordon allowed to Gregor Turnbull and William Burnley, two of the largest planters on the island.[23] While the agenda for land reform had been established before Gordon's arrival, his policies fuelled the rapid expansion of cocoa planting and the consolidation of sugar production during the 1870s.[24]

A second set of policies which Gordon inherited on his arrival in Trinidad focused on reducing the mortality amongst the indentured Indian population. After the early departure of Manners-Sutton, acting governor Edward Rushworth recommended that a ration system for newly arrived indentured immigrants be established, similar to that which he had seen in Mauritius.[25] This proposal was supported by Doctor Henry Mitchell, who had been the colony's agent general for immigration since 1850 and would play a significant role in shaping Gordon's vision of indenture in Trinidad. In May 1867 Gordon passed an ordinance requiring employers to provide one year of subsistence for indentured Indians.[26] The Colonial Office in London was opposed to making rations for immigrants compulsory; however, Gordon extended the ration system to two years in 1870 through entrenching it in a law consolidating immigration regulations.[27]

With the colonial hospital of San Fernando overcrowded with immigrants, Gordon also opportunistically seized on the retirement of the colonial health officer to increase the responsibilities of planters for medical care on the estates.[28] He reorganised the reception depot at Nelson Island to provide for the medical inspection and recovery of

---

[22] Gordon to Buckingham, 8 June 1867, CO 295/239, National Archives, London.
[23] Mitchell to Bushe, February 1869, p. 17, Box 2, Stanmore Collection, New York Public Library.
[24] H. Johnson, 'Immigration and the sugar industry in Trinidad during the last quarter of the nineteenth century', *Journal of Caribbean History* **3** (1971), p. 30; Beachey, *The British West Indies sugar industry*, p. 122.
[25] K. O. Laurence, *A question of labour: indentured immigration into Trinidad and British Guiana 1875–1917* (Kingston: Ian Randle, 1994), p. 199.
[26] Gordon to Buckingham, 24 May 1867, CO 295/239, National Archives, London.
[27] Gordon to Buckingham, 28 August 1867, Box 5, Stanmore Collection.
[28] Gordon to Buchanan, 9 May 1867, CO 295/239; Gordon to Carnarvon, 25 February 1867, Box 5, Stanmore Collection.

immigrants before their allocation to the plantations.[29] The low mortality rates amongst Indian immigrants in 1868 and 1869 were directly claimed by Gordon as resulting from greater state regulation of estate hospitals and the ration system. His 1870 consolidation ordinance converted estate doctors into government officers and provided that immigrants would not be allocated to plantations with high mortality or significantly low wages.[30] Keen to publicise his reforms in Britain, Gordon sponsored the visit of Charles Kingsley to Trinidad, whose travel narrative celebrated indentureship in the island as a well-regulated and humane system of labour.[31] Though the debate over public health in Trinidad had preceded Gordon, his immigration legislation greatly extended the intrusive powers of the state despite objections from the Colonial Office.

While attempting to reform health conditions under indenture, Gordon was also actively seeking to expand the supply of immigrant labour in the colony. In March 1867, he wrote to London requesting the transfer of indentured Indians from neighbouring Grenada to Trinidad.[32] At the same time, he supported the expansion of immigration from China, despite the widespread complaints of employers over the desertion, crime and insubordination of the Chinese who arrived in Trinidad between 1862 and 1866.[33] Gordon argued that compared to indentured Indians, Chinese immigrants were more willing to convert to Christianity and to intermarry with Afro-Caribbean creoles. Unlike the Indians, the Chinese would 'become amalgamated with the population and a permanent gain to the colony'.[34]

Gordon's advocacy of Chinese indentured labour meant little given that West Indian labour recruitment in China was effectively closed off by the Kung Convention of 1866 which provided emigrants with the right to repatriation.[35] However, Gordon was even prepared to modify the five-year contracts of service which had been offered to Chinese immigrants in 1866. He wrote in March 1867 that,

We are also willing to offer yet more advantageous terms to Chinese families willing to become permanent settlers in Trinidad. To Such, I am disposed to offer a free grant of land after one year of industrial residence and I hope this

---

[29] Laurence, *A question of labour*, p. 101.
[30] *Ibid.*, pp. 197–8.
[31] C. Kingsley, *At last: a Christmas in the West Indies* (London: Macmillan, 1887), pp. 116–20.
[32] Gordon to Carnarvon, 12 March 1867, Box 5, Stanmore Collection.
[33] Gordon to Carnarvon, 11 March 1867; Box 5, Stanmore Collection; Look Lai, *Indentured labor, Caribbean sugar*, pp. 96–9.
[34] Gordon to Carnarvon, 24 March, 1867, Box 5, Stanmore Collection.
[35] Look Lai, *Indentured labor, Caribbean sugar*, pp. 48–9.

may prove a sufficient inducement to attract a considerable number of these valuable settlers to this island.[36]

Gordon's willingness to provide land for indentured immigrants is striking, given that Henry Mitchell had informed him that planters across Trinidad saw the Chinese as unfit for estate labour.[37]

Two years after Gordon's land-for-immigrants proposal, the Crown land reforms inspired a group of twenty-five Indian immigrants to petition for their repatriation entitlements to be commuted into land grants.[38] Thirty-five Indians had already participated in the initial land purchases in the Montserrat Ward. As Charles Mitchell, the commissioner supervising the sales, reported, the Indians paid cash for their plots and 'they evinced a strong desire to form themselves into small communities, generally on the confines of the Ward, and within easy distance of some sugar estates where they may obtain employment'.[39] In May 1869, Gordon rushed to offer plots of ten acres to those immigrants whose contracts were expiring, despite the fact that this went against the existing regulations for Crown land and had not been authorised by the Colonial Office. For Gordon, land grants for immigrants represented a significant economic saving for Trinidad authorities when compared to the costs of repatriation, as well as transforming transient labour into a settled agricultural peasantry. However, Gordon's measures received ambivalent support from his successors, planters and the immigrants themselves as the quality and quantity of land offered varied during the 1870s depending on plantations' labour supply.[40]

TRANSPLANTING IMMIGRATION POLICY IN COLONIAL MAURITIUS

Gordon described his passage from England to his new post in Mauritius during early February 1871 as a 'fortnight of utter misery'.[41] Within three weeks of assuming the governorship of the colony, he was writing to family, friends and colleagues seeking a transfer to India, Ceylon, Britain or even back to his previous post in Trinidad. Complaining that the

---

[36] Gordon to Carnarvon, 12 March 1867, Box 5, Stanmore Collection.
[37] H. Mitchell, Memorandum, 15 November 1866, Box 2, Stanmore Collection.
[38] Laurence, *A question of labour*, p. 386
[39] Mitchell to Bushe, February 1869, Box 2, Stanmore Collection.
[40] Laurence, *A question of labour*, pp. 387–91, Look Lai, *Indentured labor, Caribbean sugar*, pp. 229–33; M. Ramesar, *Survivors of another crossing: a history of East Indians in Trinidad, 1880–1946* (St Augustine: University of the West Indies, 1994), pp. 82–3.
[41] Gordon, *Mauritius*, Vol. I, p. 24.

climate and high mortality of Mauritius prevented family life, Gordon was also critical of the colony's economic prospects. In the same letter in which Gordon asked his wife to lobby the Gladstones, Cardwells and Argylls for a new appointment, he requested that she

Send me out my immigration printed papers in my basket at Eccleston Square or in the drawing-room. The immigration system here is a bad one, and I should like to mend it before I go.[42]

Gordon's desires to leave Mauritius and to make a rapid impact on the colony were therefore mutually reinforcing.

The central issue facing the new governor was the public health crisis in the colony, especially in its capital, Port Louis. The population of Mauritius had been decimated during 1867–8 when an epidemic of malaria claimed over 40,000 deaths.[43] The highest mortality was concentrated amongst the impoverished Indian immigrants who had served out their indentures, and the colony's urban population. While European residents of the island had been relatively unaffected by 'fevers' in the early 1860s, the crisis of 1867–8 took a heavy toll on whites and was especially devastating for the colonial administration.[44] Alongside the demographic cost, the epidemic was an economic disaster for the colony, whose sugar exports had already been weakened by prolonged drought.

Arriving four years after the crisis of 1867, Gordon felt that the high rates of malaria were due to his predecessors' commitments to expenditure on Indian immigration without investing in the public infrastructure necessary to maintain the island's increasing population.[45] He argued that to reduce mortality rates in Mauritius would require significant long-term investment in drainage, sanitation and medical provision. Despite his earlier policies in Trinidad, his daily fears for his own health and encouragement from other local officials, Gordon did not actively pursue these reforms.[46]

Rather than public health, Gordon chose to focus his energies on indentured immigration, drawing on his Trinidad experiences and motivated by the expectation that he would quickly obtain a new post

---

[42] *Ibid.*, p. 41.

[43] *Rapport sur la fièvre épidémique de l'île Maurice adopté par la Commission d'enquête nommée par S. E. le Gouverneur Sir H. Barkly* (Mauritius: Imprimerie du Cernéen, 1868), p. 35.

[44] A. R. Barraut, *Report on the fever known in this Colony under the name of Bombay Fever* (Port Louis: Government Printer, 1864), p. 14; Carter, *Servants, sirdars, and settlers*, p. 276.

[45] Gordon, *Mauritius*, Vol. I, p. 154.

[46] B. Brereton, *Law, justice and empire: the colonial career of John Gorrie 1829–1892* (Mona: University of West Indies Press, 1997), p. 88.

elsewhere. Within his first month in Mauritius, he noted how there was relatively little state regulation of indentured immigrants after their arrival on the island.[47] Certainly, Gordon was not opposed to migrant labour *per se*, as he actively promoted the importation of Africans liberated from the slave trade for agricultural labour in the Seychelles.[48] In June 1871, when the Colonial Office in London inquired about minor reforms to the Mauritian regulations on Indian immigrant mortality, Gordon replied that the planter-dominated legislative council would certainly block such piecemeal measures and so he was in the process of formulating a far more comprehensive package of reforms.[49]

Gordon's early objections to the indentured immigration system in Mauritius were focused on the limited authority of the colony's executive to allocate immigrants and inspect their working conditions. He believed that the divergences between Trinidad and Mauritius were due to the breakdown of state regulation in the latter, however this ignored the more fundamental differences between each colony's indentured population.[50] The end of the 1850s marked the peak of indentured immigration to Mauritius fuelled by political unrest and economic dislocation in India, buoyant sugar prices, and extensive private recruiting by Mauritian planters (see Fig. 7.2). Despite this influx, the abolition in Mauritius of the right to repatriation to India meant that indentured workers were increasingly recruited from within the island rather than from outside.

By 1865, three-quarters of the plantation labour force under contract were 'old immigrants' who had already served out their first indenture terms.[51] While government regulation of indenture focused on the

---

[47] Gordon, *Mauritius*, Vol. I, p. 33.

[48] Gordon privately drafted the request for African labour in the Seychelles, which was ratified by a mass meeting in Mahé on 21 September 1871, before forwarding the petition on to London with his endorsement. Despite Henry Stanley's accusations in 1873 that Africans liberated by the British from the East African slave trade were reduced to conditions of slavery in the Seychelles, Gordon continued to defend the project – *ibid.*, pp. 45, 233; A. H. Gordon, *Mauritius: records of private and of public life, 1871–1874* (Edinburgh: Clark, 1894), Vol. II, pp. 109, 379, 688.

[49] Gordon, *Mauritius*, Vol. I, pp. 92–3.

[50] In 1909, Gordon testified that 'In the beginning … the system which was started and carried out in the West Indies, and in Mauritius, was almost exactly the same: say about 1850, they were almost identical. Then followed a period of some 20 years, from 1850 to 1870, in which they rather diverged; but the difference was this, that while in Trinidad all the alterations which were made were alterations generally in favour of greater security to the immigrant, the alterations made in Mauritius during the same period were all to the advantage of the planter, and the disadvantage of the immigrant, and consequently at the end of 20 years they were in a very different position': *Report of the Committee on Emigration from India to the Crown Colonies and Protectorates, Parliamentary Papers* **27** (1910), p. 348.

[51] R. B. Allen, *Slaves, freedmen, and indentured laborers in colonial Mauritius* (Cambridge: Cambridge University Press, 1999), pp. 59–61; H. Tinker, *A new system of slavery: the export of Indian labour*

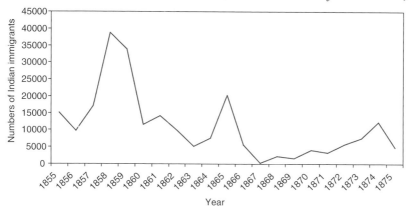

Fig. 7.2 Annual immigration to Mauritius, 1855–1875. M. Carter, *Servants, sirdars, and settlers: Indians in Mauritius, 1834–1874* (Delhi: Oxford University Press, 1995), p. 26.

transport and reception of immigrants from India, there was little supervision of the annual contracts signed by these old immigrants, or of plantation conditions such as medical care.[52] The indentured population had therefore taken on a significantly different composition in Mauritius than Trinidad, but these demographic and economic changes went largely unrecognised in Gordon's concern over the limits of his own position as governor.

Gordon's interest in the reform of indentureship ignited an explosion of debate in Mauritius. Tensions had been building in the island since 1867, when the colony's labour laws were amended to force former immigrants to return to estate work or be prosecuted as vagrants. Gordon's predecessor as governor, Henry Barkly, had implemented the measure during the malaria epidemic due to complaints of a labour shortage on the island. Like Gordon, Barkly was a transient administrator having served as governor of British Guiana, Jamaica and Victoria before he was posted to Mauritius. However, Barkly lacked Gordon's financial independence as his family fortune and career in the House of Commons had been ruined by the economic crisis that followed emancipation in the West Indies.

overseas 1830–1920, 2nd editon (London: Hansib, 1993), pp. 86, 98–102, Carter, *Servants, sirdars, and settlers*, pp. 25–7.
[52] Barraut, *Report on the fever known in this Colony under the name of Bombay Fever*, p. 15.

An absentee planter, Barkly was amongst the earliest employers of indentured Indians in British Guiana, when he hired 106 Indian immigrants for his Highbury estate during 1838 (two months before his apprenticed slaves were fully free from plantation labour). He had also sought to privately recruit Chinese immigrants from Singapore and lobbied the Colonial Office on the necessity of state-supported immigrant labour.[53] As governor of British Guiana in 1850, Barkly had sought to massively expand Indian immigration to the colony and had proposed an indentured system which gave considerably more power to planters than the Mauritian model advocated by the Colonial Office.[54] On becoming governor of Jamaica, Barkly visited Madeira in an attempt to recruit immigrants, and endorsed an extensive range of schemes for migrant labour from Central and North America.[55] Early in his colonial career Barkly had been sympathetic to coercing Afro-Caribbean labourers back onto the plantations through direct taxation, however his solution to complaints of a labour shortage in Mauritius was ultimately based on the *livret* (passbook) system of neighbouring French Réunion rather than his Caribbean experience.[56]

Facing declining arrivals from India in the late 1860s (see Fig. 7.2), and the population crisis caused by the epidemic of 1867–68, Barkly's Ordinance 31 of 1867 was intended to drive the old immigrants back onto the sugar estates. As a result of the new labour laws, vagrancy convictions skyrocketed in the colony during 1869, with almost a fifth of all Indian males charged as vagrants.[57] Within a few months of his arrival, Gordon received a mass petition from the colony's Indian population calling for the abolition of the 1867 labour laws. The public controversy over Mauritian indentureship rapidly extended during the second half of 1871 to include criticisms of the limited medical provisions for immigrants and the victimisation of Indians by the island's police. However, it is important to emphasise that Gordon saw these latter scandals as symptoms of the limited regulatory role of the state rather than the product of specific policies or social conditions.

[53] M. Macmillan, *Sir Henry Barkly: mediator and moderator 1815–1898* (Cape Town: A. A. Balkema, 1970), pp. 11, 36.
[54] *Ibid.*, pp. 41–2.
[55] R. V. Sires, 'Sir Henry Barkly and the labor problem in Jamaica, 1853–1856', *Journal of Negro History* **25**, 2 (1940), pp. 223–35.
[56] Macmillan, *Sir Henry Barkly*, pp. 37, 169.
[57] R. B. Allen, 'Indian immigrants and the legacy of marronage: illegal absence, desertion and vagrancy on Mauritius 1835–1900', *Itinerario* **21**, 1 (1997), p. 103.

Four months after arriving in Mauritius, Gordon had embarked on a comparative study of immigration schemes in the West Indies and the Mascarenes. In mid-August 1871, although his Trinidad papers had yet to arrive from Britain, Gordon sent a detailed 'sketch' to his superiors in London analysing indentureship in Mauritius, Trinidad and British Guiana. His comparative study emphasised the lower wages, inferior medical assistance, higher workloads, and more repressive labour laws of Mauritius.[58] A month later, Gordon restated his objections to indentureship in Mauritius to the Colonial Office, focusing on the State's lack of power over allocation, inspection and regulation. Strikingly, Gordon's reforming zeal did not come from direct contact with plantation conditions in Mauritius – he only visited two estates during his tenure on the island, both of which were owned by leading planters, and his papers mention no personal encounters with Indians other than his own domestic servants.[59]

In lobbying for the wholesale reform of indenture, Gordon proactively sought to shape the flow of information from the colony to the Colonial Office in London. He attacked the reports prepared by the protector of immigrants in Mauritius, Nicholas Beyts, as 'full of false figures and unsound comparisons'.[60] In mid-November 1871, Gordon forwarded Beyts' annual report to the Colonial Office, with a note stressing 'my lack of reliance on the statistical statements which are made in this Colony'.[61] He explicitly rejected its figures for labour supply, vagrancy and migrant mortality, arguing that the system of plantation inspection on the island had completely broken down. In a confidential letter to the colonial secretary, Lord Kimberley, Gordon sought to discredit Beyts as a devious Eurasian.[62] However, Kimberley and the Colonial Land and Emigration Commission in London seemed to accept some of Beyts' report in suggesting only limited reforms and in rejecting Gordon's proposal for a wide-ranging investigation of indentured immigration.[63]

Ultimately, the push for a royal commission was strengthened by demands from Mauritian planters for an enquiry that would silence their local critics.[64] Gordon was also successful in his request that the

[58] Gordon, *Mauritius*, Vol. I, pp. 92, 191.   [59] Gordon, *Mauritius*, Vol. II, p. 20.
[60] Gordon, *Mauritius*, Vol. I, p. 297.   [61] *Ibid.*, p. 315.
[62] *Ibid.*, p. 431. Beyts was the son of a customs official in Bombay and would face similar racial slurs over a decade later when governor Pope Hennessy appointed him acting colonial secretary for Mauritius: Tinker, *A new system of slavery*, p. 99.
[63] Gordon, *Mauritius*, Vol. I, pp. 396–8.
[64] *Ibid.*, p. 441.

Commission's members be drawn from the recent royal commission on indentured immigration in the Caribbean.[65] Sir William Frere of the Bombay High Court had led the investigation in British Guiana, and was chosen to head the new royal commission in Mauritius. As Henry Taylor in the Colonial Office wrote to Gordon, 'I am glad you have got the Commission for which you so dexterously procured an application, and for whose labours you have so laboriously prepared the way.'[66] In seeking commissioners with West Indian experience, Gordon sought to construct an investigation that would confirm his earlier comparative analysis of Mauritius.

One unofficial member of the 1872 Royal Commission of Inquiry was Charles Mitchell, who was the son of Trinidad's agent general for immigration. Mitchell had been educated in Scotland, before returning home to work as an assistant in the Immigration Office.[67] Gordon had appointed Mitchell as a stipendiary magistrate in 1867 to supervise the reform of Crown lands in Trinidad, despite Colonial Office objections to his educational background and lack of legal training.[68] Mitchell had been part of the British Guiana royal commission in 1871 and Gordon had lobbied for him to be a member of the enquiry in Mauritius. This appointment was blocked in London due to fears that Mitchell's close relationship with Gordon would compromise the new investigation's impartial image. Despite such concerns, Mitchell was allowed to act temporarily as deputy protector of immigrants in Mauritius so as to intensively audit plantation records for the commissioners.[69]

Gordon had initially hoped that the report of the royal commission would not only force the reform of immigration in Mauritius, but would also raise his reputation in London to speed promotion to a post elsewhere.[70] Early in its investigations, Gordon informally provided considerable amounts of material to the commissioners, even privately suggesting questions for their cross-examination of witnesses.[71] Frere's failing health meant that the royal commission would ultimately take over two-and-a-half years, and its investigation was not completed until November 1874. With such protracted delays, Gordon abandoned waiting for a report that would enhance his public image, and resigned as governor of Mauritius five months before the enquiry finished.

[65] *Ibid.*, pp. 324–5.   [66] *Ibid.*, p. 534.
[67] Gordon to Buckingham, 7 September 1867, CO 295/240.
[68] Gordon to Buckingham, 6 June 1867, CO 295/239.   [69] Gordon, *Mauritius*, Vol. I, p. 447.
[70] Gordon, *Mauritius*, Vol. II, pp. 39, 168.   [71] *Ibid.*, pp. 614–15.

ARISTOCRATIC AUTHORITARIANISM AND THE CONSTRUCTION OF
MIGRANT LABOUR IN FIJI

The start of 1874 marked a personal crisis for Gordon, who felt that his public life was over after he was passed over for the governorship of Jamaica. He was despondent that 'the qualities for command which I know that I possess should have been so wholly wasted'.[72] As he was formulating his resignation from Mauritius, Gordon began lobbying to become the first British governor of Fiji and he was officially offered this commission in November 1874.[73] The post was a significant deviation from the accepted hierarchy of colonial appointments as measured by salary and public prestige, yet to Gordon it represented the opportunity to construct a lasting legacy.

Gordon's autocratic personality and the aims of his superiors were in this case mutually reinforcing, as he was given an extreme amount of latitude in framing the objectives and personnel of his mission. As the colonial secretary, Lord Carnarvon, informed Gordon,

Whether a revenue can be raised sufficient to maintain the simplest Crown Colony Government (nothing but a despotism is thought of) seems most doubtful; as also whether the Islands can ever maintain a wealthy trading and planting community.[74]

These reservations about Britain's acquisition of Fiji were however a powerful attraction for Gordon who sought to pursue his own vision of aristocratic authoritarianism, with the maximum independence from settler society and London's bureaucracy.

This was also a strategic appointment by the Colonial Office, as the choice of a governor with a public reputation for humanitarianism helped to legitimise the imperial occupation of the Fijian archipelago. The language of antislavery had dominated debates in the House of Commons over colonial annexation, with William McArthur arguing 'that kidnapping could not be extirpated in the Pacific, unless Fiji, the great centre of the traffic, was placed under the protection of our flag'.[75] While McArthur and the Aborigines' Protection Society publicised missionary accounts attacking the Pacific labour trade, white settlers in Fiji used abolitionist discourse to call for British intervention against native

---

[72] Gordon, *Mauritius*, Vol. II, p. 387.   [73] *Ibid.*, p. 646.
[74] *Ibid.*, p. 661.
[75] *The annexation of Fiji and the Pacific slave trade: speech of Mr Alderman McArthur MP in the House of Commons on Tuesday June 13, 1873* (London: Aborigines' Protection Society, 1874), p. 2.

authorities. Influenced by both groups, Royal Navy commodore James Goodenough rejected the Fijian government of Cakobau as dependent on native slavery and proclaimed British rule in the islands.[76] Goodenough escorted Gordon to Fiji in June 1875, and the debates over Pacific slavery would continue after annexation as Gordon's policies were criticised by both missionaries and settlers.

Accompanying Gordon to Fiji was a unique retinue of officials, who had been personally selected by him based on their service in Trinidad and Mauritius. Charles Mitchell accepted a reduced salary to work under Gordon in Fiji, on the understanding that he would leave after the colony's formative period.[77] Treasurer Arthur Havelock and chief medical officer Dr William MacGregor had earlier been appointed by him to posts in the Seychelles. From Mauritius, Gordon recruited Justice John Gorrie, botanist John Horne and the lawyer Victor Williamson (who had served on the Mauritius royal commission).[78] This entourage was also strengthened in Fiji by the selective recruitment of several planters for government posts, such as long-time resident John Thurston.[79] These officials were bound together by shared Scottish or colonial backgrounds, and such close personal relationships were especially important given Fiji's isolation and lack of infrastructure.

Though the new colony began with an extremely experienced administration, its small white population of two thousand settlers was in crisis. The rapid boom and bust of cotton cultivation during the 1860s had caused the breakdown of 'race' relations as an influx of planters and adventurers attempted to forcibly claim Fijian land and labour. This frontier community was heavily shaped by the racial attitudes brought by inter-colonial migrants from Australia, New Zealand and Ceylon. While settler agitation was successful in forcing British annexation of the islands during 1873–4, the collapse of cotton prices had already begun to cause the economic and demographic decline of the white population.[80] Given Gordon's antagonism to settler democracy in New Brunswick (and later New Zealand), it is not surprising that he saw the impoverished white

[76] J. Samson, *Imperial benevolence: making British authority in the Pacific Islands* (Honolulu: University of Hawaii Press, 1998), pp. 159–67.

[77] Gordon to Hicks-Beach, 4 February 1879, CO 384/126.

[78] Brereton, *Law, justice and empire*, pp. 98–9; J. Horne, *Fiji: remarks on the agricultural prospects of Fiji* (Levuka, 1878); J. Horne, *A year in Fiji: an inquiry into the botanical, agricultural and economic resources of the colony* (London: Edward Stanford, 1881).

[79] J. Young, *Adventurous spirits: Australian migrant society in pre-cession Fiji* (St Lucia: University of Queensland Press, 1984), pp. 385–6.

[80] *Ibid.*, pp. 307–85.

planters as a doomed race.[81] Discouraging further white settlement in the archipelago, Gordon instead focused on the recruitment of overseas capital for plantation production and functionaries for government administration.[82]

Arriving in the midst of the measles epidemic of 1874, Gordon estimated that the disease had killed almost a fifth of the colony's indigenous population.[83] This demographic disaster reinforced Gordon's commitment to the paternalist protection of Fijian society, which contrasted to the impact of similar epidemics in legitimising the extension of settler society in the Australian colonies. Gordon argued that

Generally speaking, the native race has disappeared before the new comer ... Where this has been the case, however, and where injustice has been done to the original owners of the soil, I am bound to say I think it proceeds as often as not from a want, if I may say so, of the imaginative faculty rather than from a desire to do injustice. It has been from the want of consideration for differences of character, differences of race, differences of habits of all kinds. It has been expected that at once a conformity should be introduced to English habits and ideas, and in the attempt to introduce that conformity the natives have too often been improved off the face of the earth.[84]

Echoing his interpretation of indentured immigration in Mauritius, the decline of indigenous populations across the Pacific was seen by Gordon as primarily a failure of executive rule and legislation, rather than of colonial expropriation and coercion.

Two pillars were central to Gordon's vision of the preservation of indigenous society in Fiji; the recognition of native hierarchies of rule and the isolation of Fijian communities from plantation production. Gordon's transformation of chiefdoms into units of colonial administration drew on the earlier measure of Hercules Robinson, who as governor of New South Wales had negotiated the cession of Fiji to Britain. Robinson was another transient administrator, and his experiences in Ceylon of ruling though high-caste Sinhalese headmen helped shape the formation of the new colony.[85] Gordon's transformation of chiefly authority into a formal hierarchy that extended across Fijian society was also motivated by his own limited administrative resources and his preference for aristocratic patronage over settler democracy. To Gordon, this programme of native government was

---

[81] Gordon, *Fiji*, Vol. I, p. 137.
[82] A. Gordon, *Fiji: a lecture delivered before the Aberdeen Philosophical Society* (Aberdeen: Land Mortage and Agency of Fiji, 1881), pp. 20–3.
[83] *Ibid.*, p. 6.   [84] *Ibid.*, p. 13.
[85] C. Newbury, *Patrons, clients and empire: chieftaincy and over-rule in Asia, Africa and the Pacific* (Oxford: Oxford University Press, 2003), p. 226.

based on local traditions and he enthusiastically appropriated public ceremonies of deference such as *yaqona* drinking which became a daily ritual
within his own household.[86] However, critics like Methodist missionary
Lorimer Fison argued that Fijian culture under Gordon was being per-
verted into a feudal system of rule which disempowered the majority of
Fijians.[87]

Though Gordon enjoyed an unusually open mandate from the
Colonial Office when he travelled to Fiji, he was committed to creating a
colony that was economically sustainable. On his voyage to the Pacific, he
read James Money's *Java: how to manage a colony* which described how
Dutch authorities had used collective taxation paid in agricultural products to produce a thriving colonial economy.[88] Java at the time was the
world's second leading producer of sugar due to this state-regulated
system in which villages provided cane and labour for central sugar factories. Strikingly, Gordon appropriated the Dutch Cultuurstelsel system
of communal taxation to isolate Fijian communities from employment on
Fiji's emerging sugar plantations.[89] Planters labelled the governor's system
as 'slavery' for denying Fijians the opportunity of 'free labour' on the
estates, which Gordon refuted with counter accusations of plantation
slavery in lobbying the Colonial Office and the British public.[90]

The controversy over native policy increased the pressure on Gordon
to expand the colony's economy, although his commitment to an
extensive programme of migrant labour predated his arrival in Fiji. In the
weeks preceding his departure from Britain, Gordon had attended discussions over indentured labour held at the India Office.[91] In his first
meetings with planters, the new governor was careful to record those who
would be sympathetic to Indian immigration, and he later received a
letter from his private sectary on the potential for 'your plan of Indian
immigration' on the west coast of Viti Levu.[92] After two months resi-

---

[86] *Ibid.*, pp. 270, 293.

[87] L. Fison, 'Land tenure in Fiji', *Journal of the Anthropological Institute of Great Britain and Ireland*
   10 (1881), pp. 349–52; P. France, *The charter of the land: custom and colonization in Fiji* (Melbourne:
   Oxford University Press, 1969), pp. 104–10, 117–18.

[88] Gordon, *Fiji*, Vol. I, p. 196.

[89] Gordon would later acknowledge the influence of money in his autobiography; however, in March
   1879 he publicly rejected any suggestion that his communal tax was modelled on Java, stating that
   though 'there is a certain superficial resemblance, the two systems are essentially opposed in
   principle and in practice': A. Gordon, *Paper on the system of taxation in force in Fiji* (London:
   Harrison & Sons, 1879), p. 35.

[90] *Ibid.*, pp. 34–5; Arthur Gordon, 'Letter to the Editor', *Saturday Review* (1882).

[91] This meeting with Lord Salisbury was held on 25 January 1875: Gordon, *Fiji*, Vol. I, pp. 44, 53.

[92] *Ibid.*, pp. 129, 153, 338.

dency in Fiji, Gordon was officially proclaimed governor on 1 September 1875, and publicly read the colony's royal charter. The following day, he addressed a meeting of white settlers where he focused on the importance of migrant labour for the colony.

Gordon asked planters at the public meeting to indicate by ballot whether they would prefer state regulation of immigration and whether the importation of Polynesian labourers should be supplemented with indentured Indians. Comparing state and private schemes for immigration, he argued that the former were far more systematic and economical, and ensured an 'absolute guarantee against abuses'.[93] In his speech, Gordon gave considerable details on the costs of Indian immigration; emphasising that the State would pay a third of the transportation expenses, that indentured Indians were paid only five pence per day, and that their five-year contracts were considerably longer than those of the Polynesians. Gordon deliberately framed his project of state immigration in flexible terms:

If we had both systems of immigrants at work, the Government would send for such a number of Polynesians and such a number of Indians as the planters might respectively ask for. It would depend on themselves which they would have and no doubt they would ask for that which on the whole they found most advantageous to them.[94]

While publicly Gordon portrayed Indian indentureship as simply a response to local demands, he was privately critical of both the forced recruitment of native Fijian labour, and the importation of Polynesian migrant labour which he likened to a virtual 'slave trade'.[95]

Gordon's promotion of Indian immigration received little popular endorsement from white settlers who saw it as far more costly than Fijian labour. Although there had been a few isolated requests in Fiji for Asian immigration between 1867 and 1870, the majority of planters lacked the capital for the high transportation costs involved with state-sponsored migration from India. Gordon's project was also ambivalently received by the Colonial Office, due to criticisms from the Aborigines' Protection Society in early 1876 over the extension of indentured labour to new colonies.[96] While Gordon was able to overcome these metropolitan concerns by 1878, planter opposition to indentured immigration from India intensified at the end of the decade.

[93] *Ibid.*, p. 178.   [94] *Ibid.*, pp. 135, 179, 199.   [95] *Ibid.*, p. 153.
[96] K. L. Gillion, *Fiji's Indian migrants* (Melbourne: Oxford University Press, 1962), pp. 3, 13–14; O. W. Parnaby, 'The regulation of indentured labour to Fiji, 1864–1888', *Journal of the Polynesian Society* **65** (1956), pp. 1, 64.

Despite the heated debates in Fiji over state-sponsored indentured immigration, Indian migrants had been arriving in the islands before its cession to Britain. In early September 1874, six Indians had accompanied the Clarence family from Mauritius to the Rewa River on Viti Levu. Clarence was the manager of the new sugar mill at Uluicalia which commenced operation in July 1875, and given that these Indians had already worked under him for fifteen years they were probably skilled factory hands.[97] Other non-indentured Indians who preceded Gordon's arrival in Fiji, worked as cooks and domestic servants in the white settlement at Levuka.[98] At the start of 1879, thirty-one Indians were privately recruited from French New Caledonia by planters on Taveuni. These labourers had initially been indentured in Réunion, and their willingness to appeal to immigration regulations of Mauritius and elsewhere in empire quickly alienated their employers.[99]

In Levuka, Gordon's own household drew on these currents of subaltern mobility at the same time as he was promoting state-controlled indentured immigration. In late March 1876, Rachel Gordon wrote that

We have now got two Indians from Mauritius, who are excellent servants. One of them Abelak, was an old servant of ours there. Their work is to clean boots, valet all the gentleman, do all the housemaid's work, (bed and sitting rooms,) and come to the drawing-room bell. There are three Fijian footmen in smart native clothes – handsome picturesque lazy fellows who wait at table to perfection, and do nothing else whatever – and there are three foreign labour boys [Polynesians] who clean plates, wash up, and do all the dining-room work.[100]

The governor's house was therefore a microcosm for the ethnically segmented labour system he sought to impose on the colony.[101]

Fuelling the rapid construction of Indian indentureship in Fiji was the extensive experience of Gordon's official retinue with migrant labour in the Caribbean and the Indian Ocean. Charles Mitchell was

[97] Baron Anatole von Hügel, who was a house guest of the Gordons, visited the mill at Uluicalia and requested some sugar samples for the governor: J. Roth and S. Hooper (eds.), *The Fiji journals of Baron Anatole von Hügel: 1875–1877* (Suva: Fiji Museum, 1990), pp. 153–4; K. Singh, 'Uluicalia Sugar Mill and its Indian workers, 1874–1876', *Domodomo* 2, 3 (1984), pp. 113–20; J. C. Potts, 'The sugar industry in Fiji: its beginnings and development', *Transactions and Proceedings of the Fiji Society* 7, 1 (1958), p. 111.

[98] Singh, 'Uluicalia Sugar Mill', pp. 119–20.

[99] Gillion, *Fiji's Indian migrants*, pp. 68–9.

[100] Gordon, *Fiji*, Vol. I, p. 420; for a similar ethnic division of household labour see C. F. Gordon-Cumming, *At home in Fiji*, Vol. I (Edinburgh: William Blackwood, 1881), p. 52.

[101] The Gordons also recruited an Indian domestic servant from New Caledonia, while on the first shipment of indentured Indian immigrants on the *Leonidas*, eight were employed by colonial officials: Brij V. Lal, *Chalo jahaji: on a journey through indenture in Fiji* (Suva: Fiji Museum, 2000), p. 147.

described by the visiting Baron Anatole von Hügel as 'the Governor's great favourite'.[102] In Fiji, Mitchell was initially appointed as commissioner for land and then as agent general of immigration. In July 1877 he was sent to India to negotiate for the first shipment of indentured immigrants to Fiji. William MacGregor had acted as inspector of liberated Africans in the Seychelles and prepared extensive quarantine measures in Fiji before the arrival of the first indentured Indians in May 1879.[103] That the importation of indentured Indians had been driven by migrant colonial administrators was reflected by the first shipment on the *Leonidas*, where there were so few planter requests for labourers that the government had to employ over half the immigrants on public works.[104]

Despite official commitment to Indian immigration, the most immediate impact of Gordon's economic policies was to produce a new peak in the Pacific labour trade. The suppression of the abusive practices of recruiting migrant labour from the New Hebrides and the Solomon Islands had been one of the central justifications for Britain's colonisation of Fiji. After cession, the importation of 'Polynesian' immigrants became a necessary expedient for Gordon, as he sought to expand agricultural exports and maintain his native policies. Gordon's government passed a series of ordinances which were much more interventionist than Queensland in regulating the recruiting and plantation conditions of migrants from the Pacific. As well as allowing wage rates that were half those paid in Queensland, Fijian authorities also provided extensive subsidies for planters seeking to recruit and repatriate islander labour.[105] Fuelled by a five thousand pound state grant in 1877, there was a massive expansion in the numbers of islanders imported into Fiji (see Fig. 7.3), and Gordon increasingly defended the migration that he had condemned as 'slavery' when first arriving in the Pacific.[106] When concerns were raised in London about the excessively high mortality of these migrants in Fiji, Gordon argued that to increase the provision of medical care would undermine the colony's economy.[107]

---

[102] Roth and Hooper (eds.), *The Fiji journals of Baron Anatole von Hügel*, p. 124.
[103] R. B. Joyce, *Sir William MacGregor* (Melbourne: Oxford University Press, 1971), pp. 68–70.
[104] Lal, *Chalo jahaji*, p. 147.
[105] Parnaby, 'The regulation of indentured labour to Fiji', pp. 61–4; R. Shlomowitz, 'The Fiji labor trade in comparative perspective, 1864–1914', *Pacific Studies* **9**, 3 (1986), pp. 111–17.
[106] Gordon, *Fiji*, Vol. I, p. 153.
[107] Gordon to Secretary of State, 5 February 1879, CO 384/126; R. Shlomowitz, 'Epidemiology and the Pacific labor trade', *Journal of Interdisciplinary History* (1989), pp. 594–8.

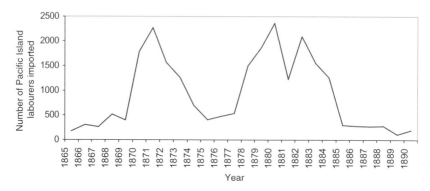

Fig. 7.3 Pacific island labourers annually imported to Fiji, 1865–1890. Jeff Siegel, 'Origins of Pacific island labourers in Fiji', *Journal of Pacific History* **20** 1–2 (1985), p. 46.

The growth of the Pacific labour trade in Fiji was reflected in John Gorrie's description of the economic expansion of Fiji under Gordon:

When a few years ago the native canoe alone was seen, or a solitary settler's boat coming up to the solitary store for a few tins of preserved meat and a case of gin, three (if not already four) first-class steamers per month from the Australia colonies now load and unload cargoes, steam launches [f]rom the neighbouring sugar mills come and go, labour schooners with Polynesian islanders enter and depart, and occasional ships with machinery, with coolies, or with general cargoes, make their appearance.[108]

It was not until 1883 that labour recruitment from Vanuatu and the Solomon Islands was surpassed by indentured Indian immigration to Fiji. This was three years after Gordon's departure from the colony, and was largely due to the commitment of the Colonial Sugar and Refining Company (CSR) to long-term indentured labour. Ultimately 61,000 indentured Indians would make the passage to Fiji between 1879 and 1916.

CONCLUSION

Gordon's passage through Trinidad, Mauritius and Fiji occurred at a time when the immigration system in each colony was being fundamentally transformed. In Trinidad, the economic boom of the late 1860s reinforced the expansion of indentured immigration and fuelled the transition to a more permanently settled population of former immigrants. In Mauritius, the radical decline of indentured arrivals created

[108] Gorrie, *Fiji as it is* (1883), pp. 160–1.

new pressures on non-indentured Indians, reflected in the harsh vagrancy laws of 1867. While Gordon sought to reform these abuses, his central concern was to extend state regulation of migrant labour on the estates, which had previously been privately negotiated through Mauritian planters and Indian sidhars. In Fiji, Gordon transplanted the indenture system as a means of isolating Fijians from settler society, against the vehement protests of the latter.

Throughout his career Gordon sought to decisively shape and reform indentureship according to his own vision of colonialism. Yet the results of his interventions are strikingly contradictory. His land reforms in Trinidad were largely ignored by his successors, while the rates of repatriation to India from the colony doubled during the economic depression of the 1880s. The extensive investigations by Gordon's royal commission in Mauritius failed to produce a radical redefinition of indentureship. Gordon's economic initiatives in Fiji fuelled the expansion of the Pacific labour trade which he had been initially commissioned to repress. His system of Indian indentured immigration would ultimately develop under successors, although at the same time they were reversing many of his earlier native reforms to protect Fijian society. While the constant migration of a governor's career allowed Gordon to carry with him common policies across disparate colonies, he often felt that his departure would mark the end for the edifice of policies and projects that he had constructed.[109]

Gordon's movements across empire reveal the range of forces which shaped the emergence of indentureship as a global system of migrant labour. Crossing between colonies, he encountered planters, administrators, missionaries, servants and labourers who were also fellow migrants. Their inter-colonial circulations meant that the indenture system was itself a product of migration. Gordon's attempts to transpose immigration policies from Trinidad to Mauritius and then onto Fiji were only partially effective, due to the distinctive environments of each colony. Equally, his awareness of colonial development projects in French Martinique and the Dutch East Indies show how schemes for indentured immigration were often influenced by debates and experiences that crossed imperial borders. Rather than simply determined by local events, the expansion of indentured labour schemes during the late nineteenth century was also fuelled by migrant administrators who played a central role in reformulating its contours and conditions.

---

[109] Gordon, *Paper on the system of taxation in force in Fiji*, p. 46.

CHAPTER 8

Sir John Pope Hennessy and colonial government: humanitarianism and the translation of slavery in the imperial network

Philip Howell and David Lambert

The arrival and departure of British governors from their colonial post-ings was a matter of importance and sensitivity. Governors, as David Cannadine puts it, 'were the centre of attention at those ceremonials when society put itself on show'; '[t]heir arrivals, departures and openings of colonial legislatures were marked with uniforms, parades, processions, salutes, at which the settler community displayed itself in ordered, layered procession'.[1] Welcomes and valedictions were not, however, merely opportunities for 'proconsular splendour as a reassertion of hierarchy'.[2] They were also important tests of local feeling – and as such not neces-sarily welcomed by Whitehall or Downing Street and not necessarily helpful to the 'projection' overseas of order and status upon which, Cannadine asserts, the British empire depended. In Mauritius, for instance, at the banquet offered in welcome of governor Sir John Pope Hennessy (Fig. 8.1) in November 1883, the chairman noted that for the first time in British Mauritian history the traditional formal toast to the governor's health might be made with sincerity and enthusiasm.[3] The genuine warmth of the welcome to Sir John was far from deferential. It was a political gesture, a pointed denunciation of the failures of previous proconsular representation. Pope Hennessy was welcomed as an antidote to the maladies associated with the alien administration of a conquered people. This was a performance, if not exactly of anti-imperial sentiment, then of a conditional loyalty which demanded constitutional concessions as much as it acknowledged imperial authority. Such an effusive welcome was an embarrassment rather than an endorsement of empire.

---

[1] David Cannadine, *Ornamentalism: how the British saw their empire* (London: Allen Lane, 2001), p. 32.
[2] *Ibid.*, p. 15.
[3] James Pope-Hennessy, *Verandah: some episodes in the Crown Colonies, 1876–1889* (London: George Allen and Unwin, 1964), p. 243.

Fig. 8.1 Sir John Pope Hennessy from frontispiece of *Souvenir de Sir John Pope Hennessy* (Ile Maurice, 1894), by permission of the British Library.

Even before Pope Hennessy had stepped onto the quayside at Port Louis, however, it was clear to Mauritians that he was never likely to exhibit proconsular indifference to the rights of colonial subjects. By 1883 Sir John was the veteran of several colonial governorships where he had gained a reputation for humanitarianism and the inclusion of indigenous peoples in government. He was already, in rumour and reputation, something of a hero to the French Mauritian community, who considered themselves 'captives in our own native country'.[4] Pope Hennessy

---

[4] *Popular banquet offered to HE Sir John Pope Hennessy KCMG, FGS, FRAS Governor of the island of Mauritius and its dependencies by six hundred and fifty inhabitants of Mauritius on the 13th September 1884 in the grounds of the Royal College Port Louis, Mauritius* (Mauritius: Mercantile Record Company's Establishment, 1884), p. 20.

was no disappointment, and quickly became associated with the reformers' rallying cry of 'Mauritius for the Mauritians'.[5] Six months after Pope Hennessy's arrival, and to mark colonial secretary Lord Derby's acceptance of a petition for constitutional reform, Sir John was fêted again with a splendid banquet in Port Louis.[6] Sir Virgile Naz, the president of the occasion, reminded the guests that Pope Hennessy had, after a distinguished parliamentary career, been favoured with colonial appointments of greater and greater prestige, in all of which he had promoted self-government and respect for the creeds, feelings and aspirations of those over whom he was placed. Sir Virgile pointed out that Pope Hennessy had fulfilled all the expectations that Mauritians had held since his appointment:

Gentlemen, the just and liberal measures of His Excellency in Mauritius are so recent that I need not remind you of them in detail. In spite of hostile preventions of which the echo had preceded him in Mauritius, the very numerous assemblage of all classes which attended his landing, cheered him from the Quay to Government House, and his first acts have justified the sympathy which he inspired at once to the Mauritians.[7]

Now to speak of 'echoes of hostile preventions' hardly did justice to Pope Hennessy's record of colonial government. Pope Hennessy was in fact infamous for stirring up trouble wherever he was appointed. In Pope Hennessy's own estimation a good governor was 'One who struggles courageously with the bureaux', and he would not have been displeased by his grandson's remark that he was 'a dedicated disturber of the *status quo*'.[8] Others spoke rather of misgovernment, or of his 'want of temper and judgment' and 'want of nice adjustment of conduct of circumstance'.[9] Even Sir John's friends candidly admitted that Pope Hennessy 'has been in trouble or hot water in every colony where he has governed'.[10] Nicknamed 'the Pope', he was derided by the Colonial Office bureaux, and British settlers in his former administrations loathed him as congenitally partial and even anti-English in his policies. Few governors can have provoked quite such strong feelings as this.

---

[5] H. T. Holland, *Despatch upon the Report of the Royal Commission of Inquiry into the affairs of the colony of Mauritius* (London, 1887); K. Ballhatchet, 'The structure of official attitudes: Colonial Mauritius, 1883–1968', *The Historical Journal* **38** (1995), pp. 989–1011; W. K. Storey, *Science and power in colonial Mauritius* (Rochester: University of Rochester Press, 1997), pp. 55, 72.

[6] *Popular banquet.* [7] *Ibid.*, p. 7.

[8] *Ibid.*, p. 27; Pope-Hennessy, *Verandah*, p. 240.

[9] *Times*, 13 July 1888, p. 7; Holland, *Despatch*, p. 1.

[10] J. Henniker Heaton, 'The suspension of John Pope Hennessy', *Times*, 10 January 1887, p. 8.

Such 'echoes' also serve here to indicate how significant was the transmission of news and rumour, hope and anxiety, from one part of the empire to another. We are concerned here as much with connections as apparently insubstantial as rumour and speculation as with the physical movement of individuals, commodities, practices and projects. Both material and immaterial translations constituted the geography of imperial governance that we examine in this chapter through Pope Hennessy's imperial career.

'HE HAD BEEN IN A GOOD MANY COLONIES'

This career was not simply a glorious procession from posting to posting, as Sir Virgile Naz suggested.[11] His journey through the British 'imperial network' was marked by constant conflict, by personal and political animosity, and even by communal violence.[12] Pope Hennessy's life and career were intricately bound up in 'the webs of Empire which traversed the vertical connections between metropole and colony' (see Map 8.1).[13] It took him to Labuan (1867–71), Sierra Leone and the Gold Coast settlements of British West Africa (1872–73), the Bahamas (1873–74), Barbados and the Windward Islands (1875–76), Hong Kong (1877–82), and finally to Mauritius (1883–89). This was not a uniquely varied career, but Pope Hennessy's protégé in Hong Kong, the sinologist Ernest Eitel, may well have had him in mind when he noted that governors were but 'transient visitors'.[14] This should not be interpreted to suggest that proconsuls made little difference to their colonies; Pope Hennessy's travels and travails certainly left his colonial postings irrevocably changed, as well as the larger project of imperial administration. It might be better to suggest that Eitel's invocation of 'transience' referred more to colonial governors' ability to set in motion profound changes in the periphery without, as

---

[11] *Popular banquet*, p. 5.

[12] Alan Lester, *Imperial networks: creating identities in nineteenth-century South Africa and Britain* (London: Routledge, 2001); Alan Lester, 'Obtaining the "due observance of justice": The geographies of colonial humanitarianism', *Environment and Planning D: Society and Space* **20** (2002), pp. 277–93; Alan Lester, 'British settler discourse and the circuits of empire', *History Workshop Journal* **54** (2002), pp. 24–48. An earlier attempt to discuss Pope Hennessy in relation to this British imperial network can be found in David Lambert and Philip Howell, 'John Pope Hennessy and the translation of "slavery" between late nineteenth-century Barbados and Hong Kong', *History Workshop Journal* **55** (2003), pp. 1–24.

[13] Catherine Hall, 'Of gender and empire: reflections on the nineteenth century', in Philippa Levine (ed.), *Gender and empire* (Oxford: Oxford University Press, 2004), p. 65.

[14] Ernest Eitel, *Europe in China: the history of Hong Kong from the beginning to the year 1882* (London: Luzac & Co., 1895), p. iii.

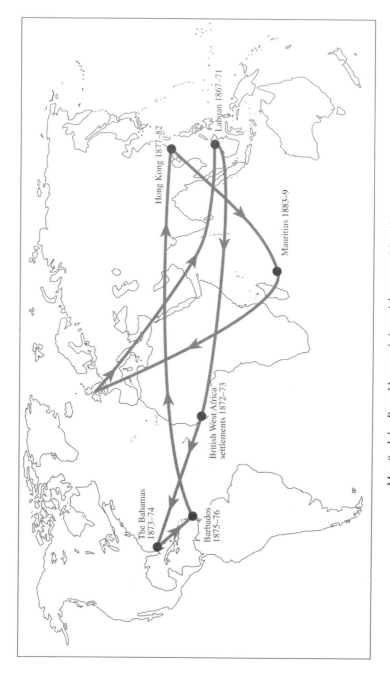

Map 8.1 John Pope Hennessy's imperial career, 1867–1889.

sojourners rather than residents, needing fully to accept the consequences of their actions. Here again, Eitel may well have had Pope Hennessy's chequered career in mind.

Governors spent much time travelling and returning from their con-sulships but Pope Hennessy was a more than usually peripatetic figure. In Mauritius, at the end of his career, the governor's comings and goings gave many occasions for his supporters to dust down the bunting. In December 1886, Pope Hennessy was suspended whilst his alleged mis-handling of affairs in the island was investigated. Those unimpressed by his radical policies accused him of partiality, cronyism, financial mis-management, and of recklessly encouraging racial and cultural antagon-ism.[15] He was held responsible for 'the intolerable yoke of despotism and political imposture under which the Colony lingers'.[16] Sir Hercules Robinson, governor of the Cape Colony, took over the reins of gov-ernment and was charged with investigating Pope Hennessy's actions. Pope Hennessy was ordered home, though his Mauritian backers hoped and trusted that this would only be a temporary absence. Pope Hennessy was eventually reinstated – censured but not charged with impropriety – and returned in December 1888 to a celebration at Port Louis astonishing for its apparent spontaneity as well as its careful orchestration.[17] A pen-nant-lined processional route welcomed him from the quayside through a series of *arcs de triomphes* erected at the Place d'Armes, and cheering crowds said to be thirty thousand strong, accompanied by a military band and a twenty-one gun salute, led him to a reception at the cathedral by the archbishop. This was a very public show of support for a man who had left the island in apparent disgrace. Once again, pomp and cir-cumstance served here to challenge as much as confirm the authority of the imperial order. This was 'ornamentalism' once more in the service of radical reform and French-Mauritian ambitions.

Such was the moment of Pope Hennessy's greatest triumph. Sir John's imperial career ended, against all the odds, in circumstances that can only have stoked his self-regard. Barely a year later, another December adieu would be played out as Sir John returned to Britain and Ireland, where he

---

[15] National Archives (hereafter NA), CO 882/5/1, 'Correspondence relating to an inquiry held by the Right Hon. Sir Hercules Robinson, GCMG, as Royal Commissioner into the condition of affairs in Mauritius' (1887).

[16] De Coriolis, letter in the *Mercantile Record and Commercial Gazette*, 26 November 1885, in NA CO 882/5/1, p. 47.

[17] Holland, *Despatch*.

campaigned and won a seat in parliament as the anti-Parnellite candidate
for North Kilkenny only to collapse of heart failure before he could
return to the parliamentary benches. But though his name may have
lapsed into obscurity at home, his reputation lived on in the colonial
world, commemorated in street names and statuary, and, at least until the
beginning of the twentieth century, in Sierra Leone's Pope Hennessy
Day, where the governor was remembered as a 'noble soul' representative
of a lost 'golden age' of colonial philanthropy and enlightened government.[18] There is no doubt that Pope Hennessy would have been greatly
gratified. He would have been equally pleased by the words of his
Mauritian historian: 'His Excellency was deeply beloved everywhere he
had been Governor.'[19]

Laughably untrue as this statement is, it suggests how Pope Hennessy
wanted to be seen. As both metropolitan politician and colonial governor
he saw himself as a humanitarian, a social reformer and lifelong opponent
of corporal punishment, an antislavery advocate who deplored the legacy
of chattel slavery and the continuing existence of forced labour practices,
and a champion of the rights of both subject races and subject peoples
(including his own native Ireland).[20] That he remained throughout his
life a Disraelian Conservative – a 'liberal', reforming, home rule, Irish
Catholic Tory no less – may appear eccentric to contemporary eyes, but
Pope Hennessy was able not just to look to Disraeli for patronage but also
for political philosophy.[21] He was able to abstract a 'persistency of purpose' from Disraeli's views on Ireland.[22] Pope Hennessy forged for
himself a similar 'persistency of purpose' in his political career, with a
self-consciously enlightened approach to the education of peoples (both
domestic and colonial), with the eventual goal of self-government and
national self-determination in mind: Kate Lowe and Eugene McLaughlin

[18] Odile Goerg, 'Between everyday life and exception: celebrating Pope Hennessy Day in Freetown,
    1872–1905', *Journal of African Cultural Studies* **15** (2002), p. 124.
[19] S. B. De Burgh-Edwardes, *The history of Mauritius (1507–1914)* (London: East and West Ltd, 1921),
    p. 89.
[20] John Pope Hennessy, *English policy in Italy and Poland, two speeches delivered by John Pope
    Hennessy, M. P., in the House of Commons, March 4th, & July 2nd, 1861* (London: Cornelius Buck,
    1861); John Pope Hennessy, *Debate upon the motion of John Pope Hennessy, Esq. (MP for King's
    County,) relating to the affairs of Poland, in the House of Commons, Friday, February 27, 1863*
    (London: Extracted from Hansard's Parliamentary Debates, Vol. CLXIX, 1863).
[21] For Pope Hennessy's relationship to Disraeli, see especially correspondence in Bodleian Library
    Special Collections and Western Manuscripts, Dep. Hughenden 131/3. Of Disraeli, Pope Hennessy
    wrote: 'My faith in him never for a moment wavered, & my devotion to him has not been
    diminished by any distant exile', letter to Lennox, 23 April 1868 (Part 6/196).
[22] John Pope Hennessy, *Lord Beaconsfield's Irish policy* (London: Kegan Paul, 1885), p. 34.

have described this as a policy of 'localisation'.[23] Pope Hennessy was far from a democrat, or indeed an anti-imperialist in any modern sense, but he was convinced that imperial ambitions should allow for the political incorporation of colonial subjects. In Sierra Leone, for example, Pope Hennessy wrote that British rule had as its object the training of natives 'so as to render them capable of Self-Government'.[24] This would, Pope Hennessy argued, safeguard the empire as much as satisfy natural justice. As he expressed it in the context of the beginnings of the 'Scramble for Africa', and in praise of the acceptance of the Mauritian petitioners' claims for constitutional reform:

The colonial world has been startled and puzzled at seeing the Prince of modern Statesmen hoisting a flag on the inhospitable coast of Africa. That is called an extension of Empire. At all events it is a geographical extension of Empire. But the Earl of Derby has now done something, perhaps not less substantial: he has extended the Empire of Queen Victoria in the hearts of Her Subjects (*loud cheers*). I prefer that extension of Empire (*great cheering*).[25]

Lowe and McLaughlin have followed Pope Hennessy's lead in discerning an essential consistency and integrity in his colonial policies. They have quoted approvingly the words of Sir John's *Times* obituary: that he 'was consistent throughout all his governorships: the indigenous or non-white inhabitants had a valuable contribution to make to the colonies and should be encouraged to join in, if not to take over, government'.[26] In parliament, it was said of Pope Hennessy that 'The House knew that he had been in a good many colonies (some ironical cheers), and no man who had been so much in the colonies could help making some mistakes', but that his mistakes 'arose only from his desire to do justice to the native population'.[27] In particular, noting the complaints of the Colonial Office and of British settlers, Lowe and McLaughlin have emphasised his 'pro-native' policies, and linked them in particular to his Irishness. The fact that Pope Hennessy was an Irish Catholic nationalist was a crucial determinant,

---

[23] Kate Lowe and Eugene McLaughlin, 'Sir John Pope Hennessy and the "native race craze": colonial government in Hong Kong, 1877–1882', *Journal of Imperial and Commonwealth History* **20** (1992), pp. 239–40.

[24] NA CO 267/317: Pope Hennessy to Earl of Kimberley, 31 December 1872, cited in Hollis R. Lynch, 'The native pastorate controversy and cultural ethno-centrism in Sierra Leone 1871–1874', *Journal of African History* **5**, 3 (1964), p. 404. Pope Hennessy supported the establishment of a higher educational institute on the West African coast. See *The West African university: correspondence between E. W. Blyden ... and His Excellency J. Pope Hennessy* (Freetown: Negro Printing Office, 1872).

[25] *Popular banquet*, p. 16.

[26] *Times*, 8 October 1891; see Lowe and McLaughlin, 'Sir John Pope Hennessy', pp. 225–6.

[27] *Times*, 10 January 1887, p. 8.

at a personal and political level, of his views on race and the rights of indigenous peoples, and of his 'radical attempts to pursue a policy of racial equality wherever he was governor'.[28] Pope Hennessy's politics may be traced to his Irish birthplace, to his already ex-centric positionality, and to his experience of being an Irish Catholic in a Protestant empire.[29]

It is certainly true that Pope Hennessy's home rule sympathies led him to link the wrongs of Ireland to the wrongs of British imperial rule.[30] Notoriously, Pope Hennessy was said to have publicly stated that Mauritius, like Ireland, had felt the heavy hand of England.[31] Pope Hennessy was a committed opponent of Anglicisation and the promotion of Protestantism, opposing the dominance of educational projects by Protestant missionaries, and removing the privileged position of the state church. His policies with regard to the funding of the religious and educational establishment in Mauritius were highly controversial. The Anglican hierarchy regarded his actions with alarm.[32] Moreover, one of the catalysts to the eventual troubles in Mauritius consisted of the appointment of a notable Orangeman as his colonial secretary. This led to the breakdown of administration in the island, and directly to Pope Hennessy's suspension. Pope Hennessy's Irish Catholic nationalist sympathies are thus inseparable from his colonial career.

However, to link Pope Hennessy's reforming policies to a transferral of Irish nationalist and 'pro-native' sympathies, or rather their *transmigration* ('many Irish carried with them their aspirations for an independent Ireland' is how Lowe and McLaughlin put it) is too simple.[33] Pope Hennessy was not merely 'an eccentric, disputatious Irishman' primed by birthright to make trouble in the empire.[34] For one thing, it is not easy, in Mauritius or in other colonies, to point in a straightforward way to who the 'natives' actually were. Mauritius was an island without indigenes, home to a sophisticated French aristocratic planter society that owed its prosperity to slavery – and the sort of people who, were they of British

---

[28] Lowe and McLaughlin, 'Sir John Pope Hennessy', p. 223.

[29] See D. G. Boyce, ' "The marginal Britons": The Irish', in R. Colls and P. Dodd (eds.), *Englishness, politics and culture, 1880–1920* (London: Croom Helm, 1986), pp. 230–53.

[30] John Pope Hennessy, *Letters from Mauritius in the eighteenth century by Grant, Baron de Vaux including an account of Labourdonnais' capture of Madras with an introduction by Sir John Pope Hennessy* (Mauritius: Printed for private circulation, 1886).

[31] See Pope-Hennessy, *Verandah*, p. 258. Pope Hennessy denied saying this: letter to Edward Stanhope, 29 September 1886, in NA CO 882/5/1.

[32] See Lambeth Palace Library, E. W. Benson papers, Vol. XIX, 28 January and 24 March 1884.

[33] Lowe and McLaughlin, 'Sir John Pope Hennessy', p. 225.

[34] Peter Burroughs, 'Imperial institutions and the government of empire', in *The Oxford history of the British empire*, Vol. III: *The nineteenth century* (Oxford: Oxford University Press, 1999), p. 177.

descent, Pope Hennessy would have routinely castigated and opposed. Mauritius was also home to the descendants of black-African slaves, and, after the abolition of slavery, to the large numbers of Indian labourers who were brought in to resolve the labour shortfall. Pope Hennessy's constitutional reforms favoured the French-creole community in the first instance, but in the long term contributed to the process of 'Indianisation', an outcome that neither followed from, nor was approved by Pope Hennessy. This puts the lie to the easy equation of anti-Englishness and policies of racial equality. Mauritius is in this regard emblematic of the difficulties faced by Pope Hennessy's diverse sympathies.

We shall return to this question but it may be helpful now to outline an alternative conception of Pope Hennessy's imperial career that links his politics to his personal journey through the imperial network. We want to demonstrate, principally through a discussion of the mapping of 'slavery' in his personal and political career, that governors and other trans-imperial figures were not just agents but also subjects of empire, both transforming and transformed. Pope Hennessy's convictions were not just taken from Ireland to the colonies. They were formulated and reformulated in both the sites and the circuits of empire. It is preferable, therefore, to return to the notion of Pope Hennessy's eccentricity and ex-centricity, but neither in the sense of the peculiarity of his politics, nor in terms of his Celtic peripheral status. Rather, we need to look to his *erratic* political trajectory in the British imperial world. We should not look too hard for consistency from Pope Hennessy; but trace the evolution and transformation, even the contortion, of his politics as his gubernatorial career unfolded. As the rest of this chapter argues, the discourses and practices associated with Pope Hennessy's government were not carried with him unchanged from colony to colony. They were instead challenged and reconfigured as they were put into operation in diverse colonial contexts. In part, we will point to the travels of discourses – notably the humanitarian discourse of antislavery – but we will also be examining the making of Pope Hennessy as an agent and subject of empire. Rather than see him as an apostle of enlightened imperialism, or alternatively as a deluded idealist and ideologue, we want to outline conflicts between principle and pragmatism as Pope Hennessy's views were tried and tested in his travels within the imperial network. We want, in short, to return the geography to Pope Hennessy's career, and to trace its implications – a return to what his grandson described as his 'thorny pilgrimage'.[35]

[35] Pope-Hennessy, *Verandah*, p. 270.

'POPE HENNESSEE HE GOOD MAN FOR TRUE'

John Pope Hennessy's early colonial career offered little indication of the troubles that were to come. It began with an appointment to the distinctly third-class colony of Labuan.[36] There Pope Hennessy steadily worked up a reputation (later challenged) for sound finances. Pope Hennessy left Labuan with commendations, to which his already established 'reputation for espousing the cause of the underprivileged' in no way detracted.[37] An appointment to the governorship of the Bahamas was his reward. Before he took up this post, however, he was seconded to the sprawling West Africa settlements of Sierra Leone, the Gold Coast, Lagos and Gambia. There, Pope Hennessy's reputation as a sympathiser with his black subjects was still a matter for recommendation rather than alarm. Pope Hennessy found a ready and fertile field for his humanitarianism and political philosophy, and he threw himself into a series of reforms, the most radical of which was the abolition of direct taxation in Sierra Leone. Unfortunately for the colonial administration, Pope Hennessy had unwisely counted on an increase in trade to make up for the fall in the revenue; fortunately for him he had already left before the fiscal chickens came home to roost.[38] The ending of direct taxation was undoubtedly popular, though, and this, combined with Pope Hennessy's humanitarian and political sympathies, rapidly ensured that the governor was fêted then and thereafter by Sierra Leoneans. The day of the abolition of the House and Land Tax, the 22nd August, became a well-established holiday:

> *Da Gov'nor lun tem, nor to so he gree*
> *Ar mean da Gov'nor, Pope Hennessee*
> *He good man for true, he write Queen say,*
> *People nor lek tax, nor mek dem pay*
> *So we 'member now and keep alladay.*[39]

---

[36] 'You must not think I am inclined to grumble, but the more I find out about Labuan the less I like it': Pope Hennessy to Disraeli, 25 April 1867, Bodleian Library Special Collections and Western Manuscripts, Dep. Hughenden 131/3 (Part 5/182).

[37] Lynch, 'The native pastorate controversy', p. 398.

[38] Goerg, 'Between everyday life and exception', p. 122. See Christopher Fyfe, *A history of Sierra Leone* (Aldershot: Gregg Revivals, 1993), pp. 387–90.

[39] Goerg, 'Between everyday life and exception', p. 130:

> The former Governor did not agree to such things
> I mean Governor Pope Hennessy
> He was a good man indeed; he wrote to the Queen saying:
> The people don't like taxes, don't make them pay.
> So now we commemorate [him] and keep a holiday.

Most significantly, though, this measure was compared at the time with the abolition of slavery four decades earlier. 'Abolition odes' confirmed the perceived link between tax reform and release from bondage, and celebrated the 'priceless worth of liberty'.[40] For an avowed opponent of slavery, this must have been particularly gratifying. So early in his imperial career, Pope Hennessy could hardly have hoped for a more flattering appreciation of his efforts. In West Africa his 'pro-native' sympathies, his philanthropy and reformism, had given him the status of a 'stalwart champion' of black Africans.[41]

After a brief uneventful stewardship of the Bahamas, Pope Hennessy was promoted to the governorship of the Windward Islands, and it was here that his troubles really began. In Barbados, the new governor's antipathy to slave societies brought him into direct conflict with a British settler population only a couple of generations removed from slave ownership. They constituted a plantocracy, conservative-minded, jealous of its privileges and inherently suspicious of any interference in the island's affairs.[42] Pope Hennessy was reportedly 'received by all classes with the utmost cordiality and enthusiasm', but many amongst the island's planter élite must already have expected the worst.[43] Primed as he was with pronounced sympathy for the subordinate races, and disdainful of white settlers' claims to racial superiority, it is hard to see how conflict could have been avoided. But Pope Hennessy was additionally authorised by the Colonial Office to attempt to reform the constitutional affairs of the Windward Islands, in the direction of federation or confederation. This would necessarily impinge on the independence of Barbados and the other islands, and even a more diplomatic governor would have faced the

---

[40] J. T. Macfoy, 'Abolition Ode', 1888, cited in Goerg, 'Between everyday life and exception', p. 131. For the significance of slavery in the post-abolition era in West Africa see: Suzanne Miers, 'Slavery to freedom in sub-Saharan Africa: expectations and reality', in Howard Temperley (ed.), *After slavery: emancipation and its discontents* (London: Frank Cass, 2000), pp. 237–64; Raymond Dumett and Marion Johnson, 'Britain and the suppression of slavery in the Gold Coast colony, Ashanti and the Northern Territories', in Suzanne Miers and Richard Roberts (eds.), *The end of slavery in Africa* (Madison: University of Wisconsin Press, 1988), pp. 71–116; Raymond Dumett, 'Pressure groups, bureaucracy, and the decision-making process: the case of slavery abolition and colonial expansion in the Gold Coast, 1874', *Journal of Imperial and Commonwealth History* **9** (1981), pp. 193–215.

[41] Lynch, 'The native pastorate controversy', p. 412; 'the self-appointed champion of African aspirations' (Fyfe, *History of Sierra Leone*, p. 390).

[42] D. Lambert, *White creole culture, politics and identity during the age of abolition* (Cambridge: Cambridge University Press, 2005).

[43] See *Memorial from House of Assembly of Barbados, to Her Majesty the Queen, relative to the conduct of His Excellency John Pope Hennessy, Esq., CMG, Governor of Barbados, and certain members of the Executive Council, with appendices* (Bridgetown, 1876), p. 1.

greatest difficulty in carrying out such a plan.[44] Barbados' planters, authorised in their turn by history, ideology and political theory, interpreted these constitutional reforms as a challenge not just to their independence but also to their dominance over the black majority. In the Barbadian assembly, and outside it through the 'Barbados Defence Association', the planters fought to retain the island's status as a self-legislating colony.[45]

Thus Pope Hennessy's government quickly became embroiled in an intense political struggle. Local planters seem to have been suspicious right from the start of Pope Hennessy's brief tenure.[46] The constitutional question was, however, inevitably entangled with the position of the island's Afro-Caribbeans; and aware as they were of Pope Hennessy's humanitarianism and philanthropy, enough black Barbadians interpreted his political efforts as an attack on planter dominance to give rise to the notion that the governor was a supporter of social revolution rather than merely constitutional reform. This misunderstanding culminated in the April 1876 uprisings that became known as the 'Confederation Riots'.[47] Though unrest had been building for weeks, riots began in earnest on the night of 17 April when workers began to gather and march, loudly proclaiming their support for Pope Hennessy and denouncing the planters' opposition to his political programme. Soon they began destroying property, seizing food, and arming. The prospect of a widespread insurgency prompted many fearful whites to seek refuge aboard ships anchored offshore. Pope Hennessy was slow – treasonably slow, from the plantocrats' view – to recognise the emergency and to take appropriate action. But when on 20 April he began to receive reports that the rioters intended to begin assassinating prominent whites, Pope Hennessy reluctantly deployed the troops and gave the orders for the riot to be put down. Calm was more or less restored by the 26th, the disturbances leaving in their wake 8 black dead, at least 36 wounded, and 450 in gaol.[48]

---

[44] On these events and the theme of constitutional crisis see Bruce Hamilton, *Barbados and the confederation question, 1871–1885* (London: Government of Barbados, 1956) and Claude Levy, *Emancipation, sugar and federalism: Barbados and the West Indies, 1833–1876* (Gainesville: University of Florida, 1980).

[45] See British Parliamentary Command Papers (C.)1539, No. 64, p. 122, Pope Hennessy to Carnarvon, 11 March 1876; C.1539, No. 8, pp. 140–1, Enclosure in Pope Hennessy to Carnarvon, 24 March 1876; *Memorial from House of Assembly of Barbados.*

[46] W. P. B. Shepheard, *Barbados and Mr John Pope Hennessy* (Manchester: J. Roberts, 1876), p. 6.

[47] 'Federation Riots' is the less common alternative.

[48] See Michael Craton, 'Continuity not change: the incidence of unrest among ex-slaves in the British West Indies, 1838–1876', in Hilary Beckles and Verene Shepherd (eds.), *Caribbean*

These disturbances, the largest since the great slave revolt of 1816, appeared to many contemporaries to be an exactly equivalent threat to white lives, property, and power. The 1816 rebellion, known to many by the name of its supposed leader, 'Bussa', was also ignited by the unwillingness of the plantocracy to enact reform.[49] Although it was put down shortly, and with great brutality, the fear and anxiety it generated were still hauntingly powerful in 1876. Not the least threatening aspect of the parallels between 'Bussa's Revolt' and the 'Confederation Riots' was the fact that the legacy of slavery seemed to have the power to reach into the post-emancipation period. Though slavery had been abolished for over forty years, the structures of power and the conditions under which the black majority laboured remained substantially the same. Richard Allen writes that

If the mid-nineteenth century did not witness the creation of 'new systems of slavery' *per se* ... it was nevertheless an era during which colonial labor relations continued to be colored by many of the attitudes, beliefs, and traditions associated with slavery.[50]

Alana Johnson has noted specifically that 'If one considers the type of freedom offered to Barbadian blacks by their former owners, it is by no means surprising that thirty-eight years after emancipation they were still equating their condition with that of slavery.'[51] Acts like the 1840 Masters and Servants Act, which required agricultural labourers to live on plantations and work there five days a week, were introduced in the immediate post-emancipation period to protect the interests of the former slavemasters. The planters' oligarchy remained firmly in place.[52] It is hardly surprising that support for and invocation of Pope Hennessy derived from the widespread perception that his policies would benefit the black majority by undermining the power of the planters. Opposition

freedom: society and economy from emancipation to the present (London: James Currey, 1993), pp. 192–206; George Belle, 'The abortive revolution of 1876 in Barbados', in *ibid.*, pp. 181–91.

[49] Lambert, *White creole culture*, chapter 4; Michael Craton, *Testing the chains: resistance to slavery in the British West Indies* (Ithaca: Cornell University Press, 1982); Hilary Beckles, *Bussa: the 1816 revolution in Barbados* (Barbados: Department of History, UWI and Barbados Museum and Historical Society, 1998).

[50] Richard B. Allen, *Slaves, freedmen, and indentured laborers in colonial Mauritius* (Cambridge: Cambridge University Press, 1999), p. 176.

[51] Alana Johnson, 'The abolition of chattel slavery in Barbados, 1833–1876', unpublished PhD thesis, University of Cambridge (1995). See also Belle, 'The abortive revolution'; Craton, 'Continuity not change'; O. Nigel Bolland, 'Systems of domination after slavery: the control of land and labour in the British West Indies after 1838,' in Beckles and Shepherd (eds.), *Caribbean freedom*, pp. 107–23.

[52] Barbados Department of Archives, Barbados Blue Book of Statistics, R.1, *Return of the population*; K.1, K.2, *Political franchise*.

to constitutional and social reform was read by Afro-Caribbean people in turn as an attempt to consolidate the power that had originally been conferred by slave ownership.[53]

Pope Hennessy was certainly quick to promote his social and political reforms by invoking the memory and legacy of slavery, criticising the Masters and Servants Act as an 'evil' that every governor since the 'abolition of slavery ... has endeavoured to get the proprietary body to recognize' but which would survive as long as the present constitutional framework remained in place.[54] His plans for abolishing flogging and reforming the prisons were also saturated by the rhetoric of antislavery:

> Soon after my arrival in the Island, in November 1875, I discovered that the number of prison offences and of prison punishments, as well as the nature of the punishments and the shocking results that in some cases followed, constituted a grave scandal, and show that in Barbados alone, of all Her Majesty's Colonies, some of the worst practices of the days of slavery still prevailed.[55]

For Pope Hennessy, opposition to these social reforms indicated that local whites continued to endorse the racialised notions of black embodiment that had typified the period of slavery.[56] This view of the planters' racial intransigence was also current in the Colonial Office, at least until the rioting in Barbados started, with one official observing laconically that 'there is a good deal of old slave dealing ferocity about the Justices [of Peace] and Prison Doctors in Barbados'.[57] Pope Hennessy's interpretation of the continuing significance of slavery was endorsed by humanitarian organisations and liberal newspapers in the metropole, by some local churches in Barbados, and by black Barbadians themselves.[58] In short, slavery set the terms of the confrontation between Pope Hennessy and the plantocracy in Barbados.

Certainly, Pope Hennessy had long been prepared to use the discourse of slavery to denounce the abuse of power: in 1866, for example, in a

[53] Belle, 'The abortive revolution'.

[54] C.1559, No. 62, pp. 158–9, Pope Hennessy to Carnarvon, 14 May 1876; C.1539, No. 77, pp. 139–40, Enclosure in Pope Hennessy to Carnarvon, 22 March 1876. On the Masters and Servants Acts, see Bolland, 'Systems of domination after slavery'.

[55] NA CO 32/3, *Barbados Government Gazette*, No. 925, Copy of Pope Hennessy's 'Minute on prison discipline', 17 February 1876; Shepheard, *Barbados*, p. 3.

[56] NA CO 321/9, Pope Hennessy to Carnarvon, 22 March 1876.

[57] NA CO 321/5, Annotation to Pope Hennessy to Carnarvon, 10 December 1875.

[58] See *inter alia*: C.1539, No. 77, pp. 139–40, Enclosure in Pope Hennessy to Carnarvon, 22 March 1876; letter from 'A Looker-On' to the Editor, *Times*, 2 May 1876; *Pall Mall Gazette*, 19 April 1876; NA CO 321/14, Committee of the British and Foreign AntiSlavery Society to Carnarvon, 19 September 1876. For Pope Hennessy's correspondence with humanitarian organisations, see Rhodes House Library (RHL), AntiSlavery Papers, MSS British empire, s.18, c.137/234–55.

speech on 'Ireland and the Manchester School', he denounced John Bright as 'a leader in the defence of the cruel old system of slavery, of disease, of ignorance, of shortened unhappy lives which the Factory Acts have successfully attacked'.[59] In the colonies, however, 'slavery' served as the most effective shorthand for continued racial inequality, a benchmark from which to judge the lack of progress since emancipation, and an indictment of white minority government based on supremacist ideologies. Later on, whilst on his way to his next governorship in Hong Kong, Pope Hennessy decided that it was the entrenched system of racial subjugation that was Barbados' greatest problem:

in all my experience I was never in a community where there was such deliberate oppression of the masses as in the community of Barbadoes [*sic*] and I did feel in the struggle in which I was engaged that it was my duty to expose to the public opinion of England, Ireland, and Scotland the real state of the case. I felt in that struggle and in the performance of that duty I would be supported by every man of right feelings at home, and especially that I would be supported by my fellow-citizens.[60]

Pope Hennessy thus regarded his offices in Barbados in terms of humanitarian reform on one side and racial supremacist retrenchment on the other. His experiences in Barbados were not only informed by his metropolitan understanding of the many evils of slavery; his personal and political instincts were confirmed in the colonial world by the recognition that slavery's legacy and memory continued to misshape Barbados' social and political order.

'A MAN WHO COULD GAIN THE CONFIDENCE OF THE NATIVES'

'Slavery' was thus a site of struggle between pro- and anti- confederationists in Barbados, and, eventually, between Pope Hennessy and the Colonial Office. In the metropole, in the aftermath of the riots, Pope Hennessy's actions, and the arguments of the Barbadian planters, began to be re-evaluated. White fears of the impact of the rhetoric of slavery on the black population prompted the Colonial Office to force Pope Hennessy to issue a proclamation to dispel popular confusion about the supposed benefits of confederation.[61] Any lingering sympathy for Pope Hennessy and his views quickly evaporated, whilst consternation at his 'pro-nativism' and lack of

---

[59] Pope Hennessy, *Lord Beaconsfield*, p. 83.
[60] NA CO 321/18, Enclosure in Thomas Daniel Hill to Carnarvon, 7 March 1877.
[61] C.1539, No. 134, p. 204, Carnarvon to Pope Hennessy, 29 April 1876; C.1559, No. 78, p. 187, Enclosure in Pope Hennessy to Carnarvon, 30 May 1876.

political judgement took its place. Dissatisfaction with Pope Hennessy's proconsular performance was loudly expressed, the beginnings of the view that he was ill-suited to be placed in charge of colonies 'where the pretensions of the natives threatened to make trouble'.[62]

In its obituary, from which these words are taken, the *Times* went on to say that the subsequent transfer of Pope Hennessy to Hong Kong said little for the intelligence or discretion with which the Colonial Office exercised its patronage.[63] For Hong Kong was a sensitive posting, with a history of suspicion between the majority Chinese population and the British colonists.[64] Unrest had already been countered there by draconian responses, and the colonial authorities continued to regard the maintenance of racial privileges as vital to the colony's security. Moreover, the Chinese community in Hong Kong was keen to develop its political influence through the promotion of individuals and institutions.[65] These were exactly the kinds of conditions least suited to a Pope Hennessy governorship, and the Colonial Office was rapidly resigned to trouble. For the bureaucrats, Pope Hennessy's demonstrably enlarged sympathy for the 'native races' could in Hong Kong only express itself as a 'Chinomania', a prospect they could only match with weary fatalism.[66] The British merchant community could indeed hardly hide its apprehensions, given the news from the West Indies. It was entirely foreseeable that the governor would become straightaway embroiled in a series of disputes that more or less paralysed colonial government. He moved to reform the more glaring abuses of power such as the widespread recourse to public flogging, and he returned to his common themes of gaol reform and prisoner amnesties.[67] The European residents of Hong Kong feared, just as predictably, that disciplinary authority in the colony was evaporating before their eyes, with crime and insubordination reaching epidemic

[62] *Times*, 8 October 1891, p. 11, quoted in John Hammond and Barbara Hammond, *James Stansfeld: a Victorian champion of sex equality* (London: Longman Green, 1932), p. 214.

[63] *Times*, 8 October 1891, p. 11.

[64] Christopher Munn, *Anglo-China: Chinese people and British rule in Hong Kong, 1841–1880* (Richmond: Curzon Press, 2001); Tak-Wing Ngo (ed.), *Hong Kong's history: State and society under colonial rule* (London: Routledge, 1999); Norman Miners, *Hong Kong under imperial rule, 1912–1941* (Hong Kong: Oxford University Press, 1987); Jung-Fang Tsai, *Hong Kong in Chinese history: community and social unrest in the British colony, 1842–1913* (New York: Columbia University Press, 1993).

[65] Elizabeth Sinn, *Power and charity: the early history of the Tung Wah Hospital, Hong Kong* (Hong Kong: Oxford University Press, 1989); Chan Wai Kwan, *The making of Hong Kong society: three studies in class formation in early Hong Kong* (Oxford: Oxford University Press, 1991).

[66] NA CO 129/189, H. K. 14124, Herbert briefing Michael Hicks Beach, 19 November 1878.

[67] See for instance NA CO 882/4/11, 'Papers relating to the flogging of prisoners in Hong Kong', Hennessy to Carnarvon, August 1877.

proportions. They reacted to Pope Hennessy's policy of promoting selected Chinese worthies with equal foreboding, fearing the beginnings of a Chinese takeover of Hong Kong.

The most controversial episode of Pope Hennessy's governorship of Hong Kong, however, was his response to the machinery for regulating prostitution in the colony. These measures had been in existence since 1857, and were intended to limit the extent of venereal disease amongst the Europeans.[68] The British response had been to license brothels, to repress unregistered women and unregistered houses, and to segregate brothels and prostitutes by clientele. Licensed brothels for European clients were allowed to practise if they ensured that their residents submitted periodically to medical inspection, and directed them to the lock hospital if they were found by British doctors to be in a contagious state. Women catering to Chinese men were exempt from sanitary inspection, though their houses still had to be licensed and to pay a levy for the privilege. The 1857 measures were replaced by a thoroughly revised 'contagious diseases' ordinance in 1867 that redrew the landscape of regulated sexuality with even greater precision: brothels for Chinese were confined as they had always been to the western district of the city of Victoria, but those for Europeans were now established in the eastern, or 'central' district.[69]

Pope Hennessy's attention was drawn to this elaborate system late in 1877, following the deaths of two Chinese women who had fallen to their deaths whilst being pursued over rooftops by policemen sent to search out unregistered prostitutes.[70] In the subsequent inquest, a number of other features of the case were revealed. It was not just the system of licensed brothels that was a matter for concern. More damningly, Pope Hennessy learned of the fact that no licensed brothels were exempt from paying fees to the government; and that since Chinese-only brothels received no medical intervention whatsoever, he could only conclude that the colony was guilty of profiting from the business of prostitution. Most worrying

---

[68] See especially Philip Howell, 'Prostitution and racialised sexuality: the regulation of prostitution in Britain and the British Empire before the Contagious Diseases Acts', *Environment and Planning D: Society and Space* **18** (2000), pp. 321–39; Philip Howell, 'Race, space and the regulation of prostitution in colonial Hong Kong', *Urban History* **31** (2004), pp. 229–48; Philippa Levine, *Prostitution, race and politics: policing venereal disease in the British empire* (London: Routledge, 2003).

[69] Howell, 'Race, space and the regulation of prostitution'.

[70] See the Hong Kong *Report of the Commissioners*. See also Parliamentary Papers 1880 (118) XLIX.69, *Report of the Commissioners Appointed to Inquire into the Workings of the Contagious Diseases Ordinance, 1867, in Hong Kong* and 1881 (C. 3093) LXV.673 *Correspondence relating to the workings of the contagious diseases ordinances of the Colony of Hong Kong.*

was the suggestion that the colonial state turned a blind eye not just to immorality but also to slavery. One of the dead women was said to have had to sell one of her children into slavery in order to pay off a previous fine. The implications of this allegation could be added to the general notion that brothels housed numbers of women who had been sold into slavery and who lived more or less in slavery. These elements of the system of regulated prostitution strongly suggested, to humanitarian and feminist critics, that the colonial state in Hong Kong was both pimp and slavemaster.

The association of prostitution with slavery is a long-standing one, and was not just used for rhetorical effect. For liberal feminist opponents of the Contagious Diseases Acts – significantly named 'abolitionists' of course – prostitution was directly linked to slavery, making state-regulated prostitution all the more obscene. This link was always evident to those who were quick to condemn the abhorrent practices of non-Western peoples, and in Hong Kong the Chinese were routinely vilified for the buying and selling of women for sex:

The most infamous traffic that has ever disgraced mankind, and the one that has brought most intense misery to its victims is the slave-trade. But a lower deep is reached when it exists to supply women and girls for the purposes of prostitution.[71]

It was satisfying to assert British moral superiority by trumpeting Britain's role in the demise of chattel slavery and denouncing other races' continuing complicity in slavery and slave trading. However, the notion that sexual slavery might exist in colonies like Hong Kong, and not merely winked at but sponsored by the British government, was an extraordinarily powerful accusation. It is one that Pope Hennessy, entirely characteristically, had no hesitation in making. The governor quickly concluded that the government-licensed brothels were quite simply a 'means of keeping Chinese girls in a state of slavery'.[72]

In this he shared a great deal in common with the international movement for the abolition of regulated prostitution. This feminist and humanitarian movement ceaselessly monitored British colonialism for complicity in state-regulated vice, and sought to expose such practices as illiberal, ineffective and illegitimate. For the men and women who took up the humanitarian crusade, Pope Hennessy was a worthy representative

---

[71] *Hong Kong Daily Press*, 16 January 1875, p. 8.
[72] NA CO 129/205, HK 12623, Correspondence of Pope Hennessy, no date; NA CO 882/5/1, *Correspondence relating to an inquiry held by the Right Hon. Sir Hercules Robinson, GCMG, as Royal Commissioner into the condition of affairs in Mauritius*, Pope Hennessy to Edward Stanhope MP, 18 January 1887.

of a moral imperialism that alone could justify the reach and power of British colonial authority. On his departure from Hong Kong, for instance, Pope Hennessy was offered congratulations from the Aborigines Protection Society, to whose activities he had long contributed.[73] Throughout his time in Hong Kong, and later in Mauritius, Pope Hennessy maintained a close correspondence with the society, even sending its secretary copies of his confidential dispatches to the Colonial Office.[74] These letters show to what great extent Pope Hennessy shared the worldview of British humanitarian discourse. Pope Hennessy was ever quick to condemn his predecessors' records, and to praise his own efforts, but he also represented himself as having constantly to combat the retrograde 'anti-native' views of the Colonial Office's officials and bureaucrats. In these letters, most tellingly, 'anti-native' and 'pro-slavery' were virtually synonymous. Whilst the claims of humanity, justice, and economy all pointed in the direction of promoting indigenous self-government, Pope Hennessy argued that what he called the 'pro slavery view of the case' amounted to nothing but prejudice, viciousness, and unnecessary expense. What was wanted, he ventured, 'was a man who could gain the confidence of the natives by strict justice & by sympathy for them. The "rod of iron" policy is a very expensive one & in truth very Anti English.'[75] Of course, Pope Hennessy saw himself in just such a role, picturing himself at the forefront of the campaign against the 'pro-slavery' party whether they were to be found in the Colonial Office or in the colonies.[76] Making common cause with the antislavery and Aborigines' protection movements, Pope Hennessy understood his reforms in Hong Kong, in parallel to his policies in Barbados, as directed at the eradication of slavery in all its forms. As in Barbados, Pope Hennessy saw cruelly confirmed all the evils of racial arrogance, and the heinous abuses of power to which they led. The British administration and the white residents of Hong Kong were complicit not only in the subjugation of the native races but also their subjection to real slavery. Opposition to his crusading reforms merely demonstrated the entrenchment of white colonial power, and the reluctance to accept that the native residents

---

[73] *Times*, 3 August 1882.
[74] See, for example, RHL MSS British empire, AntiSlavery Papers, s.18, c.137/234–255, letters from Pope Hennessy to Frederick Chesson. See also Charles Swaisland, 'The Aborigines Protection Society, 1837–1909,' in Temperley, *After slavery*, pp. 265–80.
[75] RHL MSS British empire, Anti-Slavery Papers, s.18, c.137/236, Pope Hennessy to Chesson, 1 April 1879.
[76] RHL MSS British empire, Anti-aSlavery Papers, s.18, c.137/240 & 241, Pope Hennessy to Chesson, 8 June 1884.

would need to be encouraged to participate in their own government, no longer subject races but partners.

'TO DEAL JUSTLY WITH THE SLAVERY OF CHINA WE OUGHT TO INVENT A NEW NAME FOR IT'

The campaign against regulated prostitution in Hong Kong needs to be placed more firmly however in the context of Pope Hennessy's ongoing attempts to promote self-government, principally in this case by appealing to the leading members of the Chinese community, by acknowledging their cultural and political institutions, and by appointing prominent individuals to government posts. There was nothing in the humanitarian denunciation of 'brothel slavery' to challenge Pope Hennessy's political ideal of 'localisation'. Indeed, they were perfectly consistent, and of a piece with Pope Hennessy's Barbadian experiences. However, the Aborigines Protection Society also cited the governor's discouragement of 'domestic slavery', and this was an altogether more complex matter. The complementarity of humanitarian and political aims was not so readily evident when it came to the Chinese practice of adopting children as servants: as *mui tsai* or 'little sisters'.[77] This was the name given to the practice by which Chinese children were routinely sold by their parents, and adopted by the wealthy, typically as domestic drudges, and occasionally for more sinister reasons. The issue of the *mui tsai* inevitably overlapped with the question of brothel slavery, since it was assumed that numbers of such children were bought with the intention of restocking the colony's brothels. And as such the practice was routinely condemned by humanitarian organisations keen to stamp out slavery in all its forms. As Sir Michael Hicks Beach at the Colonial Office once remarked to Pope Hennessy: 'there is nothing on which the feelings of the English people & the House of Commons are so sensitive as on this question of slavery'.[78] Slavery was simply incompatible with British jurisdiction and with the extension of civilisation that the British brought to the world.

---

[77] For general discussion of *mui tsai*, see Maria Jaschok and Suzanne Miers, 'Women in the Chinese patriarchal system: submission, servitude, escape and collusion,' in Maria Jaschok and Suzanne Miers (eds.), *Women and Chinese patriarchy: submission, servitude and escape* (London: Zed, 1994), pp. 1–24.

[78] RHL MSS British Empire, Pope Hennessy Papers, s. 409, Michael Hicks Beach to Pope Hennessy, no date.

A great deal therefore hung on the word and the concept of 'slavery'. If the custom of 'adopting' *mui tsai* was indeed a form of 'domestic slavery' then it was of course the duty of any governor to eradicate it. For an antislavery advocate such as Pope Hennessy, this might have appeared as another expression of the universally acknowledged evil of slavery. But 'domestic slavery' was different from the legacy of chattel slavery in Barbados or state-sponsored 'brothel slavery' in Hong Kong, for in this case the evil could be traced not to white colonial exploitation of subject races, but to one of those subject races themselves. This was unequivocally a Chinese social evil, not a colonial one, as the advocates of the British civilising mission were quick to point out. To act against it meant condemning the failings of Chinese society, and directly intervening in the lives and customs of the Chinese community. Unlike the campaign against 'brothel slavery', then, the claims of humanity and the policy of 'localisation' pulled in opposite directions. Pope Hennessy's 'pro-native' sympathies were here at loggerheads with a humanitarian discourse guided to such a great extent by antipathy to slavery.

Nothing that Pope Hennessy had encountered before could have prepared him for this particular dilemma. Whilst it was his custom to surround himself with like-minded allies – 'cronies', of course, to his opponents – in this case his appointees differed in their interpretation of the status of the *mui tsai*. On the one hand, as Pope Hennessy's chief justice, Sir John Smale, argued, the issue was unequivocal: the Chinese custom of buying children for adoption was nothing less than 'real slavery'. Holding forth on one of the common placards offering rewards for the return of runaway servants, Smale declared that slavery in every form in Hong Kong was illegal and must be put down. He dared his listeners to deny the existence of slavery in Hong Kong:

Has Cuba or has Peru ever exhibited more palpable, more public evidence of the existence of generally recognised slavery in these hotbeds of slavery, than such placards as the one I now hold in my hand, to prove that slavery exists in this Colony?[79]

Within the wider humanitarian discourse of antislavery, this kind of domestic servitude was comparable with the very worst exemplars of slavery. Sir John Smale went on to note that

The more I penetrate below the polished surface of our civilization [in Hong Kong] the more convinced am I that the broad undercurrent of life here is more

---

[79] C. 3185, *Correspondence respecting the alleged existence of Chinese slavery in Hong Kong*, p. 5.

like that in the Southern States of America when slavery was dominant than it resembles the all-pervading civilization of England.

Smale's comparison dismissed observations of the differences between chattel slavery and other forms of forced labour as merely a species of sophism: for 'all slavery, domestic, agrarian, or for immoral purposes, comes within one and the same category'.[80]

On the other hand, however, were those who were prepared to emphasise the distinctiveness of Chinese culture and the inappropriateness of judging the Chinese by Western standards. Here, Pope Hennessy's orientalist protégé, Ernest Eitel, was called upon to draw upon the wealth of his sinological expertise. In Eitel's academic counter argument to Smale, he claimed that it was quite useless to use such words as slavery to characterise Chinese domestic customs, this demonstrating only the linguistic and analytical indiscipline of the non-expert mind. Endorsing the kinds of cultural relativism quite characteristic of 'orientalist sociology', Eitel proceeded in his judgement to distinguish between Western forms of slavery, whose ideal type was the plantations of the southern United States, and Chinese customs:

the term 'slavery' is bound up with the peculiar development of the social life and the legal theories of the progressive societies of the West. It has, indeed, such a peculiar meaning attached to it that one ought to hesitate before applying the term rashly to the corresponding relation of a social organism like that of China, which had an entirely different history, and has hitherto been socially unconnected with those highly developed societies.[81]

Eitel argued moreover that 'Slavery in China is not an incident of race as in the West, but an accident of misfortune' so that there was 'really little in the position of a Chinese family-slave which allows a close comparison with the condition of a slave under the Roman Law, or of a negro in the hands of his West Indian or American master'. Comparison with Caribbean or American chattel slavery was simply a case of sloppy thinking. Western conceptions of property, freedom, law, the role of women, the family and the individual were not directly applicable to Chinese society, and, in any case, exploitation of racial differences simply did not enter into the question of the *mui tsai*. Thus the practice could not be 'real slavery'. The most Eitel was prepared to concede was that this was a 'Chinese analogue of slavery'. In a tellingly nominalist peroration,

---

[80] *Ibid.*, pp. 234, 2, 6.   [81] *Ibid.*, p. 50.

Eitel argued that 'To deal justly with the slavery of China we ought to invent a new name for it.'[82]

Behind the war of words lay an argument about the demarcation of discourse and the field of legitimate humanitarian intervention. The history and geography of slavery, not just the name, was central to the argument: for Smale, impatient with relativist distinctions, slavery was a stain on humanity of urgent and universal importance; for Eitel, the claims of cultural difference were paramount. In the latter formulation, a kind of discourse of differentiation is set in play, one that set limits to the applicability not just of concepts but also of political projects developed in different places, times and conditions. Although Eitel accepted and celebrated the development of the universalising moral spirit expressed in Western humanitarianism, saying that 'The natural law of reaction was set in motion by that humanitarianism which, since the end of the last century, began to permeate, like an electric current, *the whole of the western world*', he quickly followed up this observation by endowing this humanitarianism with a distinctive geography, a mapping of the limits of its legitimate application.[83] Failing or refusing to recognise this geography was to give way to sentimentalism and incoherence. As Eitel insisted when directly considering Smale's pronouncements:

I observe that in these papers the term 'slavery' is indiscriminately used, – now in a strictly legal sense, and then again in its ethical or sentimental sense. As in the latter sense the word 'slavery' can idiomatically be applied to any irksome form of drudgery people in many ranks of society have to submit to in all countries, the indiscriminate use of the terms 'slavery' or 'genuine slavery' is a source of confusion and error.[84]

This is a problem therefore of *translation*: again not just a matter of words or of discourse, conceived in the sense of semantic coherence, rather a matter of geography. The contrast drawn here between British legal and humanitarian *universalism* on the one side and an ethno-graphically informed, pragmatic cultural *relativism* on the other is highly significant, and worthy of emphasis. What might have seemed, to both contemporaries and historians, merely the natural advance of antislavery principles, an expanding social and political geography of moral and

---

[82] *Ibid.*, pp. 52, 53.

[83] *Ibid.*, p. 50, emphasis added. For discussion of the discourse of differentiation and the registers of racism, see Stuart Hall, 'The multi-cultural question', in Barnor Hesse (ed.), *Un/settled multiculturalisms: diasporas, entanglements, disruptions* (London: Zed, 2001), pp. 209–41.

[84] *Correspondence respecting the alleged existence of Chinese slavery*, p. 109.

humanitarian concern, is revealed in Eitel's construction to have an historical and cultural geography, and thus to have limits.

The *mui tsai* problem cut to the heart of Pope Hennessy's philosophy of government. For all his antislavery sympathies, it is the politics of 'localisation', informed by Eitel's argument for cultural particularism, which emerged victorious in his mind and in his actions. In the end, Pope Hennessy came down on the side of Eitel, rejecting Smale's argument and his call for the repression of 'domestic slavery' in Hong Kong. Pope Hennessy accepted the argument that a practice could not actually be called slavery 'where the individuals concerned go about our streets with a knowledge that they are free'. He contended that the existing law against slavery was enough, if properly enforced, to 'secure the real freedom of these women'. And he concluded that 'since Chinese domestic servitude differed so widely from negro slavery, police prosecution of the former under any law with reference to the latter would constitute an act of very doubtful legality'.[85]

In coming to this decision, Pope Hennessy clearly deferred to the increasingly assertive Chinese political community, whose ambitions he supported. Chinese community leaders willingly agreed to help police the traffic in prostituted women but argued robustly for special protection of the practice of adopting *mui tsai*. The leading Chinese, anxious to protect an established social institution and faced with the possibility that the *mui tsai* might be caught up in the British philanthropic net, set out to carefully distinguish legitimate and benign custom from the undoubted evil of brothel trafficking. Representatives of the Chinese merchant community petitioned Pope Hennessy to be allowed to found an institution, the *Po Leung Kuk*, dedicated to putting down the kidnapping and traffic in human beings, particularly for purposes of prostitution, but made it quite clear that the traditional custom of purchasing boys and girls for domestic servitude must be respected. The political implications of this move are clear: as Elizabeth Sinn has noted, 'In the final analysis, different views on kidnapping rested on different ideas about individual freedom and bondage. The Chinese, threatened by Pope Hennessy's attitude, may have felt compelled at this point to stem the intrusion of English law into their patriarchal system.'[86] In ultimately referring to *mui tsai* as 'so-called slavery', Pope Hennessy followed not only the

[85] Elizabeth Sinn, 'Chinese patriarchy and the protection of women in nineteenth-century Hong Kong', in Maria Jaschok and Suzanne Miers (eds.), *Women and Chinese patriarchy*, p. 148.

[86] Elizabeth Sinn, 'Chinese Patriarchy', p. 146. See also Sinn, *Power and charity*; Anonymous, *History of the Po Leung Kuk Hong Kong 1878–1968* (Hong Kong: Po Leung Kuk, no date). Lethbridge, 'The

opinion of Eitel, but also that of the *Po Leung Kuk* petitioners and that of Ng Choy, the acting police magistrate whom he had appointed as a crucial element in his project of incorporating the Chinese community into Hong Kong's government system. With the blessing of the governor, then, the Chinese patriarchal system was bolstered and politically protected from accusations of slavery, at least until its reappearance as an international humanitarian issue in the early twentieth century.[87]

Although supported by Eitel and the local Chinese élite, Pope Hennessy was nevertheless put on the defensive in his dealings with the Colonial Office. The latter, so long on the end of his criticisms of government complicity in humanitarian abuses, could hardly conceal their satisfaction at the fact that Pope Hennessy was forced finally to choose between siding with the indigenous community and siding with metropolitan humanitarianism.[88] Sir John Smale, initially encouraged by the reputation Pope Hennessy had gained in Barbados and by his crusade against 'brothel slavery' in Hong Kong, was left to bemoan the governor's actions and take whatever comfort he could from the judgement of posterity on plantation slavery.[89] For the time being, the humanitarian campaign against slavery had run up against impassable discursive and political barriers. Pope Hennessy's commitment to 'localisation', Eitel's argument for cultural relativism, and the demands of political pragmatism in the face of a newly assertive Chinese leadership ensured that any strict, legalistic adherence to antislavery principles remained a dead letter.

'MAURICE AUX MAURICIENS': 'ACCLIMATISING' HIS EXCELLENCY

If we return finally to Mauritius, bearing in mind all the controversies of Pope Hennessy's imperial career, we can see that the crisis of government he precipitated did not exactly arrive there unheralded. To MPs, civil servants and his other numerous enemies at home, the whole episode confirmed yet again that Pope Hennessy was neither suited by personality

---

evolution of a Chinese voluntary association in Hong Kong: The *Po Leung Kuk*', *Journal of Oriental Studies* **10** (1972), pp. 33–50.

[87] *Correspondence respecting the alleged existence of Chinese slavery*, pp. 4, 79, 82. For the twentieth century, see Lieutenant Commander and Mrs H. L. Haslewood, *Child slavery in Hong Kong: the mui tsai system* (London: Sheldon Press, 1930); Norman Miners, 'The abolition of the *mui tsai* system, 1925 to 1941', in Norman Miners, *Hong Kong under imperial rule*, pp. 170–90; Susan Pedersen, 'The maternalist moment in British colonial policy: the controversy over "child slavery" in Hong Kong, 1917–1941', *Past and Present* **171** (2001), pp. 161–202.

[88] *Correspondence respecting the alleged existence of Chinese slavery*, p. 81, Earl of Kimberley to Pope Hennessy, 29 September 1880.

[89] *Correspondence respecting the alleged existence of Chinese slavery*, p. 96.

nor politics to be an effective colonial governor. The governor had a long record of partisanship and antagonism behind him, and the Colonial Office had again expected the worst. Responding, for instance, to a welcome from the Mauritian *Société d'Acclimatation*, Sir Robert Herbert had noted acidly that 'We shall see how they succeed in "acclimatising" His Excellency'.[90] Whitehall could hardly have been surprised that Pope Hennessy had alienated so quickly the affections of the British community in Mauritius. Echoes of hostile preventions had poisoned the ears of these colonial subjects in more than one of his postings, leading to pre-emptive attempts in Mauritius to present Pope Hennessy as 'a dangerous man' and thus to 'discredit beforehand' His Excellency's government.[91] To these 'loyal' Britons, Pope Hennessy's record confirmed not only his 'exaggerated ideas of philanthropy', but also his Irishness, anti-Englishness, and pro-Catholicism.[92] It is no surprise that these colonists invoked the same 'yoke of despotism' that the Barbadian planters had when denouncing Pope Hennessy's confederation plans, the rhetorical pairing of liberty and slavery being so much a shared part of the pan-imperial discourse of loyalism.[93] The Mauritius crisis and Pope Hennessy's part in it were inseparable from the nature of the imperial network and the trans-imperial connections that sustained it.

What is significant here is that Pope Hennessy again fell back in his defence on the trope of slavery, returning to the themes that had animated his humanitarian critique of British rule in Barbados and Hong Kong. The exiled ex-governor stepped up his attack on the legitimacy of the royal commission appointed to evaluate the charges against him by insisting that Sir Hercules Robinson was personally disqualified to try him. Not only was Robinson a supporter of corporal punishment, and thus the very antithesis of Pope Hennessy's beau ideal of a colonial governor; he was also alleged to have a vested interest in condemning Pope Hennessy. For Sir Hercules had, in his governorship of Hong Kong (1859–65), been directly responsible for introducing the abuses of 'brothel slavery' that Pope Hennessy had exposed in parliament during his tenure

[90] NA CO 167/607, Sir Robert Herbert to Lord Derby; see Pope-Hennessy, *Verandah*, p. 233.

[91] NA CO 882/5/1, 'Correspondence relating to an inquiry held by the Right Hon. Sir Hercules Robinson', p. 88.

[92] NA CO 882/5/1, 12 April 1886, 'Complaint of four elected members of Council to the Colonial Office'.

[93] Lambert, *White creole culture*; Donal Lowry, 'The crown, empire loyalism and the assimilation of non-British white subjects in the British world: an argument against "ethnic determinism"', in Carl Bridge and Kent Fedorowich (eds.), *The British world: diaspora, culture and identity* (London: Frank Cass, 2003), pp. 96–120.

there. Pope Hennessy argued that the corrupt and demoralising ordinances that 'had created and intensified slavery in Hong Kong' were Robinson's doing.[94] Sir Hercules was ranged with the defenders of slavery and white privilege, against the interests of the indigenous races and communities. Again we observe not only the involved workings of the web of empire but also, within it, the travelling discourse of slavery. Fighting to salvage his career Pope Hennessy came back to his resolute role as an antislavery advocate, ranged against entrenched resistance to reform at home and abroad. The governor's 'pro-native' sympathies extended in Mauritius to 'the whole of the Asiatic population, immigrants from India and China' – a population, Pope Hennessy noted, that 'has received and will continue to receive my support and protection'.[95] But these sympathies easily encompassed the French and French-creole community as well. To both could the political slogan '*Maurice aux Mauriciens*' apply, and to both could Pope Hennessy promise liberation from the bonds of British slavery. In Mauritius, Pope Hennessy could reunite antislavery and pro-nativism and reconstitute his political credo.

For an avowed antislavery advocate like Pope Hennessy, colonial government could never condone the practice. In one colonial posting after another he could successfully mobilise the denunciation of slavery in the context of racial retrenchment and political exclusiveness. In this view, all his actions spoke of 'integrity', a consistency that can be traced from his experience as an Irishman of British colonial rule, through his adventures in colonial government, and back finally to Ireland and home-rule politics. But to portray Pope Hennessy's colonial governance in this way is to impart too much significance to his agency as an individual, to the formation of his ideological makeup, and to the role of the metropolis in shaping the colonial landscape. We have seen that Pope Hennessy's political ideal of localisation was not everywhere consistent with his humanitarian opposition to slavery. If we set Pope Hennessy's imperial career back within the 'geographies of colonial philanthropy',[96] we can see that whilst Pope Hennessy's previous colonial experience had reinforced his relationship to British humanitarianism, on the issue of the *mui tsai* this was challenged and tested up to the point of failure. In Barbados, the legacy and memory of slavery could be interpreted as underlying the abuses perpetrated by the white colonial community, but

---

[94] NA CO 882/5/1, Pope Hennessy to Stanhope, 18 January 1887.
[95] NA CO 882/5/1, pp. 9–10.
[96] D. Lambert and A. Lester, 'Geographies of colonial philanthropy', *Progress in Human Geography* **28** (2004), pp. 320–41.

Pope Hennessy's antipathy towards slavery and sympathy for the indigenous community pointed in a different direction in Hong Kong.

We have tried to suggest how significant were the geographies of Pope Hennessy's imperial career: not just the movement from metropolis to periphery, but also the ways in which his politics were shaped by his travels, and by the translations of humanitarian discourse itself. For it was not only governors that were 'transient visitors': so too were discourses, even such central, powerful and seemingly universalising tropes as that of 'slavery'. 'Slavery' was a profoundly contested concept, a literally mobile signifier whose application in case to case and from place to place was at issue. Slavery was a marker of the unacceptable in imperial culture, and could serve as shorthand for understanding the politics of empire, but what it *was* would continue to polarise opinion for the rest of the nineteenth century and into our own day.[97] It is no part of our intention here to try to resolve the question of what constitutes slavery.[98] What is important is to indicate how, in the spaces and places of the imperial network, the discourse of slavery was constituted and contested. We can draw attention to the fact that, long after abolition, humanitarians like Pope Hennessy drew attention to the persistence or re-emergence of slavery across the empire; and we have seen with what results. But we also want to note that humanitarian networks worked within an imperial network that consisted of diverse groups of European colonial settlers and colonised people, besides the various other metropolitan agencies. The extension of the humanitarian project of antislavery cannot be divorced from the agency of these peoples; its success or failure depended on their actions, and their place within the British imperial network. What 'slavery' meant was a production of the particular societies in which it operated or in which it had operated, and of the circuits of government, humanitarian imagination and intervention by which these places were tied together. It was, like Pope Hennessy himself, both product and producer of the tensions of empire.[99]

---

[97] See Temperley (ed.), *After slavery*.

[98] On this question see: Nancy Stepan, *The idea of race in science: Great Britain, 1800–1960* (London: Macmillan, 1982); Tommy Lott (ed.), *Subjugation and bondage: critical essays on slavery and social philosophy* (Lanham: Rowman and Littlefield, 1998), p. xviii; Frederick Cooper, Thomas Holt and Rebecca Scott, *Beyond slavery: explorations of race, labor, and citizenship in post-emancipation societies* (London: University of North Carolina Press, 2000).

[99] A. L. Stoler and F. Cooper, 'Between metropole and colony: Rethinking a research agenda', in F. Cooper and A. L. Stoler (eds.), *Tensions of empire: colonial cultures in a bourgeois world* (Berkeley: University of California Press, 1997), pp. 1–56.

CHAPTER 9

Sunshine and sorrows: Canada, Ireland and Lady Aberdeen

Val McLeish

In 1894 Lady Ishbel Aberdeen (Fig. 9.1), wife of the Governor General of Canada, crossed the Atlantic to undertake a two-week tour of rural Ireland for her Irish Industries Association. She wanted to see everything, do everything, and make each moment count. The itinerary that had been arranged for her first day – a train journey to Youghal, a church service, lunch with local dignitaries, a visit to inspect lace-making at a convent, then a drive along the Blackwater River – was altogether too gentle for her liking. It 'savoured somewhat of a Sunday excursion', she wrote scornfully, 'but I thought it best not to change arrangements'. Three days later she was 'vexed we did not manage Kenmare ... We could have done it by starting at 8 this morning [instead of 12.35], arriving at 11 and coming on by 2 [o'clock] train to Killarney.' Soon after, frustrated by some perceived aspect of Irish inefficiency or incompetence, she made a note in her journal to 'organise, organise'.[1] She ran the rest of her life in the same breathless manner, filling every moment with what she regarded as useful tasks, and urging others to do likewise. Highly intelligent, intense, serious and idealistic, she was never satisfied with second best, and expected everyone to aim for the same high standards she set herself.

Like Lady Curzon (see Chapter 10), Lady Aberdeen was a new kind of viceregal woman. Various social changes in Britain during the late nineteenth century, such as the growth of imperial fervour, the emergence of the independent 'new woman', and the professionalisation of philanthropy, all combined to influence the role of the vicereine, which earlier in the century had largely been confined to entertaining and social duties.[2] Viceregal representatives in the British colonies were appointed from the aristocracy. An aristocratic woman in Britain could not vote and had no formal political power in the nineteenth century, but her class

---

[1] 'Ishbel's journal', quotes 3–6 June 1894, Box 10/1–2, Haddo House Archives (hereafter HHA).
[2] Amanda Andrews, 'The great ornamentals: *new* vice-regal women and their imperial work 1884–1914', unpublished Ph.D. thesis, University of Western Sydney (2004).

Fig. 9.1 Lady Aberdeen wearing her Victorian era ball dress, which reflected the imperial theme of the ball and her interest in Ireland. The dress was blue and white with a red-lined train. It was embroidered with designs from the 'Book of Kells' and trimmed with Irish lace. Toronto, 1897. Reproduced by permission of Lord Aberdeen.

and social status gave her influence in other ways. She could work in partnership with her husband to advance his political career or protect the family dynasty.[3] She could wield influence as a political hostess or confidante, something that women lower down the social scale could not do.

Relatively few British women took up residence in the non-settler colonies before the 1850s: a few intrepid independent travellers, some missionaries, and those who accompanied their husbands on tours of duty from the United Kingdom. Viceregal appointees could not have functioned adequately without a wife – or a sister – to fulfil the role of hostess. Emily Eden, for example, accompanied her unmarried brother George, Lord Auckland, to Calcutta, where he was governor from 1836–42. She smiled prettily and conversed delightfully at official functions, and filled her time painting and writing novels and travelogues. In 1880, when Lord Cowper accepted the lieutenancy of Ireland he was told that his wife Katrine would 'be bored, as a lady lieutenant has no duties'. Katrine did not stray beyond the pale; it was eighteen months before she ventured out of Dublin.[4] This would not have satisfied Lady Aberdeen, who wanted to extend her own imperial career while supporting her husband. She was not prepared solely to decorate his arm.

The Aberdeens represented the crown in Ireland and Canada, and Lady Aberdeen set up organisations to improve health and rural welfare in both places. Her first overseas posting was for six months in 1886, when Lord Aberdeen was appointed lord lieutenant of Ireland. This was when her views were dramatically changed: previously disliking anything to do with Ireland, she now fell in love with the Irish people and vowed to spend her life helping them. It is impossible to understand why Ireland was so important to Lady Aberdeen without looking at that first encounter, which is discussed in detail below. The Aberdeens paid extended visits to Canada in 1890 and 1891, and spent 1893–8 there while Aberdeen was governor general. Lady Aberdeen had an imperial and political vision that complemented her husband's role: she wanted to unite people from Atlantic to Pacific as Canadians loyal to the British empire. She worked towards this through the organisations she founded for Canadian women. Then early in 1906 the Aberdeens returned to Dublin for a nine-year stay (see Map 9.1). The Liberals were back in power, home rule seemed possible once again, and Lady Aberdeen wanted to help Ireland prepare for this.

[3] K. D. Reynolds, *Aristocratic women and political society in Victorian Britain* (Oxford: Clarendon Press, 1998).
[4] Marjorie Pentland, *A bonnie fechter* (London: Batsford, 1952), p. 57. Katrine Cowper, *Earl Cowper KG* (London: privately printed, 1913), p. 538.

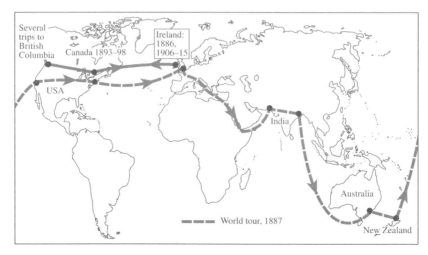

Map 9.1 Ishbel Aberdeen's imperial career and major places visited during her world tour.

A contrast will be drawn between Lady Aberdeen's more successful five years in Canada, and the difficult second Irish viceroyalty. Ideas that had previously worked well for her had to be revised and adapted to meet the different circumstances of twentieth-century Ireland. Although her problems were rooted in Irish political and social instability, the events of these years clearly indicate the vulnerability of her perceived identity as an important member of the ruling power. Her experience shows the difficulties involved in translating ideas from one imperial site to another, and the problems of returning to changing colonial sites. Lady Aberdeen found the events of these years hurtful; they were never forgotten, and perhaps never fully understood.

Lady Aberdeen was born Ishbel Maria Marjoribanks in London on 14 March 1857. It is not surprising that she had a lifelong interest in politics and empire, because generations of her ancestors had sat in the House of Commons, and much of her family's wealth had resulted from colonial adventures. One grandfather, James Weir Hogg, was an Irish lawyer who made his fortune at the Calcutta bar. On returning to England he became a Tory MP, and sat on the Indian Council. Her Marjoribanks grandfather was a Liberal MP, a barrister, a director of the East India Company, and a partner in Coutts Bank. Ishbel's father, Dudley, was Liberal MP for Berwick-on-Tweed. Her mother was a political hostess, so Ishbel was used to mixing with the many politicians who visited her parents; Gladstone was a family friend. Ishbel had deeply held religious beliefs, the result of her strict Presbyterian upbringing, and was thrilled when the year before her 'coming out' she was asked to teach at Sunday school: 'Oh lo to be made the channel through which the water of life may flow to some of these souls', she wrote excitedly in her journal.[5]

In 1877, after three years of alternating hope and despair and some matchmaking by her mother, Ishbel became the Countess of Aberdeen when she married John Campbell Gordon, the seventh Earl. Lord Aberdeen's grandfather, a Tory, had sided with the Peelites in 1846 and later presided over a coalition government. When Aberdeen entered the House of Lords in 1873 he chose the cross benches, which he described as 'a sort of "No Man's Land"', but shortly afterwards he joined the Conservatives. In December 1878 Disraeli's government declared war on Afghanistan. Ishbel, though heavily pregnant, sat through the three-day debate, and was heartened to hear her husband denounce Conservative policy. Later, describing his misery at speaking and voting against the government, he wrote that he 'felt like an outcast, almost a pariah'. Ishbel delightedly noted the event in her journal, mentioning the congratulatory letters he had received. Shortly after, he was welcomed into the Liberal party.[6] Ishbel's encouragement probably aided this conversion. She was definitely the stronger character, and those who knew the couple were well aware who ruled the roost in the Aberdeen household.[7]

After their marriage the Aberdeens travelled between England and Scotland according to parliamentary sessions. Ishbel gave birth to five children although one died in infancy. During this period she involved herself in many projects in Scotland and London, and keenly followed politics. As a Liberal, a feminist, and an ardent disciple of Gladstone, she took the Chair of the Women's Liberal Federation (WLF), which supported female suffrage. At the WLF 1888 conference in Birmingham, in one of the first political speeches to a large mixed audience by a woman, she proposed home rule for Ireland to five thousand people.[8] She was an experienced public speaker by this time, and this ability, combined with her passionate belief in liberalism, led to Gladstone choosing her to

---

[5] 'Ishbel's journal', 26 April 1874.
[6] 'Ishbel's journal', 10 December 1878; John and Ishbel Aberdeen, *We twa*, 2 vols. (London: Collins, 1925), Vol. I, p. 83.
[7] An example among many: Sinn Fein leader Arthur Griffith said that everyone knew who the *real* lord lieutenant was. Leon O'Broin, *The Chief Secretary Augustine Birrell in Ireland* (London: Chatto and Windus, 1969).
[8] Pentland, *Bonnie Fechter*, p. 73. Unfortunately Marjorie Pentland destroyed some of her mother's journals after writing this biography.

address an election meeting in Aylesbury, where she shared the platform
with Lord Ripon, governor of India during the 1880s.[9]

Although Lady Aberdeen spent most of her life in the United Kingdom
she was no 'Little Englander'. Her vision was empire wide, and she frequently made connections between different colonies. She campaigned
widely against Conservative policy during the South African wars, suggesting that military force should not be used. Until the Boers were ready
for self-government, she said, Britain should install the policies Lord
Durham had used in Canada sixty years earlier.[10]

Lady Aberdeen founded the Aberdeen Ladies' Union, which sent over
330 women emigrants to Canada and elsewhere in the empire between
1884 and 1914.[11] Many of these women had read her articles on empire and
emigration in her Scottish magazine *Onward and upward*. For over
thirty-five years between 1893 and 1937 she was president of the International Council of Women, which worked for social reform and
women's rights in the United States, the settler colonies and most European nations. When the covenant of the League of Nations was being
drafted in 1919 she headed a successful ICW deputation to Woodrow
Wilson, president of the commission, achieving the inclusion of certain
clauses favouring women.[12]

Lady Aberdeen thought devolution of the settler colonies had made
them strong, and a source of power to the United Kingdom. She believed
passionately in self-government for the British colonies, hoped that a
home-rule Ireland would win dominion status like Canada or Australia,
and even argued for 'home rule all round'. Like Gladstone, she saw the
United Kingdom as a multinational state, with the different ethnicities
within its boundaries contributing to the diversity – and also the
strength – of the nation.[13] Ireland was included in this vision, but she
clearly believed that the Irish Celt needed the 'steadying touch of the solid
Anglo-Saxon' to succeed. She wanted cooperation, not intermixing, and
wanted individual cultures to retain their separate identity.[14] She was very

---

[9] *Aylesbury Reporter*, 2 July 1892.   [10] *Aberdeen Journal*, 22 November 1901.
[11] See Marjorie Harper, *Emigration from North East Scotland*, 2 vols. (Aberdeen: Aberdeen University
Press, 1988), Vol. I, *Beyond the broad Atlantic*.
[12] Aberdeen, *We Twa*, Vol. II, p. 305.
[13] 'Lady Aberdeen's speech to the WLF', May 1892, *Speeches, addresses and articles by and on Lord and
Lady Aberdeen*, Bookcase 2A, HHA. For Gladstone's view of Britishness see D. G. Boyce, 'The
marginal Britons: the Irish', in Robert Colls and Philip Dodd (eds.), *Englishness, politics and culture
1880–1920* (London: Croom Helm, 1986), p. 235.
[14] Ishbel Aberdeen, 'The sorrows of Ireland', *Yale Review* (October 1916), pp. 61–79, quote p. 64.

careful not to reveal her opinion of Catholicism, and perhaps this in itself gives an indication of her attitude towards it. A further indication can be gleaned in a letter she received from her confidant Henry Drummond. He wrote in a style that suggests a tacit understanding between them, and in the letter he described the Irish as 'a (very) semi-Christian people'.[15]

Ishbel read Dilke's *Problems of Greater Britain* in 1890 and was greatly impressed with what he called his 'beautiful idea': that the British empire and America might form a union of English-speaking people to lead the world.[16] She often spoke and wrote on this theme, saying that 'some of us on both sides of the water may even dream of an alliance ... shoulder to shoulder before the world. God's chosen people above all others in the service of humanity.'[17] Her hope was that home rule would make the Irish peaceful and compliant, thus strengthening the United Kingdom. It would remove friction between Britain and America caused by Irish-Americans, and lead to a solid alliance with America. However her world vision of a British-led Anglo-American Christian alliance was not to be.

FEARS AND SURPRISES: IRELAND, 1886

In February 1886, Gladstone appointed Lord Aberdeen Lord Lieutenant of Ireland. Ireland had been colonised by Britain during the sixteenth and seventeenth centuries and had its own parliament until 1800, when the Act of Union incorporated it into the United Kingdom. Resistance to British rule during the nineteenth century by such events as continuing radical land agitation; efforts for the repeal of the Act of Union; O'Connell's campaign for Catholic rights in the 1830s; the Young Ireland movement of mid-century; and Fenian 'outrages' in Britain during the 1860s, culminated in the home rule bills of 1886, 1893 and 1912–14. In 1881, Catholics comprised more than three-quarters of the population of five million. The two main Protestant groups were Presbyterians and Anglicans, with most of the Presbyterians living in northeast Ulster.[18] So while there were divided and intertwined loyalties and identities in Ireland when Aberdeen was appointed, there was a dominant tradition of

[15] Henry Drummond to Ishbel Aberdeen, 4 March 1886, 'Henry Drummond letters', Box 1/7, HHA.
[16] 'Henry Drummond letters', 21 April 1890; Charles Wentworth Dilke, *Problems of Greater Britain* (London: Macmillan, 1890), p. 101.
[17] Ishbel Aberdeen, 'Speech to the WLF'.
[18] Donald Harman Akenson, *Small differences: Irish Catholics and Irish Protestants 1815–1922* (Dublin: Gill and Macmillan, 1988), pp. 155–7.

resistance to British rule: a popular Irish nationalism to which every Catholic was exposed.[19]

Lady Aberdeen had little time to prepare for the task ahead because they had to leave for Ireland quickly. She did not want to go there. Her daughter records that Ireland was 'a troublesome country for which [Ishbel] felt a strong dislike'. Years later Ishbel wrote that they had had no Irish friends and knew nothing about it. This was not quite the case. She would have been aware of the violence, evictions and the land wars of 1881–2. She would have known that in 1882 Frederick Cavendish, the new chief secretary, and his Irish Catholic deputy, Thomas Burke, had been murdered in Phoenix Park by a splinter Fenian group, the Invincibles.[20] She also knew that members of the British establishment there were subjected to heightened security. These restrictions contributed to her apprehension and aversion to Ireland. The final insult was that Aberdeen had been unable to confer with his wife before accepting the post. She wrote to Henry Drummond:

Don't you think that I ought to be very much offended at not being consulted, I who have registered a solemn vow never to set foot in Ireland? . . . how we shall ever be able to endure months of this I know not. . . . it was the very last post one would have chosen.[21]

The Aberdeens first met Drummond in 1884 when he published his theory about how the natural fixed laws of science governed the spiritual world of religion. Lady Aberdeen immediately appreciated the significance of his work for her own life. It meant that individual action was valuable, and society could progress through a combination of modern science and personal moral earnestness. This was far removed from the fierce fundamental Presbyterianism she had grown up with. Studying with Drummond renewed her faith in religion and was a turning point in her life.[22]

---

[19] They saw themselves as 'an historic people, a community whose national consciousness could be traced down the ages, and whose struggle to survive is the central theme of Irish history'. D. G. Boyce, *Nationalism in Ireland* (London: Croom Helm, 1982), p. 392. This romantic background to nineteenth-century nationalism was challenged and refuted by revisionist historians from the 1930s onwards: see also R. F. Foster's discussion of Sullivan's *The story of Ireland* (1867): *Irish story: telling tales and making it up in Ireland* (London: Allen Lane, 2001), pp. 6–10. I discuss the complex layering of Ulster identities in detail in my unpublished PhD thesis: Valerie McLeish, 'Imperial footprints: Lady Aberdeen and Lady Dufferin in Ireland, Canada and India 1870–1914' (University of London, 2002), Chapter 6.

[20] Cavendish was married to Gladstone's niece Lucy.

[21] Pentland, *Bonnie Fechter*, pp. 55–6; Ishbel Aberdeen, *Musings of a Scottish granny* (London: Heath Cranton, 1936), p. 131.

[22] Henry Drummond, *Natural law in the spiritual world* (London: Hodder and Stoughton, 1883). Theologians criticised his argument and demonstrated to their own satisfaction that it was founded on fallacy.

Her first opportunity to put Drummond's teaching into practice was in Ireland. She felt 'overwhelmed' at the prospect, but promised Gladstone she would try to see her way 'step by step in this unknown future'.[23] She squeezed in an appointment with Cardinal Manning to learn how religion affected Irish politics, and ordered green coats for her four young children to wear on their entrance to Dublin. But the green coats were hastily exchanged for cream when Ishbel discovered that green was the colour of nationalism, and would be inappropriate attire for the children of the Queen's representative. Such a potentially embarrassing faux pas was indicative of her ignorance of Irish culture and the history of its relations with Britain. However when she crossed the Irish Sea her opinions began to change. She discovered that the Irish were not the hostile or despondent simian-featured people often depicted in British newspapers and journals.[24] She told Gladstone how touched she was by the courtesy and reserve of the working classes, and how she liked the nationalist women she worked with. But the conservative Anglo-Irish aristocracy had traditionally refused to support a Liberal viceroy, and they made no exception for Aberdeen: 'The bitter hostility of the upper classes is indeed a sad feature', she continued, adding that her invitations to a dance at Dublin Castle had been spurned by several Unionists.[25]

As Lady Aberdeen became aware of the injustices Ireland had suffered as a colonised nation, she very quickly appreciated the need for home rule, which Gladstone hoped to introduce. But in August 1886 the first home rule bill was defeated. It split the Liberal party: the Liberal imperialists led by Chamberlain joined the Unionists, Gladstone resigned, and the Aberdeens were recalled to Britain. Ishbel had only just launched her Irish Industries Association (IIA), which sought to help homeworkers develop skills in such crafts as lace-making, embroidery, knitting and spinning, and set up shops to sell their products in Dublin and London. She decided to continue the work from London. Henry Drummond agreed: 'The ship seems all ready for launching and it would mean everything for the country that it should fly the Vice-Regal flag at its mast-head rather than that of the Nationalists, who would be sure to take up the thing if you abandoned it', he wrote.[26]

---

[23] Ishbel Aberdeen to William Gladstone, 11 February 1886, 'Gladstone Papers', Additional Manuscripts 44090, fo. 145, British Library.

[24] See for example *The Illustrated London News*, 7 February 1880, p. 132; 14 February 1880, p. 153.

[25] Ishbel Aberdeen, 'Gladstone papers', fo. 150. This hostility did not compare in intensity with the vitriolic campaign against the Aberdeens during their second viceroyalty.

[26] 'Henry Drummond letters', 12 July 1886.

The many cuttings in the Aberdeens' scrapbooks from all sections of the press confirmed that when they left the whole of Dublin turned out to cheer them. Aberdeen told Gladstone about the 'amazing and most impressive' farewell, and commented that '[n]ext to the enthusiasm perhaps, the most striking feature of the occasion was the entire absence of any whisper of disorder'.[27] In six short months the Aberdeens had won the popular vote, and Ireland became engraved on Lady Aberdeen's heart. She accepted her work there as a mission from God, and vowed in her journal that 'Ireland is laid on us to do all we can for her forever.'[28]

When the Aberdeens returned from Ireland, Lord Rosebery (Gladstone's foreign secretary and later prime minister) advised them to go and see the British empire first hand.[29] This they did, visiting India, Australia and New Zealand, and returning via the United States. Their reputation preceded them, for their support for Irish home rule was well known. In the antipodes they were fêted by Irish immigrants in each town they visited. This surprised Aberdeen, who told Gladstone from Sydney that their private visit 'has turned out to be quite the reverse – Irishmen especially having turned out to greet us everywhere with extraordinary cordiality'.[30] In San Francisco, Lady Aberdeen received a four-foot-high floral display in the shape of a harp from Irish Americans. Aberdeen was thrilled at their reception in America, and telegraphed Gladstone: 'From San Francisco to New York Irish addresses and proceedings eminently satisfactory and significant Irish band played God Save Queen here yesterday'.[31]

During the next few years Lady Aberdeen visited Ireland regularly on behalf of the IIA, and organised an Irish Village for the 1893 Chicago World Fair.[32] She was confident that she and Aberdeen would return to Dublin with Gladstone's new administration in 1892, and it came as a dreadful shock when they were not chosen. She wrote to Mary Gladstone:

I cannot pretend to be stoical in this matter for Ireland has been so constantly in our thoughts during the past six years that to want to work for her in a direct way has become part of one's very life . . . We know we could have been of some

---

[27] Lord Aberdeen, 'Gladstone papers', fo. 77.   [28] Pentland, *Bonnie Fechter*, p. 64.
[29] Rosebery coined the phrase 'the Empire is a commonwealth of nations': Keith Jeffery (ed.), *'An Irish empire'? Aspects of Ireland and the British empire* (Manchester: Manchester University Press, 1996), p. 8.
[30] Lord Aberdeen, 'Gladstone papers', fo. 82.   [31] Lord Aberdeen, 'Gladstone papers', fo. 89.
[32] This made a profit of £25,000 (£20,000 for the Irish workers, and £5,000 to set up a shop in Chicago).

little use there and it is miserable to seem to return the trust which has been shown us like this.[33]

In a very long letter Lady Aberdeen begged Gladstone to reconsider his decision, saying that

[W]e feel we can render you service in Ireland which perhaps at the present moment no one else can do ... [W]e know and understand the Irish to a certain degree and they know us and have shown their trust in us in a thousand touching ways.[34]

However chief secretary John Morley was not prepared to work with Lord (or perhaps Lady) Aberdeen, but wanted to take charge under a lord lieutenant who would be new to Ireland. Lord Houghton was appointed, and Gladstone sent Aberdeen to Canada.

HEALTH AND EMPIRE ON TWO CONTINENTS: GETTING
THE MESSAGE ACROSS[35]

Lady Aberdeen set out to improve health and welfare and to encourage a sense of national and imperial identity in Canada and during her second term in Ireland. She attempted to fulfil these aims through the women's associations that she established and presided over. This section provides a comparative study of the various strategies she used to promote her ideas in each place. It opens with a short discussion of her initial responses on arrival in Quebec and Dublin, and contextualises each imperial visitation with a brief historical overview. Then a sub-section on representation analyses aspects of her portrayal of Irish and Canadian people. The remainder of the section discusses the various women's organisations she founded, and how she used them to promote national unity and imperialism. It highlights the different tactics required in each place, and then considers how she coped with the opposition she received in Ireland, which severely affected her sense of self.

In September 1893, the *SS Sardinian* docked in Quebec harbour and Lady Aberdeen stepped ashore as vicereine of Canada. She immediately embraced all things Canadian. She hired an instructor to teach her the fashionable Canadian dances; engaged a French teacher to brush up the family's French; bought blanket coats, a national costume, for her children to wear in public; and she presented each of her staff with a silver

---

[33] Ishbel Aberdeen to Mary Gladstone, 'Mary Gladstone papers', Additional Manuscripts 46251, fo. 278, British Library.
[34] Ishbel Aberdeen, 'Gladstone papers', fo. 203.
[35] For more work on these topics see McLeish, 'Imperial footprints'.

maple-leaf brooch. Within a month she had been asked to help found the National Council of Women of Canada, and accepted the presidency. But she pined for Ireland: a year after arriving in Canada she told Gladstone that 'you know that we cannot pretend that our hearts are not elsewhere'.[36]

Canada was big: a land the size of Europe with a population less than that of London, and part of Aberdeen's brief as governor general was to unite the people as Canadians and encourage their loyalty to the British empire. His wife wanted to share this duty; it was not an easy task. The dominion of Canada had been created by a British act of parliament in 1867, and by 1891 contained almost five million people, predominantly rural dwellers, of whom 55 per cent were Protestant and 41 per cent Roman Catholic. Two million were of British origin, one million Irish and one-and-a-half million French Canadians. The remainder were other Europeans, Russians or East Asians or were of African or native-American origin.[37] An overarching national identity had been slow to emerge, and ethnic tensions simmered for a variety of reasons, particularly over the respective roles of religion and the state in education, and often involved discrimination against the French or the Catholics. Lady Aberdeen's enthusiastic overtures were but a small beginning to the vast work ahead.

When she returned to Ireland in 1906 she trod far more warily. On her first night in Dublin she wrote in her diary: 'Our disposition is to go very cannily and feel our way; perhaps we are too much afraid of false steps.'[38] Although she had been involved with the IIA since 1886, her visits to Ireland in the intervening years had been in an unofficial capacity amongst people who welcomed her as a friend. Now she faced a more hostile, divided country, and her position as first lady could be a dis-advantage. The friends that she had written to all confirmed that Ireland had changed. T. W. Rolleston, the secretary of the IIA, remarked that '[y]ou must have noticed that public affairs in Ireland wear a very different look from that which they bore when you were here last. New forces have arisen and old ones have decayed.'[39] James Talbot Power, owner of a distilling company and an old friend, warned her that 'you

---

[36] Ishbel Aberdeen, 'Gladstone papers', fo. 250.
[37] Ethnic origin figures are unavailable for 1891; these figures are estimated from the 1881 and 1901 censuses.
[38] Pentland, *Bonnie Fechter*, p. 152.
[39] T. W. Rolleston to Ishbel Aberdeen, 5 September 1905, Box 1/5, HHA.

will doubtless find things much changed over Here – 20 years makes great changes in People & Feelings'.[40]

Between the Aberdeens' first and second Irish viceroyalty, hopes for a constitutional settlement to the home-rule question had faded and in response the nationalist struggle had shifted from politics to culture. An awakening of interest in the Irish language, Catholicism, Gaelic games and traditions, Irish goods and industries, and a rejection of all things English, heralded the Celtic and Gaelic revivals. These influenced popular thought, polarised opinion and strengthened the southern-Irish sense of identity. In 1886 many of those who thought of themselves as Irish could feel comfortable within a wider British identity. This was scarcely possible in the years leading up to the first world war. Author Stephen Gwynn, a nationalist MP, offered Lady Aberdeen his unreserved help in attaining 'the end we are all aiming at in our different ways', but when she invited him to a meeting at the Viceregal Lodge he said:

In spite of your kindness I must stay away. This is the most jealous and suspicious country in Europe, I should think ... While we trust and honour the individual, we have not yet grounds sufficient to pay the same tribute to the office.[41]

Lady Aberdeen's different views on these imperial sites and their inhabitants are illuminated through the representations she produced in her published and private writing, through public speeches and private conversations, via the literature, theatre, art and music that she sponsored, and the organisations she founded. She came to know and love Ireland and the Irish people, but thought they were downtrodden, and inferior to the self-reliant Canadians. Her name for Canada was 'Our lady of the sunshine'. In a pamphlet entitled *Where dwells 'Our lady of the sunshine'?* she writes about a beautiful fertile land with prosperous, energetic, happy inhabitants. By contrast 'The sorrows of Ireland', which she wrote in 1916, was prompted by the Easter Rebellion and Irish war losses in Europe. This article largely suggests an unhappy nation and blames British misrule for producing a land of sullen misery.[42]

Canadians, especially the immigrant settlers, were depicted as resourceful, courageous people who took their future in both hands. In a

[40] James Power to Ishbel Aberdeen, 8 December 1905, Box 1/5, HHA.
[41] Stephen Gwynn to Ishbel Aberdeen, 17 December 1905, Box 1/5; 18 February 1906, Box 1/24, HHA.
[42] Ishbel Aberdeen, *Where dwells 'Our lady of the sunshine'?* (Toronto: Morang, 1898), and 'The sorrows of Ireland'. Her name for Canada was adapted from Kipling's poem 'Our lady of the snows'.

paper delivered to the Society of Arts in London, Lady Aberdeen described how Canadians had been 'building us an Empire in that Golden West as the result of the toil of their hands and brains ... by their high character, their endurance, their sobriety, their determination'.[43]

One reason for positive representations such as this was to encourage immigration, either from eastern Canada to the west, or from Europe. Although privately Lady Aberdeen acknowledged the harsh realities faced by immigrant families on the prairies, she believed that settlers could overcome their difficulties and this would produce the strong characters that Canada needed. She did not credit the Irish with the same sense of power over their own destiny. Like many Liberals of her generation she believed they were victims of British misunderstanding, mistreatment and misrule. She noted how embittered and mistrustful the peasantry were, yet she begged people to be tolerant, because their faults 'are those which are bred in a people who are alternately tyrannized over then cajoled; and if they seek by secret means to obtain their desires, who can blame them?'[44]

She had a sentimental concept of the rural Irish as trusting childlike people desperately trying to forge a decent life for themselves against all odds. She once described how she 'received a most genuine greeting from some dear toil-worn faces full of gladness and gratitude'.[45] Another article she wrote was entitled 'Helping Ireland to help herself', which reinforced this image of the Irish as victims.[46] Travelling from the west of Ireland to Dublin in 1894 Lady Aberdeen waxed lyrical about the scenes she saw:

The people who are working looking most picturesque, sometimes an old woman with her wheel on her shoulder returning from market, sometimes a lad with a creel and a scythe, or a pony, or a cow – or simply the people digging away at their potato patches in bright shawls and handkerchiefs over head and shoulders, generally with bare feet – or again a group of picturesque looking urchins.[47]

The only 'picturesque' people she wrote about in Canada were the native Americans and the Chinese. Yet 'picturesque' was a word she regularly used to describe Irish peasants. On the same trip she had 'photographed some picturesque old women carrying creels of turf'. But she did not mention the extreme physical effort required by the old

[43] Ishbel Aberdeen, 'Women in Canada', *Journal of the Society of Arts*, **20** (February 1903), pp. 283–91.
[44] *Women's Gazette*, 17 November 1888; Ishbel Aberdeen, 'Sorrows of Ireland', p. 71.
[45] 'Ishbel's journal', 16 June 1894.
[46] Ishbel Aberdeen, 'Helping Ireland to help herself', *The Outlook* (Dublin, March 1916).
[47] 'Ishbel's journal', 16 June 1894.

women – a full creel of turf weighed over 70 pounds (over 30kg) – or the poverty of having to dig barefoot.

Lady Aberdeen said that she was 'ashamed' of the poor children in Ottawa, and also those on her Scottish estate, yet she apparently never felt ashamed of the Irish.[48] What she was happy to see as 'picturesque' in Ireland, or amongst non-white Canadians, she clearly thought would have been a disgrace – for which she felt personally responsible – amongst white people in Scotland and Canada. The use of this word thus inscribes racial otherness, and her attitude indicates that privately she did not consider Ireland to be an equal partner in the United Kingdom, but a nation of dependent, and probably inferior people.[49] It was in marked contrast to her representations of the new Canadian nation, and the way she described the white settlers in Canada.

Lady Aberdeen's Canadian organisations provided a unifying force around which to construct a dominant identity, while also directly benefiting society. Middle- and upper-class women were the mainstay of these organisations, because philanthropy was still regarded as their social duty. In 1890, the Aberdeens bought a ranch and 13,000 acres in British Columbia, and spent several months getting to know the country, returning in 1891. On these trips they visited some of the families they had assisted to emigrate from their Haddo estate in Scotland.[50] Lady Aberdeen recruited a group of Winnipeg women to help these and other isolated settlers integrate themselves into Canadian life by sending them letters and magazines. The Aberdeen Association, as it came to be known, negotiated free postage, shipping and rail carriage, and expanded into all the major Canadian cities. In 1899 sixteen branches distributed over 20,000 parcels of reading material, flower seeds and pictures.[51] As well as the immediate benefits, Lady Aberdeen told Canadians, the association had brought 'links between east and west, between dwellers on the prairies and in the forests with those in the cities ... a very real source of strength to the country'.[52] In the early twentieth century it became a model for similar schemes in South Africa and Australia organised by the British Victoria League. Thus Lady Aberdeen's influence spread beyond

---

[48] *Ibid.*, 22 June 1894.
[49] For a different reading of the 'picturesque', one that fosters hybridity, see J. S. Duncan, 'Disorientation: on the shock of the familiar in a far-away place', in J. S. Duncan and D. Gregory (eds.), *Writes of passage* (London: Routledge, 1998), pp. 151–63.
[50] See Ishbel Aberdeen, *Through Canada with a Kodak* (Edinburgh: White, 1893).
[51] National Council of Women of Canada, *Women of Canada: their life and work* (Ottawa: The Queen's Printer, 1900).
[52] Ishbel Aberdeen, *Address at a public meeting* (Ottawa: Aberdeen Association, 1898).

Canada and into the wider British empire. The Aberdeen Association was Lady Aberdeen's first attempt to encourage Canadian unity, and it was operative until 1915.[53]

The National Council of Women of Canada (NCWC) was inaugurated in October 1893 with Lady Aberdeen as president. Each NCWC branch coordinated local philanthropic work and worked for social reform.[54] She personally oversaw the founding of nineteen of the twenty-two branches while accompanying her husband on official tours (planned to include the appropriate towns). The branches all kept in regular contact, sent delegates to the annual conferences, and offered hospitality to members away from home. These factors all helped to unite the women as Canadians. One member wrote an article entitled 'The importance of the National Council in fostering and developing the patriotism of Canadian women'.[55] Lady Aberdeen told the Regina group that

[It means] a great deal towards the consolidation of Canada, that her women from one end to the other, from Halifax to Victoria, shall be discussing one another's circumstances, and needs, and work, and are thus brought together to realize that they are one great sisterhood, with a mission to forward the welfare of this great Dominion.[56]

In January 1897, at the request of the NCWC, Lady Aberdeen produced a plan for a countrywide visiting nursing service. The Victorian Order of Nurses (VON) was founded to celebrate the Diamond Jubilee in 1897 and fulfilled a desperate need for medical provision in western Canada. It also helped Canadians to appreciate their connections with Britain and the empire: she publicised how she modelled the VON on Queen Victoria's Jubilee Institute for Nurses in Britain, right down to the nurses' uniform and the badge, and the etching of Queen Victoria that hung in their committee room. She called donations to the fund 'tributes to the Queen'.[57] The nurses' education and background ensured that they brought British ideas of culture and social behaviour into rural and backwoods Canada, and in a 1922 survey the VON was judged the most

[53] Elizabeth Riedi, 'Imperialist women in Edwardian Britain: the Victoria League 1899–1914', unpublished Ph.D. thesis, University of St Andrews (1997), pp. 101–5.

[54] For details see Veronica Strong-Boag, *The parliament of women: the National Council of Women of Canada 1893–1929* (Ottawa: National Museum of Canada, 1976); Rosa Shaw, *Proud heritage; a history of the National Council of Women of Canada* (Toronto: Ryerson, 1957).

[55] NCWC, *Annual Report* (1896), pp. 73–7.   [56] *Regina Leader*, 5 December 1895.

[57] *Boston Herald*, 25 October 1897.

important national institution for acculturating central European immigrants.[58]

Anyone could participate in these organisations, but in practice it was ladies of leisure – mainly white middle- and upper-class Protestants – who were most able to take part. French-Canadians outside Quebec were not attracted, nor were women from ethnic minorities. Few Catholics held local or national office. Participants tended to be loyal to the throne and the British empire, and patriotic towards the dominion. The Canadian identity that they helped to promote was white.

On her return to Ireland in 1906, Lady Aberdeen was able to draw on a wealth of knowledge and experience: her time in Canada, her previous Irish viceroyalty, and her ongoing work with the IIA. Her objectives in Canada had been to improve people's lives, especially in the rural hinterland, and promote Canadian unity and loyalty to empire. She was pleased with her Canadian work and had similar ambitions for Ireland. Stephen Gwynn had told her that Irish people were 'kept apart by imaginary barriers', and suggested that maybe she could draw them together.[59] She hoped that with her help the Irish people could put aside their religious differences and prepare to become a self-governing part of the United Kingdom.

During her first year back in Ireland she was approached by members of the medical profession. Tuberculosis caused one in six deaths in Ireland, mostly among young adults, she was told. Although it was on the wane over most of Europe, the death rate in Ireland was higher than in the 1860s.[60] Many, or perhaps most Irish people still held the traditional view that tuberculosis was hereditary, so afflicted families sometimes tried to hide its presence. It was necessary to create a huge shift in public awareness, and inform people that the disease was not hereditary but contagious, and could often be prevented by the adoption of simple hygienic measures.[61] Could Lady Aberdeen help? She certainly could, and after many discussions with experts in the field the Women's National Health Association of Ireland (WNHA) was inaugurated. All members pledged to fight tuberculosis, but the association had wider aims of

---

[58] John Murray Gibbon, *The Victorian Order of Nurses for Canada 50th Anniversary 1897–1947* (Montreal: Southam Press, 1947), p. 86.
[59] Stephen Gwynn to Ishbel Aberdeen, 17 December 1905, Box 1/5, HHA.
[60] John and Ishbel Aberdeen, *More cracks with 'we twa'* (London: Methuen, 1929), p. 155.
[61] Greta Jones, *'Captain of all these men of death': the history of tuberculosis in nineteenth and twentieth century Ireland* (New York/Amsterdam: Rodopi, 2001).

Fig. 9.2 Lord Aberdeen (with hat), Lady Aberdeen and the health caravan 'Eire' in Dublin, 1908. The legend on the caravan reads 'Hope and courage win the day. Our enemies are bad air, bad food, bad drink and dirt. Our weapons are pure air, pure food, pure milk and cleanliness. Victory is certain if we unite and persevere.' The same words were written in Irish on the other side of the caravan. Reproduced by permission of Peamount Hospital, Newcastle, County Dublin.

encouraging people to accept responsibility for their own health, and teaching them how to stay well and rear healthy children.[62]

The WNHA commenced operations in the summer of 1907 with an anti-tuberculosis exhibition and series of lectures in Dublin. This apparently aroused a great deal of interest, and each day's lecture was full. Spurred on by this success the WNHA caravan took the exhibition to small towns and villages, and the show was set up in a local hall (see Fig. 9.2). Irish- and English-speaking medical attendants brought rural Ireland the good news that the cure and prevention of tuberculosis was within the reach of every household, for it consisted of nourishing food, pure air and clean houses. Light entertainment such as dancing and magic-lantern shows was incorporated, and one can easily imagine the magnetism of such an event in the monotonous life of a small town. In the first year over 700,000 people visited the exhibition, and more than 100 WNHA branches were in operation.[63]

[62] Aberdeens, *More cracks*, p. 156.   [63] Pentland, *Bonnie Fechter*, p. 161.

Most branches were run by the Anglo-Irish aristocracy and gentry. Committees usually included representative churchmen, the local doctor and perhaps a local council official. Some Catholic women took part, although many preferred to join the United Irishwomen, a rural self-help group run by Sir Horace Plunkett. WNHA workers paid a 2s.6d. (12$\frac{1}{2}$ pence) yearly subscription, and were expected to subscribe to *Slainte*, the monthly WNHA magazine that Ishbel started in 1909. By contrast 'ordinary' membership was free; women often joined after door-to-door canvassing. These women, the target population, received personal instruction in their own homes in childcare, diet and hygiene.[64] WNHA workers and ordinary members were therefore not only divided along class lines, but the organisation was widely perceived to be an example of colonisers preaching to the colonised. 'A cottage', wrote the Cabinteely branch president reprovingly, 'no matter how poor its occupants may be, can still be kept neat, clean, and tidy, where the mother or wife is willing to set an example.' A sensitive area of operations was the surprise 'visitations' when committee members checked the standards of hygiene, cooking and childcare. The four members of the Cabinteely adjudicating committee visited the cottages each month 'at uncertain times and when least expected,' and awarded prizes for the cleanest homes.[65] This moral campaigning may well have upset some women: Zena Sherlock, president of the Tullamore branch, admitted that they had perhaps been too zealous and put some people off. The editor of the *Liverpool Post*, Edward Russell, told Aberdeen he was not surprised at the 'alleged bad reception of the Countess's hygienic endeavours', as the Irish were 'particularly resentful at being improved out of bad habits'.[66]

Nationalists nicknamed Ishbel 'Lady Microbe', or 'Blousy Bella', and circulated poems and jokes about her. They saw much of what she did as an attempt to impose British culture upon Irish people, and an assertion of her position as a member of the occupying power, the British establishment. In Canada, Lady Aberdeen had promoted imperialism through the women's organisations she founded, but she discovered that this was more difficult in Ireland. Invoking imperial language did not go down well, so she set up her organisations there in the name of Ireland, and did not mention the monarchy unless she had to. But as vicereine she had to drum up support for England, Britain or British royalty on various

---

[64] Ishbel Aberdeen, *Women's National Health Association of Ireland – organisation of local branches* (Dublin: no date), p. 5.
[65] *Slainte*, Vol. II (April 1910), pp. 76–7.
[66] Edward Russell to Lord Aberdeen, 3 September 1909, Box 1/5, HHA.

occasions, such as the coronation in 1911, and the visit of King George and Queen Mary shortly afterwards. Her efforts to organise an address of welcome for the royal visit backfired, as women who had unknowingly signed the address were horrified when they later learned what it was for.[67] When she requested donations from Irishwomen called Mary to buy a coronation gift for Queen Mary, the following lines (and more) appeared in the nationalist press:

> O I met with Lady Microbe and she shook me by the hand,
> And says she 'We want to compliment the Marys of your land:
> Our gracious queen is Mary too, and she is pleased to say
> She'll take a tiny gift from them on Coronation Day.'
>
> O Mary dear, you needn't fear your penny or your crown
> Will bear disease across the seas to healthy London town:
> 'Twill be surely disinfected, pasteurised, and washed with care,
> To banish all the poison of the tainted Irish air![68]

Old friend James Power told Lord Aberdeen in 1909 about the opposition faced by Lady Aberdeen:

I have mixed much with Dublin people – especially the middle classes and I was deeply pained to hear things said about Her Excellency and her labours in the cause of tuberculosis extermination in our country ... My sincere advice to Her Excellency would be ... not to force Tuberculosis any more on us. ... her hard earned popularity is at stake.[69]

In running the WNHA Lady Aberdeen also had to cope with 'bitter opposition' from Sir Henry Robinson, a British civil servant responsible for the Local Government Board. He disliked her and objected that she 'wanted to direct and dominate the Local Government Board'.[70] More controversy occurred when in 1908 the WNHA proposed the Tuberculosis Prevention (Ireland) Bill, which made notification of TB in Ireland mandatory. There was some fierce opposition from the press and some MPs, and a vigorous debate took place as the bill worked its way through parliament. Lady Aberdeen fought hard for the bill, and followed its progress carefully, even travelling to London to advise chief secretary Birrell of the tactics he should use in the House. It was finally passed in December 1908.

---

[67] *Irish Times*, 9 February 1911; *Sinn Fein*, 22 April 1911.   [68] *Irish Freedom*, March 1911.
[69] James Power to Ishbel Aberdeen, 26 October 1909, Box 1/5, HHA.
[70] Aberdeen, *More cracks*, p. 164; Henry Robinson, *Memories: wise and otherwise* (London: Cassell, 1923), p. 225.

Nationalist opposition continued. A rumour circulated in 1909 alleging that the WNHA's anti-tuberculosis campaign had damaged the image of Ireland abroad, affected tourism and the sale of Irish goods, and hurt the people whose livelihoods depended upon those industries. For these reasons the South Dublin Union Board of Guardians asked Lady Aberdeen to stop her crusade.[71] The rumours were later proved by the WNHA to be unfounded, but the damage had been done.[72]

This opposition had a variety of causes, including perceived infringement of civil liberties, but the most important seem to be resentment of Lady Aberdeen and her connections with British imperialism, and resistance to the imposition of elements of British culture. Lady Aberdeen's attempts to promote imperial interests through the WNHA in Ireland were controversial, and many failed. Some of her initiatives were unpopular because she was not sensitive enough to Irish ethnic and religious divisions. Despite her efforts to adapt successful Canadian strategies to the needs of Ireland, she was unable to win the support for crown and empire that she had hoped.

Converting colonised people away from their native religious practices and persuading them to embrace Christianity had been one of the fundamental methods of enlarging the British empire. Religion – or to be more precise, the Protestant religion – was deeply important to British colonisers and provided a way to bring indigenous peoples to an appreciation of western culture and values. Missionaries in Canada, India and elsewhere ran schools and healthcare facilities with the express purpose of attracting the local population to their churches. When Lady Aberdeen set up the National Council of Women in Canada the question of religion could not be ignored. The members included Protestants of the main denominations, Unitarians, Quakers and other sects, practising Roman Catholics and Jews. The Catholic Church opposed the organisation initially, and women needed specific permission from their bishop to join; some were refused. The Ontario Protestants insisted that their meetings should start with bible readings and a prayer, which would have presented problems for Jews and Catholics. When the Quebec group was planned Lady Aberdeen wrote in her journal: '[T]he Roman Catholics being so strong & strict, & a section of the Protestants being so narrow, would present formidable difficulties … I tremble a little when I think of

---

[71] *Slainte*, 1909, Vol. II, p. 195.   [72] *Ibid.*, p. 197.

the careful handling it will need'.[73] However the observance of silent prayers at the beginning of each meeting was a popular solution in many branches, and after a time the religious question subsided.

The difficulty of pleasing different religious communities was remembered when Lady Aberdeen returned to Ireland in 1906, and she was careful to prevent a similar situation occurring there. Although deeply religious herself, she rarely mentioned God to the Irish; the WNHA was set up without reference to religion. Whereas Canadian women had eventually become satisfied with silent prayer at their NCWC meetings, she realised this would not suit Ireland. In deciding to bypass the question of religion in Ireland Lady Aberdeen may have lost a valuable tool of persuasion, but she avoided much controversy.

One of Lady Aberdeen's successful strategies in both imperial sites was to keep firm control of her organisations. Her influence was keenly felt in the pre-planning stage. In Canada as each new NCWC branch was proposed she identified suitable influential women – those with similar ideas to herself – and suggested they stand for leadership. When the VON was planned the Aberdeens chose the provisional committee themselves, thus excluding any potential opposition. Then once cooperation was won Lady Aberdeen carefully controlled the way the organisations developed. She worked in a similar way in Ireland by attending the inaugural meetings of most groups to start them off on the 'right' track.

As well as influencing the choice of committee members it was necessary to win the cooperation of important people who would be affected by the various schemes. At the purely domestic level, for example, women who hoped to work for her organisations needed the permission and support of their husbands. In both sites of empire Lady Aberdeen stressed that looking after home and family must remain the women's top priority. This allowed men to give their support, and also encouraged conservative women to join.

Medical practitioners were an influential group in Canada, but unfortunately Lady Aberdeen did not get their support for the VON beforehand. Her initial plan was for an organisation of nurse home helpers to give emergency first aid, assist during illness and childbirth, and help with domestic tasks.[74] Nursing leaders complained that this would downgrade their profession, but the most vehement opposition

---

[73] John T. Saywell (ed.), *The Canadian journal of Lady Aberdeen 1893–98* (Toronto: Champlain Society, 1960), pp. 70–1.

[74] Ishbel Aberdeen, *The Canadian fund for the commemoration of the Queen's Diamond Jubilee, by founding the Victorian Order of Nurses in Canada* (Ottawa: Governor General's Office, 1897).

came from doctors' groups, described by Lady Aberdeen as 'organised in virulent bitterness and complete ignorance'.[75] They were fiercely opposed to the plan, believing that the nurses would undercut doctors, and fearing that in remote districts nurses would expect more autonomy. Above all they wanted to keep obstetrics for themselves. Lady Aberdeen upset them further once plans were progressing. She discarded the constitution framed for the VON by twelve Montreal doctors, preferring to copy the British Jubilee scheme set up ten years earlier.[76] The doctors had proposed a central board totally elected by subscribers, not with five members nominated by the governor general as the Aberdeens' draft constitution demanded. Lady Aberdeen commented: 'Knowing the jealousies, the evils of patronage, and the ignorance of the Local Boards we had to fight for this strongly.'[77] The doctors lost on this and other points, and Lady Aberdeen gained a board she could control. She invited Dr Worcester, who ran a school for district nurses in Massachusetts, to address doctors in Halifax, Ottawa, St John and Toronto, hoping to allay their fears and convert them to the scheme. She then ensured that the VON took the various criticisms into account. The nurses would now undergo full professional training followed by a six-month course in district nursing. In the end she won the doctors over, but she had not anticipated the strength of medical opposition in Canada, or how publicly she would have to deal with it. It was a lesson learned the hard way.

She did not repeat this mistake when she set up the WNHA in Ireland, and sought direction from the medical profession from the start. She asked eminent physicians to give papers at the inaugural Tuberculosis Exhibition in Dublin. Canadian Sir William Osler, Regius Professor of Medicine at Oxford and an international specialist in pulmonary medicine, gave the opening address, and she emphasised that her team would follow his lead. Her own physician, Sir William Thompson, became WNHA Treasurer. As each new WNHA branch was proposed she ensured that all local doctors were invited to participate.

It was inevitable that someone with as strong a personality as Lady Aberdeen would meet opposition wherever she went. Her Canadian endeavours often resulted in gossipy criticism in the newspapers, rumours that claimed the Aberdeens dined and played games with their servants. These annoyed rather than upset her, and she ignored them. The greatest opposition came from the conservative Toronto élite, who, with their

---

[75] Saywell (ed.), *Canadian journal*, p. 441.   [76] *Ibid.*, p. 438.
[77] *Ibid.*, p. 439.

often intense anti-Catholicism and Orange-style loyalism, disapproved of her liberalism and her support for Irish home rule. These people had impeccable social credentials; some were descendants of the United Empire Loyalists who settled there during the American Revolution.

Ishbel was well aware of this opposition, and thought that if she and Aberdeen could come into personal contact with the important and influential people in Toronto they could gain their support.[78] They decided to take the bull by the horns and took up residence in Toronto for six weeks. During this time Lady Aberdeen gave seven 'At Homes', a large public reception, twelve dinners, four dances, and visited all the hospitals, colleges and schools in Toronto. The visit culminated in a grand 'Victorian Era Ball' for 2,500 people which celebrated Canada, the British empire, and Queen Victoria. This strategy seemed to work. During the last few days in Toronto Ishbel noted in her journal how 'bewildering and overwhelming' was the support and kindness she received from so many people: 'It is a very solemn thing to be brought right up close to the heart of a people in this unmistakable way', she wrote. 'Words fail one to express all that comes over one – one can only feel deeply humbled & thank God.'[79]

Lady Aberdeen used this strategy in Ireland to win over influential members of the Catholic middle classes. They were flattered and impressed, but the Aberdeens were ridiculed by Irish society as a whole and the Conservative press. Lord Iveagh wrote the following scathing lines to Theresa Londonderry in 1907:

They had I hear a crowded dance last night at the VR Lodge but nobody at it that anyone had seen before – there was no supper, no champagne only marjorine [*sic*] sandwiches and jugs of milk! . . . I hear that they have chosen the new Private Secretary (who is a rabid nationalist clerk in some Government office in Dublin) because it will enable them to meet a class of people they could not otherwise have come across![80]

The Aberdeens were home-rule liberals, and so on their first tour in 1886 their entertainments had automatically been snubbed by the Protestant upper class. However the popular support the viceregal couple received had lessened the impact. When Lady Aberdeen returned to Ireland she found that many women of the same class – similar women to

---

[78] *Ibid.*, p. 409.   [79] *Ibid.*, p. 480.
[80] Lord Iveagh to Theresa Londonderry, 28 August 1907, D2846/2/25, Londonderry Papers, Public Record Office of Northern Ireland.

those who had happily joined her organisations in Canada – were against her for the same reason. Lady Londonderry, for example, organised a boycott of official entertainments in 1909. Among Lady Aberdeen's correspondence are letters from various titled ladies declining invitations to castle functions between 1907 and 1912, although most of them were anxious that the health work should continue.

It seemed to Lady Aberdeen that whatever she did or whichever way she turned she upset somebody or somebody opposed her. At first she loftily ignored the negative comments and threw herself more wholeheartedly into her work. She kept scrapbooks of favourable press cuttings in an attempt to buoy herself up, but privately she was tense and distressed, and widely reported to be suffering from stress and overwork. 'I was so vexed to observe how tired and worn you looked', wrote John Byers after a difficult visit to Portadown, where her husband had made an ill-judged speech.[81] She was advised to rest early in 1908, and told not to return to work too soon.[82] However she ignored the advice, and in July that year James Power urged her to take a break. The following year he told Lord Aberdeen that '[n]o human frame can continue to stand the labour and the strain she has passed through of late'. He wrote again saying that Lady Aberdeen 'has over "wrought" [*sic*]. Everybody notices it and she ought to take things more slowly.'[83] Her stress resulted from the unremitting opposition from all strands of society that she faced, opposition far more persistent than any she suffered in Canada.

Looking back over her life Lady Aberdeen told her grandson Archie that she knew she had made mistakes, but she liked to think that she had done more good than harm.[84] She was born before modern conveniences were invented, but using telephones and travelling by car and plane to her meetings became second nature to her in the twentieth century. She never retired. When ill health forced her to cancel a trip to Dublin to discuss tenants for some new labourers' cottages, the meeting was conducted instead at her home in Aberdeen. She died there a day or two later, on 18 April 1939, at the age of 82.

---

[81] John Byers (Professor of Midwifery at Queen's University Belfast), to Lord Aberdeen, 9 January 1908, Box 1/6, HHA.

[82] Margaret McNeill to Ishbel Aberdeen, 23 April 1908, Box 1/6, HHA.

[83] James Power to Lord Aberdeen, 21 July 1908, 26 October 1909 and 31 October 1909, Box 1/5, HHA.

[84] Reported to me in a letter from the present Lord Aberdeen.

CONCLUSIONS

Lady Aberdeen's writings indicate that much as she loved Ireland and the Irish people, she thought they were inferior to (white) Canadians, and lacked their strength of character. In each place she tried to improve lives, unite the country and promote Britain and the British empire. Her strategies in both places were similar: to provide strong and controlling leadership, to gain cooperation, and to remind people of their allegiances to monarchy and metropolis. In Canada she had gathered women together to promote a caring society. She encountered difficulties in setting up the VON, and was aware of opposition in other Canadian endeavours, but it was not serious enough to upset her and she found ways to cope with it. The NCWC and the VON – both still important today – helped to improve lives, and fulfilled her political aim of promoting a dominant Canadian identity with a Protestant Anglo-Saxon culture.

By contrast her successes in Ireland during her second term were controversial and hard won, her ideas often scathingly opposed. After her intervention the TB death rate showed a year-on-year decrease until 1914, although the historical consensus concludes that this resulted from improved living standards rather than her campaign.[85] And while the IIA continued to put pennies into the hands of peasant women this was barely significant amidst the existing rural poverty. Lady Aberdeen's work to secure decent affordable housing for poor Irish workers (not discussed here) continued all her life.

The changes in Ireland between 1886 and 1906 had led to a more divided society. From 1907 to 1914 as the pace of change intensified, support for physical-force nationalism grew, and the Unionist position hardened. There was fierce opposition from militant nationalists to Ireland remaining in the United Kingdom, or to any initiatives that even remotely smacked of imperialism. It is clear that Lady Aberdeen's actions were circumscribed in this changed social and political context. Given her relative success in Canada, and in her previous term in Ireland, much of the difficulty she had in replicating her Canadian success was caused by the volatile political situation. She was a member of the British establishment, and that was anathema to many Irish people, regardless of whether they liked her or not.

---

[85] For example Ruth Barrington, *Health, medicine and politics in Ireland 1900–1970* (Dublin: Institute of Public Administration, 1995); F. B. Smith, *The retreat of tuberculosis 1850–1950* (London: Croom Helm, 1988).

However, she brought problems upon herself. She had been warned Ireland was different, but ever optimistic, and perhaps thinking she was inviolable, she made her plans as though nothing had changed. Her dogged determination to have her own way did not help. In his memoirs Henry Robinson commented that she only listened to those 'who saw, or who pretended to see, eye to eye' with her: 'She was surrounded with advisers who gave way to her in everything ... Those who did not yield at once to her proposals were taboo, and I was unfortunate enough to be one of these, and had constant disputes with her.'[86] Her difficulties were further exacerbated by her insensitivity to the feelings of Irish men and women: her constant criticism may have been well meaning, but it was hard to take. She had some success, but unfortunately it was gained in an authoritarian manner and by riding roughshod over Irish sensibilities.

The changed Irish context since 1886 affected Lady Aberdeen's sense of self. She found the opposition deeply hurtful, and at these times she turned increasingly to prayer.[87] She adapted her ideas where she could, but as the difficulties multiplied the stresses took their toll and her vulnerability became clear. There is a certain poignancy in the fact that having devoted a large part of her life to Ireland and the Irish people, her time there between 1906–15 caused her more upset than anywhere else she had lived. In 1929 she mentioned that 'many cruel discouragements' had accompanied her welfare work in Ireland.[88] In 1917 Lord Aberdeen told Lloyd George that their 'removal from Ireland' was effected 'by a long continued and subtle campaign of disparagement, and indeed calumny ... relentless and secret plotting that was carried on against us for years, and which eventually resulted in our leaving'.[89] Despite having a band of admirers and advisers who supported everything she did, the relentless opposition dented her self-image to such an extent that she became physically ill. This is a clear indication of the fragility of her imperial identity.

The changed context also lessened her conviction that the empire was strong and united. She was deeply disheartened by the British government's handling of the devolution issue after the Home Rule Bill was passed in 1914, and believed this precipitated the Easter rebellion in 1916. When the government executed the fifteen rebel leaders in May 1916, she

---

[86] Robinson, *Memories*, p. 225.
[87] Ishbel Aberdeen, 'Notes for Matthew Urie Baird', Box 10/4/8, HHA.
[88] Aberdeen, *More cracks*, p. 313.
[89] Lord Aberdeen to Lloyd George, 20 July 1917, Lloyd George Papers, HLRO/F/1/1/2, House of Lords Record Office.

thought that Britain had lost a 'great opportunity'. Keenly aware of the contribution made to the strength of the British empire by the Irish in the settler colonies, she believed the executions had damaged relations with the overseas Irish, loyalty had been lost and the empire weakened as a result: 'Ireland and her kin beyond the sea could have been won forever', she wrote. She then told of the grief caused to 'countless thousands of British subjects both in the United Kingdom and in the overseas Dominions', who would see the executions as a snub to the 150,000 southern Irish who had volunteered to fight for small nations in Europe.[90]

Lady Aberdeen had different experiences in her three overseas postings. The first tour of Ireland, though short, had worked well for her. She was satisfied with her work in Canada. These tours both contrasted with her second posting in Ireland. This chapter has highlighted some of the difficulties involved in moving from one colonial site to another, and of returning to a changed colonial site. Lady Aberdeen's experience illustrates how important it was for British administrators to be sensitive to local opinion, to be flexible, to be aware of changing political and social climates, and adapt their plans accordingly. There was no rulebook for women like Lady Aberdeen to follow because everything had to be tailored individually to the moment and to the site of empire.

[90] Ishbel Aberdeen, 'Sorrows of Ireland', p. 63.

CHAPTER 10

Mary Curzon: 'American Queen of India'

Nicola J. Thomas

INTRODUCTION

During the first two weeks of January 1903 the population of Delhi swelled by hundreds of thousands as the princes of India, representatives of neighbouring countries, guests from the British empire, America and Europe converged to mark the coronation of Edward VII as the 'Emperor of India'. The Durbar ceremony brought India's ruling chiefs together to pay their individual 'homage' to their new emperor in the presence of each other, acting out the ritual of incorporation that the British had adopted as their own.[1] Two weeks of celebrations followed with balls and dinners, sporting events, demonstrations of military prowess and an exhibition of India's arts and crafts. Many notable people were present in Delhi for this event including the architect of the celebration, the viceroy, Lord Curzon, accompanied by Lady Curzon, the vicereine of India.

The Delhi Durbar celebrations fused the metropole and the empire together. Many people travelled to India, but also the representation of the event through word, image and film created an imaginative geography of India at 'home' which was unprecedented. The event saturated the British newspaper press and was popularly heralded as a meeting of East and West, with the ancient traditions of India being continued by the British Raj.[2] Within India a caricature (see Fig. 10.1) published in the Anglo-Gujerati journal *Hindi Punch* indicates a more critical response to the Durbar. Positioned as a labourer wearing a dhoti with the Star of India placed mockingly on his back, the viceroy is depicted building the infrastructure of the Durbar, with the vicereine above welcoming their international guests to India. The text accompanying the cartoon suggests

---

[1] B. S. Cohn, 'Representing authority in Victorian India', in E. Hobsbawm and T. Ranger (eds.), *The invention of tradition* (Cambridge: Cambridge University Press, 1983), pp. 165–210.

[2] The evolution of this discourse is detailed in T. R. Metcalf, *Ideologies of the British Raj* (Cambridge: Cambridge University Press, 1997).

Fig. 10.1 'Come Europa, come Columbia, come all nations, welcome!', *Hindi Punch*, November 1902. Reproduced in H. A. Talcherkar (ed.), *Lord Curzon in Indian caricature: Being a collection of cartoons reproduced in miniature with an elucidatory narrative* (Bombay: Babajee Sakharam & Co, 1903), frontispiece, by permission of the British Library.

Mary is 'holding agreeable converse with Divali, the Goddess of Light' about the Durbar Art Exhibition, and her patronage of the arts.[3] In a pose that parodies the Statue of Liberty, the American-born vicereine appears to have taken Divali's torch, symbolically depicting the imperial control of the British Raj.

This caricature and the accompanying text challenge the celebratory rhetoric of the Durbar, and present an anti-imperial narrative. An accompanying poem highlighted the expense of celebrating India's past traditions whilst starvation and famine threatened many people in the country. Together the image and text present the Durbar as a shared enterprise between Mary and George and raise questions that relate to the uneasy negotiation of 'race' and gender in British India. The presence of George building the Durbar beneath Mary's feet prompts questions relating to the 'incorporated' nature of Mary's position as vicereine, and her role within the government of India. The caricature makes clear the intimate fusion between India and metropole, and challenges us to see the broader links between India, America and British imperialism that Mary Curzon's position brought to attention.

These themes underpin this analysis of Mary Curzon's career as the vicereine of India. The term 'career' is somewhat of a misnomer, however. Although the honorary title of 'vicereine' had acquired a quasi-official status by the time Mary adopted it, the wife of the viceroy had no formal position within the government of India. Mary went to India accompanying her husband, who had been appointed by the Crown; her own position defined through his. Many women went to the empire as 'incorporated wives', drawing their social status from the position of their husbands and carried out duties and roles that were informally assigned to the spouse.[4] As has been amply demonstrated in recent scholarship, women such as Mary Curzon proved invaluable in the establishment and development of their husband's own careers.[5] Such women often exerted their own agency and challenged accepted gender norms. The informal

---

[3] H. A. Talcherkar (ed.), *Lord Curzon in Indian caricature: being a collection of cartoons reproduced in miniature with an elucidatory narrative* (Bombay: Babajee Sakharam & Co, 1903), p. 47. Curzon's dhoti also references the emerging swadeshi movement; a homespun dhoti became a symbol of the independence movement and a means of expressing patriotic sentiment. See Emma Tarlo, *Clothing matters: dress and identity in India* (London: Hurst and Company, 1996), p. 60.

[4] H. Callan and S. Ardener (eds.), *The incorporated wife* (London: Croom Helm, 1984), p. 1.

[5] In relation to India, this has been comprehensively addressed in M. A. Procida, *Married to the empire: gender, politics and imperialism in India 1883–1947* (Manchester: Manchester University Press, 2002). Procida's follows the work of many scholars informed by gender theory who have sought to reconsider the position of women in colonial society.

careers that women such as Mary Curzon developed were often prescribed by precedent, but also presented opportunities for individuals to craft.

A letter that Mary wrote to her parents reveals the manner in which she first received the news of George's appointment:

This is a profound *Secret*
George is going to be made Vice Roy of India ... it is the greatest position in the English world next to the Queen & the Prime Minister, & it will be a satisfaction I know to you & Mamma that your daughter Maria will fill the greatest place ever held by an American abroad – Heaven only knows how I shall do it. But I shall do my best to be a help to George & an honour to you & Mamma and I shall put my trust in Providence & hope to learn how to be a ready made Queen. We shall be out there 5 years. It seems a awful time but it is all part of George's career & a thing he has always wanted – you will come out and see us in all our glory.[6]

As Mary indicated, George's appointment as viceroy fulfilled a long-held ambition. Born in America in 1870 and brought up within the élite circles of gilded society in Chicago and Washington, it is unsurprising that Mary should display some sense of trepidation at the role she would play in the British empire. Mary was clearly aware that her parents would be pleased with the prominent position that her marriage had brought. However for Mr and Mrs Leiter, it also meant using their fortune gained from retail and real estate to supplement Mary's private income to cover expenses beyond the capacity of the viceroy's salary. This letter to her parents contains the elements that haunted Mary's negotiation of her role as vicereine over the following five years: the primacy of George's career in her life, her negotiation of her American national identity, and her sense of insecurity surrounding the role which she was about to play.

This chapter explores the incorporated career of Mary Curzon as vicereine of India; a position that prescribed her role as imperial hostess, but offered unexpected opportunities for developing her position within the imperial political structure of the Raj. It examines the letters that Mary exchanged with George, her family and friends and maps out her response to viceregal duty, and her growing appreciation of her place in the broader political culture. The letters that Mary exchanged reflect the continuous way in which the metropole and outposts of empire were tied together, not only through the material exchange of the letters, but through the interconnected lives of men and women across the British empire. As a result of

<hr>

[6] Mary to Father, undated c. 11 July – 10 August 1898, Lady Curzon Papers (LCP) 8/23–5, Mss Eur F306, Oriental and India Office Collections, British Library.

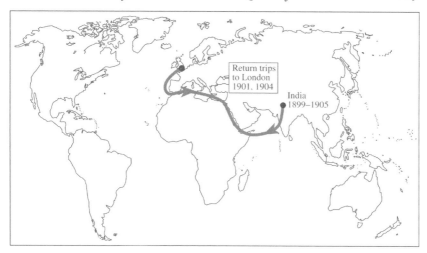

Map. 10.1 Mary Curzon's imperial career, 1899–1905.

her position, Mary's correspondence focused the attention of friends and family on India, which gave an alternative nuance to their discussions of American foreign policy. This chapter traces the time that the Curzons spent in India from their arrival in January 1899, to their departure in December 1905. Mary travelled extensively within India, and into neighbouring countries such as Burma, however her career did not extend into other areas of the British empire (see Map 10.1).

During the time Mary lived in India, she returned to Britain on two occasions, once for six months in 1901, and then again in 1904 for the birth of their third daughter. Mary died in July 1906, shortly after her return from India. Her passing was said to have been mourned in three continents marking the end of an unsought and short-lived imperial career.

BECOMING ENSLAVED TO DUTY

Following the announcement of the appointment of the new viceroy of India in August 1898, the Curzons were given widespread newspaper coverage. Mary's image appeared in many illustrated papers and magazines including the front page of *The Sketch*, which said of the 'New Vicereine of India':

Mrs George Nathaniel Curzon (nee Mary Victoria Leiter) becomes, by appointment of her husband, Mr George Curzon (MP for the Southport district of

Lancashire) as Viceroy, the most important woman socially, in a country of two hundred and ninety millions of people. As the daughter of Mr L. Z. Leiter, of Washington USA she gives fresh point to the Anglo-American Alliance.[7]

The emphasis on Mary's position within Indian society, alongside her American nationality, became enduring elements of Mary's newspaper coverage. *The Sketch* also highlighted that through George's appointment Mary was positioned at the pinnacle of society within the Raj, a culture that was obsessed with precedent, ceremony and hierarchy, but also constrained by negotiations of gender, class and 'race'.[8] In this position, Mary assumed the mantle that was already prepared for her, following in the footsteps of previous vicereines. Within the first two months Mary discovered the plethora of social duties she would undertake throughout her time in India. By day Mary would be occupied receiving visitors, visiting institutions, presenting prizes at school or sporting functions, hosting garden parties for adults and children alike, and looking after a never-ending stream of house guests. The evening events hosted by the viceroy were the principal arenas for the demonstration of the Raj's social hierarchy. These ranged in magnitude from the largest 'State Ball' and banquet, to formal dinners followed by 'Drawing Room' receptions where the viceroy and vicereine would receive guests, speaking to each for a few minutes. Smaller dinner parties and dances were scattered throughout the season. Social events followed a relentless and unchanging pattern throughout the year, whether the viceregal household was based at the winter capital at Calcutta, or the summer capital at Simla.

Having survived her first Season in India, Mary retired from the heat of Calcutta to Simla and wrote a letter to George reflecting on her initial experiences:

You made me so happy by telling me you thought I had 'made a good start' the 2 first months in India – sweet Papa! [George] anything I do seems minute beside all I want to do to help him, and India has been easy to please and I feel that I have done nothing but that Papa and only Papa has laid the foundation stone of success here.[9]

Despite George's acknowledgement of her success in the first few months, Mary demonstrates her early insecurity within her role, deprecating

---

[7] *The Sketch*, Wednesday, 17 August 1898, No. 290, Vol. XXIII, front page, photograph by Alice Hughes, author unknown.

[8] For a survey of the hierarchical society of the British Raj see David Cannadine, *Ornamentalism: how the British saw their empire* (London, Penguin Press, 2001) pp. 41–57.

[9] Mary to George, 6 March 1899, LCP 15/4–11.

her own achievements. The unrelenting social calendar meant that Mary's principal role eventually became a burden that had to be borne with fortitude. By January 1900 she indicated to her parents that the role was both demanding and inescapable: 'I am pretty well and very very busy – never a day without various duties and the constant entertaining is slavery but we go through it gladly as it is a duty.'[10] Certainly Mary's letters are liberally scattered with descriptions of her duties, although by October 1900 Mary's discontent at the 'slavery' was evident in her letters to her parents telling them:

I have refused to do anything more and although there are dances every night I have said there was an end to human endurance and I am going to bed at 10 o'clock though tonight we have a dinner of 70 people![11]

The pressure on Mary increased as she removed the burden of formal social duties from George's shoulders, representing him at functions and hosting official events when pressure of work or ill-health prevented the viceroy from attending. It would certainly appear from Mary's letters that this happened with increasing frequency during the viceregal term. In June 1902 Mary told her parents that 'George never does any social functions of any sort and they all devolve upon me and I do them all.' Mary undertook the engagements understanding that 'it is a great help to George to make the effort for him' although 'it is all work and very little pleasure'.[12] She told her parents that 'Duty is a wonderful incentive and I have inherited my devotion to it from you'; however her descriptions of 'the endlessly long list' of duties, of making 'his excuses' and 'making the effort for him' reveal a certain dissatisfaction.[13] The extent of the accommodation that they had reached was brought to George's attention when he was forced to shoulder the burden of entertaining when Mary returned to England. When George informed Mary that he had 'just returned ... from the Snowdon Garden Party which you usually take for me', Mary replied, using their familiar names for each other: 'I am so glad to hear of all Pappy's [George] gaieties ... How they must have loved Pappy coming to parties ... what a joy for them after having had to stand nothing but K [Kinkie / Mary] at former Simla frivolities.'[14]

Mary may have passed off the social events as 'frivolities' but they demanded adroit social skills. Following the 1900 spring tour to Assam,

---

[10] Mary to Mother, 11 January 1900, LCP 10/4–5.
[11] Mary to Mother, 11 October 1900, LCP 10/31–2.
[12] Mary to Father, 6 June 1902, LCP 11/112.   [13] Mary to Father, 6 June 1902, LCP 11/112.
[14] George to Mary, 22 May 1901, LCP 21/67–74; Mary to George, 28 June 1901, LCP 15/239–54.

Mary wrote to Cecil Spring-Rice, indicating something of the challenge of her social position:

> I devote all my attentions to the women and talk to them with my whole heart on subjects ranging from Jaeger's underclothes, baby food, to translations of the Vedas! I think the most satisfactory side of life is seeing shy people visibly thaw and from shaking with fright yield to intimate confidences.[15]

While such occasions may have been a source of some satisfaction Mary's continuous reference to her duties reflects, at best, her stoical acceptance of the prescribed position she occupied. Mary's conception of duty is important as it reflects her appreciation that her role was not provided for her personal amusement, but for the greater good of the Raj. This higher purpose is reflected in a response that Mary gave to her friend Pamela Tennant, visiting India for the Durbar, who had asked Mary how she coped with all her responsibilities:

> I told her that in a big life ones standpoint was not the amount of personal amusement one got out of things but how best to gratify and interest others and see far enough ahead to avoid contretemps and failures and that ones self never for a moment weighed in the larger desire to carry others pleasure to a successful issue.[16]

As a public discourse this is a worthy one although it rings hollow when set against Mary's more candid responses to her closer family and friends. Certainly, six months following the Durbar, when an extension to George's term of office was mooted, Mary clearly wished George to reject this opportunity, enabling her to return to England and also spend time with her family in America. On learning that a second term would have to be endured she wrote to Spring-Rice rationalising the situation: 'there isn't any gilding on the cake here – it is really work, work, work ... I rather hoped to go home for good next spring but I don't mind coming back ... no two people have ever been greater companions so it doesn't much matter where we are as long as we are together.'[17] In contrast Mary told her mother: 'George knows that I am miserable to come back to India but when a man has a career I fear it is all important ... I am determined to save my health but I must think of

---

[15] Mary to Cecil Spring-Rice, 19 March 1900, Cecil Spring-Rice Papers (CASR) 1/30/4, Churchill Archives Centre, University of Cambridge. Spring-Rice was a personal friend of George, whom Mary had also known independently. He held several diplomatic posts during his distinguished career at the Foreign Office, serving in Tehran, St Petersburg and Cairo during Mary's time in India.

[16] Mary to George, 16 January 1903, LCP 17/11–16.

[17] Mary to Spring-Rice, 15 June 1903, CASR 1/30/8–11.

George too as he has given me so much'.[18] While both letters reflect the true desire of Mary to return to England, they have slightly different nuances. To Spring-Rice, Mary's stress on the companionate model of marriage, with her only wish to be with George, doesn't rest easily with her real desire to return 'home' or the disconsolate reflection on her life. Mary's letter to her mother is more candid and indicates the uneven power relationship Mary shared with her 'companion', where his career was continuously accommodated at the expense of Mary's health and wishes.

The Delhi Durbar brought the necessity of Mary's role to the fore. Following the event George praised Mary's social skills as the hostess telling her the 'triumph of the social side' of the Durbar was a result of her 'absolute unselfishness in looking after others'. He also acknowledged that Mary 'lent a grace and distinction' to the public ceremonies 'the more marked from the utter inability of even the smartest and most beautiful of our English ladies to contest it'.[19] George's passion for visual displays of ceremonial power made this praise particularly welcome.[20] Mary's presence was also commended by the secretary of state of India, George Hamilton. Although he wrote to Mary, the only record of his letter survives in a comment he also wrote to George:

There was a universal acknowledgement of the admirable way in which she had discharged the multifarious and delicate duties of Viceroys wife and hostess ... I do not believe the Durbar could have been such continuous triumph if you had not been so fortunate in possessing as a wife one who was fully equal to every duty, and unforeseen difficulty which might arise.[21]

Mary sent this trophy letter to her parents telling them: 'I think you will like to hear that official approval has been given to my share in the Durbar ... I was very pleased with this as my position as an American in that vast community of English people was a very difficult one.'[22] Mary's pleasure in receiving this praise and official approval indicates the difficulty of negotiating the ambiguous role of vicereine. Mary discovered that while she was able to define her position within the confine of expectation, public criticism would come more frequently than official

---

[18] Mary to Mother, 30 June 1903, LCP 12/132–5.
[19] George to Mary, 12 January 1903, LCP 24/3–8.
[20] See David Cannadine, 'Lord Curzon as ceremonial impresario', in *Aspects of aristocracy: grandeur and decline in modern Britain* (London: Penguin Books, 1994), pp. 77–108.
[21] Mary to Parents, 13 May 1903, LCP 12/91–2.
[22] Mary to Parents, 13 May 1903, LCP 12/89–90.

approval.[23] For Mary it would appear that ensuring her public success was even more of a strain owing to her American identity. Her nationality was always present in association with her role as vicereine, and the word 'heiress' more often than not entered every article written about her.

AN AMERICAN VICEREINE

Mary had married 'away from home' and in so doing experienced the transplantation of moving away permanently from her country of birth.[24] Mary clearly felt the feelings of exile from America, telling her parents that she felt like an alien and that '50 years in a new country never alters your nationality and I shall <u>never</u> be an Englishwoman in feeling or character'.[25] On moving to India, her sense of alienation and separation from her family intensified. Mary found herself in India with a double sense of exile, from both England and America.

From the American flags flying when Mary arrived in India to the employment of an American masseuse in Simla, reminders of Mary's American identity were ever present in India. When visiting Assam she visited American missionaries, and American guests in Calcutta were sent home with items to post to her family. On 4 July 1903, Mary celebrated American independence from Britain with Lord Kitchener, commander-in-chief of the Indian Army. The irony of the situation was certainly not lost on her as she explained to her mother: 'Lord Kitchener has got a fourth of July dinner for me and had got American Flags made in my honour! So I shall celebrate our victory with a British Commander himself.'[26] Yet certain situations arose which indicated that George questioned Mary's sense of national identity. Such an occasion emerged over the American Transvaal ship, a charity ship taking aid to South Africa during the Boer War. Mary was asked to make a donation by the organiser Jennie Churchill, another American heiress who married into the British aristocracy. On asking George if he knew anything about the ship he responded to Mary:

I have not an idea what the American Transvaal ship is – possibly a ship containing books, luxuries, wine etc. for the wounded if so there is of course no

---

[23] Mary frequently reported that she felt the critical 'journalists spotlight' on her, and sought to maintain a positive image in the newspaper press. See Nicola J. Thomas, 'Exploring the boundaries of biography: the family and friendship networks of Lady Curzon, Vicereine of India, 1898–1905', *Journal of Historical Geography*, **30** (2004), pp. 496–519.

[24] Mary to Mother, undated c. November 1898, LCP 8/45–7.

[25] Mary to Mother, undated c. November 1898, LCP 8/45–7, original emphasis.

[26] Mary to Father, 1 July 1903, LCP 12/137–8.

objection to your giving though I think myself that the contributions should come rather from Americans in America than from those who have married Englishmen and still more high officials of the British Govt and have become Englishwomen in consequence. The tribute ceases in such a case to be from America.[27]

George's pompous tone reflects his unease concerning Mary's American identity, which he clearly felt she had rescinded on marriage. Mary's own feelings towards her American identity were demonstrated in her response to the assassination of American president, William McKinley in September 1901. Mary heard the news of the assassination in Scotland where she was staying with her mother and on 15 September wrote to George: 'Mamma is deeply distressed about poor Mr McKinley and so am I.'[28] Days later she asked George: 'I hope you sent an India telly [telegram] to America of grief on account of poor Mr McKinley – I have heard tellies from all corners of earth, Dublin, Ceylon, Wellington and Shanghai but no mention has been made of India I hope all the same one went.'[29] George responded that he had deliberately not sent a telegram, as 'I felt so certain that the Royal Family at home would say I was treating myself as a crowned head.'[30] Mary obviously anticipated this response as she initially highlighted the countries and capitals of the empire that had sent telegrams. George's sensitivity over Mary's American national identity clearly influenced his decision to avoid any public display of affiliation between India and America, who had after all hailed Mary as the 'American Queen of India'.[31] This regal title was often repeated; for example, in 1899 the readership of the American journal *Harper's Weekly* were treated to a series of articles titled 'American Sovereign of India' which reported in glowing terms the nature of Mary's viceregal life.[32] Within America, Mary's celebrity, took precedence over George's politics, and Mary was told on occasion: 'You don't know probably with what interest and pride Americans follow your career.'[33] Mary certainly became aware of this interest when erroneous stories were published and when she wanted to keep her failing health private.[34]

[27] George to Mary, 12 November 1899, LCP 20/74–9.
[28] Mary to George, 15 September 1901, LCP 16/135–40.
[29] Mary to George, 19 September 1901, LCP 16/142–7.
[30] George to Mary, undated c. October 1901, LCP 23/3–16.
[31] Anon, 'The American "Queen of India" and her husband' [Utica] Globe, New York, 3 December 1899.
[32] J. Ralph, 'An American Sovereign Part IV', *Harper's Weekly*, June 10 1899.
[33] Smalley to Mary, December 6 1899, LCP 32/49–55.
[34] Thomas, 'Exploring the boundaries', p. 512.

Mary actively maintained contact with her circle of American friends, particularly the journalist George W. Smalley who provided her with American novels and lusted for her reports of the 'real' India, and the cosmopolitan, historian, novelist and political commentator Henry Adams. Both men had apparently known Mary from childhood and wrote with easy familiarity. These men's letters brought news and gossip of leading figures in the American government; both commented on the latest political events; they discussed American imperialism exploring the latest turn in the Philippine-American War and pondered the relationships between Britain, America and Europe.

Smalley challenged Mary to maintain her American identity. Shortly after her marriage he had written to her of his response on reading that she was the only English woman whom the emir of Afghanistan admired: 'It gave me a shock. I suppose you are English since you have married an Englishman but I intended to claim you as an American ... I will not give you up. If you give us up that is another matter. But I don't think you will.'[35] He returned to this subject again when asking if Mary was able to follow the events in the Philippines in American papers, an area of foreign policy that concerned him: 'I don't think we have improved since the war. You are, and were a good American and would like to believe that everything is for the best in the best of all possible Republics. So should I, but can it be?'[36] With concern expressed regarding the rampant imperialism he was witnessing, Smalley invited Mary to consider whether this was in their best interests, as fellow citizens.

Adams also reflected on the rising imperialist power of America, and the growing confidence of prosperity that it brought, but also asked Mary: 'Are you anti-imperialist? I hope so. I am, so is Papa Hoare and Eugene Hale and Andy Carnegie and all the people I love most ... We all want England to take the Philippines and pay the expenses of our trade there.'[37] The fact that Adams places himself alongside other members of the Anti-Imperialist League formed in Boston in 1898 reflects his growing disenchantment with American political life, reinforced in later letters that pointedly offer no political gossip. Mary's direct responses to these men's questions are not known. However a comment by Smalley in response to Mary following an earlier discussion of the sympathy shown by some in America to the Boers illustrates that she was supportive of British policy: 'You think too much of the tales about Boer Sympathies.

---

[35] Smalley to Mary, 1 August 1895, LCP 32/3–5.   [36] Smalley to Mary, 17 June 1899, LCP 32/29–34.
[37] Adams to Mary, 13 January 1899, LCP 31/208–15.

We have not behaved altogether well but we are less black than we are painted.'[38] Mary's own letters indicate she offered unconditional loyalty to George's political outlook, which would have placed her in a certain amount of opposition with the anti-imperialist viewpoints of some American friends. The communications with Adams and Smalley in addition to news of political events from her family indicate that Mary was forced to consider the elision of American and British politics; however the absence of significant documentary evidence leaves her own response uncharted.

BECOMING A COMPANION TO STATESMEN

The political society that Mary entered on her marriage was much as Reynolds describes for the mid-Victorian period.[39] The aristocratic social and political network open to Mary offered women many opportunities for political engagement; most obviously by attending debates in the Houses of Parliament, campaigning in constituencies, and taking part in informal discussions.[40] Although Mary had not fully settled into this political culture following her marriage, she was accustomed to supporting her husband as a political incorporated wife. As vicereine, Mary continued this support, however her participation in the political sphere became of greater significance during her time in India. Mary's developing awareness of her position within imperial political culture changed in important ways depending on whether she was in India, or at 'home' in Britain, and also shifted as she gained greater knowledge and became more aware of the importance others invested in her position. Mary's movement through the spaces of empire undoubtedly reconfigured her own imperial subjectivity, and challenged her understanding of her position.

Historians anxious to uncover the nature of women's involvement in this sphere have noted that little documentary evidence remains recording the 'personal and conversational' mode of intervention by women in politics.[41] Letters exchanged between Mary and George record their thoughts on current events and offer an opportunity to eavesdrop on the conversations they shared with others. These letters are important as it is

---

[38] Smalley to Mary, 7 June 1900, LCP 32/5–61.
[39] K. D. Reynolds, *Aristocratic women and political society in Victorian Britain* (Oxford: Oxford University Press, 1998).
[40] See also J. Bush, *Edwardian ladies and imperial power* (London: Leicester University Press, 2000); P. Jalland, *Women, marriage and politics 1860–1914* (Oxford: Oxford University Press, 1986).
[41] Reynolds, *Aristocratic women*, p. 154.

possible to gain a detailed understanding of the type of female political participation at the turn of the twentieth century. Given his conservative views towards women's participation in public life, it is ironic that we gain such a full indication of Mary's activity in political society because of George's request that while she visited London in 1901 she detail 'everything, each day, each hour, everything, not a week condensed into a single sheet'.[42]

Mary's participation in the political sphere changed significantly over time while she was in India. Having arrived in India familiar with British politics, the imperial political sphere was largely uncharted territory. The first phase of Mary's active engagement in politics occurred during her first two years in India. During this period Mary was inevitably exposed on a daily level to current political affairs. The type of conversations she may have had with George are reflected in the content of the letters Mary received while they were separated; these contained full summaries of current political affairs and his response to them. Mary absorbed both Indian and British newspapers voraciously, and asked to see official government papers to understand issues more clearly. Mary's reading enabled her to become a proficient imperial hostess; it also laid the foundation for her development as a political agent.

A journalist reporting on Mary's ease in social situations in her early days as vicereine bears witness to her ability to converse within the political culture of the viceregal court:

When it fell on her lot to take the arm of a general at dinner the other night, she began at once to question him upon the trade in fire-arms in the Persian Gulf. The general was mad with delight. It happened that this was his hobby and breaking up this nefarious calling was the work he had in hand. The Vicereine found this out, but how she did it no one could imagine.[43]

Given that Mary dwelt actively in the space of imperial governance, her ability to discourse on the Persian Gulf should come as no surprise. George had addressed the threat of increasing Russian influence in the Persian Gulf region during his first year of office.[44] Mary's awareness of these matters illustrates the way in which she absorbed everyday politics and put her knowledge to her advantage in social situations. In addition, Mary had taken great pains to make herself ready for such encounters.

---

[42] George to Mary, 14 May 1901, LCP 21/59–65.   [43] Ralph, 'An American sovereign', 10 June 1899.
[44] George had published a study titled 'Persia and the Persia Question' in 1892 and continued to stress the importance of maintaining an active military and diplomatic presence in the region to secure trade and communications and to deter other imperial powers. See David Gilmour, *Curzon* (London: Papermac, 1995), pp. 76–80, 82–3, 201–3.

When Mary hinted to her father that she would learn how to be a 'lesser-queen' it is clear that she began educating herself to converse and understand both the cultural and political worlds she was entering. At Mary's request, Sir Alfred Lyall sent her a list of books about India.[45] He found it difficult to recommend a conclusive general study of 'religion and native society' as India was so 'vast and varied'.[46] He did however recommend a number of 'standard books' which were 'at any rate amusing'. Although they described India as it was fifty years previously this was not to worry Mary as Lyall explained 'the country changes very little in so short a time'.[47] As Lyall's airy colonial discourse might indicate, through these texts Mary absorbed stereotypical and orientalist views of India and its peoples. A letter to George implied that her reading matter was less than sympathetic to different religious practices: 'I finished my book on the horrors of Hinduism at 5.'[48]

During the first two years, Mary appears to have absorbed Indian politics as a way of easing social pressure and fruitfully passing the time, rather than with the notion of active political engagement. Indeed, a letter to Spring-Rice certainly suggests that her early interest in politics was fired by the need to fill the empty hours between engagements:

I am well and interested in everything from Frontier Govts. to Assam irrigation it is the only thing that keeps one going, as sometimes this life feels a very isolated one.[49]

The second phase of Mary's deeper understanding of her role as a political participant came when she visited Britain in 1901. Although George referred to her return home as a 'spree', during this time Mary was able to use the knowledge she had acquired in India, and began to question her place within political culture.[50] Indeed, it can be argued that while Mary was not performing the normal functions of the vicereine, by coming 'home' she was able to exert greater independence through her knowledge of Indian politics, applying her role as an imperial subject in a more personally meaningful way than she had in India.

---

[45] Sir Alfred Lyall had an extensive career rising through the ranks of the Indian Civil Service. He was appointed foreign secretary to the Government of India and was lieutenant governor of the North-west Provinces and Oudh before he retired to London, where he sat on the India Council from 1888 to 1902.

[46] Lyall to Mary, 1 October 1898, LCP 32/174–5.

[47] Lyall to Mary, 13 October 1898, LCP 32/176–7.

[48] Mary to George, 29 March 1899, LCP 15/30–3.

[49] Mary to Spring-Rice, 19 March 1900, CASR 1/30/4.

[50] George to Mary, 8 July 1901, LCP 22/14–21.

Mary's return to London was fêted by friends and acquaintances alike and she was sucked into the maelstrom of London political society. Her time was spent receiving callers, attending debates in the Houses of Parliament (sitting in the 'usual foul air and fussing female rows deep in the Speakers Gallery') and going to dinners that were frequently followed by a rush back to the House for the last division.[51] She also acquired furnishings for the official residences in India, and received 'Indians' as she described the British acquaintances and 'unknowns' who were home on leave from India.[52] From her initial encounters with friends Mary sweepingly stated that she was 'stupefied by the ignorance of everyone about poor India'.[53] One of her many visitors who failed to demonstrate adequate knowledge was Lord Selborne, first lord of the admiralty:

Next darling came Lord Selborne & sat for a solid hour and 1/2 discussing his [illeg.] on 'all you are doing!' I at once dropped on to the theory that he longs to succeed you but George his ignorance of India is quite amazing ... In the midst of all this in came St John [Brodrick] and before I knew where I was he had kissed me – on the cheek! ... He proceeded to sit down and talk 'haute politique'![54]

During the next few weeks, Mary had what she called 'dentist appointments' with what she called the 'aged swells.'[55] It is characteristic of Mary's ironic, self-deprecating approach to her involvement with political affairs during the summer of 1901, that she should refer to her meetings with cabinet ministers, ambassadors, senior military figures and politicians as mere 'dentist appointments'. It would appear that these figures were not simply paying their respects to Mary; they sought her company on many occasions, and spent extended periods of time with her.

A typical example of Mary's attention to recording her conversations is revealed in her description of a short exchange between the prime minister, Lord Salisbury and herself:

Lord Salisbury led through the crowd to me after lunch and asked me when I would come to Hatfield. He then proceeded to say 'How is George, he is having in my mind a very great career in India. His frontier policy will keep us India 50 years longer than we should have kept it otherwise. It is a very difficult problem – we are always trying to balance a Pyramid on its point' this I suppose

---

[51] Mary to George, undated c. May 1901 LCP 15/113–16. In his celebratory biography of Mary Curzon, Nigel Nicolson drew attention to her position within British imperial political society at this time. N. Nicolson, *Mary Curzon: a biography* (London: Weidenfeld and Nicolson, 1977), pp. 141–7, 154–6.

[52] Mary to George, 18 May 1901, LCP 15/138–65.   [53] Mary to George, 18 April 1901, LCP 5/71–2.

[54] Mary to George, 6–9 May 1901, LCP 15/99–101. St John Brodrick was serving as Secretary of State for War in 1901.

[55] Mary to George, 12–18 May 1901, LCP 15/117–33.

he meant the difficulty of holding India. He then said he strongly approved your princeling scheme ... Then he said 'G is very anxious about Persia so am I – but I don't see what I can do'. I don't feel that I have repeated this very coherently but I really couldn't hear 1/2 he said as we were standing in the middle of a huge room seething with people & every moment people would come and shake hands.[56]

This extract reveals much about the style of Mary's participation in the political culture. The importance of Mary's position is difficult to judge; however it should be appreciated that her influence continuously shifted from margin to centre according to the topic of discussion. Certainly Mary reported a number of conversations with a variety of public figures in which she was explaining policy and new measures that were being developed. One such topic was the planned military Imperial Cadet Corps which aimed to integrate the sons of Indian nobles into the Indian Army. This project had initially been met with little enthusiasm in cabinet or by King Edward VII, but was finally announced in July 1901. Through such conversations she was able to inform, reassure and also to pick up opinions that she relayed to George. For example, during a weekend visit to Windsor Castle, Mary felt the King had gained unbalanced views from various visiting Indian nobles and informed George he should write to the King countering their opinions.[57]

Throughout the summer Mary was a frequent companion of Lord Salisbury's nephew, Arthur Balfour who would become prime minister in 1902. Recording many conversations, she offered George some advice:

Arthur took me in and we talked straight through din [dinner] ... His chief interest in India is Afghanistan and what your plan of operations in the case of Amirs death, he is really keen on this as he has read an alarmist Russian book on what Russia would do. So I think if you have planned what you wd. [would] do after proclaiming Habibullah it would [be] well to write him for future use in the cabinet.[58]

Here Mary is not only relaying conversations, but also sending advice to George, raising an issue that she felt needed his consideration. In other exchanges, officials sought Mary's advice on an issue before approaching George, sometimes explicitly asking to see Mary before her weekly letter was sent to George, indicating they wished their views to be informally

[56] Mary to George, 26 May 1901, LCP 15/167–74.
[57] Mary to George, 31 May 1901, LCP 15/175–82.
[58] Mary to George, undated c. May 1901, LCP 15/117–33 . The emir of Afghanistan, Abdur Rahman, died later in 1901 and was succeeded by Habibullah. Tense differences emerged between the Indian government and the British cabinet on the way to deal with the new emir and the protection of the Indian frontier.

communicated to him. For example, St John Brodrick, secretary of state for war, approached Mary and 'in great confidence he unfolded his plan of calling upon you for your best troops in turn for the spent and jaded men in S. Africa'. Mary analysed his proposition to George noting that 'India is made a commodity of but it shows her magnificent strength that she should be squeezed in this way to fight out England's battles.' She told George that Brodrick was uncertain if he would accept the plan, and informed him that she had told St John that: 'I said you would I thought go as far as you could to help empire, but never endanger the safety of India by too great depletion her strength'.[59] Mary demonstrated her diplomacy on this occasion, responding in a positive yet guarded way to the secretary of state, and preparing George for Brodrick's suggestion. Brodrick's informal approach followed a diplomatic debacle in India that George outlined in a letter to Mary that crossed in the post.[60]

Mary clearly acted as a conduit for ideas that the politicians of the day wanted to plant in George's mind. She was particularly anxious to promote any conversation that discussed George's return to Britain; her self-interest on these occasions is undeniable. One such letter included a drafted memo written following a conversation with Lord Salisbury and Balfour that stressed George's role in future British politics and the need to maintain health for such an event.[61] Mary also manoeuvred conversations that would enable her to discover more about future changes in India, specifically in relation to the plans for Kitchener to become the next commander-in-chief of the Indian Army. Kitchener's appointment was what Mary ironically called a 'secret de Politique', as five separate statesmen had informed her of the appointment, although they each told her: 'no one knows yet'.[62] Lord Roberts, commander-in-chief of the army, was one of her informants, and Mary pressed him for information telling George: 'He spoke most warmly of Kitchener and said he had improved in 2 years and acquired greater lenience in dealing with men and his only fear for India was his attitude to native troops.'[63] A less favourable impression was gained from Sir William Nicholson who had worked alongside Kitchener in South Africa. At a private dinner Mary 'turned him [Nicholson] onto Kitchener' who lost no time in telling her 'I have worked for 2 years with K, he is not clever and can't write a dispatch, his

---

[59] Mary to George, 9 June 1901, LCP 15/193–222. George agreed on this occasion, and sent troops to help in South Africa, China and Somaliland.
[60] George to Mary, 14 May 1901, LCP 21/ 59–65.
[61] Mary to George, 19 September 1901, LCP 16/149–50.
[62] Mary to George, 18 May 1901, LCP 15/138–65.   [63] Mary to George, 18 May 1901, LCP 15/138–65.

knowledge of administration is puerile and his only one quality to praise, is his relentless determination to advance himself, in that he is the best worker I have ever known.' These vitriolic words were noted down in Nicholson's 'exact words' and followed with Mary's comment to George, 'I hope this is all a lie.'[64]

Despite the fact that Mary had been immersed in imperial politics during the summer of 1901, and had been able to contribute to debates and discussions that would have been closed to her before she went to India, her view of her position as a woman within society is telling:

A man can know a woman fairly well because her life consequently the interests which mould her mind and conceive her thoughts are more or less simple. A man's life is so complex and much of it lies outside the woman's sphere – & his mind is spiked with hundreds of magnets pointing to different possibilities that she may never know him in his entirety – but what is within her grasp has the power of making her truly happy.[65]

In this self-reflective letter Mary positions herself outside the male public sphere without acknowledging the political role she had just played within this sphere herself. Mary's actual understanding of the 'hundreds of magnets pointing to different possibilities', that she sees as representative of men's lives, is greater than she reveals. Mary played a part in influencing the direction of events during 1901, but she had not yet come to question the flexibility of the boundaries between masculine and feminine worlds.

During the third stage of her development as a political participant, Mary began to comprehend that her political understanding and individual position was exceptional, even when compared to that of her female contemporaries in Britain. Mary's role in the political process whilst in India differed from her time in England. On returning to India Mary initially resumed her role as a political confidante to George. However, the arrival of Lord Kitchener in India during 1902 prompted a new self-understanding of her role in the political sphere. Mary was able to iron out the problems between George and Kitchener, countering their differences with invitations to tea and dinner.[66] Kitchener spent much time with Mary during 1903, offering a welcome relief from the isolation of her position. In Kitchener's company, she began to reflect on her

---

[64] Mary to George, 18 May 1901, LCP 15/138–65. The warning was not unwarranted as the later events surrounding the so-called 'Kitchener conspiracy' which forced George's resignation as viceroy would prove. See Gilmour, *Curzon*, pp. 296–317.

[65] Mary to George, 14 July 1901, LCP 16/23–4. Mary edited out 'fairly' in her letter.

[66] See Gilmour, *Curzon*, pp. 250–1, pp. 296–317.

involvement in political affairs, and by June had become more outspoken about her role. Mary found Kitchener to be 'a rugged sort of social companion', and throughout the summer boasted to her mother that she had 'become a sort of necessary companion to Statesmen!' to both George and Kitchener.[67] In the same letter, Mary reflected on her new understanding:

I talk to George literally by the hour about every one of his political plans & the other Sunday K [Kitchener] sat in the garden & talked business for 3 1/4 hours with me. It is only after vast study & reading that women can ever become good companions but it is a far greater satisfaction than frivolity.[68]

By dwelling in the political atmosphere of the viceregal household, avidly reading newspapers, books, biographies and the government papers of the British government in India, Mary dissolved a boundary she had set between the female and male worlds in 1901. She clearly enjoyed the novelty of this position and regularly boasted about it to her family, for example informing them: 'I have just been talking for two hours and 1/2 to Lord Kitchener under a tree so my mind is rather military & I may burst into army reorganisation!'[69]

Although Mary dwelt constantly at the heart of imperial government, the spaces in which she negotiated her role in India were at the margins. We see her talking to Kitchener in the gardens of Mashobra, the viceregal retreat outside Simla; in other situations she talks of sharing a corner of George's study. The seeping of power into the more informal viceregal spaces can be seen in a letter from Mary to Spring-Rice, in which she describes a recent hunting tour:

Anyhow we had all been duck shooting and I have been amused first to see George blaze 300 partridges off ... and in short intervals of silence concentrate thoughts on some administrative question of his state ... I am so used to sitting for hours in a tree with George waiting for tigers and talking about land assessment that I have forever tired of frivolity and feed on the strenuous life![70]

Mary prized these rare moments of uninterrupted time with George during the tour. The repetition of forgoing frivolity and the intellectual pleasure that she gained from political engagement, reflects Mary's pride in her abilities. Mary often shared her reflections of her political life with Spring-Rice and her self-growth can be charted through such letters. A notable communication in this later phase of Mary's political

[67] Mary to Mother, 1 June 1903, LCP 12/96–103.   [68] Mary to Mother, 1 June 1903, LCP 12/96–103.
[69] Mary to Family, 8 July 1903, LCP 12/145–6.
[70] Mary to Spring-Rice, 4 December 1902, CASR 1/30/7.

development indicates that Mary considered her level of understanding to be superior to women in London:

I think one has a more honest and intelligent interest in politics when one is removed from the temptation of reading the summary in the *Times* every morning so as to be able to meet Prime Ministers at luncheon and dinner with a lame acquaintance with facts. Don't you know the London lady who gulps down politics with her morning tea and infers comprehension over political buttered toast at tea at five? Here it is a different interest that takes you through the columns of the *Times* without a break. George, Lord K [Kitchener] and I all read the speeches through in this beautiful place and then we laid down the papers and talked very hard with the sort of strenuous intense interest that Indian life gives.[71]

Mary's cutting image of the superficial political understanding of the 'London lady' is most probably an accurate reflection of her own experiences prior to going to India and something she observed in London amongst her acquaintances.

Mary's debates with Kitchener, in particular, placed her participation in politics in India outside the model of the companionate marriage, which characterised the discussions she had enjoyed with George since their arrival in India. In 1904, Mary told George that she had often been unhappy in India, however she noted: 'I was happier after K [Kitchener] came as his utter dependence upon me appealed so strongly to me – more because liking me as a woman he talked to me as a man!'[72] This feeling of equality with Kitchener prompted Mary to reassess the importance of her participation in the political sphere. Although she had privately enjoyed this relationship with George, by extending it to Kitchener she realised that her role went beyond simply supporting her husband, at which point she redefined her role within political culture.[73]

On her return to England in 1904 Mary realised that she was acquiring a name at home within political circles. Talking to Lady Lansdowne Mary was told: 'I hear you are the most helpful wife a public man ever had and a most wonderful ambassador!' Mary reported to George that she had 'laughed and said I shouldn't be either unless my efforts were appreciated, as it wouldn't be much fun to devote one['s] heart to an

---

[71] Mary to Spring-Rice, 15 June 1903, CASR 1/30/8–11.
[72] Mary to George, 7 February 1905, LCP 18/94–9.
[73] Mary's companionship with Kitchener did not enable her to anticipate Kitchener's manipulation of the army reorganisation scheme, which ultimately led to George's resignation as viceroy in August 1905. See Gilmour, *Curzon*, pp. 296–317.

unappreciative spouse'.[74] Despite her self-deprecating response, Mary sends this public recognition of her role as a trophy to George. Although Mary reduces her agency to a desire to serve her husband thus conforming to an acceptable gender model, Mary's own self-awareness of her political understanding was one of the most satisfactory elements of her life in India. Mary found her developing participation in imperial politics challenging, and her suggestion that she was exerting herself only to help George is questionable given the enthusiasm with which Mary talked of her abilities with Spring-Rice and her family.

CONCLUSION

While Mary Curzon may not have had a long imperial career, it is useful to turn the magnifying glass on the five years of her life spent as vicereine to see the change in subjectivity that dwelling in India brought. Although her position only held a quasi-official status, owing to her notoriety as an American heiress the public interest in her position was sustained. Precedent required Mary to undertake the primary duty of hosting and entertaining the viceregal court. Mary resorted to her closest confidants to rail against the pressure of her 'slavery', but the stoical demonstrations of her ethos of public duty illustrate her position as an 'incorporated' spouse to the highest degree.

Mary's American identity played a part in shaping the manner in which she undertook her duties. During an early visit from her sisters to India, Mary was forced to reprimand them for inappropriate behaviour which had been publicly noted. Mary wrote to her parents following the event and explained 'They are now as anxious as I am to keep up the dignity of the position. I told them we were the first Americans they had ever seen out here and we would just show them how nice and quiet Americans could be.'[75] The awareness of appropriate behaviour and maintaining dignity is illustrative of the nature of social expectations within the British Raj. The stereotype of American character that Mary's letter implies was clearly antithetical to this society, illustrating that Mary had to curb her own 'otherness' within a very alien environment.

The lack of enthusiasm demonstrated for formal duties was certainly supplemented by the growing enjoyment she took from dwelling in the political atmosphere of the Raj. Mary's politics were not those of the

---

[74] Mary to George, 2 March 1904, LCP 17/151–2.   [75] Mary to Parents, 6 June 1899, LCP11/112.

proto-feminist movement. Despite complaining about the role she was asked to play she seldom resisted in public, nor did she acknowledge the gender inequality of her own position. The personal role she eventually carved for herself gave satisfaction, although the continuous references to her political awareness in her correspondence indicates she required others to acknowledge and authorise her position.

Mary's letters reflect the fact that she was located in an interconnected network of people whose careers were also spent serving Britain's imperial interests. This correspondence indicates that Mary shared political news with ease and commented on unfolding current affairs with those who were crafting or delivering policy. Mary was certainly accepted within her circle, and following her visit to England in 1901 was appreciated as a pivot between Britain and George. The secretary of state for India certainly understood the leverage that her position granted her, and he attempted to use this in 1902 when he felt George was being particularly recalcitrant, writing: 'I have written at great length to him by the next mail: try and get him to give you my letter because I am sure you will take your cue from what I have said.'[76] As Mary's understanding of her expertise in political life increased she herself appreciated that her support extended beyond her marital duty to her husband.

Whilst living in Washington before her marriage Mary had forged a variety of friendships within political and diplomatic circles, from Smalley, Adams, and Spring-Rice, to the First Lady Frances Cleveland, John Hay, who would become secretary of state, and Theodore Roosevelt. Many of these friendships sustained her links to America during the viceregal years, indeed it was apparently only the small 'problem of abolishing interests' that prevented the newly elected President Roosevelt visiting Mary and 'going all through India'.[77] Following McKinley's assassination, the discussions regarding Roosevelt's appointment illustrate that Mary demonstrated her authority by presenting the unfolding events to George, sharing political gossip that she gained from her American correspondents and offering her own recollections of Roosevelt from her Washington days. The enmeshed nature of the international political web Mary was part of is seen through the linkages that are made between people and subjects at different points in time. From John Hay we hear that 'My own department going smoothly thanks to the reasonableness shown by Lord Lansdowne in the important matters we have had to

---

[76] Hamilton to Mary, June 1902, LCP 32/131–2.
[77] Roosevelt to Mary, 28 December 1901, LCP 32/219–20.

discuss.'[78] This 'reasonableness' was translated later by Mary as a policy of diplomacy that amounted to Lansdowne '[Giving] way to every country and never to stand anywhere', a less positive analysis of the relationship between Britain and America.[79] Lansdowne, himself a former viceroy of India, was within Mary's social circle, and reports of his career frequently crept into the exchanges that circulated around the correspondence network.

Mary's family reflected an important source of stability whilst she was in India. To them she could be disloyal to George and discuss the positive and negative aspects of viceregal life. In return their letters enabled Mary to bridge continents and 'spend my few minutes with you'.[80] While Mary lived in India, she frequently planned to visit America; however the extension of George's term in office prolonged her wait and prompted tortuous discussions regarding this much longed-for trip. As it became increasingly unlikely she would return to America before she left India, Mary sought to picture her family within her London home, shifting her spatial narrative of belonging away from America to the heart of the British empire. Mary bridged the divide between India, Britain and America in many ways. Smalley had once told Mary 'I try to imagine you in your new life but I have no frame to put you into. India is to me a perfectly unknown country.'[81] Like Smalley, Mary initially had no means of understanding India; however by 1905, she had travelled throughout the country, detailing her experiences in journals and letters. Those who read these texts were given a view of India that reflected the viceregal vantage point that Mary observed from. However this audience would certainly have agreed with the response President Roosevelt gave to Mary when questioned about the nature of their experiences: 'Yes, we have certainly led interesting lives.'[82]

---

[78] Hay to Mary, 16 November 1901, LCP 32/150–1.
[79] Mary to Father, 28 October 1903, LCP 12/192–3.   [80] Mary to Father, 3 June 1903, LCP 12/105–8.
[81] Smalley to Mary, 17 June 1899, LCP 32/29–34.
[82] Roosevelt to Mary, 28 December 1901, LCP 32/219–20.

CHAPTER II

Making Scotland in South Africa: Charles Murray, the Transvaal's Aberdeenshire poet

Jonathan Hyslop

In the years from 1910 to the early 1920s, Charles Murray[1] (Fig. 11.1) was the most popular vernacular poet in Scotland.[2] His work contributed to a cultural revival which fed directly into the development of modern Scottish political nationalism. Such a career might lead one to expect that Murray's life was spent in rural Scotland and literary Edinburgh. But in fact, he had lived in southern Africa since 1889. At the period of his greatest poetic fame, Murray was secretary of public works of the Union of South Africa, and was playing an important part in the development of the newly formed South African state. Scottish nationalists have tended to see their country's participation in the British empire as having led to a submergence of Scotland's political identity. To the contrary, Murray's life story confirms John MacKenzie's argument that 'Empire, far from being a source of Scots servitude, was actually a means whereby Scotland asserted her distinctiveness in relation to England.'[3]

This chapter explores Murray's career to show how vital the experiences of Scots as actors in the British empire were to twentieth century Scottish national identity. In support of this view, it seeks to make four linked arguments about the Scots diaspora at the end of the nineteenth and the beginning of the twentieth century, exemplified by Murray's life.

---

[1] Previously published accounts of Murray include: *The Star* (Johannesburg), 14 April 1941; J. F. Tocher, 'Charles Murray, CMG., LL.D.', *The Aberdeen University Review* 27 (1941), pp. 210–16; C. Christie, *Some memories of Charles Murray and a few of his friends* (Pretoria: Wallace, 1943); The editor, 'Charles Murray Memorial Trust', *The Aberdeen University Review* 37 (1957–58), pp. 361–5; J. Kidd, 'Charles Murray: author of Hamewith', *Literary Review* 22, 7 (1971), pp. 347–51; N. Shepherd, 'Charles Murray: the poet of "Hamewith"', *Leopard: Magazine for Aberdeen and North East Life* (March 1978), pp. 16–20; C. J. Beyers (ed.), *Dictionary of South African Biography*, Vol. IV (Pretoria: Human Sciences Research Council, 1981), p. 383.

[2] Unless otherwise specified, all quotations from Murray poems in this chapter are from C. Murray, *Hamewith: the complete poems of Charles Murray* (Aberdeen: Charles Murray Memorial Trust / Aberdeen University Press, 1980).

[3] J. M. MacKenzie, 'Essay and reflection: on Scotland and the empire', *The International History Review* 15 (November 1993), p. 739.

Fig. 11.1 Charles Murray (left) and the chief of the Caledonian society, the Rand, 1890s, MS.27281, f.7, by permission of the National Library of Scotland, Edinburgh.

First, for many Scots, the empire was primarily a career, a path to levels of professional and economic attainment which were blocked by economic realities and social barriers in Britain itself. Secondly, this careerism produced a pragmatic mentality which was heavily focused on personal advancement and relatively little invested in emotional identification with the empire and its ideologies. Thirdly, the combination of this pragmatic imperialism and the space of 'exile' allowed the construction by the Scots abroad of 'a certain idea' of Scotland, expressed primarily in the diasporic culture of the Caledonian societies. A vision of an imagined home country emerged, more intense and emotionally charged than that any quotidian reality could produce. This imagined Scotland was frequently in tension with, or at any rate only with difficulty reconciled to, prevailing notions of Britishness and imperialism. Fourthly, and most importantly, this diasporic cultural nationalism 'looped back' into Scotland itself, becoming an essential component in the making of the new political nationalism which emerged there in the 1920s and 1930s.

EARLY LIFE: ABERDEENSHIRE, 1866–1888

Charles Murray was born in the village of Alford, Aberdeenshire, on 5 May 1866, the child of Margaret and Peter Murray.[4] Margaret was to die of tuberculosis before her son's second birthday. I have not found a single reference to her in all his personal writings.[5] The need to cope with this trauma may have been at the psychological roots of Murray's singularly self-reliant personality.

Peter was a carpenter by trade.[6] At the time of Charles' birth, Aberdeenshire was undergoing a belated and traumatic agricultural modernisation. Smallholdings were being consolidated into large commercial estates. But some small tenant farmers, rural artisans and petty traders hung on, and it was the people of this dying world that Charles would celebrate in his poems. Ironically, Peter would, later in his career, become a landlord's agent on the large Haughton estate, and is likely in this role to have helped demolish the world his son would sing about.

In the time of Charles Murray's childhood, popular education in Scotland was notably more effective and vigorous than in England. Murray attended the village school, then went on to Gallowhill School where he found an outstanding schoolmaster, Anthony McCreadie. Murray was to develop a strong interest in Latin, which he would carry into his adult life. The literature of late nineteenth-century Scottish rural life was dominated by a school known as Kailyard – literally, kitchen garden – which was characterised by its mawkish sentimentality. One of the standard tropes of Kailyard was the story of a young man from a humble background – the 'lad o' pairts' – who would be discovered by a dedicated 'dominie' (teacher) and go on to higher education and professional success.[7] Murray's writings would later be seen as a break

---

[4] Birth certificate of Charles Murray, 21 May 1866, MS 27285/1, National Library of Scotland (hereafter NLS).

[5] Death certificate of Margaret Murray, 23 January 1866, MS 27285, NLS.

[6] Unidentified press cutting, 1926, MS 27285/50, NLS.

[7] C. Harvie, *Scotland and nationalism: Scottish society and politics 1707–1994* (London: Routledge, 1994), pp. 98–101.

from Kailyard sentimentality. His own story stands in an ambiguous relationship to the 'lad o' pairts' myth. Murray clearly was stimulated by his schooling and it certainly contributed to his later success. But, despite his ability, he did not reach university, and his subsequent achievement was not that of the Kailyard hero, who moved up through the educational system, but rather made by his own ingenuity.

In 1881, Murray became apprenticed to an Aberdeen firm of surveyors and engineers, Walker and Beattie, while continuing his education at night school. He remained with them until 1887, when he became a surveyor for an Aberdeen law firm, Davidson and Garden.[8] Murray was afflicted with deep feelings of social inferiority. In late middle age he would remember how he had been 'a village boy with patched clothes and bare legs'.[9] This feeling created a burning desire for social acceptance. In Aberdeen, he befriended a number of young upper-middle-class men. As a youth, Murray already had the gifts of the raconteur, and participated enthusiastically in local sports associations and in the local military volunteer corps.[10] His social success gained him membership of the Aberdeen Boating Club.[11] Murray was emerging as a man on the make, focused on attaining professional success and upward social mobility.

It was in 1888 that Murray took the decision to emigrate to the Transvaal, then an effectively independent Boer republic (see Map 11.1). The Aberdeen of this period was a particular centre of Scottish emigration. The travel writer and sometime Aberdeen MP, James Bryce, commented in 1912, on meeting an Aberdeen doctor in the Bolivian interior that 'Next to the Germans, the most ubiquitous people in the world are the Aberdonians.'[12] Several factors made for this propensity to migrate. The belated timing of the agricultural modernisation of Aberdeenshire, in contrast with other regions of Scotland, meant that the urbanisation which had occurred decades earlier in other regions of the country was driving numerous rural folk into the city of Aberdeen. Many of these people and their children hankered after a return to the land, and emigration to the colonies – even if it were initially to take up industrial work – was an imagined route toward this goal. But Aberdonian emigrants were also often ambitious and possessed of urban skills. The city, as the home of a major university, and a middle-range industrial centre,

[8] Tocher, 'Murray', p. 211; Shepherd, 'Murray', p. 17.
[9] Murray to Edith Murray, 15 July 1920, MS 27268, NLS.
[10] Unidentified press clipping, 1900, MS 27275/5, NLS.
[11] Tocher, 'Murray', p. 211; Shepherd, 'Murray', p. 17.
[12] J. Bryce, *South America: observations and impressions* (London: Macmillan, 1912), p. 190.

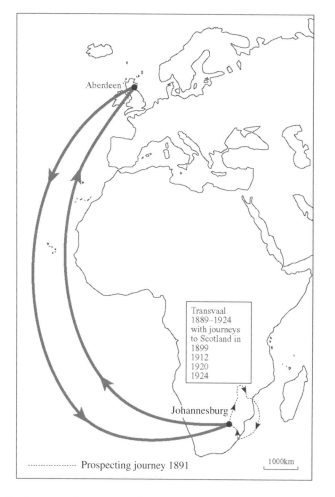

Map 11.1 Charles Murray's movements between Scotland and South Africa, and the route
of his 1891 southern African prospecting journey.

produced numerous professionals, technicians and skilled artisans. In the
context of the great depression that persisted from the early 1870s to the
1890s, Aberdeen was incapable of absorbing the skills of all these individuals. The southern Scottish industrial centres were equally affected by
the bad times, and there was a widespread awareness of the higher wages
that could be earned in the colonies and the USA. Moreover there was by
now a widespread knowledge that the less sharp social barriers of class and

the shortage of skills in the colonies made it possible for ambitious, educated men of humble social background to rise much higher in politics, administration or business than they could reasonably have hoped to do in Britain. All of this made emigration powerfully attractive to Aberdonians.[13]

A SCOT IN THE TRANSVAAL AND RHODESIA: 1889–1899

Murray's choice of South Africa as a destination was typical of Scottish emigrants at this time. Before the 1880s there had only been sporadic flows of Scots to the subcontinent. But the discovery of the Rand goldfields in 1886 changed that dramatically, prompting many Scots to take their chances in the Transvaal. Between 1893 and 1907 more Scots migrated to southern Africa than to Australia or New Zealand, and, quite incredibly, the numbers between 1895 and 1898 actually exceeded those going to Canada.[14] Within this link between Scotland and southern Africa, the synchronicity of the high level of Aberdeenshire emigration and the opening of the Rand made for an especially close set of trajectories between these two regional spaces. Aberdeenshire and the Rand were, for three decades, linked in an extraordinarily close and complex way.

Murray's health seems also to have been a factor in his decision to go to South Africa. Anyone studying late nineteenth- and early twentieth-century South Africa cannot but be struck by the extent to which the British medical profession was prone to prescribe life in the dry air of South Africa as a cure for tuberculosis (TB). Innumerable consumptives made the voyage south. Although Murray's friends were guarded about his health problems, there are references to his 'weak chest' and he was apparently known to black workers in the 1890s as 'the man with the cough'.[15] Given that his mother had died of TB, it does seem likely that he was a sufferer from the disease and that this was important in selecting his destination.

In January 1889, Murray arrived in the gold-rush town of Johannesburg.[16] There, he formed a firm of architects, civil engineers and surveyors. But he had arrived just in time for the city's first great slump.

[13] M. Harper, 'Aberdonians abroad: two centuries of human exports from North-Eastern Scotland', in T. Brotherstone and D. J. Worthington (eds.), *The city and its worlds: aspects of Aberdeen's history since 1794* (Glasgow: Cruithne, 1996), pp. 62–81.

[14] G. Donaldson, *The Scots overseas* (London: Hale, 1966), p. 187.

[15] McCreadie in A. McKie (ed.), *Dinner in honour of Charles Murray (Hamewith)* (Aberdeen: William Smith and Sons, 1912/13), p. 33.

[16] Murray, Banchory to 'Jean', 23 November 1937, MS 27268/94–5, NLS.

The readily accessible particles of gold near the surface had been worked out. From about forty metres down, the gold was contained in very low concentrations in the rock known as the Reef, and no available technology could extract it. With the gold boom appearing to be at an end, Murray accepted a job prospecting north of the Limpopo, then undergoing conquest at the hands of Cecil John Rhodes and the British South Africa Company (BSAC).

Murray left Johannesburg in April 1891, with a group of black workers. He had to learn the difficult art of managing an ox-wagon en route. At the northern Transvaal town of Pietersburg, he met up with the rest of the party, which included an Afrikaner wagon-master and three other Scots, one of them Murray's cousin. The extraordinary nature of the contemporary Aberdeenshire diaspora was demonstrated when the party crossed the Limpopo. Guarding the river were two BSAC troopers, one of whom knew Murray from Aberdeen. A few miles further on, the party encountered a trooper with whom Murray had played football in earlier years. At Fort Tuli, the post office was manned by a trooper who had worked in the same Aberdeen office as Murray.[17]

The expedition travelled north to the BSAC centre at Salisbury and then eastwards towards the highlands on the Mozambique border. As a prospecting venture the journey was a complete failure. There was no trace of the new Rand promised by Rhodes and the BSAC. The oxen became exhausted, and the party sold them at Umtali, bought pack donkeys, and set out to walk to Beira on the Mozambique coast. By the time the prospectors got there, they were in rags.[18] Thoroughly disillusioned with Rhodes and his lieutenant Charles Rudd, Murray organised a concert to raise funds for their boat fares to Durban. He penned an angry piece of doggerel which he and his friends sang:

> Then bad luck to Rudd and Rhodes, and to all those other nobs,
> Who told so many lies about the gold
> May they never make a rap,
> But be brought to mealie pap [maize porridge]
> Like us prospectors they have sold.[19]

Murray's political sentiments in the 1890s seem to have been radical liberal in British terms. There was a suspicion of capitalists – another mine magnate, J. B. Robinson is denounced for his lack of civic

---

[17] *Ibid.* [18] *Ibid.*
[19] C. Murray, *A handful of heather* (Aberdeen: privately published, 1893), pp. 35–7, MS 27258, NLS. This is probably the only surviving copy of the book.

responsibility in Johannesburg in another Murray poem of the time.[20] Murray also displayed a radical-liberal scepticism toward stridently imperial ideologies and toward the monarchy. At the time of Queen Victoria's 1897 jubilee, he wrote:

> You've passed the three score years on,
> An' work on borrowed days noo,
> Tho' its nae easy just to ken,
> Why that should merit praise noo.
> ... God bless the Queen, but damn the bells
> Clang clangin' in the steeple,
> An' God forget nae us oursel's,
> Wha made her sae – the People.[21]

Such sentiments are the more comprehensible in the context of Murray's Aberdeen, which was a bastion of Gladstonian liberalism. The Liberals attained massive majorities over the Conservatives in the city in the 1880 and 1885 parliamentary elections, and in 1886 the Tories did not even bother to stand. In 1884 there was a massive demonstration in the city in favour of the 'Grand Old Man's' new electoral reforms. Indeed Aberdeen was so solid for the Liberals that the party topped the polls in every election for the city's seats at Westminster between 1832 and 1917.[22] But Murray was driven by his careerism and ambition, and not by his political ideas. In 1893, he privately published a handful of copies of a collection of his first poems, containing both the Rhodes and the Robinson verses. Later, as a colonial civil servant at a time Rhodes had evolved into a sainted imperial figure, Murray made strenuous attempts to recover all the copies of the book, and never attempted to publish the verse about the queen or anything else that smacked of political radicalism. What the episode shows is that Murray's participation in the colonial enterprise was not rooted in any deep reverence for imperial institutions or ideals; but neither would he allow any reservations about imperialism which he may have harboured to damage his personal career.

Returning to the Rand in early 1892, Murray found a job as a surveyor on a Johannesburg mine. The mining industry was now recovering, for the discovery in Glasgow of the MacArthur–Forrest cyanide process had provided an effective means of extracting the gold from the crushed ore of the Reef. The Rand mines were developing the patterns that would

---

[20] *Ibid.*   [21] 'To Her Majesty', 22 June 1897, MS 27257/3–6, NLS.
[22] W. Hamish Fraser, 'Politics before 1918', in W. Hamish Fraser and C. H. Lee (eds.), *Aberdeen 1800–2000: a new history* (East Linton: Tuckwell, 2000), pp. 186–91.

characterise them for most of the next century, with black labourers working under white miners in deep shafts. Murray found the work gruelling and the pay unsatisfactory. But he persisted, and was eventually rewarded with the much more prestigious and better-paid post of manager at a mine in Florida, on the west Rand. The mine proved to have only low-grade ore, and closed after six months. After a period of unemployment, Murray was able to obtain a more secure manager's position on the York mine, in the west Rand town of Krugersdorp.[23]

In 1895, Murray married Edith Rogers, an Anglo-South African from an upper-middle-class background. They would have two daughters and a son. Murray seems to have regarded the marriage as another move in his search for upward social mobility. In later life, he wrote to Edith, with startling candour, that 'I always wanted to get a wife who was a lot better than myself, of finer instincts, better breeding and education & I was lucky in that.'[24]

From early in his southern African years, Murray became involved in the creation of a Scottish-exile culture. He was a member of the committee of the Caledonian society of Johannesburg and played a leading role in the activities of the West Rand Caledonian Society.[25] The Caledonian societies were a major colonial cultural movement of the late nineteenth- and early twentieth-century colonial world.[26] The Highland gatherings, St Andrew's nights and Burns nights of these organisations were far more central features of colonial life than such events were in the life of Scotland itself. An absent home is likely to appear all the more attractive: an Aberdonian admirer of Murray's work later astutely commented that 'the indelible impressions of our youth take new shapes and colour when reflected through the equatorial zone'.[27]

From 1892, the Rand Caledonians organised an annual Scottish Gathering and Games, and by 1895 they felt able to boast that this event was 'generally acknowledged as the most popular and best attended athletic function in South Africa'.[28] The Caledonians' leadership was dominated by the upper strata of the Scottish diaspora on the

---

[23] Murray to Edith Murray, 15 July 1920, MS 27268; Murray, Rome, to Bill Murray, no date, MS 27267/116, NLS.
[24] *Ibid.*   [25] *Krugersdorp Standard*, 19 August 1899.
[26] National or regional associations of United Kingdom emigrants were certainly a feature of colonial life. However Caledonianism in South Africa existed on a much bigger scale than the organisations of the Cornish and the Welsh, and the minimal Irish Catholic migration to the region meant that Irish organisations proved difficult to sustain.
[27] A. Keith, unidentified press cutting, MS 27259, NLS.
[28] *Standard and Digger's News*, 26 October 1895.

Rand: managers, professionals, minor financiers and entrepreneurs.[29] There seems to have been little representation on the organisation's committees of the substantial number of Scottish artisans who had been attracted to the Rand.

Murray was deeply emotionally committed to the Caledonians' activities. He would tell an Aberdeen audience in 1912 that:

> at home you can have no idea of the patriotism of the Scots abroad ... St Andrew's night is the day of the whole year for the Scots in South Africa ... Not a village from the Cape to the Zambesi ... if there are but two Scots there (and it is a poor *dorp* that cannot boast of that much), but will have its Caledonian Society and its St Andrew's banquet.[30]

At the Johannesburg Caledonians' 1895 St Andrew's night dinner, a verse by Murray appeared on the back of the elaborate menu, over a drawing of a misty Highland scene:

> Here on the Rand, we freely grant,
> We're blessed with sunny weather:
> Frae cauld and snaw we're well awa';
> But man, we miss the heather.[31]

This would become the epigraph of Murray's most famous volume of poetry, *Hamewith*: placed there, it positioned the author as the involuntary exile, looking toward the homeland. The St Andrew's night event revealed the political divisions of the time. A speaker who was supposed to propose a toast to the First and Second *Volksraaden* (the two chambers of the Boer legislature) launched into a full-scale attack on the Boer Republic and all its works. *Volksraad* member Carl Jeppe, responding, stoutly defended the Transvaal. The chairman, John Tudhope, tried to smooth things over when he proposed 'Scotland', assuring the gathering that the Scots in the Transvaal had thoroughly identified themselves with the country.[32] Murray had to follow, proposing a toast to 'The Land we Live in' and steered an intermediate course, delivering some truly awful doggerel gently mocking the republic's police force and its denial of the vote to British settlers (or *uitlanders* as the Boers called them), but nevertheless proclaiming it to be

---

[29] For the composition of the committee in 1895, see Caledonian Society Sports (programme), 1895, Spam 796.42 Cal., Strange Collection, Johannesburg Public Library.
[30] Murray in A. McKie, *Dinner*, p. 24.
[31] St Andrew's Night 1895, Caledonian Society of Johannesburg, MS 27285, NLS.
[32] *Standard and Digger's News*, 2 December 1895.

> A land which next to our land of birth
> Is the finest land on God's green earth.[33]

Despite being capable of such stuff, Murray was already a serious and accomplished poet. He had written a number of the poems on Aberdeenshire characters which were later to become popular in Scotland, such as 'Skeely Kirsty', 'The Miller explains' and 'The antiquary'. He also wrote a number of verses about life in South Africa, including ones on the St Andrew's night banquets and the Caledonian sports. Murray demonstrated his scholarly abilities by translating Latin verses into Scots. All three types of poems were included in the private 1893 edition of his work; the poems on life in South Africa were largely eliminated in his later publications. During the 1890s, Murray began the practice of publishing individual poems in Scottish publications, such as the Aberdeen satirical magazine, *Bon-Accord*.

Despite his tough and pragmatic personality, Murray suffered inwardly because of the way in which philistine colonial society viewed his literary activities. His humorous and self-deprecating later account of this period nevertheless hints at a difficult encounter with Transvaal definitions of masculinity, which combined the robust postures of frontiersmen, miners and 'self-made' capitalists.[34] Murray wrote:

I have always had a feeling that a man might raise chrysanthemums or even play the flute in his spare time, and still have claims to be considered a good business man, but that if his weakness was rhyming he would be set down as a 'feckless' character. Believing that this was the general feeling, I have hitherto tried to conceal my weakness from my associates, or if they did get to know of it, I tried to pass off these verses as youthful indiscretions.[35]

How did Murray place himself within the racial politics of southern Africa? The form his racism seems to have taken was that of a total exclusion of black people from his field of emotional or intellectual interest. In his personal papers and letters there are a minimal number of references to black people, despite the fact that his work as a prospector and a mine manager in the 1890s placed him in contact with many black workers. On the rare occasions that people of colour are referred to, it is dismissively, as 'niggers'.[36] Murray accepted that racial order of the day,

---

[33] *Ibid.*
[34] For an important first exploration of the history of masculinities in South Africa, see the papers collected in R. Morrell (ed.), *Changing men in South Africa* (London and Pietermaritzburg: Zed Press and University of Natal Press, 2001).
[35] Murray in McKie, *Dinner*, p. 23.
[36] Murray, Banchory, to Jean Murray, 23 November 1937, MS 27268/94–5, NLS.

but he took no active ideological part in defending it – he displayed no interest whatsoever in biological racism and other ideologies justifying the status quo. His attitude is best understood in terms of his single-minded focus on his personal interests – promotions, pay, and investments. For Murray, southern Africa was simply the available theatre for his personal ambitions. He was in that sense, the perfect colonial careerist.

The particular historical period in which he lived in southern Africa helps explain Murray's ability to exclude black people from his mental world. South of the Limpopo, black resistance to colonial conquest had been effectively crushed by the time that Murray arrived in the sub-continent. At the end of the 1870s and the beginning of the 1880s, a massive application of British military power had brought the territories of the Xhosa and the Pedi and the kingdoms of Basutoland and Zululand under white control. There was no longer any serious military threat by indigenous polities to British and Boer power. Before the First World War political organisation amongst the new black educated élite was very modest in scope, and based on seeking reforms within the imperial political framework. Trade unionism amongst black workers only started during the First World War.[37] For a quarter of a century after Murray emigrated, then, there was no major black challenge to white domination within the boundaries of what became the South African state.[38] Only in 1918–19 did militant forms of nationalism and organised labour protest emerge, and by then Murray was looking toward retirement. Because most of Murray's southern African career was located in the temporal gap between the defeat of pre-colonial polities and the emergence of modernist forms of militant black politics, he was able to act and think as if black people were not political actors of whom he had to take account.

There is no vehemence in Murray's few comments on people of colour. But there is some in his occasional remarks about Jews; for example, in a letter to his wife, he refers to someone as a 'dirty little Jew'.[39] Nevertheless, the anti-Semitism in Murray's private papers is considerably more

[37] This analysis is based on that of Shula Marks and Richard Rathbone, 'Introduction', in S. Marks and R. Rathbone (eds.), *Industrialisation and social change in South Africa: African class formation, culture and consciousness, 1870–1930* (Harlow: Longman, 1982), pp. 1–43.

[38] Apparent exceptions to this generalisation would be the African occupations of white land in the second half of the 1899–1902 Anglo-Boer War and the 1906 revolt in Natal known as the Bambatha Rebellion. But the wartime agrarian protests, made possible by the evacuation of white families to refugee camps and the disruptions of war, were easily contained once the war was ended. The Bambatha revolt involved a minimal number of white casualties and ended as a gruesome massacre of the rebels by colonial troops, without really threatening white power even in rural Natal.

[39] Murray to Edith Murray, 31 December 1900, MS 27268/36, NLS.

muted than that in the *published* writings of a figure like John Buchan. Murray's remarks reflect a shockingly conventional anti-Semitism in turn-of-the-century Scotland.

Murray was on a trip back to Scotland with his family when the South African War broke out in 1899. Returning to South Africa, he served as a lieutenant in an *uitlander* unit of the imperial forces, the Railway Pioneer Regiment. After a period in the military, he was allowed to resign early in order to join the civil service of the newly conquered Transvaal colony. In 1901 Murray became deputy inspector of mines. He was subsequently promoted to registrar of Crown titles. In 1905 he became undersecretary of public works, and was promoted to secretary in the same department when the Transvaal was granted self-government on an all-white franchise in 1907. With the formation of the Union of South Africa in 1910, Murray was made secretary of the national department of public works, and remained in this post until his retirement in 1924.

In his public works capacity, Murray supervised the construction of many of the landmark buildings of the Transvaal colony and later of the new South African state. These included, in Pretoria, the Transvaal University College and the Transvaal Museum; in Johannesburg, the law courts, the Observatory dome, King Edward VII School and Johannesburg Girls' High School; in Bloemfontein, the South African Supreme Court; in Cape Town, the new law courts and the refurbished parliament building; and numerous bridges throughout the country.[40]

By far the most significant of the projects which Murray supervised though, was the execution of Herbert Baker's design for the Union Buildings in Pretoria, which would house the South African prime minister's office and the main departments of state. In his 1911 departmental report, Murray was able to boast that the building was well under way and that it would require 14,000,000 bricks and 500,000 tons of stone to complete. The gardens were being planted and landscaped by about 100 white labourers, while 800 African and 465 white workers were busy on the building itself.[41] Murray worked closely with Baker, and

---

[40] Unidentified press cuttings, photographs, MS 27275/50, NLS. For construction in the Transvaal generally during Murray's time in the civil service, see C. Chipkin, *Johannesburg style: architecture and society 1880s–1960s* (Cape Town: David Philip, 1993), pp. 37–60.
[41] Union of South Africa, Public Works Department Report for the Year 1911, pp. 16–17, MS 27273, NLS.

successfully contained the architect's extravagance, succeeding in keeping the mammoth project within the projected costs.[42]

Murray distinguished himself as an administrator. He smoothly unified the four colonial public works departments in 1910. His performances in front of committees of the Cape Town parliament seem to have inspired some awe in contemporaries for his grasp of financial, organisational and technical detail. He took a keen interest in improving the technical aspects of building constructions, and was apparently aided in this task by his good relations with the many Scottish contractors and artisans involved in government work.[43] He seems to have derived great satisfaction from being able to hold his own amongst the corps of administrators recruited by Britain's Southern African proconsul, Lord Milner. Friends recounted the story that on one occasion, asked by an official whether he was Oxford or Cambridge, Murray gleefully replied 'night school'.[44] Whether apocryphal or not, the anecdote captures the way in which the (whites-only) egalitarianism of the colonial world provided a man like Murray with a satisfying scope for his ambitions. In Britain, he could hardly have hoped to become civil-service head of a government department.

But despite the role he played in literally creating the fabric of the settler colony, Murray continued to think of himself as a sojourner in the country. In this at least, he did not conform to the desires of his political bosses. The post-Boer War Milner administration was desperate to create a large permanent British-settler population which would outnumber the Boers and guarantee control of a future state by pro-imperial political leaders. Murray, however, was quite clear that he did not regard South Africa as his permanent home. One of the few of his poems of this period which contains specific South African references, is an explicit statement of his self-perceived position of exile, and his devotion to a maternally gendered Scotland:

> Scotland our Mither – we weary whiles an' tire;
> When Bad Luck helps to outspan, Regret brings up the fire;
> But still the hope uphaulds us, tho' bitter now the blast,
> That we'll win to the auld hame across the seas at last.

In this Murray was at cross purposes with the Milnerites. At the 1905 Pretoria St Andrew's night dinner, Patrick Duncan, one of the administration's bright young Oxford men, quoted Murray's poem, but

---

[42] Christie, *Some memories*, pp. 30–2.   [43] *Ibid.*, pp. 32–3.
[44] Editor, 'Charles Murray Memorial Trust', p. 361.

spectacularly – perhaps deliberately – missed the point, as he urged the assembled Scotsmen to root themselves in their new home:

> they were none the less Scots because they had no intention of going back ... They could remember all that Scotland means to them without doing that, just as a man remembered his mother's influence.[45]

Murray had every intention of going back. And nor, later on, would Murray display any interest in Smuts' project of fusing Anglophones and Afrikaners into a single white nation.

All Murray's spare-time activities seem to have been involved with the manufacture of colonial Scottishness. In the period immediately after the Boer War, he took part in the formation of a 'Scottish' territorial regiment on the Rand. There was already at least one such regiment in South Africa, the Cape Town Highlanders, founded in 1885, who modelled themselves on the Gordon Highlanders. Murray had already written a poem, under the title 'Bydand' – the Gordon's motto – commemorating the legend that the Duchess of Gordon had kissed each recruit when the regiment was first raised. In 1902, the Marquis of Tullabardine, heir to the Duke of Atholl, was resident on the Rand, and proposed the raising of a specifically Scottish military unit. Tullabardine addressed his idea to the Johannesburg Caledonian society, who enthusiastically took it up. Murray was the second recruit to what became the Transvaal Scottish regiment, and served as an officer until 1905.[46] Part of the attraction of the regiment to aspirant Scottish immigrants was that it enabled them to act out the part of officers of a Highland regiment, something which in the British context would have required an aristocratic, or at the very least an upper-middle-class family background. The regiment received the support of the Duke of Atholl, who gave them permission to wear the Murray tartan. This, together with the Marquis of Tullabardine's personal patronage infused the regiment's activities with a social cachet to which the managers, professionals and minor financiers who made up its officer corps could never have aspired in Scotland itself.[47] The plaid and swords which the officers wore were a connection to the dreamworld of Walter Scott, on which many of them had been raised. Murray would relax on fishing trips with friends to the artificially stocked trout streams

---

[45] *Pretoria News*, 1 December 1905.
[46] H. C. Juta, *The history of the Transvaal Scottish* (Johannesburg: Hortors, 1933), pp. 44, 46.
[47] On the South African "Scottish" regiments see J. Hyslop, 'Cape Town Highlanders, Transvaal Scottish: military "Scottishness" and social power in nineteenth and twentieth century South Africa', *South African Historical Journal* **47** (November 2002), pp. 96–114.

of the eastern Transvaal escarpment. On these outings there would be episodes of 'dressing up' as Highland chieftans and caterans.[48]

In 1900, a small Aberdeen publisher produced a collection of Murray's poems, called *Hamewith* (Homeward). The title verse was a restatement of the exile theme:

> Hot youth is ever a ranger,
> New scenes ever its desire;
> Cauld Eild, doubtful' o' a stranger,
> Thinks but o' keepin' in the fire.
> Midway, the traveller is weary,
> Fain he'd be turning in his prime
> Hamewith – the road that's never dreary,
> Back where his heart is a' the time.[49]

The volume achieved moderate sales, and began to build Murray's reputation. In 1909 Murray secured the production of a new edition of *Hamewith* by the major London publisher, Constable. This edition had a laudatory introduction by the important Scots literary figure, Andrew Lang. It comprised 45 of Murray's pieces, including his Aberdeenshire character poems, tributes to Burns and Stevenson, and translations into Scots of Virgil and Horace. The book quickly became a huge success. Over the next decade it sold about 20,000 copies – a very good sale for the small poetry market.[50] But the real impact of the work was in the way it was anthologised and taken up by teachers in Scottish schools. Murray was widely acclaimed in his homeland. On a visit home in 1912, he was fêted by the Mayor of Aberdeen at a congratulatory banquet. In 1920 the University of Aberdeen conferred an honorary doctorate on him.

How are we to account for this unexpected triumph? On the surface, it is puzzling, for on initial inspection Murray's work is likely to seem weakly sentimental to the contemporary reader. It may not seem clear what differentiates it from the literature of the Kailyard. But the second edition of *Hamewith* had appeared at a fortunate moment. A new cultural nationalism was starting to be visible in Scotland, and would gather strength over the next decade. Murray's writing tapped into a growing discontent at the way in which the educational system in Scotland dealt with the distinctiveness of the Scots language. In 1878, a centralised Scottish Education Department was set up. The department had widely

---

[48] Christie, *Some memories*, pp. 34–5.
[49] This is as it appears in C. Murray, *Hamewith* (Aberdeen: D. Wyllie and Sons, 1900); later versions substituted 'haudin', for 'keepin', and 'wanderer' for 'traveller'.
[50] Murray, Cape Town, to George Walker, 7 May 1922, MS 27266/35, NLS.

come to be seen as an agent of anglicisation, imposing 'standard' English, discouraging Scots and its regional variants, and taking no interest in local customs. It was no accident that the most popular poem in *Hamewith* was 'The Whistle', an indirect attack on the education authorities.[51] In the poem, an Aberdeenshire herd boy makes a flute on which he produces rapturous music. But when the school term starts his teacher destroys the flute. Symbolically, the creativity of rural Scotland is smashed by unfeeling bureaucracy:

> He blew them rants sae lively, scottisches, reels an' jigs,
> The foalie flang his muckle legs an' capered oer the rigs,
> The grey-tailed futt'rat bobbit oot to hear his ain strathspey,
> The bawd cam loupin through the corn to 'Clean Pease Strae';
> The feet o'ilka man an' beast gat youkie when he played –
> Hae ye ever heard o' whistle like the wee 'herd made.
> But the snaw it stopped the herdin' and the winter brocht him dool,
> When in spite o' hacks an' chilblains he was shod again for school;
> He couldna sough the catechis nor pipe the rule o' three,
> He was keepit an' lickit when the ither loons got free;
> But he afen played the truant – 'twas the only thing he played,
> For the maister brunt the whistle that the wee 'herd made.

The sheer density of the Aberdeenshire dialect effect in such poems paradoxically simply added to their wider Scottish popularity. The late modernisation of Aberdeenshire meant that it could stand, in the reader's mind, for the old Scotland, the impenetrability of its language a marker of this historic distance. A reviewer of *Hamewith* wrote that 'we who are brought much into contact with the country people of the South of Scotland cannot shut our eyes to the fact that the present system of education is killing out the beautiful soft language of the Lowlands'.[52]

Recognising Murray's critical stance toward education in Scotland also helps us to see why his work was regarded by contemporaries as a significant break with Kailyard. Kailyard proposed a stable, non-conflictual rural world in which the 'lad o' pairts' made his way upwards by conforming to the requirements of the education system. Murray instead is clearly antagonistic towards the promises of the educational order, seeing officialdom as in conflict with village culture. The herd boy is not saved from rural poverty by his schoolmaster. Similarly, in the second-most popular poem in the collection, 'The packman', a rural peddler turns

---

[51] C. Milton, 'Modern poetry in Scots before MacDiarmid', in C. Craig (ed.), *The history of Scottish literature*, Vol. IV (Aberdeen: Aberdeen University Press, 1987), pp. 26–7.
[52] *TP's Weekly*, 21 October 1910.

himself into a rich man, with a daughter married to a laird, by using his abilities to beat the system rather than by working through it. Murray's work does reflect a scepticism toward established authority and an understanding of clashing interests which was largely absent in Kailyard literature.

Another dimension of the new cultural nationalism from which Murray benefited was the Scottish literary 'Renaissance' of which much would be heard in the immediate post-First World War years.[53] An important figure in this development was John Buchan, who had been a prominent figure in Milner's Transvaal administration.[54] Internationally, Buchan today tends to be regarded as the unread author of blimpish colonial fiction. But in Scotland, he remains very much in print, and is seen by many as an author who made a substantial literary contribution to national identity, especially through his historical novels and biographical works. What accounts for this paradox is that, though a consistent champion of empire, Buchan saw it as a voluntary union of the component nations of the British Isles and the British settler colonies, in which each could participate without losing its unique identity. Through his career as a Tory MP and eventually, governor general of Canada, Buchan constantly asserted the need for a distinct Scottish place within the Empire.[55] He developed a strong interest in vernacular Scottish poetry. In the years after the First World War Buchan was active in the Vernacular Circle of the London Burns Club, which played an important public role in promoting the literary use of the Scots tongue. In 1924, he published an anthology of Scots verse. In 1925, Buchan spoke at an Aberdeen banquet for Murray, praising him effusively for his part in 'making South Africa what most parts of the British empire are today – a Scottish dependency'.[56]

Did Murray see himself as a Scottish cultural activist? Certainly, his admirers viewed him in this way. Alexander McKie, an Aberdeen headmaster and cultural broker, portrayed Murray in these terms when he introduced him at the 1912 banquet:

At a time the vernacular was under a cloud and might almost be described as moribund, in so far as it was tabooed and frowned on by most of our

[53] Harvie, *Scotland and nationalism*, pp. 102–7.
[54] A. Lownie, *John Buchan: the Presbyterian cavalier* (London: Constable, 1995).
[55] C. Harvie, 'Second thoughts of a Scotsman on the make: politics, nationalism and myth in John Buchan', *Scottish Historical Review* 70, 188 (April 1991), pp. 31–54.
[56] *Proceedings at presentation of portrait and bust to Mr Charles Murray, CMG, LL.D. and Mrs Murray* (Aberdeen: Rosemount, 1925), p. 20.

educational mentors, [Murray] breathed new life into it, and by his inimitable embodiment of it in *Hamewith* brought about a distinct and well-marked reaction.[57]

Murray's speech, which followed, was ambiguous. He disclaimed such 'laudable and patriotic intentions' in writing poetry, saying he had done it only to give pleasure to his father and because to 'throw one's mind into the old times and scenes seemed to give me something of an emotional relief . . . from the wear and bustle of colonial life'.[58] Yet he went on to complain bitterly of the difficulty he had experienced in expressing himself in standard English. And Murray added a reflection which demonstrated that it was his South African experience that had allowed him to see language as a political issue. At the time of the South African union in 1910, constitutional provision had been made for linguistic equality between Dutch-Afrikaans and English. At the time that Murray was speaking, the Afrikaner nationalist leader, General J. B. M. Hertzog, was ferociously attacking the Botha–Smuts government for, in his view, failing to honour the protected status of Dutch-Afrikaans. Murray commented:

if the Dutch language does maintain itself against the English, many of us will be tempted to wish that a similar provision had been made to preserve our Scots language.[59]

When the First World War broke out Botha, with Smuts as his minister of defence, led South Africa into active participation on the British side. The war meant a switch in the department of public works priorities from civilian to military construction. Murray was commissioned as a lieutenant colonel in 1917, and became the defence force's director of works until reverting to his civilian designation after the war.

During the World War, Murray wrote a number of poems on military themes. They appeared in newspapers including *The Times*, and were published as a collection, *Sough o' War* in 1917. The poems are patriotic – but their patriotism is exclusively Scottish. Murray's verse does not respond to the calls of imperial, British or South African loyalty. The apparently exemplary imperial civil servant displays no trace of identification either with the imperial centre or with his adopted country. The Scotland that Murray appeals to is not a political entity, but a tradition of military valour:

[57] Alexander McKie in A. McKie, *Dinner*, p. 12. [58] Murray in A. McKie, *Dinner*, pp. 22–3.
[59] *Ibid.*, p. 22.

Wha bares a blade for Scotland? She's needin' ye sairly noo,
What will ye dae for Scotland, for a' she's done for you?
Think o' the auld-time slogans, the thread runnin' throu' your plaid,
The cairns o' the Covenanters whaur the martyrs' banes are laid,
Ay, the faith o' your godly fathers, is it naething to you the day?
Wha bares a blade for Scotland? Noo is the time to say.

The poem seems to attempt to shame non-volunteers (Britain did not adopt conscription until well into the war) by playing on their fear that they fall short of the masculine fortitude of their ancestors. It neatly fuses the two opposing militant religious traditions of Scotland – Jacobite Episcopalian–Catholic Highlander (symbolised by the plaid) and millenarian Calvinist Covenanter. The radical ideological incompatibility of these two cultures is overcome by constituting devotion to a cause and physical bravery as shared Scottish characteristics. Murray was harsh on those who refused to serve. Another poem, 'Dockens Afore his Peers', set in the period after the coming of conscription, brutally satirises an Aberdeenshire farmer's attempts to obtain military exemption for his son.

What redeems Murray's poetry from simple militarism is that he did have a sense of the persistent social divisions in Scottish society masked by the patriotic unity of the war. In 'Fae France', an Aberdeenshire farm servant has been driven to poaching by a fine imposed by the sheriff. In the army the poacher serves under the sheriff's son, and rescues him during a raid on German trenches. When he receives a letter from the sheriff's wife, thanking him for saving her son, he replies:

Jist bid yer man, fan neist I'm up, ca' canny wi' the fine.

The end of the conflict seems to have left Murray bitter. In one post-war poem, Murray imagines God contemplating the world, and concludes that if he were God, he would

Tak' back my word an' sen' another spate,
Droon oot the hale hypothetec, dicht the slate.

MURRAY AND THE NEW SCOTTISH NATIONALISM

Neither Murray nor John Buchan ever fully embraced the political forms of Scottish nationalism. But the cultural nationalism which they promoted grew strongly in Scotland in the inter-war years. The position of exile enabled emigrant artists like Murray to 'see' the Scotland they no longer lived in more intensely. The cultural climate such work fostered provided a favourable context for a new politics in Scotland itself. Home rule sentiment surged in Labour and Liberal ranks, and small militant nationalist groupings emerged. In the inter-war years the dominant form of this nationalism was not a separatist one. But there was a strong desire for greater recognition for Scotland within the empire. Discourses about the Scottish contribution to empire now often contained a sting in the tale, in the form of an assertion that the British polity did not give the Scots sufficient recognition and autonomy.

The more militant nationalist groupings of this period, which were separatist, did not attain broad support, but their role was important for the future. Here again, the diaspora played a significant part. A number of the key activists of early and mid-twentieth-century Scottish nationalism had actually grown up in the dominions: Wendy Wood from Cape Town, the poet Sydney Goodsir Smith from New Zealand, T. D. Wanliss and Theodore Napier from Australia.[60] In 1933, the two main nationalist associations formed the Scottish National Party (SNP). It was long to remain a small party of activists and intellectuals. But four decades later, the SNP would at last attract mass electoral support and help to precipitate a crisis in the political unity of the British state. There is thus a real, if tenuous connection between the cultural nationalism of the early twentieth century and the coming of the Scottish parliament in 1999.

Changes in Scotland's economic position and the cultural–political shifts of the period were mutually reinforcing. The 1914–18 war marked a watershed in the relationship between the Scottish people and the empire. Before the war, Scotland had been tightly linked into the empire, supplying the dominions and colonies with the manufactures of its heavy industry, with emigrant labour and with skilled professionals. Empire meant industrial prosperity, a future for the unemployed, and careers for the middle classes. But after the war this set of interlocking interests came apart. Increased competition from Germany and America, and a growing control of Scottish manufacturing by English-based firms led to an enormous weakening of Scotland's position as an industrial exporter. To give one southern African example, between 1873 and 1910, the Cape railways bought 567 of their locomotives from Glasgow and only 118 from the rest of the world. But between 1919 and 1939, South African Railways bought only a quarter of their locomotives from the Clydeside, with 40 per cent of the purchases coming from Germany.[61] During the First World War, the dominions introduced passports for travel within the

---

[60] Harvie, *Scotland and nationalism*, p. 65.
[61] M. S. Moss and J. R. Hume, *Workshop of the British empire* (London: Heinemann, 1977), p. 46.

empire, accompanied by tighter bureaucratic controls over immigration, and with the onset of the Great Depression cut back radically on immigration. And as the dominions developed their own higher education institutions on a bigger scale, their demand for the skills of Scottish professionals began to fall. Thus in the twenties and thirties, brute economic realities contributed to a feeling that Scotland was not benefiting from imperial projects. This was articulated by the Glasgow law professor and Scottish nationalist leader, Andrew Dewar Gibb in his 1937 book *Scottish empire*. Gibb argued that the enormous Scottish contribution to the empire had mainly benefited England, and that whatever economic gains Scotland had made from the empire had been offset by the neglect of economic opportunities in Europe necessitated by alignment with England's imperial orientation.[62]

The complexity of the strengthening nationalist sentiment in Scotland, and its relation to empire, was reflected in the opening of the Scottish national memorial to David Livingstone at his birthplace in Blantyre, on the periphery of Glasgow, in 1929.[63] The memorial had been the initiative of a Congregationalist minister, Reverend James MacNair, who had conceived the project in 1925, when he visited the tenement where the missionary explorer was born (it was then still a slum dwelling). MacNair promoted the memorial specifically as a Scottish national project. In MacNair's vision, Livingstone's imperial and religious achievements simultaneously strengthened the claims of Scotland to recognition of its own national identity. For MacNair, Livingstone's memory was 'one of the most precious religious and moral assets of Scotland'. When he launched an appeal for funds for the monument, MacNair was delighted to find that 'it was evident that the explorer still had an amazing hold on the Scots' imagination'.[64] Buchan, Ramsay MacDonald and J. M. Barrie were amongst the prominent individuals who supported the project. But there was also great popular support, especially from Sunday Schools and bible classes. The initiative also reinforced the links between the Scottish diaspora and the 'home' country, with strong contributions flowing in from Canada and South Africa, and to a lesser extent Australia. MacNair presented Livingstone to his audience in the same way that Murray had framed the Scottish

[62] A. D. Gibb, *Scottish empire* (London: Alexander Maclehose, 1937).

[63] J. I. MacNair, 'The Scottish National Memorial to David Livingstone', *The International Review of Missions* **20** (1931), pp. 450–5; J. I. MacNair, *The story of the Scottish national memorial to David Livingstone* (Blantyre: Scottish National Memorial to David Livingstone Trust, 1944).

[64] MacNair, *The Scottish national memorial to David Livingstone*, pp. 450–1.

soldier; as uniting the virtues of the highland warrior and the Covenanter (conveniently, Livingstone's maternal great-grandfather was supposed to have fought at Culloden, and his paternal line to have come from the Covenanters). The memorial was a huge success when it first opened. It received 51,000 visitors in 1929–30, its importance in national identity reflected in the fact that it thereby beat Robert Burns' cottage and Walter Scott's Abbotsford, with 50,000 and 15,000 visitors respectively in the same period.[65] The politics of the memorial was part of the redefinition of Scotland's relation to empire. Through celebrating Livingstone's greatness as an imperial figure, the distinct claims of Scotland were reasserted. Livingstone became an embodiment of the nation, his achievements only possible because of his specifically Scottish character-istics. While only small nationalist and leftist vanguards wanted to ditch the empire, a much broader layer of Scottish society was indicating a desire for recognition as a distinct people within the imperial world. This viewpoint resonated with that of Murray's war poems, in which the part played by Scots in the imperial cause redounded exclusively to the glory of the Scottish nation.

Murray's work was to have a long life in anthologies of Scots verse, and in the schools. But his reputation amongst the intelligentsia as a leading Scottish literary figure collapsed in the mid-1920s. This was largely the result of the vendetta waged against Murray by one C. M. Grieve. Born in Dumfriesshire in 1892, and more or less self-educated, Grieve transformed himself, during the twenties and thirties, into 'Hugh MacDiarmid', Scotland's dominating literary figure, the creator of an indigenous modernism.[66] Grieve's career took off in 1920 when he edited an anthology of Scots verse entitled *Northern numbers*, which included work by Buchan, Neil Munro and Violet Jacob.[67] The second edition, appearing the next year, added some of Murray's best-known poems.[68] *Northern numbers* came to be seen as an important statement of Scottish cultural self-assertion and a significant moment in the country's literary renaissance. This aside, there was as yet nothing particularly radical,

---

[65] *Ibid.*, p. 450.
[66] On MacDiarmid, see D. Glen, *Hugh MacDiarmid (Christopher Murray Grieve) and the Scottish Renaissance* (Edinburgh: W.&R. Chambers, 1964); K. Buthlay, *Hugh MacDiarmid (C. M. Grieve)* (London: Oliver and Boyd, 1964) and A. Bold (ed.), *The letters of Hugh MacDiarmid* (London: Hamish Hamilton, 1984).
[67] C. M. Grieve (ed.), *Northern numbers: Being representative selections from certain living Scottish poets* (London and Edinburgh: T. N. Foulis, 1920).
[68] C. M. Grieve (ed.), *Northern numbers: Being representative selections from certain living Scottish poets* (London and Edinburgh: T. N. Foulis, 1921).

either from an artistic or a political point of view about Grieve's project. But what made Grieve's position difficult to pin down, was that he began to create a number of distinct literary personae for himself. There was C. M. Grieve, critic and poet, who wrote in standard English and was sceptical about the use of broad Scots; there was Hugh MacDiarmid, the Scots poet; and there was Isobel Guthrie, the music critic. As Grieve evolved a modernist poetics, and as Hugh MacDiarmid became his dominant voice, he turned against Murray and other conventional literary contemporaries. In 1925, Grieve launched an attack on Murray which can have few equals in the history of literary invective:

I say that Charles Murray has not only never written a line of poetry in his life, but that he is constitutionally incapable of doing so – his style of mind, his attitude to life, make him so, just as it is not in the nature of Aberdeen granite to be diamondiferous . . . his particular dialect is perhaps the poorest of them all and certainly the least capable of being used to genuine poetic purpose . . . Charles Murray has certainly made no effort to take Scottish verse out of the narrow and dismal rut in which he found it – he has done nothing to repurify a dialect which he found in a corrupt state and to put it to higher and nobler use.[69]

MacDiarmid's contempt for Murray was the result not only of his turn to modernist poetics but of his growing radicalisation. MacDiarmid would develop a Scottish nationalism so robust that in his *Who's who* entry he gave his hobby as 'Anglophobia'. By the mid-twenties MacDiarmid was active in radical nationalist groups, and by the early thirties he was identifying as a Communist.

The MacDiarmid–Murray clash raises some interesting paradoxes. Murray, who had spent his entire adult working life in southern Africa, was a champion of broad Scots; Grieve, who was never to spend a significant part of his life outside Scotland, initially championed the idea that Scots writers should use standard English. Then Grieve turned vigorously against Murray, becoming 'Hugh MacDiarmid', who wrote in broad Scots. MacDiarmid seems here to be trying to clear the ground of rivals in the field of Scots poetry. But more significantly, it is from the so-called periphery, from South Africa, that Murray's Scots poetry, which MacDiarmid is both annihilating and adopting, comes.[70] Hugh

---

[69] C. M. Grieve, *Contemporary Scottish studies: First series* (London: Leonard Parsons, 1926), p. 35.
[70] The case for a cynical interpretation of Grieve's motives is strengthened by the fact that, in the same year that he penned his attack on Murray, when trying to persuade an academic to write an introduction to one of his books, Grieve wrote of 'the Scottish literary tradition in which I would fain to have a part – Hugh Haliburton, Charles Murray and Mrs Violet Jacob': Grieve to Herbert Grierson, 30 April 1925, in Bold (ed.), *Letters of MacDiarmid*, p. 307.

MacDiarmid, Scotland's most renowned twentieth-century poet, radical nationalist and Marxist, was in some degree the product of an encounter with Charles Murray, obscure writer of Aberdeenshire verse and pragmatic imperialist.

LAST YEARS: 1924–1941

Murray remained at his post in Pretoria and Cape Town until 1924, when he retired at the age of 60. The latter years of his life were to be full of ironies. For decades he had dreamed of return to the Vale of Alford. But his South African family found the idea of settling in the village not to their taste. Edith Murray complained that she would lack company and told Charles that their daughters did not like Alford; he commented 'I suppose it is too slow for them.' And Murray himself had developed tastes and sociabilities that village life could not cater for: 'I would miss bridge and golf – a golf course in Alford would make a great diff.'[71] The dream of return faded – the senior civil servant was not the village boy, and his family were not Aberdeenshire country folk. To add to Murray's problems, having invested shrewdly and successfully, he discovered that he had not reckoned on the levels of taxation to which he would be subject on permanently returning to Britain. He and Edith spent much of the late 1920s and early 1930s travelling the world as tax exiles.[72] At last they returned to Scotland, settling in Banchory. Charles Murray died on 21 April 1941, and was buried in Alford, under the hill of Bennachie, of which he had written:

> There's braver mountains ower the sea,
> An fairer haughs I've kent, but still.
> The Vale of Alford! Bennachie!
> Yon is the Howe, an' this is the Hill.

But he had not been able to live that dream; perhaps the 'braver mountains' of Africa had more of a pull on him than he cared to admit.

Murray was a man whose life reflected much broader trends amongst Scottish emigrants. Driven by a powerful ambition and a desire to overcome the humiliations of a youth spent in poverty, he attained a success in his colonial career that would have been impossible for him at home. In pursuing his objectives he was ruthlessly pragmatic, placing his social ascent above all ideological or sentimental considerations. Yet his

---

[71] Murray, Rome, to George Walker, 8 February 1926, MS 27266/92, NLS.
[72] Murray, Christchurch, New Zealand, to George Walker, 29 April 1930, MS 27266/122, NLS.

'exile' situation provided the context in which he generated a deeply felt vision of rural Scotland which he articulated in his verse. Through his writing, his presence looped back into Scotland itself, playing a significant role in the rise of a new cultural self-assertion.

In South Africa, it is still possible to find faint traces of the world Charles Murray and the Caledonians made. A declining band of weekend soldiers still march in kilts in the South African National Defence Force's 'Scottish' units; some schools still have pipe bands; Johannesburg's upper classes often take holidays in Scottish-fantasy fishing resorts on the eastern escarpment, casting for trout by day and drinking real whisky in *faux* crofts by night. Murray's professional mark is more distinct – many of the public buildings, schools, courtrooms and bridges, the construction of which he supervised, remain in daily use. President Thabo Mbeki directs the South African state from the offices that Murray built for Louis Botha's government in the Union Buildings.

In Scotland Murray's legacy is more complicated. The poets of medieval Scotland were called 'Makars' – a title some of his friends conferred on Charles Murray. His poems are largely forgotten today. But they left a political mark, albeit a largely unintended one, in contributing to the cultural milieu in which political nationalism could grow. As a Transvaal 'Makar', Murray, in a small way, became a 'maker' of modern Scotland.

CHAPTER 12

Epilogue: Imperial careering at home; Harriet Martineau on empire

Catherine Hall

While the figures who people this volume travelled and lived across the empire it was also possible to launch a career on the basis of imperial imaginings. In this final essay I focus on Harriet Martineau, a woman who in contrast to the actors on the previous pages wrote the empire entirely from the metropole. In the process she mapped differences, both temporal and spatial, reflected on colonialism and indigeneity, and constituted herself as a woman with authority.

It was fifteen years ago that I first came across the complicated history of Edward John Eyre and was fascinated by the ways in which his life both reflected and was constitutive of shifts in racial thinking across the British empire. My initial interest in him had been as the architect of the brutal policies associated with the aftermath of the revolt at Morant Bay in Jamaica in 1865. It did not take me long to discover Eyre's very different reputation in Australia – as farmer, unsuccessful explorer and resident magistrate on the Murray river. Then came his subsequent career as lieutenant governor in New Zealand before his first appointment in the Caribbean. This led me to questions about Australia and New Zealand in the 1820s and 30s. Having started out as an historian of Britain my field was rapidly expanding as I read not only on the Caribbean but also the early colonial history of Australia and New Zealand. This was the beginning of an education in the geographies of empire and what I called 'the mapping of difference': the ways in which colonised peoples were categorised and placed in the British imagination.[1] These 'mappings' were never fixed, always mobile and contested, subject to changes, whether associated with events across sites of empire (India in 1857, Jamaica in 1865) or 'at home' (the growth of 'scientific' racism, the declining

Acknowledgments: Thanks to Jane Rendall and Cora Kaplan.
[1] Catherine Hall, *Civilising subjects. Metropole and colony in the English imagination, 1830–1867* (Cambridge: Polity, 2002).

influence of abolitionism, the concentrations of poor Irish migrants in certain towns and cities). But the construction of 'grammars of difference' as Frederick Cooper and Ann Laura Stoler classically defined them, across metropole and colony, was critically connected to both time and place, to the exercise of colonial power and forms of indigenous resistance.[2]

Eyre arrived in Australia in the 1830s, a highpoint for humanitarian thinking. For him, aboriginal people were 'children of the wilds', lost in archaic time, waiting to be brought into the modern world, or perhaps primarily construed as victims of 'new times', to be cared for, protected and made dependent for as long as they survived. Australia was an undiscovered land, a 'vacant' land waiting for its explorers and settlers, its sheep and cattle, its modern peoples with their notions of property, labour, family and civilisation. New Zealand was rather different. Maori people in his estimation were more capable of assimilation as well as being more capable of collective forms of resistance to the encroachments of the colonisers. Indeed, the Maori Wars of the 1840s were a significant challenge to settler colonialism. But Eyre's time in New Zealand was personally difficult and, despite his exploration of the arid interior, Australia remained the temperate place to which he longed to return as he languished in the tropics in the 1850s, the place which in his mind could become most like England. St Vincent, his first port of call in the Caribbean, was his troubled encounter with the tropics and with free people of colour, both black and brown. These were not 'savages' who could be dismissed as from another time. They were making claims as independent producers, seeking representative rights, ever mindful of any attempt to return to anything akin to slavery. Meanwhile, conditions were changing in the metropole and the events in India in 1857, in particular, shifted the climate of racial thinking. Erstwhile liberals on questions of race called for revenge as they consumed the horrific tales of rape and cruelty that once 'docile' sepoys had supposedly committed. The ever-present threat of racial war magnified in the minds of white people in the Caribbean and when Eyre, by then governor of Jamaica, was confronted with the rioting in Morant Bay he was convinced that 'the blacks had risen'. His brutal response, supported by the vast majority of the white population on the island, provoked a major debate in the metropole as to the proper forms of colonial rule.

---

[2] Frederick Cooper and Ann Laura Stoler (eds.), *Tensions of empire: colonial cultures in a bourgeois world* (Berkeley: University of California Press, 1997), 'Between metropole and colony. Rethinking a research agenda', pp. 1–56.

Eyre's story pointed attention to the significance of time and place and to the intersections between individual histories and larger imperial processes. Individual stories can provide a lens through which to grasp how empire was lived by particular people, in particular places, at particular times. Individual stories of colonisers who crisscrossed the empire are particularly revealing in terms of the differentiated ways in which peoples and places were constructed in their minds. What were the differences between Aborigine and Maori peoples? How did they compare with 'Bushmen' and 'Hottentots'? What were the places that could most easily be made to look and feel like England? Which were those that represented ineffable difference? There are, of course, many biographies of key colonial officials, written in the nineteenth and early twentieth centuries, which span the empire but the concerns of these studies tend to be celebratory and their focus more on the imperial centre. Issues of difference – whether of race, gender or sexuality – were not their concern. As Leigh Dale explores so effectively in her textual study of the Grey mythology, these histories themselves need to be read sceptically. In the 1990s new approaches to imperial careers have paid more attention to the specificities of place. Bridget Brereton's study of the radical colonial lawyer John Gorrie, provides an excellent example of some of the issues that could be raised by looking at his time in the Caribbean, Mauritius and Fiji.[3] Similarly, Alex Tyrrell's work on the Methodist missionary Joseph Orton traced his life across Jamaica, Australia and New Zealand. Orton took what he had learned of 'natives' back to the metropole, reporting on what he had seen, commenting on the different characteristics of African, Aborigine and Maori peoples and helping to shape the mental maps of both metropolitans and colonials.[4] Inevitably such stories are partial, and only some kinds of people can be represented in these ways since life-history materials are more likely to be available for men than women, white people rather than those of colour, anti-colonial leaders rather than the rank and file, people with power rather than those without.[5] Such stories can never supersede other kinds of history

---

[3] Bridget Brereton, *Law, justice and empire. The colonial career of John Gorrie 1829–1892* (Kingston: University of the West Indies Press, 1997).

[4] Alex Tyrrell, *A sphere of benevolence. The life of Joseph Orton, Wesleyan Methodist missionary 1795–1842* (Melbourne: State Library of Victoria, 1993).

[5] A number of feminist historians have been particularly innovative in re-evaluating archives and the ways in which they can be used to get access to women's experiences. See particularly Antoinette Burton, *Dwelling in the archive. Women writing house, home and history in late colonial India* (Oxford: Oxford University Press, 2003) and 'Archive stories: gender in the making of imperial and colonial histories', in Philippa Levine (ed.), *Gender and empire* (Oxford: Oxford University Press,

writing: those that deal with economic processes, with class relations, with wars, states and nations. But economic processes depend on people – whether capitalists and labourers, or masters and slaves; armies, states and nations are all peopled, and a grasp of the individual and the subjective, how histories were lived, is as central to our understanding of the past as are larger-scale narratives.

The collaborative project that has produced this book on imperial careering has itself crossed erstwhile imperial boundaries and linked historical geographers, historians, anthropologists and literary scholars working and living in Australia, South Africa and Britain. It is much to be welcomed. The rewriting of imperial histories, which has been such a productive field of work in the last decade, has been fed by the different preoccupations of the different disciplines. Historical geographers have been especially helpful in theorising the spatialities of empire and the networks that crisscrossed it. Literary scholars have taught us to do detailed textual reading, to think carefully about the specificities of genre and the access that imaginative writing can give to fantasy. Anthropologists have been in the forefront of directing attention to material culture and historians have been concerned with temporalities and historical change. Cutting across these disciplinary preoccupations have been the concerns of feminist and postcolonial theory which have impacted so fruitfully on the writing of imperial histories. At the same time, the interest in rethinking empire across both the metropole and the erstwhile sites of empire has inspired specific questions: in Australia and Canada the issue of indigenous peoples; in South Africa the complex colonial contestations that resulted in apartheid and eventually a new nation; in Britain the deconstruction of the myth of the homogeneous 'island race'.

The essays in this volume deal with a variety of men and women who lived and worked across imperial sites. Between them they traversed Australia, New Zealand, Canada, Cape colony, the Transvaal, the Caribbean, India, Fiji, Mauritius and the United Kingdom. Two of them

2004), pp. 281–93; Durba Ghosh, 'Decoding the nameless: gender, subjectivity and historical methodologies in reading the archives of colonial India', in Kathleen Wilson (ed.), *A new imperial history. Culture, identity and modernity in Britain and the empire 1660–1840* (Cambridge, Cambridge University Press, 2004), pp. 281–98. Individual histories are, of course, not the only way to track trans-imperial processes. Tony Ballantyne, Alan Lester and Philippa Levine, for example, have all developed ways of doing cross-imperial studies, whether focused on Aryanism, settler discourse or prostitution and venereal disease. Tony Ballantyne, *Orientalism and race. Aryanism in the British empire* (Basingstoke: Palgrave, 2002); Alan Lester, 'Settler discourse and the circuits of empire', *History Workshop Journal* **54** (2002), pp. 25–48; Philippa Levine, *Prostitution, race and politics: policing venereal disease in the British empire* (London: Routledge, 2003).

ventured even further afield, beyond the boundaries of the British empire – to Panama, the Crimea, Venezuela and other parts of central and South America. All of them, bar Mrs Seacole, came from or married into the United Kingdom, and all, again except Mrs Seacole, expected to make their fortunes or exercise power in other ways – over the souls and/or bodies of subject peoples of different kinds.

Their stories connect with larger stories of empire. Those with Scottish or Irish backgrounds or connections remind us of the critical importance of the unions with Scotland and Ireland to the making of the British empire. Richard Bourke came from the Protestant ascendancy and followed a classic route into the army and then to the new colonies of white settlement. He combined his Irishness with Britishness, as Zoë Laidlaw argues, and his knowledge of Ireland framed his understanding of empire. George Grey's experience in Ireland, as Leigh Dale explores through her rereading of the multiple narratives of Grey's formation, was critical to his colonial policies, but probably not in the humanitarian-inspired ways that previous scholars have imagined. Unlike Eyre he showed little sign of adaptation as he moved from colony to colony. Rather, Dale suggests, his ideas about 'natives' were too rigid to be open to change. For Gregor MacGregor, born in Edinburgh, the military provided access to a life across empires. His is a story, as Matthew Brown shows, that has been filtered out of national histories and can only be recovered once historians turn their attention to transnational and trans-imperial processes. Both anti-colonialist (under Bolívar) and colonialist (on the Mosquito coast) he is a complex figure whose story draws attention to crossed boundaries. Ishbel Marjoribanks married into the Scottish aristocracy and as Lady Aberdeen was to be the first lady of Canada and Ireland. Arthur Gordon came from the Scottish aristocracy. Charles Murray came from Aberdeen and became celebrated as a poet of Scotland. As Jonathan Hyslop argues, his life demonstrates the kinds of career opportunities that empire could offer and confirms John Mackenzie's view that empire provided a means for the Scots to assert a distinctive identity in relation to England. What these Irish and Scots shared was a sense that empire could offer opportunities beyond those 'at home'.

Those connected to the military (Bourke, Grey and MacGregor), remind us of the vital importance of the army, and indeed the navy (not represented here) to empire. Those connected to the aristocracy (Gordon, Lady Aberdeen and Lady Curzon) remind us of the significance of empire as a place where aristocrats could reinvent themselves, but never outside the boundaries of racial hierarchies. Gordon, as Laurence Brown demonstrates, could use his contacts as a political insider to advantage. His career across Trinidad, Mauritius and Fiji points attention both to the significance of local conditions in the translation of colonial policies and to the ways in which ideas about the different qualities of 'natives' were transported from one imperial site to another. Lady Aberdeen and Lady Curzon occupied that difficult space of the 'incorporated wife'. Lady Aberdeen assumed the rights of a grand political lady and as Val McLeish shows attempted to intervene in colonial society, whether in Canada or Ireland. The political context in which she was operating, however, changed and she was unwilling to change with it. The American-born Lady Curzon learned political confidence in India. She was able to exercise influence in the metropole, as Nicola Thomas demonstrates, in the classic mode of the aristocratic woman, that is in the dining rooms and salons of the élite.

The two missionaries – Lancelot Threlkeld and William Shrewsbury – remind us of how vital missionary testimony and networks were to the critiques of empire. In the early nineteenth century many missionaries were critical of colonial power and policy. They were crucial to the struggle over slavery, for example, because of the evidence they could produce that challenged the plantocracy's account of a benevolent system.[6] Threlkeld with his evangelical zeal and sense of righteousness is typical of this early period of missionary endeavour and as Anna Johnston argues he disturbed each of the colonial spaces in which he worked. His identification with the marginalised and the dispossessed and his critique of hierarchical relations, whether within his own missionary society or in the colonial societies he encountered, rubbed up against those who were concerned for a quieter life. In drawing our attention to the importance of the written record as a site for conflicts over colonial morality she points us to the ways in which humanitarians privileged language. Sited thousands of miles from the place where colonial policy was made (though of course it was always translated locally with varying results) they had to rely on the power of their written testimony. Missionary work, like Colonial-Office positions, meant geographical mobility and a changing sense of place and belonging as both these case studies

---

[6] Mary Turner, *Slaves and missionaries. The disintegration of Jamaican slave society, 1787–1834* (Urbana: University of Illinois Press, 1982); Emilia Viotti da Costa, *Crowns of glory, tears of blood. The Demerara slave rebellion of 1823* (Oxford: Oxford University Press, 1994); Hall, *Civilising subjects*; for an account of the shifts in missionary thinking in relation to empire over the nineteenth century see Susan Thorne, *Congregational missions and the making of an imperial culture in nineteenth-century England* (Stanford: Stanford University Press, 1999).

demonstrate. Shrewsbury's understanding of 'natives' shifted significantly with his move from the West Indies to South Africa. He was shocked by the power of black men in Xhosa country and while initially sympathetic this did not last. His failure to convert Africans led to increasing disillusionment, and this, combined with family tragedies and sharpening tensions between Xhosa and settlers led to a weakening of the humanitarian vision of his earlier years. As Alan Lester and David Lambert argue, these kinds of cases help us to think about the relation between imperial discourses operating across the empire and the specific local outcomes of colonial encounters. Figures such as Shrewsbury, they suggest, mediated between these scales during their lifetimes and an analysis of their lives enables us to do the same (this volume, pp. 88–112).

Finally, Mrs Seacole reminds us of all those women and men we would like to know more about. Herself a product of the colonial encounter, she struggled to make a place without, as Anita Rupprecht argues, being 'named', being categorised as a particular kind of subject, being placed as one of the colonised, subjected to the grammar of difference.

While the men and women documented in these essays travelled and lived across the empire, others living in the metropole occupied imperial spaces and places in their imagination. For empire was part of their everyday world. Commodities, peoples, ideas all circulated across the myriad sites of empire and knowledge of other peoples and places along with fantasies of difference were a part of metropolitan life: nothing special, just ordinary. The imperial careers documented in this book involved living in colonial spaces for extended periods, encountering 'natives' and settlers, finding and making a place in another place, telling tales of themselves and others, of what they have seen and heard and dreamed of. Their stories are necessarily interactive and sometimes involved personal transformations. An openness to change, or alternatively a rigidity and inflexibility in the face of new peoples and places, might be connected both with individual histories and subjective time – the time of the lifecycle – and with colonial time – the specificities of colonial relations, the issues of power and resistance – in particular places at particular times. While those living in the metropole did not experience the everyday realities of colonial relations in the ways that the subjects of this volume did, yet they too constructed mental maps of empire and grammars of difference, they too made stories of what they knew and imagined what they did not. These mental maps were often informed by the reports of colonial officials, military and naval officers, missionaries, merchants and the myriad others who produced written or visual representations of empire based on their experiences and what they had made of them. But they were reimagined and reconfigured in the representations of writers and artists who had never left Britain yet saw the empire as part of their world and sometimes utilised the unknown as sites of fantasy and experimentation.

Harriet Martineau was one of those who imagined the empire for both metropolitan and colonial readerships. Yet her imperial careering was done from home.[7] Born in Norwich in 1802 to a prosperous Unitarian manufacturing family, she enjoyed a good education thanks to the rational principles of her parents. From an early age she loved to read. Her deafness and associated sense of distance made intellectual activities particularly pleasurable. Encouraged by her beloved younger brother James, she began to write. In the economic crisis of 1825 the family business suffered greatly and then collapsed in 1829. At the same time her father died, defeated by the collapse of his business, and James Worthington, the young man to whom Martineau had become engaged, albeit with many scruples, went mad and died. In her autobiographical account written at a critical moment in her later life, when she thought her days were numbered and she wanted to author the construction of herself into a public intellectual, Martineau defined this horrific sequence of events as an opportunity rather than a disaster. It was the moment when she could escape the limitations of genteel femininity and begin to write to earn a living. She was convinced that 'the best happiness in this world is found in strenuous exertion on a right principle'.[8] She discovered her pleasure in being single, and in 'substantial, laborious and serious occupation', and was determined to overcome all obstacles and 'force my way to that power of public speech of which I believed myself more or less worthy'. 'My business in life', she wrote retrospectively, in celebratory mode of her independence, 'has been to think and learn, and to speak out with absolute freedom what I have thought and learned.'[9] She had already had some success in the 1820s with essays and reviews and after writing some short tales based on her knowledge of manufacturing and wages she became convinced that it would be possible to teach the principles of the new science of political economy in a similar form.

[7] In the mid-1830s Martineau went to the USA, in the 1840s she travelled in the Middle East, and twice she went to Ireland. She published on these travels. She wrote about India and other parts of empire without ever seeing them.
[8] Harriet Martineau, *Selected letters*, Valerie Sanders (ed.) (Oxford: Clarendon, 1990), p. 16.
[9] Harriet Martineau, *Autobiography* (London: Virago, 1983), 2 vols. Vol. I, pp. 133, 147.

This was the origin of her spectacularly successful *Illustrations of political economy*, a series of twenty-four tales in monthly instalments which to the astonishment of the many publishers who had evinced no interest in such a series, took the market by storm. Her plan, discussed just before tea one afternoon in the family home, was approved by both her brother and her mother – a critical necessity if she were to be able to pursue it. Martineau later recalled how in 1829 she had believed that while she had no genius,

various circumstances have led me to think more accurately and read more extensively than some women, I believe that I may so write on subjects of universal concern as to inform some minds and stir up others ... My aim is to become a forcible and elegant writer on moral and religious subjects, so as to be useful to refined as well as unenlightened minds.[10]

Thrilled by the excitements surrounding the contentious politics of reform in 1831 and 1832 she longed, as she wrote to Francis Place to be 'doing something with the pen, since no other means of action in politics are in a woman's power'.[11] While her brother could hope for a public platform through the Unitarian ministry she had to rely on writing as a way of exercising influence.

Martineau was convinced that a public awaited her – and longed for the kind of writing that she could do. Many women writers had pointed the way, from Hannah More onwards. More recently Mrs Marcet had demonstrated that it was possible for a woman author to write about political economy in such a way as to disarm the criticism of those men who thought women incapable of dealing with such topics.[12] Their forte was to popularise. Martineau's special gift was with words. 'To her', wrote her friend Maria Weston Chapman, 'words are nothing distant from life.'[13] Words were a way of making a difference in the world. In the heated debates over new theories of economy and society in the 1830s there were few educationalists and Martineau saw this as her role. She could become, as her friend and mentor W. J. Fox described her,

---

[10] Martineau, *Autobiography*, Vol. II, p. 166.
[11] Cited in R. J. Webb, *Harriet Martineau. A radical Victorian* (London: Heinemann, 1960), p. 114.
[12] See Judith Newton's discussion of the gender hierarchy around the *Edinburgh Review* and the limited tolerance for women writers who strayed on to 'serious' subjects, 'Sex and political economy in the *Edinburgh Review*', in *Starting over. Feminism and the politics of cultural critique* (Ann Arbor: University of Michigan Press, 1994). See also Jane Rendall, 'Bluestockings and reviewers: gender, power and culture in Britain, c.1800–1830', *Nineteenth Century Contexts* **26**, 4 (Dec. 2004), pp. 355–74.
[13] Cited in Shelagh Hunter, *Harriet Martineau: the poetics of moralism* (Aldershot: Scolar Press, 1995), p. 19.

'a national instructor'.[14] Teaching the new ideas of significant men was an appropriate medium for women, whereas theorising for themselves was not. Martineau could be the no-nonsense voice, the schoolmistress, who could demonstrate the truths of political economy through fable and example. Adam Smith's *The wealth of nations* was a wonderful book, as she wrote in her preface to the tales, but it was 'not fitted or designed to teach the science to the great mass of the people'. 'We want the science in a familiar, practical form', she wrote, 'we want its *picture*.' The importance of good domestic economy in the family was now understood, but 'that larger family – the nation' was not as yet so well managed. Narrative, she argued, was the best way to teach political economy, and her work would have relevance to all. Indeed, it was dedicated 'to the total population of the empire'.[15] In the struggle to tackle the visible ills of British society in the 1830s political economy was hailed by its protagonists as the way forward. Only proper understanding of social and economic principles could deliver lasting reform.

The tales were welcomed by many: 'all difficulty about getting a hearing from the public for what I felt I had to say' was over.[16] The scheme was to work systematically through the principles of Smith, Malthus, Ricardo and Mill. Martineau's plan was to map out the key principles, do the relevant reading, make a summary of the principles that the tale must cover (this she saw as the hardest and most important part of the labour), and decide how to embody these principles in people and places. The grammar of difference she produced in these tales both in relation to the nation (but that is not my concern here), and the connections between nation and empire, illustrates the ways in which one white middle-class English woman could career across the empire in her mind, mapping its peoples and places for her readers.

Up to the early 1830s relatively few white women were traversing the empire.[17] Those who did were mainly the wives and daughters of colonial officials, missionaries, merchants, military and naval men and the occasional female adventurer. Even fewer of these travellers and sojourners

---

[14] Webb, *Martineau*, p. 93.

[15] Harriet Martineau, *Illustrations of political economy* (London: Charles Fox, 1834), Vol. I, 'Preface', pp. x, xv.

[16] Martineau, *Autobiography*, Vol. I, p. 180.

[17] The numbers increased from the 1830s with emigration to the new colonies of white settlement, with the increasing use by missionary societies of women teachers and later missionaries, and after 1857 the recognition that one condition of a secure imperial presence in India was more white women. See the relevant essays in Philippa Levine (ed.), *Gender and empire*.

wrote about it for publication. Those who did were liable to encounter disapproval if they strayed on to subjects deemed unsuitable for a woman – as, for example, Maria Graham (whose work Martineau was to draw on). Graham, from a Scottish family, travelled with her father to India in 1809 and married a Scottish naval officer. Her *Letters on India* were frowned upon and her later travel writings on Brazil and Chile which discussed political matters were again deemed inappropriate by critics in the metropole.[18] Fiction or forms of what might be described as domestic travel writing, where no claims were made to deal with the serious matters written about by men, were the recognised genres for women. Mrs Sherwood's tales drawing upon her life in India had considerable success as did Emily Eden's account of her time in the governor's residence in Calcutta.

Since Martineau was writing fictional tales, she could hope to avoid the disapproval of the critics. Questions of colonisation and empire were significant to the political economists. Five of the twenty-four tales dealt with these issues and ranged across imperial sites. This was not an add on to the really important issues such as capital, labour and population. Rather, issues of empire were an integral aspect of political economy. Smith's championing of free labour and free trade, for example, and his critique of slavery and colonial monopoly, or Malthus' theories of population were basic aspects of the new science. James Mill recognised that colonies had important functions. Furthermore, by the time Martineau was writing, the efforts of Edward Gibbon Wakefield to popularise new schemes of colonial settlement were just beginning to have an impact and Australia was being reconfigured as a suitable site for respectable migrants.[19] Martineau's tales offered a simplified geography of empire for the great reading public. And unlike much previous writing it offered a secular utilitarian vision that recognised the centrality of commerce to civilisation, rather than an evangelical one. The first tale of the series, *Life in the wilds* (1832), was set in the Cape. It was concerned with some of the most basic principles of political economy: the centrality of labour to wealth creation, the significance of unproductive as well as productive labour, the importance of the division of labour. *Ireland* (1832)

---

[18] Jane Rendall, 'The condition of women, feminism and the empire in nineteenth-century Britain', in Catherine Hall and Sonya Rose (eds.), *At home with the empire* (Cambridge: Cambridge University Press, forthcoming).

[19] Bernard Semmel, *The rise of free trade imperialism. Classical political economy, the empire of free trade and imperialism 1750–1850* (Cambridge: Cambridge University Press, 1970); *The Liberal ideal and the demons of empire. Theories of imperialism from Adam Smith to Lenin* (Baltimore: Johns Hopkins University Press, 1993).

provided a critique of land policies and a disquisition on their effects in terms of indigence and immorality. *Demerara* (1833) set in that eponymous colony, later Guyana, taught the human and economic costs of slavery both for the masters and the enslaved. *Cinnamon and pearls* (1833), situated in Ceylon, critiqued monopoly as a colonial system. *Homes abroad* (1834), set in Van Diemen's Land, later Tasmania, argued for the benefits of well-organised voluntary emigration. Unreflected upon by the political economists, for this was too commonsensical a matter to merit the attention of political theorists, and indeed by Martineau in her summaries of principles, was another division of labour – that between the sexes. In these tales Martineau had much to say about a proper and desirable gender order, one in which women could be useful rather than useless. Political economy provided the set of tools that she used to think about the economic and social world, but her tools were extended as she reflected as a woman on the society she knew and the inadequacy of its guiding principles.

Martineau's preoccupation with a wider world, more specifically that ruled by Britain, was hardly something unusual, for issues connected with empire were part of the everyday politics of these years. Her *Illustrations* were written between 1831–4, when definitions of nation were themselves intimately associated with empire – whether in relation to Ireland, to the West Indies or to India.[20] Martineau had first begun to think about a possible series of tales in 1827 when Ireland was at the forefront of the imperial imagination. The activities of the Catholic Association were increasingly troubling to the governing classes and raised critical issues as to how the 'sister isle' required different forms of rule. By 1829 fears of civil war in Ireland led to the granting of emancipation and the consequent split in the Tory party: a dramatic example of the impact of a colony on the metropole. In 1831 Martineau used some prize money she had won to go to Ireland and stay with her brother James in Dublin. It was there, away from home, that she sketched out the series. Between 1830–2 the question of parliamentary reform dominated the political agenda and whether she was in Norwich, London, or Dublin, Martineau was very well aware of the dramas that were being played out. While publishers told her that the public was too preoccupied with reform and cholera for them to think her series a good financial bet she begged to

---

[20] Catherine Hall, 'The rule of difference: gender, class and empire in the making of the 1832 Reform Act', in Ida Blom, Karen Hagemann and Catherine Hall (eds.), *Gendered nations. Nationalism and gender order in the long nineteenth century* (Oxford: Berg, 2000).

differ. During the days of May in 1832 when Britain seemed close to revolution she noted that her books were selling even more. 'Everything indeed justified my determination', she wrote, 'not to defer a work which was the more wanted the more critical became the affairs of the nation.'[21]

Meanwhile, in the wake of the major rebellion of the enslaved in Jamaica in 1831 abolition became an ever-more pressing issue and across Britain antislavery groups organised meetings and petitions demanding an end to the 'stain upon the nation'. Once parliamentary reform had been won it was a matter of time before slavery was abolished, as it was in 1833. While that legislation was going through parliament the new Charter Act for India was also being debated with the two central issues under discussion being the ending of the East India Company's monopoly of the China trade and the form of government appropriate to India. This complex political conjuncture, when questions of political representation at home and in the empire were being intensively debated, provided the context for Martineau's writing. Empire was integral to the thinking of political economists and Martineau had no trouble in imaginatively taking herself to varied imperial sites as the places most suited to the principles she desired to expound. Careering across the empire *in her mind* was an ordinary thing to do.

In addition to her enthusiasm for political economy, Martineau was still at this stage in her life a Unitarian and was part of Norwich's radical dissenting culture with its commitment to better relations between the classes and the races. Being a provincial was important to her intellectual and political formation. Like many abolitionists she espoused the view that all men and women were potentially equal. It was culture and education, not innate differences, that marked off civilisation from barbarism. (It was only much later, in the aftermath of the events in India of 1857, that she faltered significantly in this view.) She had also become deeply attached in the 1820s to the necessarian philosophy of Joseph Priestley. Mental and moral life were subject to natural laws and for every effect there was a cause which could be uncovered by rational inquiry. A self-disciplined search for enlightenment was each individual's responsibility – and Martineau could assist others in the great project of education. Parts of the tales now read very didactically, with wooden characters embodying principles, lengthy set-piece conversations when 'correct ideas' were painstakingly laid out, and happy endings with resolutions of all conflicts and hopes of potential prosperity for all. But there were also

---

[21] Martineau, *Autobiography*, Vol. I, p. 216.

lively plots, evocative descriptions, interesting characters and powerful and dramatic passages – signs of the relatively successful novelist who was to come. John Stuart Mill, no favourite of Martineau's (and the feeling was mutual), thought that she made nonsense of political economy by reducing it to its most vulgar precepts and carrying all to their logical conclusions.[22] But this was the writing of a young woman, locating a market, establishing her audience, certain about her principles, not yet open to more mature or complex reflection. This case study of Martineau is not dealing with a lifetime's writing, or an imperial career on the scale of a Grey, a Bourke, a Shrewsbury or a Threlkeld. Martineau never lived outside the metropolis, never interacted with the native peoples of the empire. Yet her tales can be read for the glimpse they provide of a particular metropolitan vision, at a particular moment, of the peoples and places of empire and the relation between nation and empire.

Martineau sought information for her accounts of places and peoples from a variety of sources.[23] She was a convinced Baconian, insistent on the importance of deduction of theories from an accumulation of facts, which could then be applied to the explanation of new facts.[24] Accuracy was, therefore, important to her. She might not have been to any of these places (for even her story about Ireland was set far from Dublin), but she would do her best to establish authenticity. Blue Books and information acquired through personal connections were her stock-in-trade. The success of the series led many to write to her sending her suggestions about further tales and sharing material with her. For the Cape she read Lichtenstein's *Travels in Southern Africa*, for Demerara she read Edwards (presumably the historian Bryan Edwards) and the leading Liverpool abolitionist Mr Cropper provided her with useful statistics, for Ceylon she had the good fortune to meet Sir Alexander Johnston who had just returned from a stint as governor and was delighted to talk with her, entertain her together with a collection of Ceylonese cognoscenti, and send her a carriage full of material.[25] While the tales were structured around the principles which were laid out at the end of the story, they also depicted peoples and places. Martineau's imagined geography of empire gave her readers a picture of assorted colonies – their landscape, economic potential and native peoples. Each of the tales told of the impact of empire on both colonisers and colonised, critiqued existing

---

[22] Webb, *Martineau*, p. 109.
[23] On her use of political economy see Claudia Orazem, *Political economy and fiction in the early works of Harriet Martineau* (Frankfurt am Main: Peter Lang, 1999).
[24] Webb, *Martineau*, p. 74.   [25] Martineau, *Autobiography*, Vol. I, pp. 197–9, 245.

systems, and looked forward to better forms of colonialism (rather than critiquing empire as such). At the same time international trade outside of the frame of empire was itself seen as having civilising effects. A future world would be informed by both political economy and Martineau's own thinking on 'the woman question'. Being convinced of the pleasures of independent thought and of useful work herself she sought that for others – though her emigrant women were for the most part to be satisfied with domestic labour, and planters' wives and daughters with household management rather than the management of the nation.

In *Life in the wilds*, the story least shaped by immediate political debate, the action takes place in a small and remote settlement in the north of the Cape colony. There is a delightful climate, good air and fertile soil but many settlers are put off by 'the Bushmen', 'a race of men more fearsome than wild beasts and full of cunning'. These 'Bushmen' only appear briefly at the beginning of the story and it is their savage action in attacking the settlement, looting, burning and killing some of its members, seizing cattle and tools, that provides the backdrop to the tale. 'The Bushmen', Martineau informs her readers,

were the original possessors of much of the country about the Cape, which the British and the Dutch have since taken for their own. The natives were hunted down like so many wild beasts. This usage naturally made them fierce and active in their revenge. The hardships they have undergone have affected their bodily make also; and their short stature and clumsy form are not, as some suppose, a sufficient proof that they are of an inferior race to the men they make war upon.[26]

Here was her conviction that differences between peoples were cultural and climatic not biological. Indeed, she suggested, if Europeans had been driven into the mountains in the way in which the Bushmen had, they would probably have ended up looking like them. Having effected their savagery the 'Bushmen' are dismissed from the story. Martineau's real concern is the settlers. Faced with the loss of their homes and stock they have to begin again from the beginning, learning the most basic lessons of frontiersmen and women as to the need for human cooperation and the centrality of labour, both of head and of hand, to survival and prosperity. This is a story about how to be a good coloniser – industrious, prudent, thoughtful, and ordered, valuing labour whether productive or unproductive, establishing clear divisions between the work of women and

---

[26] Harriet Martineau, *Life in the wilds*, in Deborah Logan (ed.), *Harriet Martineau on empire* (London: Pickering and Chatto, 2004), 5 vols. Vol. I, *The empire question*, p. 5.

men, girls and boys, and recognising the possibilities for increased wealth and better lives. This was a story for potential emigrants – those who were attracted by the new possibilities of settlement on the eastern Cape, for example, and for those at home who needed to be reminded of the basic principles of cooperation and the division of labour.

Ireland was written after Martineau's visit to Dublin in 1831. Already it was crystal clear that emancipation was no panacea. The accumulated grievances that O'Connell had articulated as to be resolved through emancipation were again in the ascendant. A year after the publication of the story, in 1833, the threats to life and property posed by desperate tenants were to be met with a fearsome Coercion Act. Martineau's preface showed an awareness of the volatility of the situation in Ireland and expressed a hope (one that was not to be met) that 'the government may ere long turn from enforcing obnoxious laws to fostering the resources of the country'.[27]

In *Ireland* it is the clever young woman, Dora, who carries hope for the future of that benighted country – and that future will be in a new land to which she is transported. Dora is born in the Glen of the Echoes, on the coast of the west of Ireland. While the Cape was represented as a landscape of potential plenty, Ireland is bleak in the extreme, at least for the poor, the echoes those of grief and misery. The glen is part bog, part cultivated patches of land. There is scarcely a tree or a shrub to be seen. The huts of the poverty-stricken tenants, hopelessly exploited by landlords and the church, are 'more like tufts of black turf than human dwellings'.[28] The system of tenancy has ensured a level of subsistence barely above that of the beasts. The tenants of the glen in her story, reduced by years of political injury to 'servile dependence', face multiple miseries – imposed by middlemen, absentee landlords, Catholic priests (despite their efforts to support the peasantry) and the established church. Dora and her parents lose their home, their goods and chattels and their livestock. Dora is saved by her lover Dan, who has returned from England having earned a little money. But like her thoughtless and uneducated father he fails to secure their future against the wiles of the landlord and they too are driven from house and home. Dora and her

[27] *Ibid.*, p. 5.
[28] Harriet Martineau, *Ireland*, in *ibid.*, Vol. IV, *The Irish question*, p. 8. On the relation between homes and huts see Alison Twells, '"Let us begin well at home": class, ethnicity and Christian motherhood in the writing of Hannah Kilham, 1774–1832', in Eileen Janes Yeo (ed.), *Radical femininity. Women's self-representation in the public sphere* (Manchester: Manchester University Press, 1998).

mother are reduced to living in a cave on a cliff where the mother dies having given her last feeble efforts to support her daughter in her labour. Faced with the destruction of all their efforts her father and husband resort to drunkenness, illegality and violence. Dan, the young Irishman who has been to England, has that 'spirit of enterprise' which his people are distinguished by when there is hope of 'equitable recompense'. But once ruined he becomes a whiteboy, for 'when there was an end of justice there was an end of law'.[29] He persuades Dora (ever loyal to her family), and unlike the rest of them literate, to write a threatening letter for them. She is seized, tried and sentenced to transportation. As she is removed from the courthouse she speaks of the oppression that leads to violence and despair: 'the school in which my husband and I learned rebellion', she says, 'was the bleak rock, where famine came to be our teacher'.[30] But she is hurried out of the courtroom. Yet it is Dora who represents hope in this story – in her capacity for education, her attention to conscience, and her removal to Australia.

The hard lessons of the political economists about Ireland are carried by the young Alexander Russo, 'just from college', the son of one of the local landowners.[31] In conversations with his father, the knowledgeable and well-educated son asks leading questions, revealing the inadequacies of established views on security of property, capital investment, and overpopulation and emigration. This device of the young man with new and correct ideas is one that Martineau greatly likes: while young 'native' women could be symbols of hope it is young Englishmen who can propound the truths of the new science. It is intriguing to wonder whether the irony of the woman writer, seeking a place in the public world through popularising the works of great men and ventriloquising their ideas through the confident mouths of young men, would have been enjoyed by her women readers.

Demerara, Martineau's antislavery tale, was written when abolition was just won in Britain. But abolitionists continued to be concerned not only with the system of apprenticeship that was to be introduced in the West Indies, but also with slavery in America. Demerara, as a particular colonial space, had surfaced most significantly for the British in 1823 when the death of the missionary John Smith, languishing in gaol after a major rebellion of the enslaved, had been taken up by the antislavery

---

[29] *Ibid.*, pp. 22–3. 'Whiteboy' was the term used for rural agitators in Ireland in the early C19 on account of the white shirts they wore.
[30] *Ibid.*, p. 65.   [31] *Ibid.*, p. 20.

lobby (see chapter 3). Large public meetings, petitions and pamphlets had been organised to publicise the appalling conditions of slavery. During the 1820s abolitionist literature had poured off the presses highlighting the plight of the enslaved. A significant strand represented a sanitised and sentimental version of 'the negro' and Martineau was determined that her depiction should be more realistic. It was important, she argued in her preface, to tackle this emotive subject with reason, for 'the most stirring eloquence issues from the calmest logic'.[32] The system of slavery made the enslaved revengeful, selfish, mean, treacherous, hypocritical, indolent, conceited and sensual: she would paint it like it was. This destructive system contrasted sharply with the beauties of the tropical paradise onto which it had been engrafted:

the groves of cedar and mahogany, of the wild cotton-tree and the fig, form an assemblage of majestic columns, roofed by a canopy of foliage which the sun never penetrates, while the winds pass through and come and go as they list. In the richest regions of this department of the globe, the cane-fields look flourishing in the season, and coffee plantations clothe the sides of the hills. All inanimate things look bright; and birds of gay plumage and animals of strange forms and habits add to the interest and beauty of the scene.[33]

All inanimate things looked bright, but despondency, gloom and listlessness characterised most of the inhabitants of the colony. Alfred and Mary Bruce, the son and daughter of the owner of a coffee plantation, return to Demerara having been sent to be educated in England. They represent the voices of reason, humanity, education and civilisation, the progressive voice of the mother country, in contrast to the decadence of the planters who have degenerated in the closed West Indian world. The sun shines beautifully but the house is badly managed, the servants barely clothed; Mrs Bruce pale and vapid, yet dressed as if to go to a ball. Mr Bruce has a reputation as a kind master, his slaves only 'lightly whipped' yet still indolent. A neighbour Mitchelson, whose plantation is called 'Paradise', employs a cruel overseer renowned for his brutality. Yet whatever the punishments the enslaved will not work hard. They in turn are cruel to those below them, persecuting defenceless children and stealing from each other for 'slavery is the school of tyranny . . . the most dreadful lot on earth is to be the slave of slaves'.[34] Martineau's black figures are not Uncle Toms, suffering all with Christian fortitude. Rather some are selfish and mean, others struggling through rage and suffering to

---

[32] Harriet Martineau, *Demerara*, in Logan (ed.), *Martineau on empire*, Vol. I, p. 69.
[33] *Ibid.*, p. 71.   [34] *Ibid.*, p. 93.

realise their human potential. They are men and women with names and voices, thoughts and feelings, each with a story of a ruined life. Slavery is not only a doomed economic system, it also wrecks domestic life. Men could not protect their wives or children. 'A black man must be first a slave and then a man' says the young African Willie, who is determined not to marry.

A white woman has nobody to rule her but her husband, and nobody can hurt her without his leave; but a slave's wife must obey her master before her husband; and he cannot save her from being flogged.

'Slaves cannot love', for human relations are destroyed.[35] Slavery makes masters into tyrants, mistresses forget their household duties. The planters live in fear because of the hatred they have generated, the enslaved long for revenge, violence and brutality is the undertow of the whole society. Only the young people from England with their energy and clear thinking can save this benighted place. Alfred demonstrates the effectiveness of wages as an incentive for work, Mary vows to get the household economy in order as she has learned at home and support her father through his financial difficulties. 'I am glad I was never persuaded to send any of my children to England', says Mitchelson. 'No man is fit to be a West Indian planter who has had what is called a good education in England.'[36] The tropics bring degeneration with them, as Mary Prince argued in her *History*, published two years previously, and Brontë was to evoke so dramatically in *Jane Eyre*. Something happened to Britons when they got there and West Indians were not really Britons: only the English could be relied upon. Both colonisers and colonised are ruined by the wretched system they inhabit.

If the enslaved of Martineau's imagination are more fully imagined than those of much abolitionist literature and are granted some agency, her Cingalese characters in *Cinammon and pearls* reproduce some familiar tropes of 'the East'. They are granted 'grace' and 'indolence of demeanour', they lack violent passions and have collapsed into despair and hopelessness. Despite the extraordinary beauty and fertility of their land, another veritable paradise, they are abject.[37] Riven with superstitions, they live in 'a state of barbarism' with no incentive to toil and no capacity to think of the future thanks to the evils of colonial monopoly.[38] It is their

---

[35] *Ibid.*, p. 100. [36] *Ibid.*, p. 137.
[37] Martineau, *Cinammon and pearls*, in Logan (ed.), *Martineau on empire*, Vol. I, p. 174.
[38] *Ibid.*, p. 157.

poverty that makes them dishonest and their religion, whether Christian, Hindu, Buddhist or some amalgam, is incapable of inculcating them with proper principles. Whether diving for pearls or working on the cinnamon farms their enterprise and hope are destroyed by the cruel iniquities of the monopoly system. The duskily beautiful heroine, Marana, riven with superstition and fear, is ever watchful of her husband Rayo's safety. It is he that takes the risks and commits crimes against the monopolists. It is she who tends him, seeks help for him when he is reduced to complete dependency because of leprosy, and is willing to learn lessons from Father Anthony. It is the 'native woman' in Martineau's story, just as in *Ireland*, that represents the potential of the island.

But if this form of colonialism has degraded the natives, it has, as in Demerara, damaged the colonisers too. Mr Carr, the East India Company agent on the cinnamon plantation, has learned a haughty manner with his servile dependants, and passed this bad example on to his precocious daughter, Alice. In her grandma's field in England she could be simple Alice Carr: in Ceylon the 'black people' bowed before her and treated her as if she were a princess. Her mother, meanwhile, lived in indolence and luxury, anathema to Martineau. Mrs Carr,

did not know that she had ever enjoyed her way of life more ... than since she had come to Ceylon. She liked lying down for the greater part of the day, and being sure of seeing something beautiful from the verandah when she could exert herself to look abroad from it. She liked being fanned by the punkah, and waited upon by five times as many servants as she wanted, and amused by Alice, and flattered by her husband's station; none of the troubles of which devolved upon her.[39]

Interestingly, in this tale it is the American missionaries, husband and wife, who speak for reason and humanity.

Reflecting perhaps on the Charter Act of 1833 which abolished the East India Company's monopoly on the China trade, Martineau settled for a happy ending with the monopoly on cinnamon abandoned and the Cingalese enthusiastically looking forward to the time when 'every man should sit under his vine and his fig-tree, and none should make him afraid'.[40] Those English who are wise, comments the Christian Father Anthony who has struggled to inculcate the virtues of honesty and obedience amongst his flock, see 'that to make a colony poor is to make it unprofitable, and that colonies cannot be very rich while they are dependent'. Colonies should be cherished until they could take care of

[39] *Ibid.*, p. 187.   [40] *Ibid.*, p. 201.

themselves: to do otherwise would be folly. 'It is as if every man here should keep his grown-up son in the bondage of childhood. Such fathers and sons can never be prosperous and virtuous.'[41] Again, colonial monopoly is the wrong form of colonialism. The natural resources of the island should benefit its inhabitants. If the Cingalese could enjoy the fruits of their labour they would soon learn to understand comfort, care for luxuries and assume the duties and desires of a more advanced state. Free trade would mean that Britain could 'disburthen her conscience of the crime of perpetuating barbarism in that fairest of all regions, for whose civilization she has made herself responsible'.[42]

While the Cingalese were relatively ready for grown-up treatment in Martineau's view, her picture of aboriginal people was very different. *Homes abroad* was her story of poor Kentish labourers, suffering from an abject poverty in 'the fair and fertile county of Kent' who turned to emigration rather than Captain Swing. Frank, the responsible and industrious carpenter who can get no work, and his dairymaid sister Ellen, decide under the tutelary guidance of their curate, an enthusiast for Australia, that emigration might provide the cure to their woes. Since their two young brothers, reduced to crime, have been sentenced to transportation to Van Diemen's Land, they decide they will settle in the same area. Again the country is a place of plenty in Martineau's vision, (the family settle on the aptly named Dairy Plains), but the natives are 'little better than wild beasts' who would 'soon die out as their wild cattle had done'. Their warfare was 'horrible, – their movements being stealthy, their revenge insatiable, their cruelty revolting'.[43] They would hover for days awaiting an opportunity and then seize on their victims at their most defenceless moment. A traumatic encounter for Ellen on her wedding morning (she is to marry an industrious young emigrant, Harry, who has paid off his passage) marks the entry of aboriginal people into the white world of the Dairy Plains. Hearing a strange sound very early one morning on the farm she finds in the cowshed, 'something ... which she mistook for a little black pig, till its cry made her think it was something much less agreeable to meet with. Stooping down, she saw that it was certainly a black baby; ugly and lean and dirty; but certainly a baby.' The baby cries, 'in much the same style as if it had had a white skin' and she lulls and rocks 'the little woolly-headed savage'. Then another strange

---

[41] *Ibid.*, p. 200.   [42] *Ibid.*, p. 157.
[43] Martineau, *Homes abroad, illustrations of political economy* (London: Charles Fox, 1834), Vol. 4, pp. 72, 89.

sound, like that of a bird, sends Harry rushing off in full pursuit 'of something which leaped like a kangaroo through the high grass'. He shoots to kill. Ellen, meanwhile, sitting in her new cottage (built by her brother and husband-to-be) with the baby sees,

the black form she dreaded to see ... A crouching, grovelling savage, lean and coarse as an ape, showing his teeth among his painted beard, and fixing his snake-like eyes upon her, came creeping on his knees and one hand, the other holding a glittering hatchet. Ellen made neither movement nor sound. If it had been a wild beast she might have snatched up a loaded musket which was behind her, and attempted to defend herself; but this was a man, – among all his deformities, still a man.

Harry, however, seeing his wife at risk, shoots again to kill. Martineau represents aboriginal people as bestial, ugly and insentient – to be killed as easily as if they were not human. But at the very same time she insists on their humanity – 'this was a man' to Ellen, despite his deformities. Yet Harry can simply kill him, just as he has killed the kangaroo-like creature who turns out to be the mother of the 'woolly-headed savage', because they are seen to have threatened his young white wife and their pristine home.

Meanwhile, one of Ellen's convict brothers, Jerry, is discovered to be responsible for this horror. He had stolen a black man's wife and in revenge they were attacking the white settlement. He is discovered,

smoking his pipe, drinking rum, and doing what he pleased, with a black wife who, having skinned the kangaroo and lighted the fire squatted down on the turf, waiting for further orders. If it had not been for the child she carried in a hood of hide on her shoulders, she would have been taken for a tame monkey, so little was there human in her appearance and gestures; but the tiny face that peeped over her shoulder had that in it which bespoke humanity, however soon the dawning rationality might be destined to be extinguished.[44]

This is a very different picture of a 'native' woman from that of Dora or Marana. She is from another time – and a time that is soon to be over. She has no name, she is scarcely human, and she services her white master, himself degraded by his theft of another man's (and a savage at that) property. Her child will soon lose all claim to be like a baby with a white skin. This is Martineau's harshest picture of racial difference: here are savages who can only be expected to die out and leave the land for those more suited to its proper use. Yet still she feels impelled to tell her

[44] *Ibid*, pp. 89–102.

readers that the newly-weds managed to return the baby to its tribe – though it is now an orphan since its mother and father have been killed.

In concluding the tale brother Frank discourses on the differences that emigrants will find across the empire:

> If a man quits England through intolerable poverty, he must not expect to find everything to his mind and abundance besides. If he goes to Canada he may gain what he emigrates for, – food for himself and prosperity to leave for his children; but he must put up with tremendous toil and hardship till he can bring his land in to order, and with long, dreary winters, such as he had no notion of before. If he goes to the Cape, he finds a better climate and less toil; but from the manner of letting land there, he is out of the way of society and neighbourhood, and cannot save so as to make his children richer than himself. If he comes here, he finds the finest climate in the world.[45]

Here he can hope for much. But still there will be convicts to be suffered and occasional murders by marauding native survivors. Government action, however, is reducing the dangers as the 'natives' are driven farther into the bush and their numbers decline. Martineau looks ahead to a future with no 'natives' and industrious and domesticated white settlers living in their newly built homes and establishing a new population. As she noted in her summary of principles at the end of the volume, both capitalists and labourers were required to create a balanced and orderly society and they should be 'young, healthy and moral persons'.[46] Later on that same year when she concluded her sequence of tales with *The moral of many fables* she noted, having read the reports of the emigration commissioners for 1832, that perhaps her optimism was somewhat overstated. Her picture of the position of indentured workers had been too rosy. Life might not be quite as full of promise in Van Diemen's land as she had hoped.[47]

The picture of empire that Martineau constructed in the early 1830s was from inside the metropole. Her move from Norwich to London during the period she was writing had significant effects, not least in her access to publishers, a literary world, colonial officials and ideas. Her picture of the networks of empire was one that flowed unproblematically from the centre to the peripheries: from England to the Cape, from England to Ireland, from England to Demerara, from England to Ceylon, from England to Van Diemen's Land – these were the spokes of the wheel, moving out from the heartlands. There were no webs for her

---

[45] *Ibid.*, p. 105.   [46] *Ibid.*, p. 127.

[47] Harriet Martineau, *The moral of many fables. Illustrations of political economy* (London: Charles Fox, 1834), Vol. 9, p. 77.

connecting one site to another. Each site was imagined as a place that could be transformed for the better by the right kinds of official policies, the right economic practices, the right settlers. The violence that hovered over them, whether of coloniser or colonised, the whiteboys, the cruelties of slavery, the rebellions of the enslaved, the attacks on settlers by indigenous peoples, all this could be eradicated. The Cape would be fertile with hard-working colonists building a better future. Ireland would no longer be stalked by misery once good English landlords had marked the way forward and 'surplus' population had gone to Australia. Demerara would fulfil its promise of tropical beauty once slavery was abolished and black labour able to work for wages. Ceylon would be governed in such a way as to benefit and civilise its peoples. Van Diemen's Land would be transformed from vacant land to a dairy plain populated with white settlers. 'Natives' who could be improved would be, the rest would disappear. Martineau's bird's eye or panoptical view placed the metropole firmly at the centre of the map and constructed a form of imperial knowledge complete with racial, gender and class hierarchies. Irish, Cingalese and African peoples had names and voices, hopes for the future. Bushmen were banished to the hills while aboriginal peoples tested the terrifying boundaries of humanity.

The *Illustrations* was a very ambitious writing project which Martineau carried to a triumphant conclusion. It marked the beginning of her writing career. It was perhaps her most confident moment in relation to empire: Catholics had been emancipated, slavery had been abolished , the nation and its empire were capable of reform. She looked forward to an optimistic future with free trade expanding, civilisation extending, and savage peoples disappearing in the face of progress. There was nothing dismal about the science of political economy as far as she was concerned. At the heart of this future was England, and people like herself – forward looking, educated, rational and believing in a better world once the evils of slavery and colonial monopoly, which degraded both men and women, colonisers and colonised, had gone. In the years that were to come both her own experiences and changes in the wider world made her less optimistic. In her travels in the USA her encounters with the enslaved further disturbed her picture of 'the negro' and the effects of slavery though she remained fully committed to abolitionism. On her journey across Ireland in 1852 she was still hopeful that changes would come, but mindful of the scale of the problems. At the time of the Civil War she was a keen supporter of the North. The events in India in 1857 precipitated a view of racial difference much less tolerant than the one she had previously espoused (as for so many in Britain). For a short period she called for revenge in her *Daily News* editorials and she wrote in strong support of the East India Company.[48] Like Eyre, her vision of other peoples and the grammars of difference that she constructed shifted over a lifetime, though never so dramatically as his.

The lives of men and women such as the ones studied in this collection remind us of the complexities of thinking about race and empire, the shifts over time that take place both for individuals and in collective discourses, and the profound debates that these issues engendered then as now.

---

[48] Logan (ed.), *Harriet Martineau on empire*, Vol. 5.

Select bibliography

Ambrosius, L. E., *Writing biography: historians and their craft* (Lincoln, NB and London: University of Nebraska Press, 2004).

Backscheider, P. R., *Reflections on biography* (Oxford: Oxford University Press, 1999).

Baigent, E., 'The geography of biography, the biography of geography: rewriting the *Dictionary of national biography*', *Journal of Historical Geography* **30** (2004), pp. 531–51.

Baker, A., *Geography and history: bridging the divide* (Cambridge: Cambridge University Press, 2003).

Baldwin, J., 'Stranger in the village', in *Notes of a native son* (Harmondsworth: Penguin, 1953), pp. 151–65.

Ballantyne, T., *Orientalism and race: Aryanism in the British empire* (Basingstoke: Palgrave, 2002).

Beales, D., 'History and biography', in T. C. W. Blanning and D. Cannadine (eds.), *History and biography* (Cambridge: Cambridge University Press, 1996), pp. 266–83.

Bell, M., ' "Citizenship not charity": Violet Markham on nature, society and the state in Britain and South Africa', in M. Bell, R. Butlin and M. Heffernan (eds.), *Geography and imperialism, 1820–1940* (Manchester: Manchester University Press, 1995), pp. 189–220.

Bertaux, D. (ed.), *Biography and society: the life history approach in the social sciences* (London: Sage, 1981).

Blanning, T. C. W. and Cannadine, D. (eds.), *History and biography: essays in honour of Derek Beales* (Cambridge: Cambridge University Press, 1996)

Blunt, A., *Travel, gender, and imperialism: Mary Kingsley and West Africa* (New York: Guilford Press, 1994).

Boehmer, E., 'Global and textual webs in an age of transnational capitalism; or, what isn't new about empire', *Postcolonial Studies* **7**, 1 (2004), pp. 11–26.

'Introduction' to R. Baden-Powell, *Scouting for boys* (Oxford: Oxford University Press, 2004; originally published 1908), pp. xiv–xviii.

The books in this select bibliography are derived from the literature discussed in the introduction to this volume.

Empire, the national and the postcolonial, 1890–1920: resistance in interaction (Oxford: Oxford University Press, 2002).

Colonial and postcolonial literature: migrant metaphors (Oxford: Oxford University Press, 1995).

Boehmer, E. and Moore-Gilbert, B., 'Postcolonial studies and transnational resistance', *Interventions* **4**, 1 (2002), pp. 7–21.

Bridge, C. and Fedorowich, K. (eds.), *The British world: diaspora, culture and identity* (London: Frank Cass, 2003).

Brown, M. and Roa, M. A. (eds.), *Militares extranjeros en la independencia de Colombia: nuevas perspectivas* (Bogotá: Museo Nacional de Colombia, 2005).

Buettner, E., ' "We don't grow coffee and bananas in Clapham Junction you know!": imperial Britons back home', in R. Bickers (ed.), *Settlers and expatriates: Britons over the seas* (Oxford: Oxford University Press, forthcoming).

Bunkše, E. V., *Geography and the art of life* (Baltimore: Johns Hopkins University Press, 2004).

Burton, A., 'Archive stories: gender in the making of imperial and colonial histories', in P. Levine (ed.), *Gender and empire* (Oxford: Oxford University Press, 2005), pp. 281–94.

'Introduction: on the inadequacy and indispensability of the nation', in A. Burton (ed.), *After the imperial turn: thinking with and through the nation* (Durham, NC: Duke University Press, 2003), pp. 1–26.

Burdens of history: British feminists, Indian women and imperial culture (Durham, NC: University of North Carolina Press, 1994).

Cain, P. J. and Hopkins, A. G., *British imperialism: crisis and deconstruction, 1914–1990* (Harlow: Longman, 1993).

British imperialism: innovation and expansion 1688–1914 (Harlow: Longman, 1993).

Carlyle, T., *On heroes, hero worship and the heroic in history*, 4th edition (London: Chapman and Hall, 1852).

Clayton, D., *Islands of truth: the imperial fashioning of Vancouver Island* (Vancouver: University of British Columbia Press, 2000).

Clifford, J., ' "Hanging up looking glasses at odd corners": ethnobiographical prospects', in D. Aaron (ed.), *Studies in biography* (Cambridge, MA: Harvard University Press, 1978), pp. 40–58.

Cobley, A. G., 'Forgotten connections, unconsidered parallels: a new agenda for comparative research in Southern Africa and the Caribbean', *African Studies* **58** (1999), pp. 133–55.

Colley, L., *Captives: Britain, empire and the world, 1600–1850* (London: Jonathan Cape, 2002).

Cook, S. B., *Imperial affinities: nineteenth century analogies and exchanges between India and Ireland* (New Delhi: Sage, 1993).

Cotterill, L. and Letherby, G., 'Weaving stories: personal auto/biographies in feminist research', *Sociology* **27**,1 (1993), pp. 67–80.

Daniels, S. and Nash, C., 'Life paths: geography and biography', *Journal of Historical Geography* **30** (2004), pp. 449–58.

Darwin, J., 'Imperialism and the Victorians: the dynamics of territorial expansion', *English Historical Review* (June 1997), pp. 614–42.

Davidson, J., Bondi, L. and Smith, M. (eds.), *Emotional geographies* (Aldershot: Ashgate, 2005).

Davis, N. Z., *Women on the margins: three seventeenth-century lives* (Cambridge, MA: Harvard University Press, 1995).

Dirks, N. B., 'Introduction: colonialism and culture', in N. B. Dirks (ed.), *Colonialism and culture* (Ann Arbor: University of Michigan Press, 1992), pp. 1–26.

Drayton, R., *Nature's government: science, imperial Britain, and the 'improvement' of the world* (London: Yale University Press, 2000).

Driver, F., 'Distance and disturbance: travel, exploration and knowledge in the nineteenth century', *Transactions of the Royal Historical Society* **14** (2004), pp. 73–92.

  Geography militant: cultures of exploration and empire (Oxford: Blackwell, 2000).

  'Henry Morton Stanley and his critics: geography, exploration and empire', *Past and Present* **133** (1991), pp. 134–66.

Edel, L., *Writing lives: principia biographica* (New York: W. W. Norton, 1984).

Elbourne, E., 'The Eastern Cape and international networks in the early nineteenth century', Fort Hare Institute of Social and Economic Research, Working Paper series, WP 43 (August 2003), University of Fort Hare, South Africa.

Epstein, W. H., *Recognizing biography* (Philadelphia: University of Pennsylvania Press, 1987).

Evans, J., *Edward Eyre: race and colonial governance* (Dunedin: University of Otago Press, 2005).

Fieldhouse, D., 'Can Humpty-Dumpty be put together again? Imperial history in the 1980s', *Journal of Imperial and Commonwealth History* **12**, 2 (1984), pp. 10–23.

Findlay, A. M. and Li, F. L. N., 'An auto-biographical approach to understanding migration: the case of Hong Kong emigrants', *Area* **29** (1997), pp. 33–44.

Fuchs, M., 'Autobiography and geography: introduction', *Biography* **25** (2002), pp. iv–xi.

Gallagher, J. and Robinson, R., 'The imperialism of free trade', *Economic History Review*, 2nd series, **6**, 1 (1953), pp. 1–15.

Gay, P., *The bourgeois experience: the cultivation of hatred*, Vol. III (London: W. W. Norton, 1999).

  The bourgeois experience: Victoria to Freud – tender passion, Vol. II (London: W. W. Norton, 1994).

Gupta, A. and Ferguson, J., 'Beyond "culture": space, identity, and the politics of difference', *Cultural Anthropology* **7** (1992), pp. 6–23.

Hall, C., *Civilising subjects: metropole and colony in the English imagination, 1830–1867* (Cambridge: Polity, 2002).

    'Introduction: thinking the postcolonial, thinking the empire', in C. Hall (ed.), *Cultures of empire, a reader: colonizers in Britain and the empire in the nineteenth and twentieth centuries* (Manchester: Manchester University Press, 2000), pp. 1–36.

    ' "Going-a-trolloping": imperial man travels the empire', in C. Midgley (ed.) *Gender and imperialism* (Manchester: Manchester University Press, 1998), pp. 180–99.

    White, male and middle class: explorations in feminism and history (Cambridge: Polity, 1992).

Hopkins, A. G. (ed.), *Globalization in world history* (London: Pimlico, 2002).

Israel, K. A. K., 'Writing inside the kaleidoscope: re-representing Victorian women public figures', *Gender and History* **2** (1990), pp. 40–8.

Kamuf, P. (ed.), *A Derrida reader: between the blinds* (New York: Columbia University Press, 1991).

Kennedy, D., 'Imperial history and post-colonial theory', *Journal of Imperial and Commonwealth History* **24**, 3 (1996), pp. 345–63.

Laidlaw, Z., *Colonial connections, 1815–1845: patronage, the information revolution and colonial government* (Manchester: Manchester University Press, 2005).

Lambert, D., 'The counter-revolutionary Atlantic: white West Indian petitions and proslavery networks', *Social and Cultural Geography* **6** (2005), pp. 407–22.

    White creole culture, politics and identity during the Age of Abolition (Cambridge: Cambridge University Press, 2005).

Larson, M. S., *The rise of professionalism: a sociological analysis* (Berkeley: University of California Press, 1977).

Lee, H., *Body parts: essays in life writing* (London: Chatto and Windus, 2005).

Lester, A., 'Imperial circuits and networks: geographies of the British empire', *History Compass* **3**, 189 (2005), pp. 1–18.

    'Missionaries and white settlers in the nineteenth century', in N. Etherington (ed.), *Missions and empire* (Oxford: Oxford University Press, 2005), pp. 64–85.

    'British settler discourse and the circuits of empire', *History Workshop Journal* **54** (2002), pp. 27–50.

    Imperial networks: creating identities in nineteenth century South Africa and Britain (London and New York: Routledge, 2001).

Mackillop, A. and Murdoch, S. (eds.), *Military governors and imperial frontiers, c. 1600–1800: a study of Scotland and empire* (Leiden: Brill, 2003).

Marcus, L., *Auto/biographical discourses: theory, criticism, practice* (Manchester: Manchester University Press, 1994).

Massey, D., *For space* (London: Sage, 2005).

Mathurin, O. C., *Henry Sylvester Williams and the origins of the Pan-African movement, 1869–1911* (Westport, CT: Greenwood, 1976).

McEwan, C., ' "The Mother of all the Peoples": geographical knowledge and the empowering of Mary Slessor', in M. Bell, R. Butlin and M. Heffernan (eds.), *Geography and imperialism, 1820–1940* (Manchester: Manchester University Press, 1995), pp. 125–50.

McKenzie, K., *Scandal in the colonies* (Melbourne: University of Melbourne Press, 2004).

Mein Smith, P. and Hempenstall, P., 'Australia and New Zealand: turning shared pasts into a shared history', *History Compass* (2003), http://www.history-compass.com, accessed 11/07/05.

Ogborn, M., 'Writing travels: power, knowledge and ritual on the English East India Company's early voyages', *Transactions of the Institute of British Geographers* **27** (2002), pp. 155–71.

Painter, N. I., 'Writing biographies of women', *Journal of Women's History* **9** (1997), pp. 154–63.

Parke, C. N., *Biography: writing lives* (New York: Twayne Publishers, 1996).

Porter, A., *Religion versus empire: British Protestant missionaries and overseas expansion, 1700–1914* (Manchester: Manchester University Press, 2004).

Potter, S., *News and the British world: the emergence of an imperial press system* (Oxford: Oxford University Press, 2003).

Pratt, M. L., *Imperial eyes: travel writing and transculturation* (London: Routledge, 1992).

Rawley, J., *London, metropolis of the slave trade* (Columbia: University of Missouri Press, 2003).

Rhiel, M. and Suchoff, D. (eds.), *The seductions of biography* (London: Routledge, 1996).

Richardson, B. C., *Igniting the Caribbean's past: fire in British West Indian history* (Chapel Hill: University of North Carolina Press, 2004).
    'Detrimental determinists: applied environmentalism as bureaucratic self-interest in the *fin-de-siècle* British Caribbean', *Annals of the Association of American Geographers* **86** (1996), pp. 213–34.

Robinson, R., 'Non-European foundations of European imperialism', in E. R. Owen and B. Sutcliffe (eds.), *Studies in the theory of imperialism* (London: Longman, 1972), pp. 117–42.

Robinson, R. and Gallagher, J. with Denny, A., *Africa and the Victorians: the official mind of imperialism*, 2nd edition (Basingstoke: Macmillan, 1981).

Said, E. W., *Culture and imperialism* (London: Chatto and Windus, 1993).
    'Traveling theory', in *The world, the text and the critic* (London: Faber and Faber, 1983), pp. 226–47.
    Orientalism: Western conceptions of the Orient (London: Penguin, 1978).

Saunders, C., 'From Trinidad to Cape Town: the first black lawyer in the Cape', *Quarterly Bulletin of the South African Library* **55**, 4 (2001), pp. 146–61.

Seeley, J. R., *The expansion of England: two courses of lectures*, 2nd edition (London: Macmillan, 1895).

Shortland, M. and Yeo, R. (eds.), *Telling lives in science: essays on scientific biography* (Cambridge: Cambridge University Press, 1996).

Smith, S. and Watson, J. (eds.), *Getting a life: everyday uses of biography* (Minneapolis: University of Minnesota Press, 1996).

Söderqvist, T., 'Existential projects and existential choice in science: science biography as an edifying genre', in M. Shortland and R. Yeo (eds.), *Telling lives in science: essays on scientific biography* (Cambridge: Cambridge University Press, 1996), pp. 45–84.

Spiers, E., *The Victorian soldier in Africa* (Manchester: Manchester University Press, 2004).

Stanley, L., 'On auto/biography in sociology', *Sociology* **27**, 1 (1993), pp. 41–52.

    The auto/biographical I (Manchester: Manchester University Press, 1992).

Steedman, C., 'Difficult stories: feminist auto/biography', *Gender and History* **7** (1995), pp. 321–6.

    The radical soldier's tale: John Pearman, 1819–1908 (London: Routledge, 1988).

    Landscape for a good woman: a story of two lives (London: Virago, 1986).

Stoler, A. L., 'Tense and tender ties: the politics of comparison in North American history and (post) colonial studies', *The Journal of American History* **88**, 3 (2004), pp. 830–65.

    Carnal knowledge and imperial power: race and the intimate in colonial rule (Berkeley: University of California Press, 2002).

Stoler, A. L. and Cooper, F., 'Between metropole and colony: rethinking a research agenda', in F. Cooper and A. L. Stoler (eds.), *Tensions of empire: colonial cultures in a bourgeois world* (Berkeley and London: University of California Press, 1997), pp. 1–58.

Strachey, L., *Eminent Victorians* (London: Chatto and Windus, 1993; originally published 1918).

Thomas, N., *Colonialism's culture: anthropology, travel and government* (Cambridge: Polity, 1994).

Thomas, N. J., 'Exploring the boundaries of biography: the family and friendship networks of Lady Curzon, Vicereine of India, 1898–1905', *Journal of Historical Geography* **30** (2004), pp. 496–519.

Tuchman, B. W., 'Biography as a prism of history', in M. Pachter (ed.), *Telling lives: the biographer's art* (Philadelphia: University of Pennsylvania Press, 1981).

Whitlock, G., *The intimate empire: reading women's autobiography* (London: Cassell, 2000).

Wilson, K., *The island race: Englishness, empire and gender in the eighteenth century* (London: Routledge, 2003).

Wolf, E., *Europe and the people without history* (London: University of California Press, 1982).

Index